VOLUME FOUR

DISCARD

GENERAL EDITOR
J. I. Packer

EDITOR
J. Isamu Yamamoto

AREA EDITORS

Old Testament: Bruce K. Waltke
New Testament: Harold W. Hoehner
Church History: Nathan O. Hatch
Systematic Theology: David F. Wells
Ethics/Spiritual Life: Donald G. Bloesch
Pastoral Psychology and Counseling: David G. Benner
Missions: C. Peter Wagner
Homiletics: Haddon W. Robinson
Christian Education: Kenneth O. Gangel

ADMINISTRATIVE EDITOR
Marty L. White

Carol Stream, Illinois

THE BEST IN THEOLOGY
Volume Four

Published by Christianity Today, Inc.
Distributed by Word, Inc.

Cover Design: Dwight Walles

ISSN 1041-3898

Printed in the United States of America

CONTENTS

iv

Section 6: PRACTICAL THEOLOGY: PASTORAL PSYCHOLOGY AND COUNSELING

Section 7: PRACTICAL THEOLOGY: MISSIONS

Section 8: PRACTICAL THEOLOGY: HOMILETICS

Section 9: PRACTICAL THEOLOGY: CHRISTIAN EDUCATION

INTRODUCTION

J. I. PACKER
General Editor, *The Best in Theology*
Sangwoo Youtong Chee Professor of Theology
Regent College

I.

Once again it is my privilege to compose a verbal trumpet-flourish heralding *The Best in Theology*, CT's fourth annual collection of the year's brightest journal articles. Once again, as I have read through the material, I have rejoiced in the discriminating diligence of the section editors and their friends (for the wise section editor pulls in his friends to help in this job): once again they have tracked down cartloads of first-class stuff. From their selections, plus the up-to-date surveys of their disciplines that some of them threw in for good measure, I have learned a lot. Others, I think, will have the same experience and echo my thanks to these learned men.

One new selector, Donald Bloesch, joined the team this year, to look after Ethics/Spiritual Life. It is good to have him, but the occasion of his coming is sad: His predecessor, Klaus Bockmuehl, died of cancer on June 10, 1989, at the age of 58. Undervalued, as it seems to me, in North America, Klaus, who served as Professor of Theology and Ethics at Regent College from 1977, was a brilliant analytical thinker, a masterful teacher, a superb colleague, and a holy servant of God, and it is right that I should pay tribute to him before I go any further.

II.

"Writing maketh an exact man," said Bacon. Klaus was evidence for this dictum: He was an eminently exact man, who was always writing. In faculty and seminar discussions he used to jot down just about everything that was said. In the motel room that we once shared, I sat on my bed for morning devotions, but Klaus went to the table and wrote, evidently following the old Oxford Group/Moral Re-Armament discipline of putting on paper all that God seemed to say in, through, and *à propos* of the Scriptures that one read in one's quiet time. (Klaus owed something to Moral Re-Armament from his earlier years.) At his last public appearance, as speaker at Regent College's

Spring Convocation, a month before he died, he sat in his wheelchair with pen in hand, amending his script. As for exactness, he combined the deep learning and rigorous antithetical thinking of the German academic with a clarity, precision, and gracefulness of speech that was almost French. There was never any doubt about his meaning or the direction of his thought; he knew his own mind and could express it with a simple, pointed elegance, grave and witty by turns, that made him an impressively strong communicator. Shyness made him seem remote at first, but his warm-hearted generosity soon banished that impression. Scrupulous integrity, and care—care for his family, his students, and the College; care for the cause of God and the millions enmeshed in liberal theology and Marxist ideology—marked all that he did. Fortitude—uncomplaining courage and resilience—marked him too. His evangelicalism lost him a university position. He was a martyr to migraines for much of his life. Although North American publishers would not produce his books for a long time (though he was an established writer, whose German works had gone into Dutch, Finnish, Italian, Portuguese, and French, as well as English), he wrote on steadily, completing his last book just before his death. The constant pain of his final months produced exhaustion, but not bitterness. As the end approached, he often repeated the words, "Hold Jesus dear." He lived to God in thankful obedience and service, and he died to God in peace.

Klaus's evangelical theology was academically impeccable, but not in the least academic in the sense of detached from life. Ethical standards, both personal and socio-political, on the one hand, and spiritual life on the other, were central interests of his, as can be seen from his 1986 book *Living by the Gospel*, and which will soon be seen from the book that he struggled to complete before death claimed him, *Listening to the God Who Speaks*. He was a pietist in the noble sense in which Spener and Francke, Whitefield and Wesley, Edwards and Brainerd, were pietists: That is to say, he was as far as possible from complacency, obscurantism, sectarianism, and sloth, and he was moved by his personal knowledge of God's grace and forgiveness to all kinds of compassionate efforts for others' benefit. I am sure that I am the better for having known him, and that many others are too.

Klaus's last speech, which was printed in full in the June 1989 edition of *Crux* under the title "Let Us Be Listeners," was a gem. Addressed, characteristically, to "dear students, colleagues, and friends," it speaks wisdom to pastors too, and I make no apology for quoting some of it here.

Starting with a call to thank God for what has been good and seek each other's forgiveness for what has not been so good, Klaus then zeroed in on the thought that waiting on God till we are able to act on the basis of what we have actually received and heard is our first task. "I have come to think that among the multitude of God's mercies (Ps. 106:7) which I have received, my recent illness was to teach me this lesson . . . in the past, if someone had called me a workaholic, I would secretly have responded: 'Of course, what else?' A workaholic in the kingdom of God, that was a title of honour! I saw my Christian and human dignity, my self-confidence, and reason for self-respect in being a 'worker' in God's vineyard. . . . Let us beware of the seductive glory of Christian workaholism, of the moments when we tell ourselves secretly, how wonderful it feels to be exhausted in the work of the Lord. . . . No, it is far better to do a few inconspicuous things but to do them under God's instruction. Christian commitment is not primarily towards Christian activism—that would be a basic misreading of Christianity. Listening to the voice of God comes first and must precede all motion."

Activism, therefore, as a way of life will not do for Christians. "It goes hand in hand with the technological bent of modern secular civilization. Its pragmatism and its utilitarianism emphasize what is useful and what is practical. The many books suggesting 'How To' do and effect something are witness to this. This attitude has pervaded much of Western Christianity, too." But "we are to listen to God and not to rush into things which have a momentary Christian appeal."

"*Passivism*, also sometimes called *Quietism*" is, however, a trap too. "It conceals in effect the human propensity to sin, and ignores the biblical task of the sanctification of the believer. Asking man to do nothing but 'repose in redemption,' it fuels the already existing human 'sloth-factor.' Also, nicely fitting with the philosophy of today's individualism, it gives people the impression that salvation ends with *me*, with the individual, and makes them forget the perspectives of the Kingdom of God. In the person of Jesus, however, we . . . see that the attitudes of listening and of action go hand in hand, and are not set against each other."

Nor can any aping of the Enlightenment quest for freedom through personal autonomy lead Christians along the path of life. "Self-determination is a quest which sees listening and liberty of decision as incompatible . . . much can be said in a positive appreciation of the Enlightenment's search for human identity, dignity, freedom, and the programme of a comprehensive development of the self. The question is: how far is it possible? . . . total human liberation and autonomy are not available to us. Man's manifold and fundamental interrelatedness with nature through body and soul will at times be felt as an irremovable alien domination. In addition, we are only just beginning to see today how much the liberated individual can be taken captive again by a return of collective forms of the same self on a larger scale, e.g., in nationalism, racism, class consciousness, and warfare. These are among the mighty forces which the New Testament sums up under the name of 'powers and principalities.'

"Yet personal freedom, *a freedom going together with listening* and devotion to God, are seen to be in agreement in the person of Jesus. Listening to God and obeying, Jesus was free of human determinations, individual or collective. . . . If there is one faculty we need to have for the next phase in life, it is not the sharp teeth and swift legs needed for the 'rat race,' but the *listening heart* (1 Kings 3), for which King Solomon asked, when he was granted a wish from God."

Golden words to all groups present rounded off the address.

"For their own and for their students' sake, teachers need silence and frequent times of quiet and prayer, to find, receive, and know what their 'statement of purpose' . . . is to be. Then students must ask themselves the same question. . . .

"From a practising Christian one may expect radiation of light and warmth, giving to others both orientation and an experience of shelter. Those who listen to God promote healing instead of creating new problems. They truly become spiritual *resource people*, i.e., constant sources of inspiration instead of a constant source of irritation in their surroundings. Remember, however, that this is not a matter of human endeavour and achievement. It comes from listening; it is the outcome of communion with Christ."

Thus Klaus, though dead, yet speaks, and all of us who are or hope to be in any form of Christian ministry do well to listen. In him we lost a wise, good man, and *The Best in Theology* will never carry better theology than this, his final message.

III.

Klaus regularly used to teach the doctrine of God, that dazzling, dizzying exercise of looking, as it were, at the sun, and this is the theme on which I shall focus for the rest of my Introduction. Why? For a very basic reason, namely, that this is a focus we need. The relatively small space that most theology textbooks allot to the doctrine of God tells its own story, and the fumbling way in which evangelicals commonly speak of God shows that more thought and clarity are needed here. A firm grip on the doctrine of God is needed for fitting into place the material brought together in a book of journal articles like this, along with the lines of thought found in one-man books of theology (I hope, dear readers, that you do tackle one-man books of theology, as well as reading articles?). And the study of God is just as necessary for achieving and maintaining a God-centered religion, as distinct from a man-centered and indeed self-centered one; which is a matter of even greater importance than God-centered orthodoxy, even though without the latter you are unlikely to attain the former.

Is there a difference between God-centered and man-centered evangelical piety? I'll say there is! God-centered piety, like God-centered theology, exalts God directly, celebrating, adoring, magnifying, and glorifying him in every way; it breathes the spirit of worship, and it leads to a constantly enriched appreciation of the wonder and grandeur of being a human individual made in God's image—an appreciation that led preachers and teachers of former days to dilate on "the greatness of the soul" (when did you last hear a sermon on that?) and "the infinite value of the person." But man-centered religion, fed usually by man-centered theology, starts by shrinking and domesticating, and purporting to harness and control God, and ends up in cahoots with popular secular culture (the media, paperback fiction, mass magazines) to sentimentalize and superficialize humanness itself, so that life is made to seem trivial. How egghead Enlightenment secularism can lead up—or, rather, down—to this point was recently illuminated by Paul Johnson's brilliant eye-opener, *Intellectuals*, which I urge you to read if you have not yet done so. How popular worldliness can achieve this effect was explored earlier by Christopher Lasch, a contributor to this volume, in *The Cult of Narcissism*. How orthodox evangelicalism can do it has been shown by the sad sagas of the Bakkers and some other televangelists. But in truth only an adequate view of God can save any of us from cheapening ourselves and our life under God in the manner indicated. "There but for the grace of God. . . !"

Card-carrying evangelicals, preachers, teachers, youth workers, writers, singers, vie with each other to maximize vividness in their presentations of the Father and the Son as heavenly pals who are there to give us a good time. This is disturbing. On my study door at Regent College is a cartoon of a beaming believer standing in a Roman arena, his back to the approaching lion, assuring his panicky friend, who can see the lion, "Don't forget, brother, being saved is fun!" Callers are meant to read, mark, learn, and while giggling inwardly digest. Surely it is infantile to think that real life in the real world could ever be all fun; surely it borders on blasphemy to enlist God in order to make it so. We evangelicals seem to need a freshening of our vision of God more, perhaps, than believers of any other stripe.

Spirituality, the study of communion with God in all its aspects, has become a focus of interest in the world church, and particularly in recent years among evangelicals, for whom Merton and Nouwen are becoming household names. This development, which much in the present volume reflects (see especially the pieces by Shogren, the late Albert Outler, Rice, Adams, Hellwig, and Helminiak), is basically healthy; it is a quest for spiritual reality. But it cannot be pursued with any sureness of touch where the doctrine of God, the God with whom one communes, is deficient.

What, then, must we be clear on regarding God? Producing at this point from my professional pocket a preacher's pabulum of sweet P's, I offer a four-heading answer, thus.

First: God is *plural*. God is not just personal, but tripersonal; not just one, but triune. The truth of the Trinity—that threeness is as basic to God's being as oneness, so that God in his unity is as much "they" as "he"—is clear in both the facts and the words of the New Testament, and is basic to understanding God and godliness. Scripture presents the plan of salvation, the Christian life, and the original creation and coming re-creation of the cosmos, in trinitarian terms. Father, Son, and Holy Spirit, coequal and coeternal in the unity of their togetherness, appear as the only God there is. So where the Trinity is not well stated, everything that depends on the revelation of God's threeness will be stated more or less badly. That is inevitable.

Second: God is *powerful*. God is the self-sustaining sovereign Lord (God who *lives* and *reigns*, as Scripture puts it), everlasting, unchanging, infinite, and unlimited by any created reality; present everywhere, cognizant of everything, and able to do all that he wills to do. In every divine relationship and activity God is fully involved, since the three who are he always and in everything move together, as it is their nature to do.

Third: God is *perfect*. God, the Three-in-One, is perfect in the goodness, faithfulness, love, and mercy by which he saves; perfect in the holiness, purity, and justice by which he judges; perfect in the wisdom by which he chooses the best goal for us and for himself, and the best means for achieving it. He does all things well; he could not be better than he is.

Fourth: God is *praiseworthy*. The triune Lord shows us glory in his self-disclosure, the glory of him who is them, Father, Son, and Spirit together; and for this we give him glory, the glory of celebratory praise, loyal homage, and glad service directed to the three in both their distinctness and their unity.

Why is it important to be thus clear about God? Why, when God is spoken of, is it vital to focus at once on the transcendent Trinity? Several answers may be briefly given.

(1) From the revelation of the Trinity we learn that God's own internal, self-generated life—his mode of personal existence, as we might say—consists of endless expressions and interchanges of love between three persons, in each of whom the fullness of deity is found; whence it appears that God's purpose in creating rational beings, angelic and human, was to extend this circle of love by including them in it. Thus, this is the destiny for which we were made, and, as the Book of Revelation supremely shows, this heavenly life, starting here and perfected hereafter, is that for which and into which we have been redeemed.

(2) From the revelation of the Trinity we learn, in face of the contrary noises made by spokesmen for liberal, existentialist, and institutionalist forms of Christianity (sub-Christianity, rather), that Jesus is more than a historical memory, and the Holy Spirit is more than an uplifting influence. Both are living, distinct persons, and are to be honored as such here and now. Believers enjoy personal fellowship with the Father and with his Son Jesus Christ through the personal ministry of the third person of the Godhead. God above us is one person, God with us (beside us) is a second, and God in us is a third. We are to think of our communion with God, and the consequent supernaturalizing of our lives, in terms that are neither unitarian nor binitarian, but trinitarian. Knowing God does not mean acknowledging the Father without reference to the Son, as liberal teachers seem to think, nor does it mean recognizing the Father and the Son without regard for the Spirit, as nonexperiential evangelicalism appears to suppose. Knowing God in

volves conscientiously venerating and consciously trusting all three persons together.

(3) From the revelation of the Trinity we learn that God's plan of salvation is (to speak boldly) a team job, in which Father, Son, and Spirit work together for our salvation in the unvarying relational pattern that the church fathers called the *economy*. In this pattern the Father's role is to initiate, and accordingly he has schemed out everything, honoring the Son by appointing him to become the Savior of those given to him. Then the Son, whose nature it is always to follow the Father's lead, acts as the Father's agent, and so he has become man, died for sins, risen, ascended, and begun to reign; one day he will return to judge and will take believers to be with him in endless joy in a renewed creation. Finally, the Spirit's role and nature is to be the executive of the Godhead, doing the will of the Father and the Son, and hence he has been busy since the Pentecost of Acts 2, illuminating sinners to see the glory of Christ the Savior, inducing in them faith, hope, and love directed to Christ, plus all the character qualities that Paul calls the Spirit's fruit, and implanting the skills for service that Paul calls spiritual gifts. Scripture indicates that the same economy operates in creation and providence too, but it is in the realm of redemption that we are shown it most clearly. Nontrinitarians are, quite simply, nonstarters when it comes to comprehending the plan of grace.

(4) From the revelation of the Trinity we learn the essentially relational character of God, which confirms the primacy of relationships—specifically, love-relationships—for the fulfilling of our destiny as God's image-bearers. By the same token, it highlights the perversity of shrinking from love-relationships or reducing them to role- or rule-relationships, out of a belief that that is what God wants. "Love" here means (need I say?) not sexual desire, but the non-exploitative purpose of making the beloved one great, and I have in view here the whole gamut of relationships between spouses, between friends of both sexes, and between adults and children. Be it said, however, that sexual affection in marriage is given us to help us forward not only in our love-relationship to our spouse, but also thereby in our love to God himself, that is, to Father, Son, and Spirit—as we have been saying.

(5) From the revelation of the Trinity we learn that a church is not just a club or an interest group that is there for us to join or not join as we fancy; rather, it is a local microcosm of a worldwide macrocosm, a current organ of an age-long organism that is itself a mystery of new creation by the holy three, a trinitarian reality still in process of completion—"built on the foundation of the apostles and prophets, with Christ Jesus himself as the chief cornerstone. In him the whole building is joined together and rises to become a holy temple in the Lord. And in him you too are being built together to become a dwelling in which God (the Father) lives by his Spirit" (Eph. 2:20–22; one sentence, expressing one thought, in the Greek). So the essential supernaturalness of the local church's life must never be forgotten, even where it is more a matter of faith than of sight, and the categorical obligation

of every believer to be part of some local church or other, so as to share in the corporate manifesting of the mystery of new life in the Body of Christ through the Spirit, must always be stressed. The life of the church is as truly a trinitarian reality as is the life of the Christian individual, and it must never be seen as anything less. Thus the truth of the Trinity safeguards the divine dimension of church worship, as well as of the believer's personal existence, fellowship, and work.

(6) From the revelation of the Trinity we get our bearings and our balance for studying, on the one hand, the public realities of redemption (Old Testament, New Testament, systematic theology, church history) and, on the other hand, the personal realities of salvation (communication, mission, spiritual life, pastoral care). The economy of the Trinity—that is, the Father glorifying the Son through the Spirit—is the real subject matter in both fields of study, and the one-sidedness of embracing one and ignoring the other would be indefensible. So it is ultimately the truth of the Trinity that requires you to explore all the sections of *The Best in Theology* and forbids you to leave any untouched on the grounds that it is not your field of concern.

So dive in, drink deep, and prosper! I will not keep you from 1989's best in theology any longer.

About the General Editor

J. I. Packer (B.A., M.A., D.Phil., Oxford University) is the Sangwoo Youtong Chee Professor of Theology, Regent College (Vancouver, B.C., Canada). He was ordained in the Church of England, and now attends Saint John's (Anglican) Church, Shaughnessy, B.C. Many will have read several of his earlier books: *"Fundamentalism" and the Word of God* (1958), *Evangelism and the Sovereignty of God* (1961), and *Knowing God* (1973). His recent books include *Keep in Step with the Spirit* (1984), (with Thomas Howard) *Christianity, the True Humanism* (1985), *Your Father Loves You* (1986), and *Hot Tub Religion* (1987).

OLD TESTAMENT

Bruce K. Waltke, area editor

OLD TESTAMENT

BRUCE K. WALTKE
Professor of Old Testament
Westminster Theological Seminary

Introduction

Periodical literature tends to be of two sorts: either it addresses a particular exegetical, archaeological, or historical problem, or it aims to reflect on the present state of a discipline by raising hermeneutical, methodological, and/or organizational questions.[1] *The Best In Theology* focuses on the latter kind, as it aims to inform its readers about the contemporary shape of the various disciplines and subdisciplines.

During the past decade, Old Testament specialists have observed paradigm shifts occurring within their subdisciplines. In higher criticism a literary-artistic study of the final text has gained ascendancy over the historical and diachronic study of the text—the regnant "scientific" method of the preceding century, while sociological criticism has joined forces with literary and form criticisms to refine historical criticism. In hermeneutics, feminists uniquely use biblical criticism and contextualization in an attempt to relativize the Old Testament patriarchialism, while evangelicals are accepting a more symbolic, rather than a woodenly literalistic, interpretation of the early chapters of Genesis. In Hebrew prosody the "b" verset of a parallel is now understood as transforming the poetic line into living color, and not as a black-and-white shadow. In the history of Israel "the settlement model" of Israel's emergence in the land about 1200 B.C. is presently triumphing over "the conquest model." Archaeology now serves as a corrective against a purely textual reading, by illuminating the historical context. In textual criticism, which has overtaken literary criticism, the task is now often conceptualized as reconstructing a book's final texts (plural), calling into question the meaning of an original autograph.

In this issue of *The Best in Theology* this editor selects and mentions outstanding articles giving insight into these paradigm shifts or challenging them. These new models heuristically force the Church to become hermeneutically self-conscious, to distinguish between its traditional understanding of Scripture and the intention of the infallible Word of God, and to prove what is good in the new and to hold on to what is good in the old.[2] This editor calls special attention to G. J. Wenham's[3] sensible introduction to biblical criticism, republished here.

In literary criticism the German tradition of *Redaktionskritik* focuses on isolating original small textual units and discovering the diachronic complex stages through which the text reaches its present shape. The method that focuses on a synchronic reading of the text's final literary-aesthetic form and/or its components, however, has rocked this tradition during the past two decades. Skepticism about historical criticism and the insights afforded through rhetorical criticism, canonical criticism, new criticism, structuralism, and reader-response theory has abetted this modern method. This new method has yielded an astounding number of insightful articles during the past decade. C. C. Black II[4] succinctly identifies the major streams of rhetorical research during the past two decades, indicates their ripples through the canon, and suggests some of their strengths and weaknesses. Here we focus on outstanding applications of the method during the past year.

The best in this category is that of T. C. Eskenazi,[5] also republished here. Eskenazi applies the new literary approach to Ezra-Nehemiah, especially to the repeated lists of returning exiles in Ezra 2 and Nehemiah 7, the occasion "for scholars who rely on source criticism . . . for dissecting the text and distributing its components to different sources. . . . According to contemporary literary criticism, however, repetitions are significant vehicles for the text's intention." Through this new strategy, Eskenazi transforms these "most uninviting portions of the Bible to the modern reader" into an exciting mystery and through them gains profound insight into the text's structure and meaning. Her brilliant study lays a firm foundation upon which future studies of Ezra-Nehemiah must be built.

The new method also is unlocking the structure and meaning of other biblical books, once closed by searching for sources in a diachronic analysis. For example, W. Bruegmann[6] finds that in the appendix to 2 Samuel "David has now become Israel's true king, and the one Samuel envisioned, the one who claimed, presumed, and possessed nothing, but who trusted and cried out to Yahweh, and obeyed. . . . David becomes the approved king because he has become more like Hannah, Samuel's mother. Like her, he is empty-handed, utterly needful, utterly trusting. These narratives of Hannah and David petitioning and being heard provide an *inclusio* for the Samuel narrative about power and the transformation of power." K. I. Parker[7] argues against most biblical scholars that the narrative of 1 Kings 1–11, instead of being a heterogenous mix of legends, prophecy, archaeological data, lists, and sermonic prose, "contains a unified and coherent structure." C. R. Seitz[8] debunks historical critical analysis of the Book of Job, which assigns the book's different times and/or rearranges them. By insisting on the book's unity, Seitz gains new and profound insights into the relationship between God and a righteous and wise sufferer, which led this reader to worship, even though Seitz detracts from his work by disallowing God's sovereignty. J. W. Roffey,[9] having explored the nature and function of literary discourse in Scripture, interprets as the major issue of the Book of Jonah that prophet's failure in his prophetic duty of intercession: "He knew God's merciful nature, but saw only its implications for himself as God's messenger." In that light, the gourd scene at the end of the book, an old *crux interpretum*, makes sense.

Others argue that modern scholars have overreacted against historical criticism and source criticism. S. Boorer[10] in an attempt to defend the value of the diachronic approach treats her readers to succinct presentations of the source criticism of the Pentateuch by Wellhausen, Noth, Van Seters, and Rendtorff. Although she shows the importance of these approaches to interpretation of the text, she misses the obvious point that their radical differences in reconstructing the text's history shows that the approach is arbitrary. More convincingly, J. A. Emerton[11] examines five attempts to defend the unity of the flood narrative against those who believe it to be composed of two sources, and he gives reasons for finding none of them convincing.

The "Fiftieth Anniversary Volume: Scripture Issue" of *Theological Studies* splendidly summarizes historical criticism, sociological criticism, feminine criticism, and narrative criticism. J. A. Fitzmyer[12] defends the historical-critical method as valid within the Roman Catholic Church because the method is neutral and must be guided by Christian presuppositions according to him. Classically, however, naturalism has been chosen over supernaturalism. In the same volume, C. Osiek[13] surveys the origins, development, and present state of sociology's contribution to enter and interpret a world from thousands of years ago. This method also shares the presuppositions of German rationalism and refines the History of Religion School as exemplified in the work of Troeltsch, Harnack, and the American. pragmatists. Osiek makes no attempt to "sanctify" the method.

Computerized statistical analysis of the text places the study of the text's composition on a relatively more objective basis. G. J. Wenham[14] reviewed the full work of Y. T. Raday, *et al.*, who subjected Genesis to a computerized stylistic analysis of the composition.[15] First, he clearly summarizes the methods and conclusions of the study, and then he suggests some areas for critical scholarship. Although it unfortunately does not sample Genesis 1, this new approach observed distinctions in style between narrative and dialogue among the material in Genesis 2–11, 12–36, and 37–50, especially the break between chapter 11 and chapter 12, and between J/E and P, but it detected no distinction between J and E. Raday interpreted the distinction between J/E and P as due to genre effect, but Wenham leaves undecided whether it is due to different genre and/or to different authors.

Feminine hermeneutics is attempting a paradigm shift, but it is being robustly challenged. Pheme Perkins, professor of theology at Boston College, rightly noted: "Perhaps no question on our cultural and theological agenda divides church communities more quickly than the topic of women in the Bible." *Dialog*, a Lutheran journal, devoted at least four articles during the past year to the issue.[16] The editors of *Interpretation* devoted Volume 42

(January 1988) to a study and evaluation of the way feminist advocates have interpreted the Bible. Two articles are outstanding for mapping and evaluating this new hermeneutic. G. W. Stroup,[17] building on C. Osiek's typology of models of biblical authority within feminism, trenchantly criticizes four themes which have dominated the discussion and development of feminist hermeneutics.

E. Achtemeier[18] takes up the almost impossible task of evaluating the feminist approach to the Bible and theology by dealing with the views of a few leading feminists. This editor, while disagreeing with Achtemeier's revisionist tendencies, namely, her acceptance of Fiorenza's explication of how feminine freedom was suppressed by the time of the writing of the New Testament Pastoral Epistles (p. 46), her willingness to ordain women (p. 47), her inadequate concept of canon (p. 51), and her acceptance of progressive revelation (pp. 52f), nevertheless, finds her essay superior to many which claim an evangelical pedigree.[19] Achtemeier's clear and cogent essay critically appraises feminist interpreters both for their positive contribution through illuminating insights in the Bible and for their errors, namely, their removing authority from the givenness of the canon to subjectivity, their rejection of the lordship of Jesus Christ, and their introduction of pagan theology by introducing inclusive language. Her polemic against inclusive language for God is based on biblical theology. R. M. Frye,[20] Professor of Literature, Emeritus, University of Pennsylvania, insightfully developed this position on the basis of a fine distinction between the half-dozen maternal similes for God and the two hundred and fifty paternal metaphors for God.

A responsible theological understanding of creation based on a proper interfacing of Genesis 1–2 with the scientific endeavor has been a vexed question in contemporary literature. C. H. Pinnock,[21] republished here, intelligently presents a nonconcordist approach to the first two chapters of the Bible while ably maintaining that they present history *in their own way*. One caveat, however, to his essay is U. Cassuto's *Genesis*, which demonstrated that 2:5–6 do not presuppose a totally different order from Genesis 1. His essay has intrinsic value, but it is also significant because of the volume in which it was published. Traditionally nonevangelicals dismiss evangelical writings, but in a rare break with that tradition the editors of *Interpretation* 43/2 (April 1989) devoted the issue to "articles by evangelicals engaged in interpreting and applying the biblical witness to some of the more difficult and convoluted problems of contemporary theological reflection."

Beyond the personal battle between J. Kugel and R. Alter regarding Hebrew parallelism,[22] in which J. Gammie[23] awards the decision to Alter, A. Berlin[24] advanced our understanding of Hebrew parallelism in one of the most important applications of Prague-type structuralism in American biblical scholarship.[25] S. Segert[26] comprehensively reviewed her work and significance. J. Bazak[27] introduces a new method of numerology into Hebrew poetry. According to him, as renowned poets such as Edmund Spenser, John

Milton, Geoffrey Chaucer, and others organized some of their compositions along numerical principles, so also Israel's poets used numerological techniques in some psalms. For example, in Psalm 23 the central expression "for you are with me" begins 26 words after the beginning of the psalm and ends the same number of words from the end of the psalm. He also notes that the numerical value of the Tetragrammaton is 26, a fact that has frequently been mentioned in the traditional literature of Judaism. Psalm 136 repeats the refrain "For his grace is for ever and ever" 26 times. This editor found his work convincing because independently he observed similar phenomena in the Psalter.

I. Finkelstein,[28] author of *The Archaeology of the Israelite Settlement*,[29] presents the most compelling evidence for a late date "settlement" of Israel in the land based on the sudden emergence of dozens of hill-country sites dated to the Iron Age I (ca. 1200–1000 B.C.). The "early date conquest model," on the other hand, suffered a serious setback when D. P. Livingston, after six seasons of excavations at Khirbet Nisya, failed to validate archaeologically the identification of biblical Ai with Kh. Nisya instead of with traditional Et Tell, which shows no Canaanite occupation. Livingston turned up some Canaanite pottery sherds, giving it some advantage over Et Tell, but no architecture from their era.[30] This editor, having served as an external examiner in June 1989 of Livingston's Ph.D. dissertation at Andrews University, on the basis of the archaeological evidence, essentially corroborates A. F. Rainey:[31] "No honest stretch of the imagination can turn Khirbet Nisya into a fortified royal city like the one that Bimson and Livingston assume for the Biblical Ai." Although describing the site as "a small, isolated, highland agricultural settlement," Livingston argues that the Canaanite walls and buildings were robbed out. Nevertheless, archaeology continues to be used both to confirm the historicity of the Hebrew Scriptures and to clarify them; noteworthy examples are articles by A. R. Millard[32] regarding Solomon's gold and P. Albenda[33] about Assyrian reliefs.

Aramaic is one of the three languages in which the Bible was originally written. By the beginning of the seventh century B.C. it was the lingua franca of the ancient Near East; the Jews adopted it after the Babylonians defeated them in 586 B.C. Moreover, Jesus spoke Aramaic. S. C. Layton[34] introduces his readers to the oldest phase (925–700 B.C.) of this remarkable language, so important to biblical studies. D. Sheriffs[35] goes beyond using isolated ancient Near Eastern texts to elucidate particular Old Testament passages. In his hands Babylonian documents about its nationalism and imperialism afford a profound insight and comparison "in seeing biblical material as an engaged and contextualized theology worked out by a process of polemic against deviant Israelite and Near Eastern alternatives."

Since no single essay during the past decade has mapped the changed contours of the present state of Old Testament textual criticism, although one could discern it from *Ezekiel and His Book: Textual and Literary Criti-*

cism and Their Interrelation,[36] this editor[37] wrote "The Aims of Textual Criticism" to fill the void. This editor takes this opportunity to notify readers that Gawdat Gabra,[38] the director of Cairo's Coptic Museum, dates a Coptic book of the Psalms from Oxyrhynchus to the second half of the fourth century; as such it vies with Codex Vaticanus and Codex Sinaiticus to be the oldest book in the world.

Here are some outstanding particular studies. In a biographical study of Abraham, B. W. Anderson[39] movingly encouraged this editor to walk by faith. In a study of Job, S. Lasine[40] modified the common view that the divine speeches belittle or shrink a "swelled up" Job. Rather, he broadens Job's narrow, distorted perspective with the insight that "he [as a prophet] is also a man who sees inversions of justice and then intervenes with the all force of his particular human personality to right them in God's name. If he sees under the aspect of eternity, he responds under the aspect of urgency." Thus, Job, like a prophet, learns to see the world with the eyes of God. In an exegetical study of Proverbs 22:6a, T. Hilderbrandt[41] validates the word *train* to mean "dedicate publicly," the word *child* to mean something like "cadet," and the phrase *in the way he should go* to mean "in what is demanded of him." If he is right, the verse commends a ceremony similar to the Jewish Bar Mitzvah. A. M. Harman[42] exegetically defends the Larger Catechism (Question 113) of the Westminster divines, who taught that the third commandment forbids "making profession of religion in hypocrisy."

Serious expositors will be delighted to learn that W. G. Hupper,[43] by indexing over 600 periodicals, going back to the eighteenth century, with a concentration on nineteenth-century literature, is doing for the Old Testament and the Ancient Near East what Bruce Metzger[44] has done for part of the New Testament. The first volume of many (the number of which is not clear) of this series, and the result of "sixteen years of labor," has now appeared.[45]

Finally, we celebrate that the editors of *Iraq* dedicated Vol. 50 (1988) to Lady Mallowan and Professor Donald J. Wiseman as a tribute to their services and achievements on behalf of the British School of Archaeology in Iraq, of which Professor Wiseman is Chairman.

Notes

[1] Cf. Elisabeth Schuessler Fiorenza, "The Ethics of Biblical Interpretation: Decentering Biblical Scholarship," *Journal of Biblical Literature* 107/1 (1988) 3.

[2] Cf. David E. Holwerda, "Hermeneutical Issues Then and Now: The Janssen Case Revisited," *Calvin Theological Journal* 24/1 (April 1989) 7–34.

[3] G. J. Wenham, "The Place of Biblical Criticism in Theological Study," *Themelios*, April (1989) 84–88.

[4] C. Clifton Black II, "Rhetorical Criticism and Biblical Interpretation," *The Expository Times* 100/7 (1989) 252–57.

[5] Tamara C. Eskenazi, "The Structure of Ezra-Nehemiah and the Integrity of the Book,"*JBL* 107/4 (1988) 641–56.

[6] Walter Bruegmann, "2 Samuel 21–24: An Appendix of Deconstruction?" *Catholic Biblical Quarterly* 50 (1988) 383–97.

[7] Kim Ian Parker, "Repetition as a Structuring Device in 1 Kings 1–11," *Journal for the Society of the Old Testament* 42 (1988) 19–27.

[8] Christopher R. Seitz, "Job: Full-Structure, Movement, and Interpretation," *Interpretation* 43 (1989) 5–17.

[9] John W. Roffey, "God's Truth, Jonah's Fish: Structure and Existence in the Book of Jonah," *Australian Biblical Review* 36 (1988) 1–18.

[10] Suzanne Boorer, "The Importance of a Diachronic Approach: The Cases of Genesis–Kings," *Catholic Biblical Quarterly* 51/2 (April 1989) 195–208.

[11] J. A. Emerton, "An Examination of the Flood Narrative in Genesis," *Vetus Testamentum* 38 (1988) 1–21.

[12] J. A. Fitzmyer, "Historical Criticism: Its Role in Biblical Interpretation and Church Life," *Theological Studies* 50/2 (June 1989) 244–59.

[13] Carolyn Osiek, "The New Handmaid: The Bible and the Social Sciences," *Theological Studies* 50/2 (June 1989) 260–78.

[14] G. J. Wenham, "Genesis: An Authorship Study and Current Pentateuchal Criticism," *Journal for the Study of the Old Testament* 42 (1988) 3–18.

[15] Y. T. Radday, and H. Shore, with D. Wickmann, M. A. Pollatschek, C. Rabin, and S. Talmon, *Genesis: An Authorship Study*, Analecta Biblica 103 (Rome: Biblical Institute Press, 1985).

[16] See also Sandra M. Schneiders, "Feminist Ideology Criticism and Biblical Hermeneutics," *Biblical Theological Bulletin* 19/1 (1989) 3–10 and Phillis Trible, "Five Loaves and Two Fishes: Feminist Hermeneutics and Biblical Theology," *Theological Studies* 50 (1989) 279–95.

[17] George W. Stroup, "Between Echo and Narcissus: The Role of the Bible in Feminist Theology," *Interpretation* 42 (1988) 19–32.

[18] Elizabeth Achtemeier, "The Impossible Possibility: Evaluating the Feminist Approach to Bible and Theology," *Interpretation* 42 (1988) 45–57.

[19] Cf. *What's Right with Feminism*, by Elaine Storkey and *All We're Meant to Be: Biblical Feminism for Today* (rev. ed), by Letha Dawson Scanzoni and Nancy A. Hardesty, reviewed by Martin Van Campbell in *Journal of the Evangelical Theological Society* 31 (1988) 96–98.

[20] Roland Mushat Frye, "Language for God and Feminist Language: A Literary and Rhetorical Analysis," *Interpretation* 43/1 (1989) 45–57.

[21] Clark H. Pinnock, "Climbing Out of a Swamp: The Evangelical Struggle to Understand the Creation Texts," *Interpretation* 43/2 (April, 1989) 143–55.

[22] Cf. Bruce Waltke, *The Best in Theology*, Volume Two (Carol Stream, Ill.: Christianity Today, 1987).

[23] John Gammie, "Alter vs. Kugel," *Biblical Review* 5/1 (1989) 26–33.

[24] Adele Berlin, *The Dynamics of Biblical Parallelism* (Bloomington: Indiana University, 1985).

[25] Cf. S. Segert, "Prague Structuralism in American Biblical Scholarship: Performance and Potential," C. L. Meyers—M. O'Connor, eds. *The Word of the Lord Shall Go Forth* (Winona Lake, Ind.: 1983) 697–708, esp. 700–1, 703.

[26] S. Segert, *Archiv fuer Orient Forschung* (1987) 89–91.

[27] Jacob Bazak, "Numerical Devices in Biblical Poetry," *Vetus Testamentum* 38 (1988) 333–37.

[28] Israel Finkelstein, "Searching for Israelite Origins," *Biblical Archaeological Review* 14/5 (1988) 34–45.

[29] Israel Finkelstein, *The Archaeology of the Israelite Settlement* (Jerusalem: Israelite Exploration Society, 1988).

[30] For a convenient summary of the issues and evidence see William H. Stiebing, Jr., "New Archaeological Dates for the Israelite Conquest: Part II: Proposals for an MB IIC Conquest," *Catastrophism and Ancient History* 10/2 (1988).

[31] Anson F. Rainey, "Letter to the Editor: Rainey on the Location of Bethel and Ai," *Biblical Archaeological Review* 14/5 (1988) 67–68.

[32] Alan R. Millard, "Does the Bible Exaggerate King Solomon's Golden Wealth?" *Biblical Archaeological Review* 15/3 (1989) 20–34.

[33] Pauline Albenda, "The Gateway and Portal Stone Reliefs from Arslan Tash," *Bulletin of the American Schools of Oriental Research* 269 (1988) 5–30.

[34] Scott C. Layton, edited by Dennis Pardee, "Old Aramaic Inscriptions," *Biblical Archaeologist* 51/3 (1988) 172–89.

[35] D. Sheriffs, "A Tale of Two Cities," *Tyndale Bulletin* 39 (1988) 19–57.

[36] *Ezekiel and His Book: Textual and Literary Criticism and Their Interrelation*, ed. by J. Lust (BETL 74; Leuven: Peeters/Leuven University Press, 1986).

[37] Bruce K. Waltke, "The Aims of Textual Criticism," *Westminster Theological Journal* 51 (1989) 93–108.

[38] Gawday Gabra, *Biblical Review* 5/2 (1989) 4–5.

[39] Bernhard W. Anderson, "Abraham, the Friend of God," *Interpretation* 42 (1988) 353–56.

[40] Stuart Lasine, "Bird's-Eye and Worm's Eye View of Justice in the Book of Job," *Journal for the Study of the Old Testament* 42 (1988) 29–53.

[41] Ted Hilderbrandt, "Proverbs 22:6a: Train Up a Child?" *Grace Theological Journal* 9/1 (1988) 3–19.

[42] A. M. Harman, "The Interpretation of the Third Commandment," *The Reformed Theological Review* 47 (1988) 1–7.

[43] William G. Hupper (ed.), *An Index to English Periodical Literature on the Old Testament and Ancient Near Eastern Studies*. Vol. I (ATLA Bibliography Series, No. 21; Metuchen, N.J. and London: The American Theological Library Association and The Scarecrow Press, 1987).

[44] Bruce Metzger, *Index to Periodical Literature on Christ and the Gospels* (Leiden: E. J. Brill, 1966).

[45] Reviewed by John Wright, *Australian Biblical Review* 36 (1988) 69–71.

About the Area Editor

Bruce K. Waltke (Th.M., Dallas Theological Seminary; Th.D., Dallas Theological Seminary; Ph.D., Harvard University) is professor of Old Testament at Westminster Theological Seminary. He is affiliated with the Orthodox Presbyterian Church. Until 1985 he was assistant editor of the Expositor's Bible Commentary. He currently serves on the Committee for Bible Translation of the *New International Version of the Holy Bible.* He is a contributor of the notes for the books of Psalms and Proverbs for the *New American Standard Study Bible.* His books include *Theological Word Book of the Old Testament* (1980); *Micah* in the Tyndale Old Testament Commentary series (Leicester: InterVarsity Press, 1989); and *Intermediate Hebrew Grammar* (Winona Lake: Eisenbrauns, 1990).

THE PLACE OF BIBLICAL CRITICISM
IN THEOLOGICAL STUDY

GORDON J. WENHAM
Senior Lecturer in Religious Studies
College of St. Paul and St. Mary
Cheltenham, England

Article from *Themelios*

"'Tis mystery all! The immortal dies.
Who can explore his strange design?"

These great lines of Charles Wesley's draw attention to the greatest of all mysteries in Christian theology, the death of Christ. How could the eternal Son of God, the agent of creation, die? How could the Son who always enjoyed perfect union with the Father cry out, "My God, my God, why hast thou forsaken me?"

Wherever we look in the doctrines of the Trinity and incarnation, we are faced with paradox and mystery. "That the Father is God, the Son is God, that the Holy Ghost is God, and yet they are not three Gods, but one God" (Athanasian Creed). Our human minds cannot comprehend how God can be both three persons, but only one. We cannot understand how Christ can be both fully God and fully man. If he is not omnipotent can he be truly God? But if he is, is he really human? Such dilemmas try to perplex us at every turn in theology. We are tempted to deny one truth in order to uphold another. But this is not the course taken by mainline Christian orthodoxy. With great persistence the church has insisted on maintaining both Christ's full humanity and his full divinity.

Mystery—A Characteristic of Christian Doctrine

But the necessity of holding in tension apparently mutually irreconcilable doctrines is not confined to Christology and Trinitarian thought. It is found in many other areas of doctrine as well. The doctrines of divine sovereignty and human responsibility may be logically incompatible, but a Christian is not free to reject either. If we deny that God is in control of all events, we become virtual atheists, or at least we deny the value of all intercessory prayer; for why pray, if God cannot respond to our prayers and do something about what we ask? Conversely the denial of human responsibility undercuts all exertion in any direction. We shall become fatalists unwilling to throw ourselves into evangelism or any good works: "what will be, will be" will be our motto and nothing will get done! But Scripture and Christian theologians assert both doctrines are essential and mutually complementary, even if they are not logically reconcilable.

We could go on: the doctrines of grace contain similar tensions, antinomies, paradoxes, or mysteries, describe them how you will. Both Jesus and Paul teach that God freely forgives sinners; both teach that all men, even believers, will be judged by their works and rewarded. It was Paul who said, "Being justified by faith, we have peace with God" (Rom. 5), who also said, "We must all appear before the judgment seat of Christ, so that each one may receive good or evil according to what he has done in the body" (2 Cor. 5:10). If mediaeval Christianity tended to overlook the doctrine of justification by faith, I fear twentieth-century Christians play down the doctrine of judgment. The doctrines are certainly very difficult to reconcile, so it is not surprising if we cleave to the one and reject the other. But fidelity to our Lord and the apostles surely involves upholding both.

Often it is the discovery that we have grasped only half the truth of a particular doctrine that makes theological study so uncomfortable. There must have been many theological students who have been dismayed to discover that the Christology they have assumed for years is technically heretical. Christians from a conservative background may come to realize that their beliefs about the Trinity are essentially modalist, that is that the Father, the Son, and the Spirit are merely different descriptions of the one God. Whereas those from liberal backgrounds are liable to discover that their Christology is adoptionist, i.e., that Christ became fully Son of God during his ministry, or Arian, i.e., that Christ is not God to the same degree as the Father. And if you avoid falling into one of these errors you may well discover you have embraced some other position such as monophysitism or nestorianism, gnosticism or montanism, pelagianism, or antinomianism, that no orthodox right-thinking Christian should dally with.

And it can be a painful process adapting our thinking to the truth of revelation. It requires humility to recognize and accept that what we believed in the past is not the whole truth, and then to reprogramme our minds and wills to the new truth. For Christian doctrines have an ethical as well as an intellectual dimension. To affirm that Jesus Christ is fully God as well as fully man means committing oneself unreservedly and totally to his teaching and obeying it to the letter. Similarly the doctrines of original sin and human depravity will affect profoundly our actions and attitudes across a wide range of social, political, spiritual, and pastoral issues. And adjusting ourselves to these new aspects of truth can be a very painful process.

But I suspect that if either you or your lecturers discover during your study that you are a Sabellian montanist or semipelagian gnostic, it will not cause over-much excitement. Such deviants are commonplace today and in this pluralistic society are usually accepted without much fuss. However, should you be diagnosed as a fundamentalist your fate may be very different. In the modern theology faculty fundamentalism is the great heresy. It is regarded as nearly as dangerous as the HIV virus and is treated with similar fervour but with rather less tack and sympathy. Fundamentalists will find themselves denounced in lectures and tutorials, and doubtless be encouraged to read James Barr's books on the subject. And those of this persuasion or even simply brought up in a fairly traditional church may well find their studies rather difficult in consequence. I still remember with sadness two of my tutorial partners at Cambridge. Neither could have been branded fundamentalist, but both were devout Christians intent on ordination. However, as a result of their study they both lost their faith and neither entered the ministry.

So what is this fundamentalism that causes so much controversy? The term "fundamentalism" has been called a theological swear-word, and it is used differently by different people—usually in abuse. Sometimes the term is used in a narrow sense to describe an exceptionally literalistic and wooden approach to the interpretation of the Bible; in this sense the name would be disowned by many evangelical Christians. But the word is commonly used much more broadly, for example, by Barr, to refer to Christians who hold to most traditional Christian doctrines and who in particular insist on the truthfulness of the whole Bible as God's written word. It is on the doctrine of Scripture that the critics of fundamentalism focus. For them the Bible contains essentially a variety of viewpoints, some of which contradict each other. It is not always reliable historically or theologically. To understand the Bible aright, all the tools of biblical criticism need to be employed. They will allow us not simply to correct the errors in the biblical text, but help us to read Scripture in context as a book of its time, with the assumptions and limitations of the age in which it was written. It is the rejection of biblical critical method and the naïvety of fundamentalist interpretation that is the focus of modern theologians' complaints.

Is criticism the indispensable tool for understanding Scripture as its protagonists argue, or is it, as it so often appears to the theological student, just a means of relativizing the Bible so that we cannot be sure what we should believe about anything? These are the issues on which I wish to focus.

Scripture—A Divine and Human Work

The role we ascribe to biblical criticism depends to a large extent on our understanding of the nature of Scripture. Is it a divine book or a human one? Is the fundamentalist right to insist on the divinity of Scripture, or the biblical scholar more correct in underlining its humanity? I wish to argue here that such antitheses are wrong: it is not the case of either divine or human, but it is a case of both human and divine. As in many other aspects of Christian doctrine, the incarnation, the Trinity, grace and law, we are confronted with two truths, both of which need to be affirmed; neither can be dispensed with, yet they cannot be fully reconciled by mortal man. In the doctrine of Scripture we confront another antinomy, paradox, or mystery, of a book that is at once fully human and fully divine.

Perhaps before considering what implications this view of Scripture has for its interpretation, we should very briefly review the evidence for its being both a divine and a human work. The Old Testament constantly claims divine authorship. Most of the laws begin "the LORD said to Moses," while the Ten Commandments are said to have been written by the finger of God. The prophets typically introduce their messages with "thus says the LORD," while the narrator of the historical books adopts an omniscient perspective.[1] He describes the secret thoughts of men's hearts and also analyses the divine intentions, something beyond the scope of any human author. Within the New Testament the divine authorship and authority of the Old Testament is always assumed and frequently asserted. For Jesus the Old Testament is the word of God (Mark 7:13; John 10:35). According to St. Paul it is all inspired by God (2 Tim. 3:16). And the claim that the New Testament comes from God too is also clear in many passages (Matt. 5:22, 28, 32, 34, etc.; 1 Cor. 14:37).

This attitude towards the Bible was continued by the early church. Kelly writes, "It goes without saying that the fathers envisaged the whole of the Bible as inspired . . . their general view was that Scripture was not only exempt from error but contained nothing that was superfluous."[2] According to Jerome, "In the divine Scriptures every word, syllable, accent and point is packed with meaning."[3]

If the divine character of Scripture has been affirmed by believers throughout the ages, its human qualities are equally apparent to careful readers, even though this aspect has only attracted detailed attention in the last two centuries. Most obviously, the fact that we have four gospels demonstrates the humanness of Scripture. Here we have four portraits of our Lord by four authors each with their own particular slant and emphasis. Then the epistles are addressed to different churches each with their own special problems, each demanding a response by the apostle to their particular needs. The variety of styles, the tendency for the writers to go off at tangents, all attest the fact that we are dealing with human compositions by human authors each with their own idiosyncrasies. Indeed, the more you think about it, the more obvious it is that Scripture has to be a human book, if it is to communicate with man. For if it had been written in God's language as opposed to Israelite Hebrew or Koine Greek, no one could have understood it without first learning God's language. But written in Hebrew the Old Testament was at least immediately intelligible to an ancient Israelite, while the New Testament was equally accessible to first-century readers of Greek.

So then, Scripture is both a completely divine book and a totally human book. Neither aspect should be overlooked in the study of Scripture. We must bear both in mind as we read it and seek to apply it today. The dual nature of Scripture causes various problems, but none of the tensions are intrinsically any worse than those posed by the other doctrines mentioned earlier. We face paradox and mystery here, just as we do in understanding the incarnation and atonement. But if we acknowledge that we do not understand how the immortal could die, we will not despair when confronted by the mystery of Scripture's dual nature.

The Indispensability of Biblical Criticism

What then is the place of biblical criticism in the study of Scripture? Very important, indeed indispensable, but not all-important. Biblical criticism is essential to the understanding of Scripture as a divine work. Let me elaborate.

I have already said that if God was to be understood by man, he had to speak in a human language. Had he addressed us in the language of the angels we would have been little the wiser. He chose rather to reveal himself to particular people in particular situations in their own language, in their own dialects and idioms. So if we are to understand those messages, we must somehow seek to put ourselves back into the situation of the original recipients of the Word. We must discover exactly what the original authors of the Scriptures meant by their words. And this is where the arts of biblical criticism become necessary.

Let me list and illustrate some of the branches of biblical criticism that aid the interpretation of the Bible. There is first of all textual criticism. Whenever documents are copied, especially when copied by hand, mistakes are liable to creep in. And even in this age of computer typesetting I have found some very odd mistakes in my proofs from time to time. Similar things have unfortunately happened in the copying of the biblical text. We do not have the original text of Isaiah or St. Paul's epistles, only copies; indeed in most cases copies of copies of copies, so that there has been plenty of chance for errors to creep in. This is particularly the case in the New Testament, partly because there are many more manuscripts of it and partly because Christians were less careful copiers than the Jews! However, thanks to the skills of the textual critics these errors can be spotted and the text restored to very nearly its original purity. To quote F. F. Bruce, "The various readings about which any doubt remains . . . affect no material question of historic fact or of Christian faith and practice."[4] We can in other words be very confident that our restored texts are so close to the original that there is no significant difference in meaning between them and the originals.

But once we have our restored texts, as near as makes no difference to the original, how do we establish what they mean? This brings us to the science of philology and linguistics, which has been most fruitfully applied to the understanding of the Bible; in particular James Barr has here made an immense and positive contribution to biblical interpretation. His studies[5] have transformed our approach to determining the precise meaning of words in Scripture. So often sermons are based on sloppy etymologies or words or phrases taken out of context, but linguistics has shown that this is quite mistaken. So quite central terms in the Bible's theological vocabulary, e.g., faith, soul, redemption, justification, may have been misunderstood by amateurs who fail to understand how language works. Modern linguistics has taught us to examine the context in which words are used rather than their etymology to determine their meaning. It has taught us to study language synchronically before studying it diachronically. In practice this means we must examine the usage of a word in a particular book of the Bible before examining its usage and meaning elsewhere. Just because a word means one thing in one writer, it does not necessarily follow that another writer uses it in exactly the same way. And once we recognize this principle we may well be on the way to resolving the apparent contradictions between different parts of Scripture, for example between Paul and James.

The next area of biblical criticism has burgeoned in the last decade. It is the new literary criticism, especially associated in Britain with Sheffield University. It is, I believe, one of the disciplines in biblical criticism of most potential value to would-be biblical expositors in that it opens up whole new vistas in the biblical narratives so that characters in the story come alive as real people not as mere names on the page. The new literary criticism has made us much more sensitive to the inner feelings of the actors in the Bible so that we can identify with them more closely.

Let me give a short example. Literary critics insist that repetition within a story often offers very valuable clues to the attitudes of the people involved. We must examine closely who says what, and what phrases they use.

For example, after God has promised Sarah a child, she laughs in disbelief. The RSV says, "After I have grown old, and my husband is old, shall I have pleasure?" And it is remarkable that such brazen unbelief should be treated so mildly by God. Think of Isaiah's rebuke of King Ahaz when he refused to believe his message (Isa. 7:13). But Sarah apparently gets away with it. Why?

A careful examination of the phraseology here gives the answer. The narrator first of all gives an objective, almost clinical, account of Sarah's situation: "Abraham and Sarah were old, well on in years. Sarah had stopped having periods." But Sarah describes herself more colourfully: "After I am worn out, shall I have pleasure? And my husband is old too."

From her language we see her real state of mind. It is not blind unbelief, rather it is the hopelessness of a woman exhausted by life who has been disappointed so often that she dare not believe things will change. And this is why God in his mercy treats her so gently and in the face of her doubts and lies reaffirms his promise and indeed quickly fulfills it.

In some ways this new-style literary criticism is a reversion to the older exegetical methods used before the nineteenth century. Reading the older commentaries, e.g., of Calvin or the mediaeval rabbis, one sometimes comes across interpretations like this. But this new-style criticism is a great advance over these old works. Their insights rested on the imagination of the commentator, and one is therefore never really quite sure whether Calvin's interpretation would have met with the biblical writers' approval. But the new literary criticism is based much more closely on hints contained within the text itself, so I dare to hope it is indeed enabling us to recover the original writers' understanding.

Next I should like to turn to an area of criticism that sometimes raises problems, but again has produced many valuable insights, indeed is indispensable to a fair and accurate understanding of Scripture. It is historical criticism. Under this heading I shall mention source criticism, issues of dating biblical books, and the writing of biblical history.

To understand the message of the Bible it is absolutely essential to have some understanding of the social setting in which its books were written. Otherwise we shall import our own twentieth-century models, impose them on the text, and come up with quite a misleading interpretation. For example, Genesis 2:24 makes a very significant comment about the nature of marriage: "For this reason a man leaves his father and mother and cleaves to his wife, and they become one flesh." But what exactly does it mean? A Westerner reading this passage might well conclude that it is endorsing our practice of setting up home independently of our parents, often indeed a long way from them. Indeed I remember reading a book by a missionary in Nigeria who criticized Nigerian men for continuing to live near their parents after they married. This he said was unbiblical and harmful to the marriage relationship! In fact, what the Nigerians did was precisely what the Israelites did! On marriage it was the woman who moved, not the man. The man stayed put, because he would succeed to his father's job and land, and the new wife moved in with him. In a literal physical sense the ancient Israelite man did not leave his family at all. So what is Genesis 2:24 really saying? Something far more profound than telling you where to live when you marry: it is talking about priorities and commitments. Before marriage a man's first obligations are to his parents. In the Ten Commandments, "honour your father and mother" comes immediately after our obligations to God and before "Thou shalt not kill." In the ancient world filial duty was regarded as the supreme obligation. But according to Genesis 2:24, marriage changes this. Now a man's first duty is to care for his wife, and secondarily to care for his parents. "He leaves his father and mother and cleaves to his wife." Read in the context of Old Testament society, rather than modern ideas, we see that Genesis 2:24 is a statement that revolutionizes the status of married women. Wives are not mere appendages or chattels of their husbands, rather the welfare of his wife must be a man's first concern.

Perhaps I may give another illustration of the necessity of understanding the social setting of the Bible if we are to grasp its intentions correctly. Leviticus 19:9–10 says, "When you reap the harvest of your land, you shall not reap the field to its very border. . . . " The motive of this law is then explained: "You shall leave them for the poor and the sojourner [i.e., the immigrant]." But J. V. Taylor in his book *Enough Is Enough* expounded this text as proof of the Bible's ecological concern, that we should not exploit the earth to its limits. And in a lecture I heard him say he was outraged at visiting an agricultural show where combine harvesters which boasted of their ability to reap right up to the edge of the field were on display. How unbiblical, he said! But he had failed to grasp the purpose of the law and the difference between our society and theirs. The law is designed to help the poor of ancient Israel, who were scattered throughout the land and could indeed easily go into the countryside and glean in the fields of the well-to-do neighbours (see the book of Ruth). But the poor of our society are in the cities, far from the fields. To leave the edges of our fields unreaped would not help them in the least. We must devise quite different welfare measures in our society to help our poor. So I believe historical criticism has a most important role to play in delineating the nature of biblical society. Without such sociological study we are liable to make terrible mistakes in interpreting and applying Scripture today.

The disciplines of source, form, and redaction criticism can also contribute to our understanding of the Bible. Form criticism has made us aware of the conventions that guided the biblical authors. It enables us to appreciate why they arranged material in the way they did, for example in the laws, the psalms, and the epistles. Through form criticism we can be more clear about the writers' intentions: why they included certain details and omitted others. And this knowledge should keep us from misinterpreting and misapplying biblical texts today.

Source and redaction criticism can again be valuable aids to interpretation. Source criticism is concerned with elucidating the sources used by the biblical writers. For example, the book of Kings often refers to the royal annals of Judah and Israel, suggesting that if one wants further details about the events recorded, these annals should be consulted. And for a historian concerned to reconstruct the exact course of Old Testament history, source criticism is clearly very important if he wants to come as close as possible to the earliest account of events. In the gospels some critics do their best to recover the exact words of Jesus, as opposed to the edited version offered by the evangelists.

But clearly what the editors do, whether they be Matthew, Mark, Luke, and John, or the compiler of Kings, is also of great concern to Bible readers. By comparing their work with their source we can discover what their special interests are. We can see what they have left out, what they have added from another source, what aspects of the original they have played up, what they have played down. In this way we gain a much clearer insight into the editor's theological viewpoint and the message he is trying to convey. And this investigation, what is termed redaction criticism, has proved extremely fruitful for more clearly understanding the text.

Genesis 1–11 shows how source and redaction criticism can help to elucidate the purpose of this important but perplexing part of Scripture.[6] Several ancient Near Eastern texts from 1600 B.C. or earlier contain an account of world history that runs roughly parallel to Genesis 1–11. But it is quite unlikely that any of these texts serve as the direct source of Genesis 1–11; rather they show us the sort of thing people in the ancient Near East believed in the second millennium B.C. when Genesis originated. And by comparing Genesis 1–11 with these other texts we appreciate more precisely what it is saying and what ideas it was trying to confute. For example, these nonbiblical texts paint a picture of evolutionary optimism, from a primitive world where life was hard and difficult to the comforts and sophistication of Mesopotamian civilization. Genesis, on the other hand, shows a world that was created very good progressively being corrupted by sinful man. On the other hand, while Mesopotamians regarded the creation of man as a divine afterthought, Genesis portrays him as the summit of God's creative purpose to which everything else is an accessory.

We are also presented with a very different picture of the supernatural world. Whereas the ancient Orient believed in a multitude of competing, lustful gods and goddesses limited in their powers, Genesis 1–11 shows that there is but one God, omnipotent and holy. Up to a point this theology is apparent to the simple reader of the Bible ignorant of source and redaction criticism, but it seems much more obvious when read against the views of Israel's neighbours. Indeed, until the discovery of the Atrahasis epic, it had hardly been appreciated that the command given to Adam to "be fruitful and multiply" showed Genesis rejecting the ancient fear of a population explosion.

Some Limitations of Criticism

But with source criticism we must be careful. C. S. Lewis, surely one of the greatest critics of English literature, was not at all impressed with the pretensions of biblical critics. His splendid essay, *On Fern Seed and Elephants*, ought to be compulsory reading for all students of theology. There he argues that theologians are often over-subtle in their source analysis. They claim to be able to spot fern seed but cannot recognize an elephant ten yards away!

The other reason we must not overrate source criticism is that the Christian is interested not so much in the sources that lie behind Scripture but in the text of Scripture itself. This is, I suppose, obvious in the case of Genesis 1–11. We are not interested in the Near Eastern myths used by the writer but the present composition. But it is easy to forget when we look at other parts of the Old Testament. Students of the prophets spend much time trying to distinguish between the pure original words of Isaiah and Jeremiah and later editorial traditions. But it is not the words of Jeremiah as recovered by John Bright or Ernest Nicholson that should be our chief interest: rather it is the present book of Jeremiah, whether it is all by Jeremiah or not, that is the canonical authoritative text for us today. Similarly in the gospels, it is not the words of Jesus as reconstructed by Joachim Jeremias or Ed Sanders that really matter, but the total portraits offered by Matthew, Mark, Luke, and John.

Finally we come to that aspect of biblical criticism that is often the most sensitive. This concerns the question of the dating of the biblical material and the attempt to assess its historicity. Establishing the historical setting of a book is often of great value in interpreting it. For example, it makes a great difference to the interpretation of the book of Revelation whether we date it before A.D. 70, when Jerusalem fell, or afterwards. On the former view we can read it as a prophecy of the fall of Jerusalem, of the great whore Babylon. Dated later it is more natural to read it as an anticipation of the end of the Roman empire. And there are many other books in the Bible where it makes a considerable difference to our understanding of them, when we date them. I think it is very natural for Christians to want to date the gospels as close as possible to the life of Christ, for then surely there is less chance of distortion and corruption creeping in. We can be more confident of the accuracy of the gospels if they were written around A.D. 50 than if they were written around A.D. 90. A similar motive surely underlies Jewish reluctance to give up the Mosaic authorship of the Pentateuch rather than with many Christian scholars to suppose it reached its final form nearly 1,000 years after Moses. For if it was written so late, who can be sure which stories, if any, bear any resemblance to historical reality?

Now I fear that some of your biblical courses may well spend a large amount of time on some of these issues. Which gospel was written first? Does Q exist? Were all the Pauline epistles written by Paul? Who were J, E, D, and P? How many Isaiahs were there? and so on. These are all perfectly legitimate questions, and the answers we give to them are often illuminating. But by way of conclusion, I should like to encourage you to keep these discussions in perspective.

First remember that the theories of authorship and dating are not as securely based as is sometimes claimed. The assured results of criticism are not quite as sure as they seem. Commenting on the source criticism of the Pentateuch, Professor Rendtorff of Heidelberg has written: "We possess hardly any reliable criteria for the dating of pentateuchal literature. Every dating of the pentateuchal sources rests on purely hypothetical assumptions which only have any standing through the consensus of scholars."[7] And in his book *Redating the NT*, J. A. T. Robinson makes much the same point. He wrote, "Much more than is generally recognized, the chronology of the New Testament rests on presuppositions rather than facts. What seemed to be firm datings based on scientific evidence are revealed to rest on deductions from deductions. The pattern is self-consistent but circular. Question some of the inbuilt assumptions and the entire edifice looks much less secure."[8] So my first caveat when faced with some critical theories about the dates of the biblical books is, "Do not be bowled over by them." These theories may not be as securely based as they sound.

The second thing to bear in mind is that historicity is not everything. It of course matters whether Jesus lived, died, and rose again. But there is a Jewish scholar, Pinhas Lapide, who believes in these facts without being a Christian. And I suppose that if the Turin shroud had proved to be genuine, it would not have persuaded many unbelievers that Jesus was indeed resurrected. It is most heartening when archaeologists find evidence corroborating the historical record of the Bible, whether it be the names of the patriarchs, the ashes of towns sacked by Joshua, the pool of Bethesda, or the house of Peter in Capernaum. All these discoveries confirm our faith in the historical reliability of the Bible. But the Bible is more than a human history book. Throughout, it claims to be offering a divine interpretation of public historical events, an interpretation that is beyond the scope of human verification. Take, for example, the book of Kings. It ends with recording the sacking of Jerusalem by Nebuchadnezzar and Jehoiachin's release from prison. These are events that are beyond dispute because they are also mentioned in contemporary Babylonian records. However, these events are not recorded in Kings just because the writer wanted to mention them as important events. He has included them because they reveal God's attitude to Israel, that he was angry with them for breaking the covenant, that he was fulfilling the warnings made much earlier by Moses. Now who can check whether this interpretation is correct? Obviously no one. We cannot telephone God to check if that was his attitude or not. We simply have to accept or reject the view of the book of Kings. We have no means of checking his view. It is beyond the possibility of human verification. But that does not make it unimportant or insignificant: clearly it was the main theological point being made in Kings that Israel and Judah were punished for their sins. So let us keep the issue of historicity in perspective. As Christians we shall wish to maintain that where the Bible is relating historical events they really happened,[9] but let us bear in mind that it is not so important that they occurred so much as what they teach us about God and his purposes and how we should respond.

Finally, my third caveat. Let us not spend too much time on the critical issues: it can easily divert us from the purpose of Scripture. Like the Jews we should be searching the Scriptures to find eternal life. Or as St. Paul said, "Whatever was written in former times was written for our instruction, that we might have hope" (Rom. 15:4). The purpose of the Scriptures is not simply to stimulate us academically, or to provide a living for professional biblical scholars. It is to lead us to God. Biblical criticism offers us indispensable aids to the interpretation and understanding of the Bible. But often instead of being the handmaid of Scripture it has become its master. I suppose that in the last 200 years there have been more than a hundred scholarly books discussing the criticism of Deuteronomy, its date, authorship, sources, and so on. But very few have focused on its theology, or the meaning of its teaching and laws for today. And there is a similar imbalance in some biblical courses, too—plenty on critical theory, and little on theology and its application. Yet what is the chief concern of Deuteronomy? "Hear O Israel: the LORD our God is one LORD, and you shall love the LORD your God with all your heart and with all your soul and with all your might."

When the academic study of Scripture diverts our attention from loving God with all our heart, soul, and strength, I think we should pause and take stock. We should ask ourselves whether we are using it as it was intended. As I said at the beginning, it is both a divine book and a human book. Because it is a human book we cannot understand it unless we employ all the types of biblical criticism to the full. But because it is also a divine book we must recognize that these tools are insufficient by themselves for us to grasp and apply its message. To do that we must have a humble mind and a heart open to the guidance of the Spirit.

Notes

[1] For further discussion of the omniscience of the biblical authors, see R. Alter, *The Art of Biblical Narrative* (New York, 1981), pp. 23–46; M. Sternberg, *The Poetics of Biblical Narrative* (Bloomington, Ind., 1985), pp. 23–57.

[2] J. N. D. Kelly, *Early Christian Doctrines* (London, 1960), p. 61.

[3] Ibid., p. 62.

[4] F. F. Bruce, *The New Testament Documents: Are They Reliable?* (London, 1960), pp. 19–20.

[5] J. Barr, *Biblical Words for Time* (London, 1962); *The Semantics of Biblical Language* (Oxford, 1961). For a compact modern discussion see M. Silva, *Biblical Words and Their Meanings* (Grand Rapids, Mich., 1982).

[6] For further treatment see G. J. Wenham, *Genesis 1–15* (Waco, Tex., 1987), pp. xlv–1.

[7] R. Rendtorff, *Das überlieferungsgeschichtliche Problem des Hexateuch* (Berlin, 1976), p. 169.

[8] J. A. T. Robinson, *Redating the NT* (London, 1976), pp. 2–3.

[9] Here we of course beg the question of genre. Though in most parts of the Bible it is quite clear whether or not Scripture is intending to describe historical events, there are of course some very problematic fringe cases, e.g., Genesis 1–11 or the book of Jonah. It is an important task for commentators to establish the genre of such books. But here as elsewhere what Christian readers should be most concerned about is what these books teach us about God and his purposes.

THE STRUCTURE OF EZRA-NEHEMIAH
AND THE INTEGRITY OF THE BOOK

TAMARA C. ESKENAZI
Assistant Professor and Director of the
Institute for Interfaith Studies
Center for Judaic Studies
University of Denver

Article from *Journal of Biblical Literature*

Debates about the integrity of Ezra-Nehemiah and its relation to Chronicles continue. On the one hand, the pervasive view for the past 150 years has been that Ezra—Nehemiah and Chronicles form a single book, authored by the Chronicler.[1] This theory had been challenged in recent decades by the pioneering work of S. Japhet, a challenge corroborated also by H. G. M. Williamson and others.[2] Nevertheless, a lively discussion concerning the relation of Ezra-Nehemiah to Chronicles persists and the issues seem far from settled.[3]

On the other hand, Ezra-Nehemiah is commonly divided into two distinct books, Ezra and Nehemiah. These two are printed separately in nearly all modern translations of the Bible even though such division runs counter to the earliest LXX manuscripts and the MT, where Ezra-Nehemiah appears as a single work.[4] Ezra-Nehemiah thus receives a peculiar treatment and appears to have indeterminate boundaries.

The structure of Ezra-Nehemiah becomes a pivotal issue in attempting to respond to the dual pull of scholarly debates: the drive to submerge Ezra-Nehemiah in Chronicles or to dissect it into Ezra and Nehemiah. Yet little progress has been made in clarifying such a structure. Although it is no longer fashionable to recompose Ezra-Nehemiah into a presumed, pristine "original," as L. W. Batten, for example, had done,[5] very few scholars explain or even describe the present form of the book. Most commentaries on Ezra-Nehemiah simply follow the sequence of chapters in the book with but an occasional glance at what the overall design might be. They describe some of the major blocks in terms of literary or historical categories, noting the confusing peculiarities in the book (such as the dispersion of the Ezra material in the Nehemiah memoirs) without coming to conclusions about the nature of the present composition of the book.

Notable exceptions to these general tendencies are B. S. Childs and Japhet.[6] Each, in a brief study of Ezra-Nehemiah, proposes in passing an overall structure and alludes to an organizing principle. The very brevity of their studies and the absence of developed details heighten rather than diminish the need for an analysis of the structure of the book.

This paper uses literary tools to explicate Ezra-Nehemiah's distinctive structure and point of view by focusing on one aspect of Ezra-Nehemiah, namely, the lists of people. I intend to show how these lists, often considered one of Ezra-Nehemiah's most exasperating features, are in fact an important key to the structure and hence the meaning of Ezra-Nehemiah. The lists, I argue, shape the book, affirm its integrity, and help differentiate Ezra-Nehemiah from Chronicles. They also express one of Ezra-Nehemiah's major themes, that is, the shift away from individual heroes to the centrality of the people as a whole.

My method is literary in adhering to the kinds of criteria that critics such as R. Alter, A. Berlin, and M. Sternberg have used for other biblical narratives.[7] My text is the MT, wherein Ezra-Nehemiah appears as a single book, as the masoretic notations indicate. In the MT, Ezra-Nehemiah is also separate from Chronicles, which follows it.[8] Although my paper thus presupposes—and therefore cannot also claim to prove—the integrity of Ezra-Nehemiah and its separateness from Chronicles, it nevertheless contributes to that discussion: It presents a particular structure which accounts for Ezra-Nehemiah's peculiarities, a structure that is independent from that of Chronicles. In so doing, the paper illustrates a coherence to Ezra-Nehemiah that renders a connection to Chronicles unnecessary and less plausible.

I

The predominance of lists constitutes one of Ezra-Nehemiah's most familiar features. Approximately one quarter of the book is made up of lists, mostly lists of people. The major ones are as follows:

Ezra 1:9–11: list of returned vessels
Ezra 2:1–70: list of returned exiles
Ezra 8:1–14: list of Ezra's companions
Ezra 10:18–44: list of men who separated from foreign wives
Neh. 3:1–32: list of builders of the wall
Neh. 7:5–72: repeated list of returned exiles
Neh. 10:2–29: list of signatories to the pledge
Neh. 11:3–36: list of settlers and settlements
Neh. 12:1–26: list of cultic personnel
Neh. 12:32–42: list of parading members of the community

The prevalence of lists has frequently been used as an argument for unity of Ezra-Nehemiah with Chronicles. E. L. Curtis, for example, mentions fondness for lists and genealogies as the trademark of the Chronicler that is found in both Chronicles and Ezra-Nehemiah.[9] Such a claim needs to be reexamined. Ezra-Nehemiah, in fact, has but a single, brief genealogy (Neh. 12:10–11); the rest are lists and occasional pedigrees (i.e., a line of ascent from the present to the past, such as Ezra's lineage going back to Aaron in Ezra 7).[10] In this sense, Ezra-Nehemiah is already different from Chronicles, where the genealogies (tldôt), especially in chapters 1–9, dominate.[11]

At the same time that the lists have been claimed as evidence for *unity* of Ezra-Nehemiah and Chronicles, the repetition of the list of returnees (Ezra 2 and Nehemiah 7) has influenced scholars to *divide* Ezra-Nehemiah itself into two books. The repetition has been understood as a vestige of an earlier, separate circulation of Ezra and Nehemiah, preserved by scribes too pious to omit either of these venerable documents.

Such arguments lose much of their power precisely on account of books such as Chronicles. The very existence of Chronicles, with its bold modifications of the sacred traditions, and also the existence of 1 Esdras, should teach us that the ancients were quite willing to tamper with sacred traditions in order to express their distinctive views. The preservation of the two lists, therefore, must point to something else. In what follows I shall suggest what that "something else" might be.

Literary criteria invite us to look at the lists as a deliberate strategy rather than as a frozen remnant. Even though, as Williamson wisely observes, chapters like Ezra 2—and perforce also Nehemiah 7—"are among the most uninviting portions of the Bible to the modern reader,"[12] they are literarily important. Their prominence compels us to consider their significance to the overall intention and message of the book.

In order to understand that overall intention, we will explore the nature and function of the repeated list of returnees, Ezra 2 and Nehemiah 7. The lists of returnees, in terms of content, focus on the people and record the people according to class, families, geography, and numbers, and occasionally according to profession. The lists include a wide range of categories of persons who now form the people of Israel and who have returned to their home. Heading the lists are eleven and/or twelve men, their number presumably reflecting a new configuration in order to retain symbolically the traditional twelve-tribe division. The parallels between the lists are so great that we can call them a repetition, their divergence notable mostly at the concluding sections (Ezra 2:68–69; cf. Neh. 7:70–71).

R. W. Klein's meticulous study of the lists analyzes the text of the lists and their relation to each other (and to 1 Esdras), aspects which I need not recount here.[13]

The setting of the lists and their original purpose have been explored as well.[14] There appears to be a consensus that each of the lists is a composite.[15] Social and political, as well as economic, concerns most likely lurked in the background and explain their origin.[16]

Whatever the original sense, one must nevertheless still ponder the role of the repetition of the list in the book's final form. This concern is all the more relevant when we take into account the fact that Ezra 1–6, according to Japhet and Williamson, constitutes the latest stratum of the book.[17] The repetition is therefore not simply the product of an unyielding respect for sources but a voluntary and thus presumably deliberate act of the author/compiler. Williamson raises the question from a canonical perspective,[18] but relies on A. H. J. Gunneweg's limited answer, namely, the reiteration that the purified community is the same as the community which had first returned and undertook the building of the Temple.[19] This explanation is probable but insufficient.[20]

A full study of the repetition of the lists in Ezra 2 and Nehemiah 7 requires some discussion of the ways repetitions function in narrative. For scholars who rely on source criticism, repetitions most often signal insertions; they frequently become occasions for dissecting the text and distributing its components to different sources. This approach characterizes most studies of Ezra-Nehemiah, even when undertaken by scholars who have applied new literary tools to other biblical works. As a result, as noted earlier, Ezra-Nehemiah's most outstanding repetition typically turns into evidence for the initial independence of the books of Ezra and Nehemiah. S. Talmon sums up a representative view: "If indeed Ezra and Nehemiah at one time were two separate works written by different authors, this could help in explaining the duplication of some events and the literary units in both, such as the list of returning exiles (Ezra 2–Nehemiah 7)."[21]

According to contemporary literary criticism, however, repetitions are significant vehicles for the text's intention. Literary studies confirm and amply demonstrate the ingenious and sophisticated use of repetition in biblical narrative to convey meaning.[22] As Adele Berlin notes, repetition "is one of the most extensive devices in the Bible, taking many different forms. . . . It should not be mistaken for ancient redundancy, or even as simply an aesthetic device. It is a key to perception, to interpretation."[23] Since repetition in literature serves no single function,[24] one cannot apply an automatic or mechnical interpretation to this particular repetition. Instead, specific meanings have to be tested out on the basis of patterns found elsewhere. It should be clear, however, that the lists, by virtue of being an overt and major repetition, are important as a distinctive *literary* strategy. They articulate, thereby, something central to the book as a whole. Our task is to determine what this might be. I identify at least six important points that the repetition of the lists articulates.

First, structurally speaking, repetition as an *inclusio* unifies material.[25] *Inclusio* and chiasm are major devices for defining units in ancient literature. As H. Van Dyke Parunak observes, "An inclusio is a three-membered (A B A) chiasm whose outer members are short, compared with the center member."[26] As an *inclusio*, as well as a chiasm, repetition signals conclusion of a unit.[27] The weighty repetition of the lists in Ezra-Nehemiah, as a literary technique, defines the structure of the narrative. It establishes boundaries and compresses all the material that has been "bracketed" within the repetition. The repetition of the list frames the intervening material, binding it more closely together, forming a unit from Ezra 2 to Nehemiah 7.

The section thus formed is the longest in the book. It is the heart of the book and its central event. We can discern three distinct subunits or stories within this largest section. Each story contains a specific cast of characters and a clear task with complication and resolution. The first story tells of the building of the Temple by the returnees, with Zerubbabel and Jeshua. The second describes the return of Ezra and the children of exile who build up the community according to the Torah. The third recounts the adventures of Nehemiah and the Judeans who build the wall.[28]

These three sections, typically understood as mere succession despite some chronological disarray, are firmly clamped together in Ezra-Nehemiah by the repetition. The repetition of the list indicates that these diverse stories finally constitute a single major event: the building of God's house by the people of God in accordance with a decree (see Cyrus's declaration).

For Ezra-Nehemiah, the house of God is not simply the Temple but rather comes to encompass the city as a whole.[29] The repetition of the list is one of several ways that Ezra-Nehemiah expresses this idea. The list confirms formally and structurally what Ezra 6:14 expresses thematically, namely, that building the house of God extended over a long period, spanning the reigns of Cyrus, Darius, and Artaxerxes, whose decrees sustained these activities.

The repetition allows us to discern the shape of Ezra-Nehemiah, making what precedes into an introduction and what follows into a conclusion. This observation leads to the following overall structure of Ezra-Nehemiah:

I.   An introduction which sets an agenda: Cyrus's decree calls God's people to build the house of God in Jerusalem (1:1–4)
II. The actualization of the decree in Ezra 2–Nehemiah 7 or Ezra 1:5–Nehemiah 7:72 (see below for the more precise boundaries)
III. The celebration of success: God's people celebrate and dedicate the house of God (Neh. 8–13)

Because Ezra 2 through Nehemiah 7 constitutes ultimately a single event, the grand celebration does not take place after the completion of the Temple in Ezra 6 but awaits and comes only after the completion of the whole project. At that time the completed house of God, Temple, people, walls, are sanctified (Neh. 12:30). Hence, according to Ezra-Nehemiah's structure, all of these developments between Ezra 2 and Nehemiah 7 are necessary elements of the full realization of Cyrus's decree. Only when they have been executed can the great fanfare of the dedication proper take place. Nehemiah 8–13 is that dedication. The repetition of the list is thus the key to Ezra-

Nehemiah's structure. This may constitute its first and foremost significance.

Second, repetition indicates emphasis. Repetitions most frequently occur in order to stress something important. Biblical narrative, as well as other ancient and modern literature, characteristically repeats ideas, information, or phrases that are significant (note the repeated stories of creation and the Ten Commandments, etc.). In Ezra-Nehemiah, the repetition then emphasizes the significance of the persons named in the lists. The repetition keeps numerous persons and names firmly before the readers' eyes, drawing attention to the multitude that constitutes the people of Israel. Josephus, as *via negativa*, helps us appreciate the import of the lists and of their repetition. His own account of the return omits the list of returnees with the following rationale: "But I have thought it better not to give a list of the names of the families lest I distract the minds of my readers from the connexion of events and make the narrative difficult for them to follow" (*Ant.* 11.3.10 §68).

The difference from Ezra-Nehemiah could not be more telling. Josephus, in his rush to continue the main story line, refuses to linger on what for him comprise the less important details, that is, the lists. Ezra-Nehemiah, however, keeps the readers' mind *precisely* on such lists because they are the bearers of the narrative line. It is the names in this duplicated list (and other such lists) that disclose the characters whose adventures are recounted. For Ezra-Nehemiah, the people, not simply their illustrious leaders, are the main characters in the book. By repeating, the book underscores this point, emphasizing the role of the people as a whole.

Third, as an emphasis on the people as a whole, the list also expresses Ezra-Nehemiah's view of the wholeness of the people. Chronicles, by way of contrast, assumes the twelve-tribe schema for Israel even after the demise of the northern kingdom. Consequently, Chronicles includes members of the northern tribes in the return (e.g., 1 Chron. 9:3). Ezra-Nehemiah offers a different notion of who Israel is. For Ezra-Nehemiah, as Japhet, for example, has shown, only the returned exiles now constitute Israel.[30] These comprise the Judeans, Benjaminites, priests, and Levites (Ezra 1:5). By enumerating the composition of the people twice, Ezra-Nehemiah stresses the nature of this reconstituted community.

Fourth, the repetition bridges past and present. Talmon has shown that resumptive repetition can convey contemporaneity of events.[31] Something akin to this happens here. The repetition of Ezra 2 and Nehemiah 7 links people and events of the past with those in the present. Nehemiah 7 literally brings the earlier returnees into the present and combines them as participants in the subsequent event(s): namely, celebration and dedication. All that transpired between the "brackets" (i.e., the two lists) now joins with what follows. The structure suggests that all the groups have had a specific role in the "process of actualization." All the people thereby gather together to celebrate "success." Just as the later rabbis saw "all Israel" standing at

Sinai, including all those who followed since Moses, so Ezra-Nehemiah, by repeating Ezra 2 in Nehemiah 7, makes all those who preceded take part in the ensuing celebration of the reading of the Torah and the dedication of the walls, that is, in the completion of the house of God and its dedication. Celebration waits until such conjoining takes place. The list at this juncture not only stresses the importance of the people as a whole but also unites them in time and place.

Fifth, the repetition suggests the broadening of communal participation. This meaning can be gathered from looking at differences in details, since repetition sometimes draws attention to important differences by establishing an initial commonality followed by variations.[32] One detects within the lists slight differences in names and numbers which are most easily explained as textual corruptions.[33] The more obvious difference concerns the reports of the initial activities in the land (Ezra 2:68–69; Neh. 7:69–71). These differences include variant details of who did what, and who contributed what. The amount of contributions differs. The most dramatic differences are the priests' garments and gold darics.[34] As for the contributors, Ezra 2 mentions only "some of the heads of families" (Ezra 2:68), whereas Nehemiah 7 mentions the heads of the ancestors' houses, the governor, but also *"the rest of the people"* (Neh. 7:71). The rest of the people contribute as much as the heads of the houses and much more than the governor.[35] Galling explains these variations on the basis of historical issues, whereas Japhet grounds them in ideology.[36] From our perspective, one may conclude that the differences cited express in Nehemiah 7 the broader participation of the populace in the task of building.[37] Not only are the leaders involved, but the people as a whole make substantial contribution.

Sixth, and more speculative, interpretation of the repetition implies that the list sets equivalencies between Torah reading and sacrifices. This interpretation is based on the recognition that repetitions establish at times analogies, equivalencies, or substitutions between those things that follow, to which the repetition points.[38] Ezra 2 immediately leads to the building of the altar and to worship. Nehemiah 7 directly leads to the ceremony of the reading of the Torah. This arrangement suggests a relation between altar building and Torah reading. One could postulate that here we find an earlier version of a view that later becomes normative, that is, that the study of Torah replaces the offering of sacrifices. Such a conclusion is attractive all the more when one notes how rare and briskly reported are the sacrifices in Ezra-Nehemiah, especially after Nehemiah 8. The idea is indirectly supported by the location of the reading of the Torah in Nehemiah 8. As H. L. Ellison has suggested, "In the choice of site we have Ezra's deliberate proclamation that the Torah was greater than the Temple and its sacrifices, indeed that the Torah as such was above anything it might contain."[39] This use of the repetition to replace cult with Torah is too subtle, however, to constitute a major focus. At best one can argue for a beginning of such analogies and possible shift in cultic orientation which later generations utilized.

We have looked at what the lists accomplish as repetition. They bind the intervening material together, leading to the conclusion that what is embraced within the brackets belongs together and articulating several compounded meanings.

II

We now turn to the larger context, looking at what precedes and what follows each of these lists in order to discern the book's pattern with greater precision. We need to examine the context where the first list (Ezra 2) appears and then the context where the second list (Neh. 7) ends. First we must ask whether the unit begins with the list itself in Ezra 2 or at an earlier point. This involves determining the place of Ezra 1:5–11, the report of the return and the list of vessels returned by Cyrus. Three possibilities typically have been proposed concerning 1:5–11. (1) It is common to divide the passage into two segments: Ezra 1:5–6 and 1:7–11. Ezra 1:5–6 has been considered a part of the introduction together with Cyrus's decree (Ezra 1:1–4), whereas 1:7–11 has been linked with the list of Ezra 2 (so most commentaries). (2) Ezra 1:5–11 as a whole has been included as part of the introduction, Ezra 1:1–4.[40] (3) Ezra 1:5–11 has been attached to the list of returnees and joined with Ezra 2.

I suggest that the third possibility is the best, but I intend to develop it further and show how Ezra 1:5–11 is connected to what follows. Like most narratives, Ezra-Nehemiah is a story.[41] The basic components of story can be delineated as follows: (I) Potentiality (objective defined); (II) Process of Actualization; (III) Success (objective reached).[42] This is the structure which the repetition of the lists (Ezra 2 and Neh. 7) indicates.

Cyrus's decree (Ezra 1:1–4) by itself forms the first part of the book, standing as a separate introductory unit. This unit sets up the agenda for the book by declaring what God and Cyrus have decreed. The material within the repeated lists depicts the actualization of the decree in three stages. However, this process of actualization is first introduced by a proleptic summary, Ezra 1:5–6. As a proleptic summary, these verses state in an embryonic fashion what Ezra 1:7–Nehemiah 7:72 elaborates in detail. They announce the fulfillment of Cyrus's decree. As the decree had summoned a people to go up and build the house of God in Jerusalem which is in Judah (Ezra 1:1–4), Ezra 1:5–6 reports that a community rose up promptly to execute this decree, going up to build.

The structure of this proleptic summary essentially parallels the decree, stressing thereby the close correspondence between the decree and its fulfillment. The jussives "let him go up" (wy⁢ᶜl) and "let him build" (wybn) in Cyrus's edict (Ezra 1:3) become the infinitives "to go up" (lᶜlôt) and "to build" (lbnôt) in the people's response (Ezra 1:5). The exhortation to neighbors to support the returnees with freewill gifts of silver, gold, goods, and livestock (Ezra 1:4) is matched by the report that the neighbors strengthened the returnees with silver, gold, goods, and livestock (Ezra 1:6).

This introduction specifies that "the people" comprise the heads of ancestors' houses of Judah and Benjamin,[43] priests and Levites and every one (lkl) who had been stirred up by God. All of these people are the central subject of Ezra-Nehemiah. What will follow is their story.

As God had stirred up the spirit of Cyrus (Ezra 1:1), so does God stir up the spirit of the returnees (Ezra 1:5). The parallel confirms that the response by the community to the decree is prompted by the same divine power responsible for the decree itself, reiterating the connection between decree and fulfillment. In addition, as the proleptic summary of the process of actualization, this repetition consigns all subsequent events in Ezra 1:5–Nehemiah 7:72 to the workings of the same divine intitiative.

The decree is fully actualized by three movements: each involves a beginning in the Diaspora with the transfer of material from the Persian king to the returned exiles (see, e.g., Ezra 7:12–26, esp. 16). For this reason it seems best to understand the list of vessels which Cyrus transfers to the returnees as the introduction to the first movement rather than as a conclusion of the previous section. Given this understanding, the structure of Ezra-Nehemiah can be described as follows:

I.   Potentiality (objective defined): decree to the community to build the house of God (Ezra 1:1–4)
II. Process of actualization: the community builds the house of God according to decree (Ezra 1:5–Neh. 7:72)
     A. Introduction: Proleptic summary (Ezra 1:5–6)
     B. First movement: the returnees build the altar and the Temple according to the decree and the Torah (Ezra 1:7–6:22)
     C. Second movement: Ezra and the exiles build the community according to the Torah (Ezra 7:1–10:40)
     D. Third movement: Nehemiah and the Judeans build the wall (Neh. 1:1–7:5)
     E. Recapitulation: list of returnees (Neh. 7:6–72)
III. Success (objective reached): the community dedicates the house of God according to Torah (Neh. 8:1–13:31)

We turn now to the context of the concluding list, Nehemiah 7. Traditional assessment of Nehemiah 7's relation to its context usually focuses on questions of priority vis-à-vis Ezra 2. Some scholars argue that the seemingly tight connection of Nehemiah 7 with what follows shows that Nehemiah 7 is prior to Ezra 2.[44] Others (e.g., U. Kellermann) argue for a closer integrity of Ezra 2 with its context, and they grant, therefore, priority to Ezra 2.[45]

Such inconclusive debates, which mix historical and literary questions, serve to illustrate the complexities and ambiguities in the text. They reveal, in this particular case, that both Ezra 2 and Nehemiah 7 are in some respects well integrated into their respective contexts and that, in others, they stand apart from their surrounding.

The list in Nehemiah 7 is particularly perplexing, although its beginning is clear. Nehemiah reports: "And I found the book of the genealogy of those who came up at the first, and I found written in it" (Neh. 7:5). The phrase, "and I found written in it" [w^ɔmṣ^ɔ ktûb bô] is an *un*ambiguous clue that what follows is a quoted document. The conclusion of the quotation, however, is obscure. There are no indications that one thing has ended and another one has begun. As a result, scholars break the units in different ways.

No formulaic language or any other literary markings indicate the conclusion of the unit. The last identified speaker/writer was Nehemiah (Neh. 7:5). One would have expected him to resume once his quotation concluded, possibly in Nehemiah 7:72. Yet it is not self-evident where the list does conclude. One cannot immediately determine whether the report about the gathering on the first day of the first month in Nehemiah 8:1 belongs still to the document which Nehemiah introduced and quoted or whether it is a resumption of Nehemiah's own memoirs. Only further reading yields the necessary conclusion that *neither* is the case. The reference to Ezra in Nehemiah 8:2 indicates that the scene belongs to a time later than the first return and therefore in the reign of Artaxerxes, wherein all subsequent events transpire.[46] This confirms the view that Nehemiah's quotation of the older document had come to conclusion at an earlier point.[47] The reference to Nehemiah in the third person (Neh. 8:9), however artificial, indicates that he is no longer the narrator. Consequently, it is clear that a definite transition occurs between Nehemiah 7 and 8, but the exact location of that transition remains unclear. The customary scholarly designation of Nehemiah 8 as part of the Ezra material acknowledges the transition.[48]

What is striking here is the remarkable *seamlessness* of this particular transition. Such seamlessness is all the more astonishing in a book so rife with obvious seams. It is at this juncture that "confluence" appears as the most apt description. A probable explanation of this peculiar confluence of the texts—peculiar all the more in view of Ezra-Nehemiah's rough transitions elsewhere—is that it expresses syntactically what is also expressed through the repetition: the flowing together of persons and events embraced in the preceding section into the present event of Nehemiah 8–13. Like a funnel, Nehemiah 7 channels persons and events from Ezra 2 through Nehemiah 7 into the final celebration which comes next to conclude the book.

It is no mere accident therefore that Nehemiah 8:1 reports, for the first time in Ezra-Nehemiah, that "*all* the people gathered as *one*." This "all . . . as one" indicates the efforts and participation of all who preceded, all of whom are embraced within the repeated lists and join in the celebration.

The main results may be summarized as follows: The repetition of the list of returnees defines the shape of the book and articulates several important ideas. The shape is a tightly constructed book with an objective defined in Cyrus's decree, actualized in Ezra 1:5–Nehemiah 7:72, and celebrated in Nehemiah 8–13. A repeated emphasis is given to the people as a whole.

III

The other lists in Ezra-Nehemiah continue to restate the importance of the people as a whole. Their strategic placement shows that each act, from the building of the Temple to the final celebration, is performed by many individuals whose names and number literally and literarily at times submerge those of the leaders (see, for example, the climactic encircling parade of Neh. 12:32–42 in which Ezra and Nehemiah are virtually "lost" to the reader in the crowd). The message is thus clear: the people are the important ones. The people "go up" and the people "build"—as Cyrus and the Lord have commanded. The additional list in Ezra 8 reiterates another "going up." The list of builders (Neh. 3) spells out who were the numerous participants responsible for restoring the wall. The pledge to the Torah and to the house of God comes with a long list of signatures (Neh. 10:2–29). The list of settlers and settlements (Neh. 11:3–36) continues to keep diverse persons before the readers' eyes. Each and every important event in the book has its list of participants to indicate that the activities were not the actions of famous individuals but included the less known members of the society. In many respects, Ezra-Nehemiah's account of the restoration is analogous to the Vietnam War Memorial: events are recalled by commemorating the names of many who have been otherwise lost to the communal memory. This can be contrasted with another form of remembering, reflected in our culture by the Washington Monument, which celebrates the great hero. Such heroic mentality characterizes Josephus's and 1 Esdras's accounts of the return and restoration of postexilic Israel, where great men, such as Zerubbabel, remain in the limelight.[49] For Ezra-Nehemiah, glory goes to the countless people who actually shaped the details of the events, not simply to their leaders. The book painstakingly insists that future generations recognize the communal participation in the re-creation of the nation's life.

The use of one particular list in Nehemiah 12:1–26 provides a final clue to the structure of the book and its independence from Chronicles. This list of cultic personnel is situated in the last major unit of the book, Nehemiah 8–13, wherein the celebration of the fulfillment of the decree and the dedication of the house of God take place. Before it, come several ceremonies (Neh. 8–10); after it, comes the grand finale of Nehemiah 12:27–13:3. Between the ceremonies themselves and the grand finale we find the lists of Nehemiah 11:1–12:26.

These lists, like the repetition of Ezra 2 and Nehemiah 7 weave characters together in relation through time and space. Thus Nehemiah 11 links people and land, whereas Nehemiah 12 braids the present day with the beginning of the book, recording the network of cult personnel that spans the unified era. The point to note is that the era it unifies is from Zerubbabel and Jeshua (Neh. 12:1) to Ezra and Nehemiah (Neh. 12:26).

The list of cultic personnel in Nehemiah 12:1–26 provides closure, tying together the loose ends of the tapestry. As the book comes to an end, Nehemiah 12:1–26 explicitly retraces these threads back to Ezra 2:1, recapitulating lines of cultic personnel back to those who came up in the first wave of return.[50] The network of priests and Levites unifies the earlier and later periods into a single, continuous event: the actualization of Cyrus's edict. Having begun in the days of Zerubbabel and Jeshua (Neh. 12:1; cf. Ezra 2:1), the list concludes with "in the days of Nehemiah the governor and of Ezra the priest the scribe" (Neh. 12:26). This articulates, as did the repetition of the lists, the oneness of the intervening generations and activities.

The lists of priests and Levites in Nehemiah 12:1–26 pose many historical and textual problems that have remained unresolved.[51] As Williamson has shown, there is no relation between these priestly lists and the priestly courses in 1 Chronicles 24:1–18.[52] From a literary perspective it is important to note the book's concern with recapitulating the era through such lists, however awkward this proves to be.[53]

The fact that the concluding recapitulation links the conclusion to the beginning of Ezra-Nehemiah itself, and not to some events in Chronicles, shows that Ezra-Nehemiah is a self-standing book and not the continuation of Chronicles. Nehemiah 12 thus confirms the structure of Ezra-Nehemiah which the repetition of the list defined; it thus helps illustrate the integrity of the book. Most of all, Nehemiah 12:1–26 serves to sever Ezra-Nehemiah from a relation to Chronicles by showing that this book's conclusion returns to its beginning.

All these lists in Ezra-Nehemiah, recounting past figures and linking them in the present, establish the harmonious whole which is the restored community. Together they set the stage for the communal celebration of the completed task. The united community, a community whose many members Ezra-Nehemiah's extensive lists diligently honor, is now ready to meet the new day with unmitigated joy (Neh. 12:43).[54] Cyrus's decree has at last been fulfilled.

Notes

[1] The theory of common authorship for Ezra-Nehemiah and Chronicles was set forth by L. Zunz, "Dibre hajamim oder Bücher der Chronik," *Die gottesdienstlichen Vorträge der Juden, historisch entwickelt* (Berlin: Louis Lamm, 1832, 1919 ed.) 12–34. This seminal article quickly established the unity of Chronicles and Ezra-Nehemiah as the normative view. As H. G. M. Williamson observes, "Although there had been some who earlier hinted at this idea, it was in

1832 that L. Zunz set out the evidence which, with later additions and refinements, convinced the overwhelming majority of scholars. Confirmation of this statement may be found by reference to virtually any modern commentary or introduction written from that time down to the present" (*Israel in the Books of Chronicles* [New York: Cambridge University Press, 1977] 5).

[2] Japhet, *The Ideology of the Book of Chronicles and Its Place in Biblical Thought* (Jerusalem: Mosad Bialik, 1977) [Hebrew]; see also idem, "The Supposed Common Authorship of Chronicles and Ezra-Nehemiah Investigated Anew," *VT* 18 (1968) 330–71; Williamson, *Israel in the Books of Chronicles*, esp. pp. 1–70.

[3] Note, for example, the special "Chronicles, Ezra, Nehemiah Consultation" at the Annual Meeting of SBL in Atlanta in 1986, devoted to the question of the relation between Ezra-Nehemiah and Chronicles: "The Unity and Extent of the Chronicler's Work" with P. R. Ackroyd, S. Japhet, and B. Halpern representing different positions.

[4] The division into Ezra and Nehemiah is first attested by Origen (see Eusebius *Hist. eccl.* 6.25.2) and was later accepted by the Vulgate. For a recent discussion of this development, see H. G. M. Williamson, *Ezra, Nehemiah* (Word Biblical Commentary, 16; Irving, TX: Word Books, 1985) xxi-xxiii.

[5] Batten, *A Critical and Exegetical Commentary on the Books of Ezra and Nehemiah* (ICC; New York: Scribner, 1913).

[6] B. S. Childs, *Introduction to the Old Testament as Scripture* (Philadelphia: Fortress, 1979) 624–38; S. Japhet, "Biblical Historiography in the Persian Period," in *World History of the Jewish People* (ed. H. Tadmor and I. Ephal; Jerusalem: Alexander Pelei, 1983) 6. 176–88; see esp. pp. 178–79 [Hebrew].

[7] R. Alter, *The Art of Biblical Narrative* (New York: Basic Books, 1981); A. Berlin, *Poetics and Interpretation of Biblical Narrative* (Sheffield: Almond, 1983); M. Sternberg, *The Poetics of Biblical Narrative: Ideological Literature and the Drama of Reading* (Bloomington: Indiana University Press, 1985).

[8] The ancient manuscripts of the LXX and the oldest extant Hebrew manuscripts unanimously attest the unity of Ezra-Nehemiah on the one hand and its separation from Chronicles on the other. See, e.g., Codex Alexandrinus and the Aleppo Codex.

[9] Curtis, *A Critical and Exegetical Commentary on the Books of Chronicles* (ICC; New York: Scribner, 1910) 4.

[10] See R. R. Wilson, *Genealogy and History in the Biblical World* (New Haven: Yale University Press, 1977) for the taxonomy of genealogies.

[11] See also M. D. Johnson, *The Purpose of Biblical Genealogies with Special Reference to the Setting of the Genealogies of Jesus* (Cambridge: University Press, 1969) esp. pp. 69 and 80, on the internal differences between Ezra-Nehemiah's lists and pedigrees and those of Chronicles.

[12] Williamson, *Ezra, Nehemiah*, 38.

[13] Klein, "Old Readings in 1 Esdras: The List of Returnees from Babylon (Ezra 2/Neh. 7)," *HTR* 62 (1969) 99–107.

[14] C. C. Torrey assumes that the lists are fictitious (*Ezra Studies* [Chicago: University of Chicago Press, 1910] 250). W. Rudolph thinks that the lists are genuine but composed of different records between the years 539–515 (*Esra und Nehemia* [HAT 20; Tübingen: Mohr-Siebeck, 1949] 17). According to A. Alt, Zerubbabel compiled the list in order to legitimate land rights ("Die Rolle Samarias bei der Entstehung des Judentums," in *Kleine Schriften zur Geschichte des Volkes Israel* [Munich: Beck, 1953] II, 316–18). For G. Hölscher, this is a tax list drawn by the Persians ("Die Bücher Esra und Nehemia," in *Die heilige Schrift des Alten Testamentes* [ed. E. Kautzsch; 4th ed.; Tübingen: Mohr, 1923] 504). K. Galling sees the controversy between Samaria and Judah as the background for the list. It is drawn to demonstrate the right and ability of the Judeans to rebuild the Temple and resettle the land (cf. Tattenai's request for names in Ezra 5:10). The list makes clear both the legal and ecclesiastical structure of the community ("The 'Gola List' According to Ezra 2/Neh. 7," *JBL* 70 [1951] 153–54).

[15] Williamson, *Ezra, Nehemiah*, 28–29.

[16] Carl Schultz, for example, connects the list with the rejection of the adversaries' building

participation: "Clearly the builders of a temple had a monopoly, and in the case of the Jerusalem temple it was composed of the returning exiles. No outside assistance was allowed or wanted. Even as in the Craftsmen's Charter, so in the Golah list ancestry is traced, frequently in terms of skill" ("The Political Tensions Reflected in Ezra-Nehemiah," in *Scripture in Context* [ed. C. D. Evans, W. W. Hallo, and J. B. White; Pittsburgh: Pickwick, 1980] 227). The returnees alone had a monopoly; others may not be included. Schultz bases his work on David E. Weisberg's study of ancient guilds (*Guild Structure and Political Allegiance in Early Achamenid Mesopotamia* [New Haven: Yale University Press, 1967] 1–4), which attests to building monopolies and rights concerning sanctuaries.

[17] S. Japhet, "Biblical Historiography in the Persian Period," 128; H. G. M. Williamson, "The Composition of Ezra i–vi," *JTS* ns 34 (1983) 1–30.

[18] Williamson, *Ezra, Nehemiah*, 269.

[19] Ibid., 269. Cf. Gunneweg, "Zur Interpretation der Bücher Esra-Nehemia," in *Congress Volume: Vienna, 1980* (VTSup 32; Leiden, Brill, 1980) 156.

[20] See below, my third function of the repetition.

[21] Talmon, "Ezra and Nehemiah (Books and Men)," *IDBSup* 318. Elsewhere historical and textual questions and implications preeminently occupy the discussions of these lists. See, for example, Galling, "The 'Gola List,' " 149–58; and Klein, "Old Readings in 1 Esdras."

[22] See Alter, *Art of Biblical Narrative*, 88–113; Sternberg, *Poetics of Biblical Narrative*, 365–440; S. Talmon, "Presentation of Synchroneity and Simultaneity in Biblical Narrative," in *Studies in Hebrew Narrative Art Throughout the Ages* (ed. J. Heinemann and S. Werses; ScrHier 27; Jerusalem: Magnes, 1978) 9–26.

[23] Berlin, *Poetics and Interpretation*, 136.

[24] See J. Hillis Miller, *Fiction and Repetition* (Cambridge, MA: Harvard University Press, 1982) esp. pp. 1–21. See also Sternberg, *Poetics of Biblical Narrative*, 365–440.

[25] See H. Van Dyke Parunak, "Oral Typesetting: Some Uses of Biblical Structure," *Bib* 62 (1981) esp. p. 158 n. 8. Parunak adds in n. 9: "The notion of the inclusio as a segmenting device has been discussed extensively in the literature. The more important works are listed in B. Porten, 'The Structure and Theme of the Solomon Narrative (1 Kings 3–11),' *HUCA* ?8 (1967) 94 note 2."

[26] Ibid., 158.

[27] Ibid., 158; see also p. 168. Parunak calls attention to the fact that repetition cannot only mark a unit but also indicate secondary material (158–61). He therefore distinguishes between what he calls internal and external *inclusios* and develops guidelines for differentiating between the two. Ezra 2 through Nehemiah 7 clearly fits the definition of demarcated unit rather than peripheral material.

[28] For a detailed structure of the subunits, see T. C. Eskenazi, *In an Age of Prose: A Literary Approach to Ezra-Nehemiah* (SBLMS 36; Atlanta: Scholars Press, 1988) esp. chapter 3, pp. 37–126.

[29] Ibid., 37–126.

[30] Japhet, "People and Land in the Restoration Period," in *Das Land Israel in biblischer Zeit* (ed. N. Kamp and G. Strecker; Göttingen: Vandenhoeck & Ruprecht, 1983) 112–18; so too Williamson (*Ezra, Nehemiah*, 32) who ties it in with the Exodus (see below).

[31] Talmon, "The Presentation of Synchroneity and Simultaneity in Biblical Narrative," esp. p. 17.

[32] See Berlin, *Poetics and Interpretation*, 76–79.

[33] See Klein, "Old Readings in 1 Esdras."

[34] There are 597 priestly garments in Nehemiah 7, against 100 in Ezra 2; 41,000 gold darics in Nehemiah 7 against 61,000 in Ezra 2.

[35] Unless the priestly garments were valued in 10,000 gold darics (which seems unlikely), the governor's contribution is the smallest. That of the heads of the ancestors' houses and that of the rest of the people appear to be comparable. The numbers themselves are large and imply a great deal of wealth being contributed to the project.

[36] Galling, "The 'Gola List' According to Ezra 2/Nehemiah 7"; Japhet, "People and Land in the

Restoration Period," 112, 123 n. 46.

[37] See D. J. A. Clines, *Ezra, Nehemiah, Esther* (NCB; Grand Rapids: Eerdmans, 1984) 60–61 for an interesting attempt to reconcile these numbers.

[38] See, e.g., Sternberg's discussion "Repetition with Variation: Forms and Functions of Deviance," in *Poetics of Biblical Narrative*, 390–93.

[39] H. L. Ellison, *From Babylon to Bethlehem* (Atlanta: John Knox, 1979) 47.

[40] So Williamson, *Ezra, Nehemiah.* Williamson combines Ezra 1:5–11 with Cyrus's decree because he finds the theme of the return as the new exodus unifying the whole passage. According to Williamson, these verses, which build upon an available list, are "a highly charged theological interpretation" of the sources of 1:1–4 and 1:9–10 (p. 8). Several elements develop the decree and the list to articulate the exodus motif. The language recalls the despoiling of the Egyptians (cf. Exod. 3:21–22) (p. 16); the specific references to vessels also connect these passages of Exodus with Ezra 1:5–11 (and also with Isa. 52:11–12). Even the reference to *Nasi* contributes to this. The journey itself parallels that of the wilderness, where, according to Numbers 2:3–31; 7:11–83, we find lists of princes of various tribes (as well as references to donated vessels in Num. 7:84–86) (p. 18). The final sentence, Ezra 1:11, uses the passive of h'lh, "were brought up," deliberately to echo, e.g., Exodus 33:1 (p. 19). It seems to me that these allusions are suggestive but too subtle to constitute a major theme of the passage.

[41] Story in this sense is not a genre definition but a description of one of the three constitutive elements of narrative (see S. Rimmon-Kenen, *Narrative Fiction: Contemporary Poetics* [London: Methuen, 1983] 3). This use of story is to be differentiated from that of B. O. Long, for example, for whom it designates a specific genre (see B. O. Long, *1 Kings with an Introduction to the Historical Books* [Forms of Old Testament Literature, 9; Grand Rapids: Eerdmans, 1984] esp. pp. 30–31 and 261).

[42] I owe the terminology to C. Bremonds's definition of the components of "story." See S. Rimmon-Kenen, *Narrative Fiction: Contemporary Poetics*, 22.

[43] For details of the meaning of this category, see J. P. Weinberg, "Das *beit 'ābōt* im 6. -4. JH V.U.Z.," *VT* 23 (1973) 400–414.

[44] See Clines, for example (*Ezra, Nehemiah, Esther*, 44–45).

[45] See U. Kellermann, *Nehemia: Quellen, Überlieferung und Geschichte* (BZAW 102; Berlin: Töpelmann, 1967) 25.

[46] The exact date is obscure. If Nehemiah 7:72b belongs to the subsequent assembly, then the date appears to be the seventh month of the twentieth year of Artaxerxes (see Neh. 6:15). But Nehemiah 13 frustrates the attempt to accept this date by its repeated references to "that day," which refer, in their present context, to the celebration of the dedication of the walls. It also mentions, however, Nehemiah's activities after his return at least twelve years later (Neh. 13:6). Perhaps all that we can conclude from this is that the book is not interested in ascertaining this date in its vertical dimension but prefers to focus on the cyclical dimension of the ritual season.

[47] One might seek to argue that Nehemiah has resumed his memoirs somewhere before Nehemiah 8:2. However, the reference to Nehemiah in the third person (Neh. 8:9) implies that the depicted episode in Nehemiah 8:2–12 cannot be an entry in Nehemiah's memoirs.

[48] The arrangement in 1 Esdras, where the parallels to Nehemiah 8 follow the parallel to Ezra 10, indicates to many scholars that Nehemiah 8 has been dislodged from its original position, which was initially after Ezra 10. See K.-F. Pohlmann, *Studien zum dritten Esra* (FRLANT 104; Göttingen: Vandenhoeck & Ruprecht, 1970) 127–43, for a thorough discussion of this point; cf. Williamson's critique in *Israel in the Books of Chronicles*, 22–25.

[49] For the specific focus of 1 Esdras, see my article, "The Chronicler and the Composition of 1 Esdras," *CBQ* 48 (1986) 39–61.

[50] Note Nehemiah 12:1: "These are the priests and the Levites who came up with Zerubbabel the son of Shealtiel and Jeshua: Seraiah, Jeremiah, Ezra, Amariah, Malluch, Hattush. . . ."

[51] See J. M. Myers, *Ezra, Nehemiah* (AB 14; Garden City, NY: Doubleday, 1965) 196, for a good discussion of some major problems. Prominent among them is the near repetition of many of the names. The list of the earliest priests (Neh. 12:1–7) is suspiciously like the list of the later priests

(Neh. 12:12–21). W. Rudolph has suggested that the compiler had in his possession lists of priests for the time of Joiakim (Neh. 12:12–21) but not for the earlier time. Lacking one for the earlier era, he simply copies material from the available list (*Esra und Nehemia*, 196). This is not implausible. See, however, C. Fensham's cautionary remarks, *The Books of Ezra and Nehemiah* (NICOT; Grand Rapids: Eerdmans, 1982) 252.

[52] Williamson writes that the study of the list in Nehemiah 12 "... should remove any lingering temptation to compare this list with the twenty-four priestly courses known from 1 Chronicles 24:7–18 and later times; neither names nor numbers are now even remotely similar. The added six names, however, mark a clear step in that direction" (*Ezra, Nehemiah*, 360–61).

[53] The lists demonstrate that Ezra-Nehemiah is committed to describing the links in terms of numerous people who hold the events together, even if this means tampering with priestly lists.

[54] Note the fivefold repetition of the root śmḥ, "rejoice" in Nehemiah 12:43.

CLIMBING OUT OF A SWAMP: THE EVANGELICAL STRUGGLE TO UNDERSTAND THE CREATION TEXTS

CLARK H. PINNOCK
Professor of Christian Interpretation
McMaster Divinity College

Article from *Interpretation*

An esteemed evangelical geologist and son of the late conservative Old Testament scholar E. J. Young has written: "The evangelical community is still mired in a swamp in its attempt to understand the proper relationship between biblical interpretation and the scientific endeavor;" and he added, there seems to be more effort being put into name calling than into finding higher and firmer ground to stand upon.[1]

The problem Davis Young identifies is the proclivity of evangelicals to treat the creation texts of early Genesis as a source of usable scientific concepts and accurate historical information which can be employed in dialogue with modern science. This tendency is well known and has been dramatized for the public by the recent Arkansas court case,[2] the resurgence of creationist fervor in its many forms,[3] and by an acquaintance with popular fundamentalism, one of whose prominent traits in recent years is its stubbornly anti-evolutionary streak.[4]

So, to write about the evangelical interpretation of creation texts means that one has to probe an area of sensitivity and unsolved difficulty for evangelical hermeneutics. It will dramatize the fact that evangelicals have devoted much more time and energy to defending the inerrancy of the Bible than to interpreting it impressively.[5] One is thus required to deal with a malady in interpretation rather than a serious interpretation of the doctrine of creation itself. Fortunately more and more evangelicals are asking themselves if they ought to be looking to the Bible for answers to scientific questions and embroiling themselves in these awkward debates. They are searching for ways to back out of a dead-end street.[6]

The Present Situation

The situation at present is roughly the following.[7] On the one hand, there are various kinds of *concordists* who try in different ways to harmonize the results of exegesis and science. They understand early Genesis to be giving a more or less historical chronicle of what happened in the past and try to demonstrate a concordance of correspondence between Genesis and the actual events of creation. One of their difficulties is that there is little agreement among concordists on how to achieve this. One group practices narrow concordism. They take the days of Genesis 1 to be literal twenty-four hour days and appeal to the tradition of flood geology to explain the difficulties this creates. Why does the earth appear to be so old if it is not? Where did the enormous amounts of water which would be required in a universal flood go afterwards? Though this approach bears tremendous intellectual burdens and requires major leaps into speculation to deal with some of the problems, this is the approach presently enjoying considerable popularity.[8]

Another group practices broad concordism. More liberal in exegesis and more comfortable with the present scientific consensus, they construe the days of Genesis 1 as long periods of time or as intermittent days of creation amidst the lengthy process of billions of years. In this way they are able to accept much of the evolutionary picture, picking fault with it only in a general way, though they seem forced to stretch the text to achieve the concordance.[9]

On the other hand, there are evangelical nonconcordists who do not read early Genesis to gain scientific information or to discover history as it really was. They read it more as a theological text, best understood in its own context, and therefore do not come into such severe conflict with modern knowledge. These scholars are of the opinion that the various efforts at concordance have failed rationally because they were misinformed literarily. It was a mistake ever to have supposed that scientific questions could be answered using biblical data.[10] Davis A. Young can speak for the nonconcordists:

> I suggest that we will be on the right track if we stop treating Genesis 1 and the flood story as scientific and historical reports. We can forever avoid falling into the perpetual conflicts between Genesis and geology if we follow those evangelical scholars who stress that Genesis is divinely inspired ancient near eastern literature written within a specific historical context that entailed well-defined thought patterns, literary forms, symbols, and images. It makes sense that Genesis presents a theology of creation that is fully aware of and challenges the numerous polytheistic cosmogonic myths of Mesopotamia, Egypt, and the other cultures surrounding Israel, by exposing their idolatrous worship of the heavenly bodies, of the animals, and of the rivers, by claiming that all of those things are creatures of the living God. The stars are not deities. God brought the stars into being. The rivers are not deities. God brought the waters into existence. The animals are not deities to be worshipped and feared, for God created the animals and controls them. Even the "chaos" is under the supreme hand of the living God. Thus Genesis 1 calmly asserts the bankruptcy of the pagan polytheism from which Israel was drawn and that constantly existed as a threat to Israel's continuing faithfulness to the true God of heaven and earth.[11]

Why is it, we may ask, that evangelicals are so powerfully drawn to the concordist pattern of trying to integrate modern science and Holy Scripture? There are at least two sets of presuppositions which encourage it—one is traditional and the other modern. First, evangelicals are theological traditionalists or conservatives, and therefore the mere fact that a Calvin or a Luther, for example, had no qualms about reading Genesis to be saying that God created the world in seven ordinary days impresses them, whether it should do so or not.[12] Then there is the fact that what Charles Darwin was proposing did administer a severe jolt to the premodern outlook and posed an apparent threat to traditional dogmatics, particularly at the point of the uniqueness of the human and the historicity of the fall into sin. Furthermore, when evangelicals look at what liberals have done when they accommodated to this new way of thinking in relegating biblical truth to the realm of the existential, threatening the historical reality of the entire biblical narrative, they become understandably nervous.[13]

Second, there is a modern set of presuppositions, linked to the realist epistemology most evangelicals favor, which has a profound influence on their exegesis. Having a realist epistemology means that they will tend to favor truth of a factual and scientific kind and not be quite so open to truth of a more symbolic or metaphorical type. One sees it in the evangelical doctrine of biblical inspiration, which is protective of cognitive truth in general and factual inerrancy in particular. It means hermeneutically that the "natural" way to read the Bible is to read it as literally and as factually as possible. In apologetics too evangelicals like to appeal to empirical reason: They like to ask, If you can't trust the Bible in matters of fact, when can you trust it? In many ways then, evangelicals are in substantial agreement with the modern agenda which also prefers the factual and the scientific over the symbolic and figurative. What could be more modern than to search for scientific truth in text three thousand years old? Such a modern presupposition will demand the right to read the Bible in modern terms whatever the authorial intention of the text might be. It just assumes that our values must have been the same as those entertained by the ancient Israelites.

The influence of these presuppositions and this mindset is overwhelmingly powerful, and the difficulty standing in the way of evangelicals transcending it is enormous. Changing one's presuppositions is a painful business, and it will not be easy for evangelicals to listen to the Bible's own agenda and to put their own on the shelf. Yet it can be done, and it is happening.[14]

Getting Out of the Swamp

The way out of the swamp is to begin reading early Genesis appropriately in its own context, in the setting of the life of ancient Israel, and to stop forcing modern agendas upon it. Evangelicals who are supportive of the final authority of the Scriptures over all the other sources of human understanding ought to be open (at least in principle) to such a strategy. If they are sincere in wanting to submit their minds to Holy Scripture, then this is something they will have to learn to do in the case of the Genesis creation texts.

Does Scripture help us to decide about its own original intentions, or is it helpless in the face of contemporary reader interests? Are there indications in Genesis which support the suspicion that an attempt to find science in Genesis is likely to be a modernity-driven agenda? If there are such indications, it would be ironic, insofar as evangelicals believe it is exactly the opposite, namely, that people are attracted to a literary reading of early Genesis, not because the text requires it, but because they are over-awed by modern science. Let me explain the basis of my conviction that the text invites a literary reading which does not call for a close scientific concordance.

First, evangelicals need to attend to the purpose and function of the Bible and of the creation texts in that context. As Van Till puts it: "Taking the Scriptures seriously involves affirming its status as Word of God and covenantal canon."[15] The Bible's purpose is to present a covenantal relationship between the Creator and his creatures. Genesis 1–11 in particular is a preamble to God's calling of Abram (12:1). It answers questions which have to do with God's decision to call him. Its purpose is not to inform us about history or scientific process as a modern scholar might investigate it but to explain how it came about that God issued this call to the patriarch. It also tells us how Israel came to exist and sets her election against the background of the creation and the fall into sin, thus helping us to understand the purposes of God in redemption. Genesis 1–11 sets the stage for what follows in the rest of the Bible. It places the drama of salvation in the universal context of the creation of the world, the nature of the human, and the fall of the whole race into sin. Its purpose first and foremost is to teach certain theological truths which lie behind God's striking a covenant with Abraham and his seed.[16]

One should add, in order to allay genuine fears, that this does not mean that one has the right to create an ironclad rule for Scripture as a whole that in no circumstances should readers ever "allow" the text to make historically and scientifically relevant claims. This would be to substitute one kind of imperialism for another and drive a false wedge between religious and factual truth. For even though the purpose of Genesis 1–11 is other than scientific, these texts are still talking about the real world and its history *in their own way*. After all, the creation of the world is the beginning of God's purposeful temporal activity in relation to history and the event of the world's coming into being. My point is more modest, that we should be guided in a general way by the macro-purpose of the Bible and the Book of Genesis and not unduly influenced by debates which have their meaning largely in the context of modern society.

This impression about the function of the Bible is reinforced by specific signals in the text itself which should alert us to it in other ways as well. The fact that God made the sun, moon, and stars on the fourth day, not on the first, ought to tell us that this is not a scientific statement (Gen. 1:14–19). This one detail in the narrative suggests that concordism is not going to work well and that the agenda of the writer must have been something other than one of describing actual physical processes.

Second, the original purpose of the writer of Genesis 1 is brought out rather forcefully in several ways. For one thing, there are numerous indications that he wanted to combat the errors contained in the creation myths of the ancient world such as the Babylonian Enuma Elish. When placed alongside this document, Genesis 1 reads like a strong polemic against the kind of pagan ideas we find there.[17] In general, it thoroughly demythologizes nature and sees it as the creation of the one true God. It presents the one God who created all things and who exists independently of nature. It says that there are no warring deities, and no monster goddess needing to be subdued and cut in half. It describes the separation of the primeval waters as a peaceful operation because the chaos is not a powerful force. Creation is by God's effortless word and requires no struggle at all. The text tells us that the heavenly bodies which the ancients worshipped and feared are just lights in the heavens (cf. Deut. 4:19) and that the great sea creatures are God's workmanship too and not mythical monsters. Most important of all, it teaches us that human beings are not a divine afterthought, created to do the dirty work of the gods. They were created to be lords of the world, because they are personal agents just like God is.[18]

The micro-purpose of Genesis 1 then is to counter false religious beliefs. The author wants to undermine the prevailing mythical cosmologies and call for a complete break with them. The chapter is not myth but antimyth. It is not history either in the modern sense, and it is mistaken to construe its interpretation in terms of the debate over Darwin. The text tells us all this, if we would only listen.

Third, the purpose of Genesis 1 is brought out rather plainly by evidences of literary artistry in its construction. In so many ways it shows itself to be a carefully composed and systematic essay. From one angle the text moves from what is farthest from God (v. 2) to what is nearest and dearest to him (v. 26). It moves from the inanimate to the animate, from chaos to Sabbath rest.[19] There is also an impressive pattern running through the passage: the announcement of God speaking, the command to let something be, the report that it was so, the evaluation that it was good, and the temporal framework of evening and morning. Most impressive of all, however, is the parallelism between the first (1-3) and second triad of days (4–6). The author is using the Hebrew week as a literary framework for displaying the theology of creation. First God creates the spaces, and then he populates them with inhabitants. God deals with the challenge posed by the world being "without form and void" by providing first the form and then the fulness.[20]

To spell it out, the first problem God confronts is one of darkness, and he overcomes it by creating the light on one day and by making the sun, moon, and stars on day four. The second problem is posed by the watery chaos, and God deals with it by creating a firmament to divide the waters on day two and by making birds for the sky and fish for the seas on day five. The third problem is the formless earth, and God takes care of that by separating the waters a second time and forming dry land with vegetation on day three and then making the animals and human beings to dwell upon it on day six. The author is obviously a literary architect who has created a framework which serves magnificently for presenting the totality of creation at the hand of God.[21]

The antimythical agenda coupled with the strong suggestion of literary artifice leads to the conclusion that the logic of Genesis 1 is primarily theological rather than historical or scientific. It is the evidence of the text rather than the desire to avoid modern criticism from science which ought to move evangelicals away from misreading the creation account as a scientifically informative tract and burdening themselves with enormous and unnecessary difficulties.

A Similar Pattern in Genesis 2

A similar pattern emerges when we examine the evangelical interpretation of Genesis 2. What the genre suggests comes into conflict with what these modern readers seek, and one is forced to choose between the intent of the text and reader presuppositions. The situation in this case is actually worse in that the passions are even more heated and agitated, because even more is thought to be at stake. Therefore, the dire warning is frequently issued that the moment one begins to move away from a literal, historical reading of Genesis 2, the floodgates of criticism will open and threaten to overthrow the fundamental doctrines of Christianity. Listen to Francis A. Schaeffer: "If Paul is wrong in this factual statement about Eve's coming from Adam, there is no reason to have certainty in the authority of any New Testament factual statement, including the factual statement that Christ rose physically from the dead."[22] In a similar vein, John Meyer speaks of the text providing reliable historical and scientific information and insists on maintaining its historical accuracy and inerrancy.[23]

Why would evangelicals respond so strongly to this issue? Part of the explanation relates to what has already been noted in connection with their interpretation of Genesis 1, that is, the expectation on the part of evangelical readers of finding historical fact and scientific information in the biblical text. It is an expectation which leads them, not surprisingly, to some remarkable speculations including: (1) The notion that Genesis 2 is just an explication of the sixth day of Genesis 1, which conveniently ignores the fact that verses 5–6 presuppose a totally different order.[24] (2) Efforts to date the appearance of Adam and Eve in history. James O. Buswell, Jr., puts it at 30,000 B.C. on the basis of the supposed rise of language, even though this creates another problem, namely, the neolithic cast of the Genesis 4 account, leading Millard Erickson to admit: "This is an area in which there are insufficient data to make any categorical statements. It will require additional study."[25] (3) The location of the Garden of Eden. In Iran, says Ramm; but Archer demurs, claiming that it cannot now be located because the geological conditions which the account assumes no longer obtain.[26]

In addition to expectations of accurate information, there are other powerful assumptions at work as well. (1) There is deep resistance to the idea that Scripture might resort to myth, legend, or saga in order to communicate its truth. Although there is no a priori reason to exclude this possibility, there is the fear of liberal theology and what admitting such a thing here could lead to.[27] (2) There is fear that the uniqueness and the unity of the human will be jeopardized if we grant a theory of evolutionary origins. (3) There is also fear that the fall into sin as a historical event will be lost sight of and with it the evangelical soteriology dependent on it. Again, there is much by way of presuppositions to prevent a patient hearing of the text. The impression is given that the whole gospel depends on a literal reading of Genesis 2.

Here again the solution is to listen to the text and not let modern presuppositions overwhelm it. First, readers need to acknowledge what a very different narrative of creation this is in comparison to Genesis 1. The focus is narrower, on the creation of man, not the cosmos. It asks the human, not the cosmological, question: How did we come to be? It begins by describing a very inhospitable earth without any vegetation or rainfall and then describes the creation of a man from the clay. The origin of woman is entirely unique. The whole ethos of the passage is pastoral. It describes the world of the shepherd, with its concerns about dry earth, abundant waters, fruited trees, and serpents.

Second, we have to be straightforward about the symbolic character of this narrative. This is a story with the following features: a talking snake, symbolic trees, Eve's origin through divine surgery, cherubim, a flaming sword, God walking in the garden, God modeling Adam from the clay and breathing into his nose, a perfect garden, the world rivers, the parade of animals. It is a story in which God is described very anthropomorphically as potter, as surgeon, and as gardener. Ramm suggests that one might view the account as a nonpostulational literary vehicle for conveying truth, the language of theological symbolism rather than literal prose. He mentions James Orr's view that this was "old tradition clothed in oriental allegorical dress."[28] Even J. I. Packer, a strong inerrantist, admits: "There is nothing inconsistent in recognizing that real events may be recorded in a highly symbolic manner."[29]

The symbolic form of the account of course does not rule out the possibility that the fall into sin was a historical event. One of the purposes of Genesis 2 surely was to explain what went wrong in God's good creation. As Nahum Sarna says, "The story of the Garden of Eden is the answer of Genesis to this problem. It wishes to indicate very simply that man, through the free exercise of his will in rebellion against God, corrupts the good and puts evil in its place."[30] James Orr, Bernard Ramm, and James Packer are all concerned to defend the event character of the fall into sin, and properly so in my view; but this does not necessitate misconstruing the nature of the Genesis record. Our Christian belief in the historical fall of humanity into sin rests on a good deal more than Genesis 2 and does not require us to distort that narrative in order to protect this doctrine. In a real sense, the fall is the silent hypothesis of human history, and is one of the most empirically verifiable doctrines of all.

Concluding Remarks

1. Evangelicals as a group have to receive low marks for the performance in this area of biblical interpretation. It is certainly not their finest hour. Many are still burdening their exegesis with presuppositions which need to be critically reexamined. The result is a set of interpretations badly flawed and a warfare with modern science and with one another which creates a bad impression.

2. In this, they are behaving contrary to their own principles of theological method and operating below their own ideal of letting Scripture speak definitively above the noise of human opinions. On this subject indeed they tend to act like certain religious liberals in allowing the modern demand for scientific information and accuracy to silence the agenda of God's Word.

3. This area of hermeneutics also reveals the "docetic" potential very near the surface of the evangelical doctrine of Scripture, an unconscious wish not to have God's Word enter into the creaturely realm.[31] A strong emphasis on the divine inspiration of the text naturally tends to overshadow the obligation to read the Bible in its own human and historical setting in order to grasp its truth. It encourages readers to seek the pure divine message to themselves here and now and to assume they will grasp its meaning best by reading the text in the most "natural" way, which means, in a way congenial to the assumption of the reader, maximizing the danger of text manipulation.[32]

4. Inevitably this also leads to theological impoverishment. So much time and energy is consumed tilting at windmills that little gets said about the actual doctrine of creation. Look at this article, or pick up an evangelical book on creation, and you will seldom find a discussion of the issues which properly belong to the heart of the doctrine: our relationship with God the

creator in contrast to systems of dualism and pantheism; the meaning and destiny of our own existence grounded in the purpose of God; the goodness of our created lives; creation as the basis of the belief in the intelligibility of our world. Evangelicals themselves are forced to turn to nonevangelical authors such as Barth, Torrance, and Gilkey.[33]

5. One of the reasons many evangelicals are hesitant to grant that the creation texts ought to be read on their own terms and not anachronistically in the context of modern science is valid. They object to the way in which liberals tend systematically to transform biblical claims into existential symbols, not just when the text suggests it, but whenever it is convenient and practically across the board.[34] This means that they have difficulty accepting the idea that texts like Genesis 1–3 might be more theological than factual, despite the evidence in favor of it, due to their (warranted) anxiety on this score. Here is a case of a presupposition, born out of the painful experience occasioned by liberal theology and quite appropriate in the circumstances, being applied unwisely. Even though it may be valid to be wary of existential hermeneutics, that does not give anyone the right to twist Scripture into a convenient polemical instrument without exegetical permission. Besides, reading Genesis 1–3 in the way it itself commends does not negate the major factual issues. For when all is said and done, Genesis 1 still affirms a creation event and Genesis 3 still asserts a fall into sin at the beginning of human history. Evangelicals are understandably nervous about existential hermeneutics, but that is no reason to overreact and make the Bible a victim.

6. By placing the Bible and modern science in a strongly adversarial relationship, evangelicals have also created a problem surrounding the place of reason in their theological method. Normally reason plays a useful ministerial role in theology as faith seeks critical understanding in its assertions. The effect of this searching for scientific information in the biblical text is that it results in a much higher level of tension with current scientific endeavor than is necessary, which in turn gives the impression that reason plays no positive role in Christian interpretation. Of course Calvin took the days of Genesis 1 to be ordinary days, but after all he had no reasons to doubt that. The data had not accumulated which would have required him to deal with the issue of the age of the earth or the processes in its formation, but we are in the position of having to take seriously the information scientists have gathered from a careful study of God's world. Have astronomy and geology not told us some things which suggest it would be wiser not to regard Genesis 1–2 as a chronicle of creative acts but in some other way? Have not the broad concordists admitted as much when they stretch out the narrative to include billions of years unknown to premodern exegesis? One thing is certain—they did not find out about an ancient earth from reading Genesis. Scientists do not need any defense from me, but something has to be said on behalf of the freedom human beings enjoy to explore God's world without the clergy looking over their shoulders.[35]

7. The lesson to be learned here is the principle of allowing the Bible to say what it wants to say and not impose our imperialistic agendas onto it, squeezing it into our molds. I am not for a moment suggesting that religion and science occupy entirely different realms and never touch; or that evolutionary theory, when it puffs itself up and pretends to offer us a worldview which can take the place of biblical theism, is not something to be fought against; or that Christians ought not to raise questions about the hard evidence which is said to favor a purely naturalistic account of origins. My intention is to make the simple plea for the sovereignty of the biblical text over reader agendas. Our exegesis ought to let the text speak and the chips fall where they may.

Notes

[1] Davis A. Young, "Scripture in the Hands of a Geologist," *Westminster Theological Journal* 49 (1987), 1. This is a long two-part article which traces the centuries-old effort to harmonize the Bible and modern science and which, according to the author, has failed (pp. 1–34, 257–304).

[2] See Langdon Gilkey's racy account of his experience at the creationist trial in December 1981, *Creationism on Trial: Evolution and God at Little Rock* (Minneapolis: Winston Press, 1985). For another view, see Norman L. Geisler, *The Creator in the Courtroom* (Milford, Mich.: Mott Media, 1982).

[3] Ronald L. Numbers, "The Creationists" in *God and Nature: Historical Essays on the Encounter Between Christianity and Science*, ed. David C. Lindberg and Ronald L. Numbers (Berkeley: University of California Press, 1986), pp. 391–423.

[4] George M. Marsden, *Fundamentalism and American Culture: The Shaping of Twentieth Century Evangelicalism 1870–1925* (New York: Oxford University Press, 1980), pp. 212–15.

[5] There are hopeful signs this may be changing; see, for example, Moises Silva, *Has the Church Misread the Bible? The History of Interpretation in the Light of Current Issues* (Grand Rapids: Zondervan Publishing House, 1987) and Anthony C. Thiselton, *The Two Horizons* (Exeter: Paternoster Press, 1980).

[6] This is one of the areas of change which Hunter notes in recent evangelical thinking; see James D. Hunter, *Evangelicalism: The Coming Generation* (Chicago: University of Chicago Press, 1987), pp. 27–28, 33, 120, 132–33.

[7] Davis A. Young's articles are helpful for background, and *Christianity Today* published a major debate on these matters, "How It All Began," August 12, 1988, pp. 31–46.

[8] Henry M. Morris, *The Genesis Record* (San Diego: Creation Life, 1976) and *Scientific Creationism* (San Diego: Creation Life, 1974); Donald W. Patten, *The Biblical Flood and the Ice Epoch* (Seattle: Pacific Meridian Publishing Co., 1966); Norman L. Geisler and J. Kerby Anderson, *Origin Science: A Proposal for the Creation-Evolution Controversy* (Grand Rapids: Baker Book House, 1987).

[9] Nineteenth-century evangelicals practiced broad concordance before the battle lines hardened: David N. Livingstone, *Darwin's Forgotten Defenders: The Encounter Between Evangelical Theology and Evolutionary Thought* (Grand Rapids: Wm. B. Eerdmans Publishing Co., 1987). Recent exponents would include Bernard Ramm, *The Christian View of Science and Scripture* (London: Paternoster Press, 1955); Pattle P. T. Pun, *Evolution: Nature and Scripture in Conflict?* (Grand Rapids: Zondervan Publishing House, 1982); John Wiester, *The Genesis Connection* (Nashville: Thomas Nelson Publishers, 1983); Robert C. Newman and Herman J. Eckelmann, *Genesis One and the Origin of the Earth* (Downers Grove, Ill.: InterVarsity Press, 1977). Davis A.

Young himself was formerly of this persuasion, *Creation and the Flood* (Grand Rapids: Baker Book House, 1977).

[10] Nonconcordists would include N. H. Ridderbos, *Is There a Conflict Between Genesis 1 and Natural Science?* (Grand Rapids: Wm. B. Eerdmans Publishing Co., 1957); Howard J. Van Till, *The Fourth Day: What the Bible and the Heavens Are Telling Us About the Creation* (Grand Rapids: Wm. B. Eerdmans Publishing Co., 1986); Henri Blocher, *In the Beginning: The Opening Chapters of Genesis* (Downers Grove, Ill.: InterVarsity Press, 1984); Meredith G. Kline, "Because It Had Not Rained," *Westminster Theological Journal* 20 (1958), 146–57; J. I. Packer, "The Challenge of Biblical Interpretation: Creation" in *The Proceedings of the Conference on Biblical Interpretation 1988* (Nashville: Broadman Press, 1988), pp. 21–33.

[11] "Scripture in the Hands of Geologists," p. 303.

[12] What they do not pause to notice is that Calvin also says in his commentary on Genesis that we should look elsewhere if we wish to know about astronomy and that Genesis 1 was using the language of ordinary description and not teaching us science.

[13] Langdon Gilkey makes this plain, *Religion and the Scientific Future* (New York: Harper & Row, 1970), Chap. 1.

[14] Conrad Hyers makes this point gently but insistently, *The Meaning of Creation: Genesis and Modern Science* (Atlanta: John Knox Press, 1984).

[15] *The Fourth Day*, p. 78.

[16] Van Till leans on Meredith G. Kline for this perspective, *The Structure of Biblical Authority* (Grand Rapids: Wm. B. Eerdmans Publishing Co., 1972), pp. 53–57.

[17] Nahum M. Sarna, *Understanding Genesis* (New York: Schocken Books, 1970), Chap. 1.

[18] The character of Genesis 1 as antimythical polemic was brought out by Adventist evangelical scholar Gerhard F. Hasel, "The Polemical Nature of the Genesis Cosmology," *Evangelical Quarterly* 46 (1974), 81–102. Bruce K. Waltke echoes the same point in *Creation and Chaos: An Exegetical and Theological Study of Biblical Cosmogony* (Portland, Oreg.: Western Conservative Baptist Seminary, 1974).

[19] This majestic movement from chaos to order, which is preserved even when one opts for a literal interpretation of Genesis 1, opens the door to concordism again, but in a very general way and one which does not require Scripture twisting.

[20] This literary framework is noticed by Ridderbos, *Is There a Conflict?* pp. 29–55; Blocher, *In the Beginning*, pp. 49–59; and Derek Kidner, *Genesis: An Introduction and Commentary* (Downers Grove, Ill.: InterVarsity Press, 1967), p. 46.

[21] It is not at all unusual for biblical writers to arrange their materials artificially in order to make some point; see Ridderbos, *Is There a Conflict?* pp. 36–40; and Robert H. Gundry, *Matthew: A Commentary on His Literary and Theological Art* (Grand Rapids: Wm. B. Eerdmans Publishing Co., 1982), "A Theological Postscript," pp. 623–40.

[22] *No Final Conflict* (Downers Grove, Ill.: InterVarsity Press, 1975), pp. 33–34.

[23] "How It All Began," pp. 33–34.

[24] Compare Gleason L. Archer, *Encyclopedia of Bible Difficulties* (Grand Rapids: Zondervan Publishing House, 1982), pp. 68–69.

[25] *Christian Theology* (Grand Rapids: Baker Book House, 1987), p. 487.

[26] Ramm, *The Christian View*, p. 231-32; Archer, *Encyclopedia of Bible Difficulties*, pp. 69–70.

[27] My suggestion that Scripture ought to be permitted to employ whatever forms of literary composition it chooses encountered a cool response, *The Scripture Principle* (San Francisco: Harper & Row, 1984), Chap. 5.

[28] *The Christian View*, pp. 223–24. More recently he speaks of Genesis 2 as "divinely inspired reconstruction" and theology in the form of narration, *Offense to Reason: The Theology of Sin* (San Francisco: Harper & Row, 1985), pp. 68–75.

[29] *"Fundamentalism" and the Word of God* (London: InterVarsity Fellowship, 1958), p. 99. He continues to hold this view; see *The Proceedings of the Conference on Biblical Interpretation 1988*, pp. 30–33.

[30] *Understanding Genesis*, p. 24.

[31] G. C. Berkouwer, *Holy Scripture* (Grand Rapids: Wm. B. Eerdmans Publishing Co., 1975), pp. 17–38.

[32] The obvious parallel is the evangelical hermeneutics of eschatological assertions which displays the same insensitivity to the all-important historical background of the symbols being employed by the biblical writers, Stephen Travis *I Believe in the Second Coming of Christ* (Grand Rapids: Wm. B. Eerdmans Publishing Co., 1982), Chap. 4.

[33] Millard Erickson comments on some of these issues, but his discussion is limited as to space and overshadowed as to content by the strong presence of concordist concerns, *Christian Theology*, Chaps. 17 and 22.

[34] Langdon Gilkey, *Naming the Whirlwind: The Renewal of God-language* (Indianapolis: Bobbs-Merrill, 1969), p. 76–77.

[35] Thomas Oden's treatment of the Wesleyan quadrilateral of sources for the theology including reason is helpful here, *The Living God: Systematic Theology* (San Francisco: Harper & Row, 1987), I, 330–44.

SECTION TWO

NEW TESTAMENT

Harold W. Hoehner, area editor

NEW TESTAMENT

HAROLD W. HOEHNER
Chairman and Professor of New Testament Studies
Director of Th.D. Studies
Dallas Theological Seminary

Introduction

Trying to narrow down New Testament articles to the best three in the field is like asking for the universe in its context. After looking in nearly fifty journals from July 1988 to July 1989, about sixty articles were worthy of consideration, and by the process of elimination about twenty-five articles could be considered as excellent contributions to the field of New Testament. Choosing the three that were to appear in this work was extremely difficult. Some of those not appearing in this volume are mentioned because they are worthy to be read. One factor in deciding which were to appear is the avoidance of an overemphasis on any aspect within the discipline of New Testament. For example, selected New Testament articles must not concentrate only in the Gospels or Paul's letters, or even on subjects like Paul and the Law or the New Testament's use of the Old Testament.

The first selected article discusses a problematic passage of Ephesians 4:26 regarding Paul's statement about the believer's anger and the injunction not to sin.[1] Daniel B. Wallace carefully examines the various approaches that the students of the New Testament have used and then by the process of elimination he concludes that it should be rendered as a command imperative: "Be angry, and do not sin." Having come to that conclusion, he gives further support for that view. Here is a good model of careful exegesis.

The second article deals with a practical pastoral problematic passage—James 5:14–16a.[2] Gary S. Shogren discusses different interpretations regarding the function of oil in relationship to the sick, and he concludes that this function is a sign of God's healing power. He shows believers how to apply this passage in a pastoral situation.

The third article explores the biblical implications regarding the present-day problem of homosexual behavior.[3] James B. DeYoung examines the use of the word *nature* in relation to homosexuality in the Greek and Jewish settings, and then he investigates its usage in the New Testament and specifically discusses Romans 1:26–27, where Paul uses the term in the context of homosexual relationships.

Several other articles could have been reprinted but for various reasons

53

are not included. They are, however, worthy of due consideration. Professor Morna Hooker delivered the presidential paper of the Society of New Testament Studies in Cambridge, England, in August 1988.[4] She asked the student of the New Testament to consider the genitival relationship of faith to Christ, which is normally rendered in present-day translations as an objective genitive "faith in Christ" rather than a subjective genitive "faith or faithfulness of Christ." Professor Hooker states that the objective genitive view became prominent at the time of the Reformation, and the other alternative needs to be considered. However, she does not go to the other extreme but rather posits the idea of an interchange of opposites; namely, that there may be a combination of the objective and subjective genitive. She suggests that because of the believer's participation in Christ, he or she has faith in Christ and is participating in the faith/faithfulness of Christ. This view has some interesting possibilities.

Two other articles are well done but too long for inclusion. The first one is by Craig A. Evans, who interacts with E. P. Sander's contention that Jesus' action in the temple was not a cleansing but a prophetic demonstration or portent of the temple's destruction.[5] Evans concludes that the traditional view of the cleansing of the temple better fits the evidence than Sander's reconstruction. The second one is by Richard Oster who attempts to demonstrate that the Roman practice of men wearing devotional head coverings had spread throughout the Mediterranean area. He proposes that Paul did not want this custom practiced in the Corinthian church because man's uncovered head demonstrated his headship over the woman.[6]

Three other thought-provoking articles should be pondered, although they are at times rather technical: two on textual criticism and one on the canon. The two articles on textual criticism do not favor the Majority text as the "true" text of the New Testament. First, Kurt Aland gives a brief history of the textual tradition from Luther to the present time and shows that the Majority text was not the generally accepted text of the Byzantine church until the ninth century.[7] Second, Daniel B. Wallace attempts to demonstrate that the Majority text differs from the Textus Receptus in almost 2000 places—which means that a reexamination of the Byzantine text-type is needed; that the Majority text differs from the critical text in more than 6500 places; that in over 650 readings it has shorter reading than the critical text; and that Hodges, who is considered the main proponent of the Majority text view, is inconsistent in carrying out his textual theory.[8] Finally, in the article on the canon, Robert E. Picirilli demonstrates that early apostolic fathers alluded to 2 Peter, although one must be careful not to try to prove too much from their writings either positively or negatively.[9]

Interest in Paul and the Law continues. Thomas R. Schreiner argues that since the new age of the Messiah has come, the present-day believer is not under the ritual demands of the Mosaic Law but is under the moral demands of the Mosaic Law, which are fulfilled by walking in the power of the Spirit.[10]

Furthermore, interest in "reader" or "audience criticism" goes on. John Paul Heil states that the reader is to respond to Jesus' irony before the Sanhedrin differently than the Sanhedrin responded.[11] Joanna Dewey proposes that the Gospel of Mark was composed for a listening and not a reading audience.[12]

Since this year marks the hundredth anniversary of *Expository Times*, two interesting series of general articles in biblical studies have appeared, entitled "They Set Us in New Paths" and "Today and Tomorrow in Biblical Studies." Three articles on New Testament studies are in the first series: I. Howard Marshall begins the series by discussing the six most significant works on the New Testament written in English, excluding commentaries;[13] Kenneth Grayston gives his opinion as to which are the most significant New Testament commentaries in the English language in the past century;[14] and James D. G. Dunn lists not only some of the great works that have been translated into English from other languages but also great works that have never been translated and in his opinion should have been.[15] In the second series two articles are to be considered: A. T. Hanson discusses biblical studies of today and tomorrow specifically related to the New Testament;[16] and J. L. Holden thinks that the future study of the New Testament will be truthful in that it will be done with less prejudicial bias in a university setting than within confessional settings, and that Christianity will be compared with other religions much like it has been done with Judaism.[17]

Notes

[1] Daniel B. Wallace, "Ὀργίζεσθε in Ephesians 4:26: Command or Condition?" *Criswell Theological Review* 3 (Spring 1989) 353–72.

[2] Gary S. Shogren, "Will God Heal Us—A Re-Examination of James 5:14–16a," *Evangelical Quarterly* 61 (April 1989) 99–108.

[3] James B. DeYoung, "The Meaning of 'Nature' in Romans 1 and Its Implications for Biblical Proscriptions of Homosexual Behavior," *Journal of the Evangelical Theological Society* 31 (December 1988) 429–41.

[4] Morna D. Hooker, "ΠΙΣΤΙΣ ΧΡΙΣΤΟΥ," *New Testament Studies* 35 (July 1989) 321–42.

[5] Craig A. Evans, "Jesus' Action in the Temple: Cleansing or Portent of Destruction?" *Catholic Biblical Quarterly* 51 (April 1989) 237–70.

[6] Richard Oster, "When Men Wore Veils to Worship: The Historical Context of 1 Corinthians 11:4," *New Testament Studies* 34 (October 1988) 481–505.

[7] Kurt Aland, "The Text of the Church?" *Trinity Journal* 8 (Fall 1987) 131–44. This article only recently appeared although it has a 1987 date.

[8] Daniel B. Wallace, "Some Second Thoughts on the Majority Text," *Bibliotheca Sacra* 146 (July–September 1989) 270–90.

[9] Robert E. Picirilli, "Allusions to 2 Peter in the Apostolic Fathers," *Journal for the Study of the New Testament* 34 (June 1988) 57–83.

[10] Thomas R. Schreiner, "The Abolition and Fulfillment of the Law in Paul," *Journal for the Study of the New Testament* 35 (February 1989) 47–74.

[11] John Paul Heil, "Reader-Response and the Irony of Jesus before the Sanhedrin in Luke 22:66–71," *Catholic Biblical Quarterly* 51 (April 1989) 271–84.

[12] Joanna Dewey, "Oral Methods of Structuring Narrative in Mark," *Interpretation* 43 (January

1989) 32–44.

   [13] I. Howard Marshall, "They Set Us in New Paths: I. The New Testament: Paths without Destinations," *Expository Times* 100 (October 1988) 9–13.

   [14] Kenneth Grayston, "They Set Us in New Paths: III. A Century of New Testament Commentaries," *Expository Times* 100 (December 1988) 84–87.

   [15] James D. G. Dunn, "They Set Us in New Paths: VI. New Testament: The Great Untranslated," *Expository Times* 100 (March 1989) 203–7.

   [16] A. T. Hanson, "Today and Tomorrow in Biblical Studies: I. The Present State of New Testament Studies," *Expository Times* 100 (June 1989) 324–28.

   [17] J. L. Holden, "Today and Tomorrow in Biblical Studies: III. A Future for New Testament Studies," *Expository Times* 100 (August 1989) 405–8.

About the Area Editor

Harold W. Hoehner (B.A., Barrington College; Th.M., Th.D., Dallas Theological Seminary; Ph.D., Cambridge University; postdoctoral work at University of Tübingen and Cambridge University) is director of Th.D. studies and also department chairman and professor of New Testament Studies, Dallas Theological Seminary. He was ordained in Grace Bible Church. He was on the board of the International Council on Biblical Inerrancy. Two of his writings are *Herod Antipas, XVII* in the Society of New Testament Studies Monograph Series (Cambridge, 1972, reprinted by Zondervan, 1980), and *Chronological Aspects of the Life of Christ* (Zondervan, 1977). He has also contributed to various publications, including the *Expositor's Bible Commentary*, the revised *International Standard Bible Encyclopedia,* and *Oxford Companion to the Bible*.

'ΟΡΓΙΖΕΣΘΕ IN EPHESIANS 4:26:
COMMAND OR CONDITION?[1]

DANIEL B. WALLACE
Assistant Professor of New Testament Studies
Dallas Theological Seminary

Article from *Criswell Theological Review*

It would be very appropriate to develop in this paper something of a "theology of anger," or, more specifically, a "theology of righteous *human* anger." Such a study is sorely needed. But it must be built on the exegesis of several key passages. Our goal, therefore, is far more modest: We wish to focus on only one text which, nevertheless, contributes heavily to such a theme. Ephesians 4:26 is arguably the *crux interpretum* in the New Testament regarding the validity of man's δικαία ὀργή (as the Greeks put it)—man's righteous indignation.

Why is this so? How can this one verse be regarded as so crucial to the issue? It is simply because we have great difficulty finding explicit statements in the New Testament in *praise* of human wrath. (One overly zealous writer went so far as to use the anger of the king in the parable of the wedding feast [Matt. 22:7] as a proof-text for the validity of righteous *human* indignation[2]—in spite of the fact that most would view the king as representative of God.) Consequently, the imperative ὀργίζεσθε, "be angry," in Ephesians 4:26, *if taken as a command*, becomes the most explicitly positive statement of human anger in the New Testament.

I. Possible Syntactical Nuances for 'Οργίζεσθε in Ephesians 4:26

That ὀργίζεσθε is a command is by no means a settled issue among the commentators; in fact, some even doubt that it is an imperative. Altogether I have found in the commentaries *seven* different syntactical options—five of which treat the form as imperative, two as indicative:
1. Declarative indicative: "You are angry, yet do not sin."
2. Interrogative indicative: "Are you angry? Then do not sin."
3. Command imperative: "Be angry, and do not sin."
4. Permissive imperative: "Be angry (if you must), but do not sin."
5. Conditional imperative: "If you are angry, do not sin."
6. Concessive imperative: "Although you may get angry, do not sin."
7. Prohibitive imperative: "Do not be angry and do not sin."

In order to make this discussion manageable, we need to pare down the field. We will do this in two ways: first, three options will be quickly dismissed since their exegetical bases are tenuous at best; second, three nuances will be grouped as one because in this passage there is very little difference among them.

A. Implausible Options

The two approaches which treat ὀργίζεσθε as an indicative and the one which sees it as a prohibition are implausible on their face. I have seen but one commentator treat the verb here as a declarative indicative. R. O. Yeager argues that "ὀργίζεσθε in our verse can be present middle indicative. Taken with concessive καὶ such a translation makes as good sense [as an imperative] and fits the context well."[3] He translates it, "Although you are provoked, do not go on sinning," rendering this not materially different from a concessive imperative.[4]

There are three primary[5] difficulties with this view however: (1) ὀργίζεσθε is in the thick of an overtly parenetic section, Ephesians 4:25–32, being surrounded by ten imperatives and two hortatory subjunctives; though there are three indicatives[6] here, they all speak of positive realities which God has effected for the believer and as such constitute the basis for the parenesis.[7] The flow of argument, therefore, is decidedly against an indicative ὀργίζεσθε. (2) To treat the καὶ which joins ὀργίζεσθε to μὴ ἁμαρτάνετε as concessive (or adversative) is doubtful enough between two imperatives (ἀλλα or δὲ would be expected), but to consider it as introducing the abrupt shift from indicative to imperative seems especially unnatural.[8] (3) Finally, the entire clause, ὀργίζεσθε καὶ μὴ ἁμαρτάνετε, exactly reproduces the LXX rendering of Psalm 4:4, where it must be taken as an imperative.[9] Whether or not the apostle intentionally alluded to this text is not the point here: Even if he used it rhetorically, it is a supreme case of *petitio principii* to view the formal correspondence with the Psalm as having *no* effect on the syntax in the Ephesians passage.[10] This approach, therefore, must be judged highly improbable—at best.

The second view, that ὀργίζεσθε is an interrogative indicative (held by Beza, Meyer, and J. Eadie),[11] comes under the same judgment for the same reasons: It would be an uneasy indicative in the midst of imperatives, the allusion to Psalm 4:4 shows that an imperative is in Paul's mind, and the use of καὶ in the sense of "then" or "therefore" is not natural here.[12]

The third implausible view is the prohibitive imperative view—i.e., that the negative μὴ governs both ἁμαρτάνετε *and* ὀργίζεσθε.[13] This view takes a "180-degree" turn from treating ὀργίζεσθε as a positive injunction. In spite of the theological difficulty caused by the *prima facie* reading of "be angry" as a command, this view is impossible grammatically.

B. Permissive, Conditional, and Concessive Grouped Together

On a popular level especially, the permissive, conditional, and concessive views are all neatly separated. But several writers hold out for the distinction, at least, between permissive and conditional.[14] Thus, J. L. Boyer states that "in Ephesians 4:26 it is difficult to understand 'Be angry and sin not' as a command or even a permission, expecially [sic] in light of the context. . . . It is much easier to take it as a condition. . . ."

This distinction is usually made because the imperative can have a permissive or conditional nuance. Grammarians, however, make no distinction between a conditional imperative and a concessive imperative.[16] And semantically, of course, concession is one *kind* of condition. In this context, since ὀργίζεσθε is followed by a prohibition, any real difference between condition and concession is imperceptible. Consequently, we will treat the conditional view and the concessive view as one and the same.

But what about the difference between permission and condition? Many grammarians make a distinction between these two.[17] But not all do. No less an authority than the grammar by Blass-Debrunner lumps the permissive, concessive, and conditional uses together.[18] M. Barth, in his meticulous commentary on Ephesians, does the same: he translates ὀργίζεσθε "if you are angry," labels it a "concessive imperative," then defines what he means by saying that "a factual *permission* is granted by this imperative" (italics mine).[19] It may be significant that, almost universally, those who distinguish the two opt for the conditional nuance, arguing that permission is closer to command. C. L. Mitton is representative: "It is quite wrong to take it as a command or even a permission to be angry . . . here the quotation means: 'If you do get angry. . . .' "[20]

In this context, however, one has difficulty even determining the difference between permission and condition. This is due to the following prohibition, μὴ ἁμαρτάνετε, which somehow governs the opening imperative. There is very little difference between "be angry, if you must, but don't sin" and "if you are angry, don't sin." Nevertheless, the semantic situation found in Ephesians 4:26 (viz., imperative + καὶ + a second verb) fits the pattern required for a conditional imperative, though it is quite rare for permissive imperatives.[21] Consequently, we will treat permissive and conditional as one—and, out of deference to conditional advocates, call this approach simply the conditional view.

To sum up, the live options in Ephesians 4:26 are only two: Either ὀργίζεσθε is a command or a condition. We now need to examine several factors which may help us to come down from the fence on one side or the other.

II. Factors Contributing to the Use of 'Ὀργίζεσθε in Ephesians 4:26

There are four major factors which help shape our understanding of the nuance of ὀργίζεσθε in this text: (1) the use Paul makes of Psalm 4:4; (2) the context; (3) the general biblical teaching on man's anger; and (4) the specifics of the syntax of the construction. For reasons which should soon become obvious, we will treat the first two in this section and treat the syntax separately. However, as our purpose is to see what contribution Ephesians 4:26 makes toward the biblical teaching on human anger, and not vice versa, we can only touch on this third category in our examination of the context.

A. Paul's Use of Psalm 4:4

As we mentioned earlier, Paul quotes verbatim the LXX rendering of Psalm 4:4: ὀργίζεσθε καὶ μὴ ἁμαρτάνετε. There are problems with this translation, however. ὀργίζεσθε renders *rgzû*, which though an imperative, might not mean "be angry." The basic significance of the stem, *rgz*, is simply "tremble, shake,"[22] which may involve—in a given context—shaking out of fear, trembling in awe or reverence, or shaking in anger. Though the LXX renders *rgzû* as "be angry," the Targum as well as Aquila opt for "tremble [in fear/reverence]."[23] The commentaries are divided on the issue,[24] though those who affirm the LXX's rendering tend to do so precisely because Paul quoted it. Whether this Psalm is to be connected with the previous one,[25] and if so, whether verse 4 is addressed to Absalom's men[26] or David's companions,[27] are questions difficult to answer. My tentative preference is to opt for the meaning "tremble (in awe)," for *rgzû* because (1) the nuance of anger is rare for *rgz* and is perhaps never found in the Qal stem;[28] and (2) the parallel with the rest of verse 4 ("meditate . . . and be still") seems to be a fitting balance with the idea of "tremble (in awe) and do not sin."[29] But even if "be angry" is the meaning of *rgzu*, because of the question mark over who is being addressed as well as the object of the anger, we cannot be dogmatic about the force of the Hebrew imperative.[30].

All of this, however, is a moot point. Paul does not here use one of his standard introductory formulas;[31] he is not putting his apostolic stamp of approval on the LXX's rendering. In my judgment, Abbott's dictum is correct: "It is . . . superfluous, as far as the present passage is concerned, to inquire what the meaning of the original is. St. Paul is not arguing from the words, but adopting them as well known, and as expressing the precept he wishes to inculcate."[32] His use of the Psalm is, therefore, rhetorical. Hence, we need to look at the context into which Ephesians 4:26 is set for further clues on the use of ὀργίζεσθε.

B. The Context of Ephesians 4:26

There are at least seven contextual factors, of varying weight, which may be helpful in shaping our understanding of this elusive imperative.

1. *Parenetic Section.* As we have already mentioned, Ephesians 4:25–32 is a specifically parenetic section in this epistle. On a mechanical level, this might tend to favor the command view, for the other ten imperatives here

must all be taken as commands (or prohibitions).[33] At the same time, none of the imperatives—except ὀργίζεσθε—fits the *structural* requirements for a conditional imperative (viz., imperative + καί + second verb), which might indicate that a conditional imperative was on the apostle's mind.

2. *Community of Faith*. Not only is verse 26 in a parenetic section, but it is in one which addresses the relationship of individual believer to individual believer. It begins and ends with two indicatives ("we are [ἐσμὲν] members of one another" in verse 25; "God in Christ *has forgiven* [ἐχαρίσατο] you" in verse 32), which speak of the divine initiative toward those who now constitute the believing community. All this is to say that, however we take ὀργίζεσθε, it should be seen as anger directed within the church. By extension, perhaps, it can apply to those outside the faith, but I doubt if that is the apostle's primary point. Consequently, those who argue for the command view on the basis of a righteous indignation toward unbelievers have missed the thrust of the apostle here.[34] But this cuts both ways: If Paul is not here speaking about judging the world per se, then arguments against the command view which presuppose that he is are equally invalid.[35]

3. *A Specific Situation in View?* Not to be discounted entirely is the possibility that Paul has in mind a specific situation in 4:25–32. Formally, all the injunctions are directed toward the group except one. ὁ κλέπτων (v. 28) may well refer to a specific individual. Not only is it singular, but the negative μηκέτι ("no longer") indicates that the stealing was already taking place.[36] If this exegesis is valid, then the entire pericope might center on this problem, and the injunction in verse 26 would then probably mean "be angry about the fact of such sin in your midst and do something about it!"[37]

However, identifying a specific problem in this epistle is notoriously difficult. It depends not only on taking ὁ κλέπτων as referring to an individual (rather than generically), but on seeing other specific problems addressed in this epistle,[38] as well as viewing Ephesians as primarily intended for one church.[39] More than "one thief" will be required to overturn the well-worn view of the epistle as some sort of circular letter.[40]

Consequently, this parenetic section is probably very loosely organized. The rapid-fire imperatives march on asyndetically;[41] these staccato exhortations are typically Pauline.[42] But even this tends to support the command imperative view, though hardly conclusively.[43]

4. *Ephesians 5:1*. Barth brings 5:1 ("as beloved children, be imitators of God") into the discussion: "Among the saints who are 'God's imitators' (5:1) such anger cannot be excluded any more than in God himself . . . or in the Messiah (Mark 3:5, etc.)."[44] This, too, would tend to support the command imperative view[45]—if all the moral attributes of God are to be copies by the believer. But, at best, this is only an inference.

5. *The Audience*. One factor rarely considered is how the audience would have understood Paul's words. Assuming that it was largely Gentile, it may be significant that, among the Greek philosophers, only the Stoics

categorically condemned human anger.[46] Though the general tenor among the Greeks was a negative assessment, "the moral wrath which protects against evil"[47] was seen as entirely legitimate in the realm of government and "even necessary for great acts and virtues. . . ."[48]

With reference to the Jewish contingency among Paul's addressees, both the Old Testament [49] and rabbinic literature[50] considered righteous human indignation to be legitimate.[51] On the other hand, Philo had a difficult time accepting either human wrath or divine wrath as a righteous emotion/act.[52] This, of course, is in keeping with his Stoic training.

In other words, few Jews or Gentiles in the first Christian century would flinch at reading ὀργίζεσθε as a command. In the least, since the Stoics and Philo stand apart from the rest of the ancient world, those exegetes who would absolutely prohibit human anger[53] might do well to take stock of the company they keep! Nevertheless, what the original audience would think is not conclusive for what an author meant. Two final (and related) contextual arguments are usually judged as decisive clues to Paul's meaning here.

6. Ὀργή *Prohibited in Verse 31.* What is normally perceived to be the strongest argument[54] against taking ὀργίζεσθε as a command is the prohibition against anger in verse 31: "Let all bitterness and wrath and *anger* [ὀργή] and clamor and slander be put away from you, with all malice."[55] Formally, it is not just ὀργή that is prohibited—but πᾶσα ὀργή ("all anger").

Verses 26 and 31 clearly stand in tension. Just as it would be wrong—by appealing only to 26a—to say that *all* anger is a righteous duty laid on the believer at all times, so too it would be wrong—by appealing exclusively to verse 31—to say that *all* anger is wrong and utterly sinful at all times. Indeed, there are two internal clues which help to resolve the tension created by verse 31.

First, as many commentators point out,[56] this verse apparently gives a progressively climactic and inherently cohesive list of vices; hence, the ὀργή which springs from θυμός (which, in turn, is rooted in πικρία) is to be shunned at all times. As C. Hodge points out, "Verse 31 is not inconsistent with this interpretation [viz., that there is a righteous anger], for there the context shows [that] the apostle speaks of malicious anger—just as 'all hatred' means all malice, and not the hatred of evil."[57]

Second, the very fact that Paul distinguishes between anger and sin in verse 26 indicates that there is an anger which is *not* sinful. Now it might be objected that this is begging the question because it presupposes an injunctive flavor for ὀργίζεσθε. But that is not the case. Even if we assume the conditional view, "*if* you are angry, then do not sin" at least implies that it is possible to be angry without sinning. As A. Tholuck has aptly remarked, "Spricht Paulus von einem verwerflichen Zorne, wie kann er das Sündigen vom Zürnen trennen?"[58] And once it is recognized that the apostle admits of a non-sinful anger in verse 26, then it must be conceded that he does not *absolutely* prohibit anger in verse 31. Therefore, "conditionalists" who appeal to verse 31 prove too much: They undercut their own view of ὀργίζεσθε in the process.

7. *Ephesians 4:26b–27.* Finally, conditionalists appeal to verses 26b–27 as an argument against the command view. Boyer asks, ". . . if this is a command to show 'righteous indignation,' why is the warning added to end it before the sun goes down?"[59] In response, four things can be said.

First, if, as Boyer believes, Paul is condemning all human anger, why would he allow it to last until sundown? Would it not be more to the point for him to have said, "Do not get angry in the first place"? By setting a temporal limit[60] the apostle lays down a restriction, but not a prohibition.

Second, no one who maintains the "command" view would see ὀργίζεσθε as an unqualified exhortation. Unless it is impossible for a command to have a limited and occasional application, it is difficult to see the validity of Boyer's point. If I am commanded to "weep with those who weep," is this not a limited command? Or if parents are told not to spare the rod for that would spoil the child, does this mean that all discipline must be corporeal—or worse, that the only way they are to relate to their offspring is with a whip in hand? Surely the imperative is flexible enough, in a given context, to make demands which are limited by time and/or occasion.

Third, no one but the Stoics and Philo would deny God the right—even the obligation—to be angry at times. Yet few would say that anger is God's leading attribute. Isaiah 28:21 speaks of the exercise of God's wrath as his "strange"[61] or "unusual"[62] work. The point is that a command to be angry—and yet to limit that anger—is in keeping with God's character and may well be, as Barth has noted, a specific application of Ephesians 5:1: "become imitators of God." Does not the psalmist say, "His anger is but for a moment, His favor is for a lifetime"?[63]

Finally, entirely apart from these considerations is the possibility that we have misconstrued the limitation in verse 26b. Paul might not be placing a temporal limit on one's anger. When he says "do not let the sun go down on your anger," he does not use the obvious cognate, ὀργή. Instead, he uses παροργισμός. This is a rare term which has been found to date only in biblical Greek.[64] "In the LXX it is used as a rule with an active meaning. . . ."[65] In fact, we may go so far as to say that the term always has an active meaning except for one variant found in codex Alexandrinus.[66] It may thus be translated "the cause of provocation," and always refers[67] to the external cause by one party (usually Israel) which aroused the wrath of another (usually Yahweh). παροργισμός is used but once in the New Testament, in Ephesians 4:26. Perhaps commentators are too hasty to label it a passive—viz., the feeling of being provoked.[68] If it bears its normal sense of "that which caused provocation," Paul might well be saying, "Deal with the cause of your anger immediately." And if that cause is another brother (as would be most natural in this section), the point might well be the same as Matthew 18:15: "If your brother sins, go and rebuke him." Verse 27 then would have the force of "don't let the devil gain a foothold in the assembly by letting sin go un-checked."[69] Further, μὴ ἁμαρτάνετε in this view would have the force of "do not sin by doing nothing—act quickly to discipline your brother." If this reconstruction is correct, then ὀργίζεσθε would have to be taken as a command.[70]

Perhaps we are reading too much into the text in this approach. But suffice it to say here that, whether 26b is a temporal limit on one's anger or whether it is an incitement to carry out church discipline quickly, there is no good reason to object to ὀργίζεσθε as a command.

To sum up the contextual arguments: none of the seven points we have made is decisive. At this stage, ὀργίζεσθε could be either a command or a condition, though I am inclined to think that the command view has the edge.

III. The Syntax in Ephesians 4:26

The final factor deals specifically with the syntax of ὀργίζεσθε καὶ μὴ ἁμαρ-τάνετε. There are three arguments to consider here, though the first two are of minor importance.

A. Aspect

The aspectual forces of the imperative are often treated in relation to present time. Thus, the aorist imperative is usually considered to mean "start to do X," while the present imperative bears the sense, "continue doing X." The aorist prohibition[71] has the force "don't start to do X," while the present prohibition means "stop doing X."[72] If this meaning were pressed in Ephesians 4:26, the idea might be "keep on being angry, but stop sinning."

But recent studies have shown that this way of viewing the imperatives is quite incorrect,[73] for the time element is entirely incidental to the tense used and is to be derived from the context. As K. L. McKay points out, "In the imperative the essential difference between the aorist and the imperfective [i.e., present] is that the former urges an activity as whole action and the latter urges it as ongoing process."[74] Consequently, this is a moot point for our present passage.

B. The Connective Καὶ

Several commentators who favor taking ὀργίζεσθε as a command make much of the conjunction joining the two imperatives. Meyer is representa-tive: ". . . the mere καὶ is only logically correct when both imperatives are thought of in the *same* sense, not the former as permitting and the latter as enjoining, in which case the combination becomes *exceptive* ('only, how-ever'), which would be expressed by ἀλλά, πλήν, or μόνον. . . ."[75] This is not a very strong argument for the simple reason that καὶ is not here connecting two naked imperatives, but an imperative on the one side with μὴ plus the imperative on the other. The negative disrupts any simple connection and, in fact, probably lends a mildly adversative force to καὶ: "Be angry, and *yet* do not sin." Still, the presence of καὶ cannot be construed as an argument *against* the command view and, in all probability, leans toward it. Nevertheless, neither of these first two grammatical arguments is very decisive.

C. The Semantic Situation of Conditional Imperatives

The final syntactical argument, however, may well be decisive. Those who hold that ὀργίζεσθε is a conditional imperative must reckon with the fact that it is followed by another imperative. This would seem unnatural, as we might expect a future indicative—thus, in John 2:19 we read, "Destroy this temple and in three days I will raise it up [λύσατε . . . ἐγερῶ]." In Boyer's exhaustive study on imperatives in the New Testament, in fact, he states the following:

> Probably the strangest and most controversial category of imperatives is that which seems to express some conditional element. Here it is necessary to distinguish two groups. The first is neither strange nor controversial; it includes a large number of instances (about 20) where an imperative is followed by καὶ and a *future indicative* verb [italics mine]. . . .
> The second group consists of a few passages where condition has been proposed to explain a difficult passage.[76]

Boyer then lists only three passages[77] which belong to this questionable category. Ephesians 4:26 gets the greatest amount of coverage—and here Boyer comes out strongly, on contextual and theological grounds, for a conditional ὀργίζεσθε. The point is that one of the leading advocates of the conditional view—and the only one to categorize every imperative in the New Testament—was unable to find any other conditional imperatives which was followed by καὶ and another imperative. Boyer has clearly felt the force of this syntactical argument and has found that his only recourse is to argue on the basis of other factors.

But, to be sure, there are grammarians who argue that a conditional imperative can be followed by another imperative. A. T. Robertson has made perhaps the most cogent statement along these lines:

> Sometimes two imperatives are connected by καὶ when the first suggests concession. Thus Ephesians 4:26, ὀργίζεσθε καὶ μὴ ἁμαρτάνετε. So also ἐραύνησον καὶ ἴδε (John 7:52). Cf. ἔρχου καὶ ἴδε (John 1:46). *This seems simple enough* [italics mine].[78]

Robertson thus gives two examples (besides Eph. 4:26) of a conditional imperative followed by another imperative. But what "seems simple enough" to Robertson does not help the cause of a conditional imperative in Ephesians 4:26 for three reasons.

First, Robertson's identification of ἐραύνησον in John 7:52 and ἔρχου in

John 1:46 as conditional imperatives is highly debatable, for even Boyer—
who would like to find such a tidy semantic parallel to Ephesians 4:26—is
unable to admit that any construction other than imperative + καὶ + *future
indicative* involves a conditional imperative.[79]

Second, even if we assumed that Robertson's proof-texts were valid, a
proper parallel has not been drawn for us. In John 1:46 we read ἔρχου καὶ ἴδε
("come and see"). This is Philip's response to Nathanael's challenge, "Can
any good thing come out of Nazareth?" If we see ἔρχου as a conditional
imperative, rather than entreaty, then Philip's response means, "If you come
you *will* see." In John 7:52, the Pharisees suspect that Nicodemus has become a disciple of Jesus. They ask, "Are you from Galilee, too?" Then they
declare, "Search and see [ἐραύνησον καὶ ἴδε] that no prophet comes from
Galilee." Again, if ἐραύνησον is conditional, the Pharisees' retort means, "If
you search, you *will* see." In other words, in both of Robertson's proof-texts
the second imperative functions *semantically* as a *future indicative*.[80] If we
applied that principle to Ephesians 4:26, we would get "If you are angry, you
will not sin"!

Third, there is an additional problem with Robertson's proof-texts. The
very fact that there is some doubt concerning the label of conditional imperative for ἔρχου and ἐραύνησον is not because others would give them a
radically different nuance. The idea of injunction or condition in these two
texts is not very far apart at all. But this is not due to a blurring in the
distinction between the categories (or, more accurately, nuances) of command and condition—otherwise exegetes would not spill so much ink over
Ephesians 4:26.[81] Rather, it is due to the fact that these conditional imperatives have not lost their natural injunctive force. And it is probable that this is
due to their being linked by καὶ with another imperative. We might even
paraphrase John 1:46 as "If you come—and I urge you to—you will see" and
John 7:52 as "If you search—as well you should—you will see." If this were
applied to Ephesians 4:26, it would mean, "If you are angry—and you should
be"!

Perhaps we are being unfair to Robertson, however. After all, he only
supplied two proof-texts, implying that there may be others. Because of this
possibility it is necessary to examine every imperative + καὶ + imperative
construction in the New Testament. Altogether, there are 187 imperatives +
καὶ + imperative constructions in the New Testament.[82] This certainly
seems like a large enough data base from which to draw some fairly firm
conclusions. I examined each one to determine whether we can add any
more *potentially* conditional imperatives to Robertson's list. The answer is a
qualified yes. In addition to John 1:46 and 7:52, 21 more imperatives can be
added to the list[83] of *potential* conditional imperatives. I broke these down
into two groups: those which only had a slight chance of deserving the label
and those which, in their contexts, looked like good candidates. In the first
group belonged 17 imperatives.[84] For example, Mark 2:9 has "rise and take up

your bed and walk." It is just possible that the force is, "If you rise and take up your bed, you will walk." Yet, the whole tenor of the pericope seemed to render this unlikely.[85] In Luke 24:39 Jesus, in his resurrected body, says "Touch me and see . . ."; the force could possibly be "If you touch me, you will see." But again, the tone of the passage seems to be against this.[86]

In the second group—the likely candidates—belonged, besides John 1:46 and 7:52, only two other texts. In Luke 7:7 we read of the centurion's request that Jesus heal his servant: "Say the word and let my servant be healed." Many scribes changed ἰαθήτω ("let him be healed") to ἰαθήσεται ("he will be healed"),[87] indicating that the second imperative is virtually the equivalent of a future indicative. "If you say the word, he will be healed," is not an inappropriate rendering, therefore.[88] John 11:34 reproduces the verbage of 1:46 ("come and see") and consequently may well imply a conditional nuance.

Significantly, of all 21 potential examples, only two were as convincing as Robertson's two alleged proof-texts. Thus, out of 187 imperative + καὶ + imperative constructions in the New Testament, four *probably*—or, at least, quite possibly—involve conditional imperatives. Yet each of these four could be construed as conditional imperatives precisely because the trailing imperative functioned as a *future indicative*—a semantic situation which finds no parallel in Ephesians 4:26.

However, among the 17 mildly possible conditional imperatives, I found a different phenomenon. In four passages,[89] assuming that the first imperative was conditional, the second still, most naturally, bore its injunctive force, thus paralleling Ephesians 4:26. However, there were two major problems with all these examples: First, they were exceedingly doubtful as legitimate candidates for conditional imperatives; and second, the conditional imperative nuance still carried with it the full force of a command. Two examples should suffice. In Mark 5:19 Jesus told the formerly demon-possessed man, "Go home and tell them what the Lord has done for you." If we read ὕπαγε conditionally, we would have, "If you go home, tell them. . . ." Though a command would thereby be preserved in the apodosis, only with great ingenuity could we construe ὕπαγε as a mere option.[90] Luke 5:4 suffers the same judgment, for Jesus' command to Peter to "Put out into deep waters and lower the nets" can hardly, without torture, be rendered, "If you put out into deep waters, lower the nets." The context must virtually be suffocated to get this idea out of the verse.[91]

It must be readily admitted that these examples are very difficult to swallow. They are included in this discussion to show that only by great mental gymnastics is one able to show legitimate parallels to a conditional ὀργίζεσθε in Ephesians 4:26.

To sum up the major syntactical argument we can make the following three points:

1. All the *positively* identified conditional imperatives in the New Testa-

ment are followed by καὶ + future indicative.

2. All four of the *probable* conditional imperatives in imperative + καὶ + imperative constructions require the second imperative to function semantically as a future indicative (i.e., stating the consequence/fulfillment of the implied condition).

3. All of the 21 *potentially* conditional imperatives in imperative + καὶ + imperative constructions retained their injunctive force.

These three syntactical facts I consider to be *decisive* against a conditional ὀργίζεσθε because the semantic situation of conditional imperatives is so radically different from what we see in Ephesians 4:26.[92] (In light of this, we might well consider the distinct possibility that what the phenomena of the New Testament display is hardly unique to itself: The semantic pattern of conditional imperatives found in the New Testament might just be an aspect of universal grammar as well.) Furthermore, the normal expediency of appealing to the use of Psalm 4:4, the context, or the general biblical teaching on human anger as that which must override any notion of command in ὀργίζεσθε is inconclusive at best, and, as we have hopefully shown, more than likely supports the command view. Ephesians 4:26, then, can be taken at face value: "Be angry and do not sin."

IV. Conclusion and Application

In Ephesians 4:26 Paul is placing a moral obligation on believers to be angry as the occasion requires. As his injunction is in a parenetic section dealing with how believers are to interact with each other—rather than with the world—he probably has in mind a righteous indignation which culminates in church discipline, though not necessarily in a formal way. Since this righteous indignation is a part of our response to imitate God, it must be an "enlightened wrath, the wrath *whitened* by grace."[93] As God himself does not dwell in anger, neither should we. As anger is the dark side of God—his strange work—so too wrath must never characterize the believer. However, if we fail to obey this injunction, not only will the enemy continue to make well-ploughed inroads into our churches, but we ourselves will, by suppressing our holy indignation, be but "a maimed sample of humanity."[94]

Notes

[1] This is a revision of a paper read at the annual meeting of the Evangelical Theological Society held at Gordon-Conwell Theological Seminary (December 5, 1987).

[2] H. C. Hahn, "Anger, ὀργή," in *The New International Dictionary of New Testament Theology* [= DNTT] (3 vols.; ed. C. Brown; Grand Rapids: Zondervan, 1975) 1.110. Further, even if the king in this parable could be interpreted as representing man (rather than God), the incidental comment by Jesus of the king's wrath (ὠργίσθη in Matt. 22:7; ὀργισθείς in Luke 14:21) is hardly

adequate as proof of his sanction of human anger, for elsewhere he uses questionable moral models in his parables as an illustration in a different realm of a good moral virtue (cf. the parable of the workers in the vineyard [Matt. 20:1–16]: he is not advocating that every landowner pay the same wage to all-day and part-day workers; and the parable of the talents [Matt. 25:14–30]: surely he is not here equating wealth with righteousness [cf. also Luke 16:1–9]. Our point is simply that the parables do not always have a direct, literal application—often, if not usually, they are illustrative of a truth in an entirely different realm).

[3] R. O. Yeager, *The Renaissance New Testament* (18 vols.; Gretna: Pelican, 1983) 14.307.

[4] Yeager apparently is uncomfortable with the concessive imperative view: "There is nothing in the imperative mode itself to imply consent or permission" (ibid.), which has probably prompted him to attempt to make his view rest on more solid syntactical ground (since declarative indicatives, unlike concessive imperatives, are common).

[5] A fourth difficulty (though less significant) also presents itself: Yeager's view tends to see Ephesians as written to a specific, identifiable situation (for anger is stated as a present problem in the community), rather than as a circular letter. Attempts to treat Ephesians as addressed to a specific community with a specific set of problems/needs have not been entirely persuasive. See later discussion.

[6] ἐσμὲν in v. 25; ἐσςραγίσθητε in v. 30; and ἐχαρίσατο in v. 32.

[7] If ὀργίζεσθε as a declarative indicative were treated the same way, then anger would be seen as a permanent and positive moral virtue (and one which, incidentally, believers did not possess before salvation).

[8] Further, we would most naturally expect the concession to come at the beginning of v. 26–either implicitly (e.g., instead of ὀργίζεσθε we might expect Paul to have written ὀργιζό-μενοι) or explicitly (e.g., καίπερ).

[9] Athough there is doubt over the lexical choice of the LXX translator, he has correctly rendered the syntax of the Hebrew Qal imperative *rgzû*.

[10] H. A. W. Meyer (*Ephesians* in MeyerK, 254) argues cogently against the interrogative indicative view on the basis of the quote of Psalm 4:4: "Against this we cannot urge—the objection usually taken since the time of Wolf—the καὶ, which often in rapid emotion strikes in with some summons . . . ; but we may urge the fact that Paul *reproduces a passage of the LXX* (which, it is true, is quite arbitrarily denied by Beza and Koppe) in which ὀργιζ is *imperative*, and that such an abrupt and impassioned question and answer would not be in keeping with the whole calm and sober tone of the discourse." Similarly, cf. J. P. Lange, *Ephesians* in *Commentary on the Holy Scriptures* (Grand Rapids: Zondervan, n.d.) 170; T. K. Abbott (*Ephesians* [ICC; Edinburgh: T. & T. Clark, 1987]) 140.

[11] See MeyerK, 252 and J. Eadie, *A Commentary on the Greek Text of the Epistle of Paul to the Ephesians* (reprint ed.; Grand Rapids: Baker, 1979) 342 for a list of names. The view is no longer popular.

[12] Not only would we normally expect ἄρα or οὖν here, but in Paul's usage especially we are accustomed to seeing explicitly paratactic structure if that is what he meant.

[13] C. Hodge seems to entertain this view (*A Commentary on the Epistle to the Ephesians* [New York: Robert Carter and Brothers, 1856] 269) when he writes:

> . . . the words of the apostle may mean, do not commit the sin of being angry. To this it is objected, that it makes the negative qualify both verbs, while it belongs really only to the latter. It is not necessary to assume that the apostle uses these words in the precise sense of the original text; for the New Testament writers often give the sense of an Old Testament passage with a modification of the words, or they use the same words with a modification of the sense.

[14] Aquinas embraced the permissive view; more recently, cf. H. Alford, *The Greek Testament*, vol. 3: *Galatians–Philemon* (3 vols.; rev. E. F. Harrison; Chicago: Moody, 1958) 125 (though he

calls it "assumptive"); R. P. Martin, *Ephesians* in *The Broadman Bible Commentary* (12 vols.; Nashville: Broadman, 1971) 11.161 (though he seems to lump conditional, concessive and permissive ideas together, his translation reflects the permissive idea: "You may be angry . . . if you can't help it . . ."). Others have held the conditional view, considering it as different from the permissive view: cf. C. L. Mitton, *Ephesians* (NCB; ed. M. Black; London: Marshall, Morgan and Scott, 1973) 168: "It is quite wrong to take it as a command or even a permission to be angry"; J. Gnilka, *Der Epheserbrief* (in HTKNT) 235, asks, "Wird hier der Zorn für gewisse Fälle konzediert?" ("Is the anger allowed here for particular cases?") He answers in the negative because anger in v. 31 is prohibited.

[15] J. L. Boyer, "Other Conditional Elements in New Testament Greek," *GTJ* 4 (1983) 185.

[16] E.g., A. T. Robertson, *A Grammar of the Greek New Testament in the Light of Historical Research* (4th ed.; Nashville: Broadman, 1934) 948, calls his fifth category of usage "Concession or Condition"; cf. also J. M. Stahl, *Kritisch-Historische Syntax des Griechischen Verbums der Klassischen Zeit* (reprint ed.; Hildesheim: Georg Olms, 1965) 239, 362; W. D. Chamberlain, *An Exegetical Grammar of the Greek New Testament* (New York: Macmillan, 1941) 86; C. Vaughan and V. E. Gideon, *A Greek Grammar of the New Testament* (Nashville: Broadman, 1979) 107; B. L. Mandilaras, *The Verb in the Greek Non-Literary Papyri* (Athens: Hellenic Ministry of Culture and Sciences, 1973) §729.

[17] See n. 15.

[18] BDF §387. They list three uses: command, request, concession. In discussing John 2:19 they consider λύσατε to be equal to ἐὰν καὶ λύσητε (which they call concessive). And regarding our passage, they argue that it "most probably means 'you may be angry as far as I am concerned (if you can't help it), but do not sin thereby' "—a rendering which is normally equated with the permissive view. Cf. also H. Schlier (*Der Brief an die Epheser* [Düsseldorf: Patmos, 1963] 224, n. 3) who, though calling the imperative concessive, cites Blass-Debrunner in support.

[19] M. Barth, *Ephesians 4–6* (AB; 2 vols.; Garden City, N.Y.: Doubleday, 1960) 2.513. So also N. Hugedé, *L'Épître aux Éphésiens* (Geneva: Labor et Fides, 1973) 187: "L'impératif ὀργίζεσθε en soi n'était pas un ordre, mais une concession . . . : si vous vous emportez, ne péchez point" ("The imperative ὀργίζεσθε is not in fact a command, but a concession . . . : "If you are angry, do not sin").

[20] Mitton, *Ephesians*, 168.

[21] But cf. John 19:6 (λάβετε . . . καὶ σταυρώσατε) and Revelation 22:11 (ἀδικησάτω . . . καὶ . . . ῥυπανθήτω); yet even here these "permissive" imperatives bear the sense of reluctance or toleration rather than positive permission.

[22] A. Bowling in *Theological Wordbook of the Old Testament* (ed. R. L. Harris, G. L. Archer, and B. K. Waltke [Chicago: Moody, 1980] 2.830) states, "The primary meaning of this root is to quake or shake, from which ideas such as shaking in anger, fear, or anticipation are derived." Cf. also BDB, 919; KB, 872.

[23] *z'w mnîh wl' thtôn* ("tremble [in fear] and you will not sin"); κλονεῖσθε.

[24] In defense of "be angry," cf. F. Delitzsch, *Psalms* (vol. 5 in *Commentary on the Old Testament* by C. F. Keil and F. Delitzsch [reprint ed.; Grand Rapids: Eerdmans, 1976]) 114–15; W. Kay, *The Psalms* (London: Rivingtons, 1871) 14; in defense of "tremble (in awe)," cf. C. A. Briggs, *Psalms* (ICC; Edinburgh: T. & T. Clark, 1907) 34; H. C. Leupold, *Exposition of the Psalms* (Columbus, Ohio: Wartburg, 1959) 68–69.

[25] So Delitzsch, *Psalms*; differently, Briggs, *Psalms*.

[26] So Delitzsch, *Psalms*.

[27] So Kay, *Psalms*.

[28] "*be angry*, AV. is sustained by Isaiah 28[21] of God's anger and Proverb 29[9] of man's. But in these cases it is rather the quivering and trembling of passion, which is justifiable; and is regarded by many as Hiph v. BDB" (Briggs, *Psalms*, 34).

[29] Not only are the imperatives taken naturally as commands, but "tremble (in awe)" and "meditate" are both God-ward actions. The NEB translation ("However angry your hearts, do not do wrong; though you lie abed resentful, do not break silence") seems a bit forced.

[30] Even if addressed to Absalom and his men, the idea may well be "be angry (at your own wrong-doing) and stop sinning." Yet, if these are the addressees, Paul's use of it is decidedly rhetorical, for he is addressing the community of believers. In large measure, the use of *rgzû*, just like ὀργίζεσθε, is a problem of syntax (see section III for discussion of both).

[31] In Ephesians, however, he uses an IF only twice (4:8; 5:14). See J. P. Sampley, "Scripture and Tradition in the Community as Seen in Ephesians 4:25ff," *ST* 2 (1972) 101–9, for an interesting view on Paul's use of the Old Testament in this section.

[32] Abbott, 139–40. Cf. also MeyerK, *Ephesians*, 252; Lange, *Ephesians*, 169. This is not to say that the quote has *no* significance, for the very familiarity of the Psalm (at least to Paul) renders the two indicative views (discussed earlier) as highly unlikely.

[33] This argument is helpful against seeing ὀργίζεσθε as an indicative here, but probably not against taking it as a specific type of imperative.

[34] So E. K. Simpson (*Ephesians* [NICNT; Grand Rapids: Eerdmans, 1957]) generalizes the passage so as to include individual nations as well as the world (108–9); cf. also C. R. Erdman, *The Epistle of Paul to the Ephesians* (Philadelphia: Westminster, 1974) 102.

[35] So Yeager, *New Testament*, 308: "Why should he allow his anger to persist until it has him shouting at the poor defenseless slaves of Satan who cannot help behaving as they do since they are only unregenerated human flesh?" J. L. Boyer, too, seems to hold this view ("A Classification of Imperatives: A Statistical Study," *GTJ* 8 [1987] 39).

[36] The substantival participle also implies this.

[37] On the assumption that the thief had not yet been identified, the pericope might have the following force:

v. 25: Each man should be open and honest with his neighbor—and not suspect everyone in the community of stealing—because we are members of each other.

vv. 26–27: Either "be angry" at the fact of such sin within the community of believers (cf. 1 Cor. 5:1–5) and resolve to do something about it quickly; or, less likely, "if you are angry" stop sinning by allowing your anger to be vented on everyone you suspect.

v. 28: Rebuke of the thief directly, which fits in well with the command imperative view (at least for Paul; again cf. 1 Cor. 5:1–5).

vv. 29–31: Rebuke of the congregation: the rest of you have sinned, too. As the thief has robbed you physically, you have robbed yourselves spiritually (note the interchange between χρεία in v. 28 and v. 29)—by suspicious innuendo (v. 29) and an escalating vituperation (v. 31)—which grieves the Holy Spirit (v. 30).

v. 32: Because of this one thief in your midst, you have forgotten Christian graces. But, remembering what God in Christ has done for you, forgive one another.

[38] But cf. C. Rogers, Jr., who makes a plausible argument for the problem of drunkenness due to the Dionysian cult in 5:18 ("The Dionysian Background of Ephesians 5:18," *BSac* 136 [1979] 249–57); nevertheless, the Dionysian cult was not a problem unique to Ephesus.

[39] Even if ἐν Ἐφέσῳ in 1:1 is original, this does not, of course, mean that the letter was not intended to be circular.

[40] Cf. D. Guthrie, *New Testament Introduction* (Downers Grove: InterVarsity, 1970) 515. Moving even further away from a specific destination/specific occasion view, W. G. Kümmel, citing J. N. Sanders, argues that Ephesians may well be "the spiritual testament of Paul to the church" (*Introduction to the New Testament* rev. ed.; Nashville: Abingdon, 1975]) 355 (see his discussion on 352–55).

[41] Note vv. 26, 28, 29, 31.

[42] Cf. 1 Thessalonians 5:15–22; Romans 12:9–17.

[43] See n. 32.

[44] Barth, *Ephesians*, 2.513.

[45] However, Barth himself sees ὀργίζεσθε as permissive (= conditional).

[46] H. Kleinknecht, "ὀργή," *TDNT* 5.384–85.

[47] Ibid., 384.

[48] Ibid.

49 Cf. Exodus 32:19; Judges 9:3; 1 Samuel 11:6; 2 Samuel 12:5; Nehemiah 5:6. J. Fichtner points out that "Saul's wrath against the Ammonites . . . is attributed to the Spirit of Yahweh (1 Sam. 11:6)" (ibid., 394), and further that ". . . one can speak especially of holy and righteous anger when it is a matter of directly championing the cause of Yahweh . . ." (ibid.; see references there).

50 See references in Str-B 3.602 (on Eph. 4:26).

51 The Old Testament, however, seems to view it, at times, as a virtue, while the rabbinic material simply allows for it.

52 *TDNT* 5.417.

53 Boyer, "Conditions," though he advocates the conditional view, categorically prohibits anger to men: "it seems impossible to understand this in a good sense. . . . 'righteous indignation' seems never to be approved for men" (39).

54 So Gnilka, *Epheserbrief*, 235.

55 RSV translation.

56 Eadie, *Ephesians*, 348–49; B. F. Westcott, *St. Paul's Epistle to the Ephesians* (London: Macmillan, 1906) 74; Barth, *Ephesians*, 2.521.

57 Hodge, *Ephesians*, 270.

58 "If Paul speaks [only] of a reprehensible anger, how can he distinguish between sinning and being angry?" A. Tholuck, *Philologisch-theologische Auslegung der Bergpredigt Christi nach Matthäus* (Hamburg: Friedrich Perthes, 1833) 186. The underlying difficulty for the conditional view, in this regard, is that it cannot handle the apodosis, μὴ ἁμαρτάνετε. To maintain both a conditional ὀργίζεσθε *and* an absolute prohibition of anger requires a declaration in the apodosis, not a prohibition: "If you are angry, you are sinning."

59 Boyer, "Imperatives," 39.

60 Which is more than likely not literal, the point being that one ought not to allow anger to fester so as to become sin. Even righteous anger, then, can degenerate, if not properly guarded.

61 So NEB.

62 So NASB.

63 Psalm 30:5 (NASV).

64 As well as in patristic comments on Ephesians 4:26. My perusal of *Thesaurus Lingua Graece* (via the *Ibycus* computer-generated concordance) turned up no new instances.

65 J. H. Moulton and G. Milligan, *The Vocabulary of the Greek Testament* (reprint ed.; Grand Rapids: Eerdmans, 1976) 496.

66 Cf. 3 Kingdoms 15:30; 4 Kingdoms 19:3; 23:26; Nehemiah 9:18, 26. The variant reading is found in Jeremiah 21:5. As well, the close cognate, παρόργισμα is also found only with an active meaning (3 Kgdms. 16:33; 20[21]: 22; 2 Chron. 35:19).

67 The *v. l.* excepted.

68 For an active sense, cf. H. C. G. Moule, *Studies in Ephesians* (reprint ed.; Grand Rapids: Kregel, 1977) 122; Westcott, *Ephesians*, 73.

69 See n. 37 for a possible reconstruction of the incident, if any, that the apostle might have had in mind.

70 What might give further support for this view is the fact that ὀργίζω, rather than θυμόω, is used. If a distinction can be made between these two—though, admittedly, there is a great deal of overlap—ὀργιζω tends to accent the volition, while θυμόω tends to stress the emotion (though it is probably impossible to extricate emotions entirely from ὀργίζω's connotations). If such a volitional emphasis is on the apostle's mind (a nuance difficult for English-speaking natives to grasp for "anger, be angry"), then the link with decisive action, justice, (informal) church discipline is thereby strengthened.

71 In the New Testament, all aorist prohibitions in the second person employ the subjunctive rather than the imperative.

72 Cf. H. E. Dana and J. R. Mantey, *A Manual Grammar of the Greek New Testament* (Toronto: Macmillan, 1927) 299–303; J. A. Brooks and C. L. Winbery, *Syntax of New Testament Greek* (Washington, D.C.: University Press of America, 1979) 116.

[73] Cf. K. L. McKay, "Aspect in Imperatival Constructions in New Testament Greek," *NovT* 27 (1985) 201–26; Boyer, "Imperatives," 35–54.

[74] McKay, "Aspect," 206–7.

[75] Meyer, 253–54.

[76] Boyer, "Imperatives," 39.

[77] Strangely, he includes John 2:19 in his dubious list, as well as 2 Corinthians 12:16 and Ephesians 4:26.

[78] Robertson, *Grammar*, 949. Cf. also A. Buttmann, *A Grammar of the New Testament Greek* (Andover: Warren F. Draper, 1873) 290.

[79] Boyer considers ἐραύνησον καὶ ἴδε (John 7:52) to be ambiguous semantically, fitting either the "command" or "condition" category; he does not deal with John 1:46.

[80] It should be noted here that conditionalists who base their view on a supposed conditional imperative in Psalm 4:4 must also reckon with the fact that the same semantics are operative in Hebrew. Abbott (*Ephesians*, 140) aptly points out:

> The phrase is frequently explained by reference to what is called the Hebrew idiom (which is by no means peculiarly Hebrew) of combining two imperatives, so that the former expresses the condition, the latter the result, as in Amos v. 4, "Seek Me and live." But this would make the words mean, "Be angry, and so ye shall not sin."

As well, in all 17 examples listed in *GKC* of this idiom, none broke away from the "condition-consequence" idea (§110.2(a)). Indeed, they noted that "In this case the first imperative contains, *as a rule*, a condition, while the second declares the consequence which the fulfilment of the condition will involve" (italics mine). (See also n. 22.)

[81] Cf. also John 2:19 where such a blurring of nuances would wreak exegetical havoc.

[82] These data were derived from Gramcord. Gramcord is a copyrighted software package which is able to perform grammatical searches in the Greek New Testament. It is distributed solely by the Gramcord Institute, 2065 Half Day Road, Deerfield, IL 60015.

By creating a contextfield of twelve words, 289 imperative + καὶ + imperative constructions were found. We made it this broad in order to pick up every legitimate construction. Gramcord, however, did not discern whether such imperatives belonged in the same clause; as well, it multiplied the examples when more than two imperatives were used (e.g., Mark 2:9 [which reads ἔγειρε καὶ ἆρον . . . καὶ περιπάτει] was listed four times). Consequently, this list of raw data was pared down to 187 legitimate examples.

[83] Ephesians 4:26 being omitted from consideration as that is our target passage.

[84] Cf. Matthew 9:5; 11:29; 15:10; Mark 2:9; 5:19; 7:14; 9:50; Luke 5:4, 23; 24:39; John 4:35; 5:8; 20:27; 1 Corinthians 11:28; 15:34; Galatians 5:1; Ephesians 5:14.

[85] σοὶ λέγω in v. 11 sounds like it introduces a command; the man's immediate response suggests that he viewed it as a command; and the fact that Jesus stresses his own authority (v. 19) would best fit a command imperative. See also Matthew 9:5; Luke 5:23; and John 5:8 for the same expression.

[86] The parallel in v. 39a and the apparent eagerness of Jesus to get his disciples to believe in him are decidedly on the side of seeing entreaty/command here.

[87] In fact, only P[75] B L 1241 cop[sa,bo] are listed in *UBSGNT*[3] in support of the imperative. A quick check of *The New Testament in Greek: The Gospel According to St. Luke*, Part One: Chapters 1–12 (IGNTP; Oxford: Clarendon, 1984) revealed no more MSS.

[88] Cf. also the *v. l.* in Galatians 6:2 (ἀναπληρώσατε) where the *UBSGNT*[3] (= NA[26]) text has the future indicative.

[89] Matthew 15:10; Mark 5:19; 7:14; Luke 5:4.

[90] Jesus had just prohibited him from coming with him. This alternative, then, is not "if you go home rather than coming with me" because the latter was already forbidden.

[91] In particular, Peter's response in v. 5 indicates that he would have been unwilling to do this

except that Jesus commanded him.

[92] If one wishes to debate whether this verse or that belongs in the category where I have placed it, such would not invalidate these three points. We could just as easily drop the numbers and say, "All of the potentially conditional imperatives, . . ." etc.

[93] M. B. Lang, "Isaiah 1:18 and Ephesians 4:25–29," *ExpTim* 8 (1896–97) 405.

[94] Simpson, *Ephesians*, 108.

WILL GOD HEAL US—
A RE-EXAMINATION OF JAMES 5:14–16a

GARY S. SHOGREN
Teaching Fellow of New Testament
Conservative Baptist Seminary of the East
Worcester, Massachusetts

Article from *The Paternoster Press*

James 5:14–16a (author's rendering):

> Is any among you ill? Let him summon the presbyters of the Church and let them pray over him after anointing him in the name of the Lord with olive oil. And the prayer offered in faith will deliver the sick, and the Lord will raise him up; and if he is in the state of having committed sins, they will be forgiven him. Therefore confess (your) sins to each another and pray for each other so that you might be healed.

James 5:14–16 is intriguing on several counts: (1) because it seems to give an unqualified promise of answered prayer, as in John 14:13–14; (2) because it involves physical healing; (3) because Roman Catholicism bases two of its sacraments on it; (4) and more excitingly, because anointing with oil seems exotic to many evangelical Protestants. The need for a careful study of James 5 is all the more valid in an age when medical technology has taken on religious connotations of its own, when religion and science are neatly divided into Cartesian categories, with healing generally falling into the realm of science. The issue is further heightened with the latter-day spread of holistic treatment, 'inner healing,' and the 'Health and Wealth Gospel' with its sporadic rejection of medical technology,[1] movements which soften the distinction between supernatural healing and natural law.

The very strangeness of James' instructions may trigger an emotional bias which will force us to conclude that 'James cannot mean that' to the violation of our own interpretive principles. This is a plea, therefore, not for a renewal of the healing *charisma*, but for an approach to James 5:14–16 which sees the passage as the battleground for a sound hermeneutic.

In 5:14 we have the third piece of advice James gives to people in different situations in the Church (*en humin*, 'among you,' is used five other times in James 3–5 to speak of the 'congregation'). James' third question and his instructions for the ill continue throughout 5:16a. James uses a common word for sickness (*astheneō*, 'to be weak, sick') which here denotes physical ailment, not spiritual distress (cf. 13a); its meaning is confirmed by the participle of *kamnō* ('the one who is ill, sick') in 15.[2]

His prescription is to 'summon' (*proskaleō*) the elders of the Church. The fact that it is the body of presbyters that is called,[3] and not a charismatic healer, is highly suggestive for two reasons. First, James was almost certainly written within the first century, and probably before the controversy over Gentile admission to the Church.[4] Since the gift of healing was known in the Church throughout the first century, James is signalling a course of action which circumvents the charismatic healer in favor of Church officers.[5] Second, he has the patient call for his own presbyters, the very people who would be best equipped to inquire about hidden sins (15b).[6]

The elders are called upon to anoint the subject with 'olive oil' (*elaion*); the aorist participle *aleipsantes*, 'having anointed,' probably denotes an action antecedent to prayer. They are then to invoke the name of the Lord. The name of the Lord Jesus is surely meant here (see Mark 16:17 [longer ending]; Acts 3:6, 16; 16:18);[7] the invocation of his name stamps the use of oil as a Christian religious act, 'an opening to the power of God for him to intervene.'[8]

Let us examine four possible interpretations of the function of the anointing with oil: (1) the oil is purely medicinal; (2) the oil is sacramental (Extreme Unction); (3) the oil is a psychological reinforcement; (4) the oil is a symbol of divine favor.

1. The Oil Is Purely Medicinal

Olive oil was widely used both for hygienic and medicinal purposes. It was popular as a sort of body rub or lotion for use after bathing or between baths (cf. 2 Sam. 12:20). It was also used in the treatment of flesh wounds, skin afflictions, sciatic pain, and violent headaches. In such cases the oil would be applied to the part of the body where it would do good. In the Roman world, some healers anointed to drive out the spirit that was thought to have caused the illness.[9] The Jews too seem to have used oil as a part of exorcism; according to the Midrash on Ecclesiastes, Hanina is put under a spell (by a Galilean Jewish Christian) and rides an ass on the Sabbath; his uncle Joshua anoints him, whereupon he recovers from the spell (cf. *Midr. Qoh.* I, 8).[10]

The proponents of the 'medicine' view imply that in the first century olive oil was used as a cure-all.[11] The point that is made is that James is promoting the best of both worlds: good medicine in conjunction with prayer. Therefore, the argument runs, a modern Christian should seek the best medical attention (certainly not olive oil!) while praying for healing.[12] This interpretation coincides well with our Western regard for the medical profession.

The 'best medicine' approach, however, has several important flaws. First, oil was by no means regarded as a panacea in the first century; we need not suppose that the medical profession of those days was that primitive. While oil was helpful in some cases (as in giving immediate roadside treatment for wounds, Luke 10:34), it would have been next to worthless for broken bones, heart trouble, or infectious diseases such as leprosy. Why too would James invite the charge of quackery by having Church elders give whatever medicine they thought best? This is especially pertinent in a society where a variety of other more suitable cures was recommended. Anointing is not the best medicine, and in most cases it is not even good medicine.

The modern misunderstanding of anointing arises when one culls the ancient references in Strack-Billerbeck's *Kommentar* or in the entry on *aleiphō*, in the *Theological Dictionary of the New Testament* by Schlier, who is himself almost wholly dependent upon Strack-Billerbeck. Some authors refer the reader to the first-century Celsus, who in his *De Medicina*, Books I–IV, gives some attention to anointing with oil. Wilkinson thus quotes from *De Medicina* II, 14, 4 (Spencer's translation) 'it is desirable that even in acute and recent diseases the whole body should be anointed' to prove that anointing was a panacea. But not only does Wilkinson disregard the fact that Celsus used all sorts of natural oils (not necessarily olive oil), he quotes only the positive part of the opinion; Celsus goes on to say '. . . but only during remissions and before food. But prolonged rubbing is unsuitable in acute and increasing diseases . . . it should never be applied whilst a fever is increasing.' He recommends anointing for headaches and for pain in a bodily member, but not when the pain is at its peak. No one who reads Celsus' arcane remedies at any length could assert that he thought of oil (let alone olive oil) as a cure-all. Galen's approach in his *On the Natural Faculties* is similar.

The Jews' approach to medicine was also fairly sophisticated: the Babylonian Talmud records all sorts of remedies, of which anointing with oil plays a minor role. Oil is often cited as an aid to good hygiene, but healing is said to result from proper diet, hygiene, and folk remedies, e.g.; 'Six things cure an invalid from his sickness, and their remedy is an efficacious remedy: cabbage, beet, a decoction [i.e., being boiled down] of dried poley, the maw, the womb, and the large lobe of the liver. Some add: also small fish (*b. Ber. 57b*).'[13] *b. 'Abod. Zar.* 28b–29a recommends vinegar rinses and potions, a good diet, herbs and leaves. To be sure, *Test. Adam* 1:7 states that at the seventh hour of the night 'the waters [from above the heavens] (can be) taken up and the priest of God mixes them with consecrated oil and anoints those who are afflicted and they rest.' But this reference ascribes the rest to the celestial waters rather than to the oil, and the whole section is less than literal at any rate.

Therefore, both Hellenistic and Jewish sources indicate that a first-century author could easily have said 'use the best available medicine, then let the elders pray' if that is what he meant. With that in mind, is it feasible to claim that oil was the best medicine available and thus provide an analogy to modern medicine? Would it not be equivalent to a modern pastor telling the sick to take two aspirin and pray about it?

Second, it is the prayer that saves the sick, not the oil; note the emphatic position of *hē euchē tēs pisteōs*, 'the prayer of faith.' In the plan for healing in James 5, oil or medicine simply play no efficacious role. James is certain that prayer saves the sick. Of course, he does not rule out medicine either.[14]

Third, some of the illnesses in question are caused by a spiritual problem—by the Lord's chastisement for unconfessed sins. Anointing does no good for disciplinary illness if confession and repentance are lacking.

Fourth, the 'best medicine' view cannot explain the parallel passage in Mark 6:13—'And (the apostles) were casting out many demons and were anointing with oil (*ēleiphon elaiō*) many sick people and healing them.' Since these apostolic healings were miraculous, it must be asked why the apostles would use the best medicine if they were healing through the direct power of God? Anointing in Mark 6:13 is hardly as a perpetual sacrament (since it is the only such reference in the gospels to anointing), nor is it medicine. While we have said that the healing in James 5 was not charismatic, the role of the oil is similar: James underscores the fact that it is the prayer which effects the healing, not the oil.

Fifth, the anointing is to be accompanied by the invocation of the name of the Lord, implying that the oil does no good without the Lord's intervention. Jay Adams, however, claims that 'what James advocated was the use of consecrated, dedicated medicine. . . . But when medicine is used, it must be used in conjunction with prayer. That is why James said that the prayer of faith makes the sick well.'[15] But why then, we must ask, does modern medicine cure those who do not pray?

Sixth, a whole-body anointing offends our sense of propriety if male elders performed it themselves (the participle would certainly imply that they do).

Here is where a problem of hermeneutical presupposition must be raised. Might we not be assuming that James advocates the 'best medicine' along with a general prayer precisely because that is what twentieth-century Christians do? The evidence against that position is all but insurmountable, and it behooves us not to assert its truth against the clear data.

2. Oil Denotes the Sacrament of Extreme Unction

The Catholic Church formally made Extreme Unction (the so-called 'Last Rites,' but known since Vatican II as the Anointing of the Sick) a sacrament in A.D. 852, and reaffirmed it at Trent (Session XIV, 1); it also drew the sacrament of Auricular Confession from James 5:16. This sacramental anointing accompanies a final confession of sins before death. God will forgive these last sins, he will be 'saved' and 'raised up' (i.e., resurrected).

This sacerdotalist view directly contradicts James' expectation of healing, not of a better state of preparedness for the after-life.[16] The illness is not necessarily life-threatening,[17] and a soteriological understanding of 'save' and 'raise up' damages James' discussion of physical healing through 16 (note his use of *iaomai*, 'heal').[18]

Sophie Laws suggests that those who rule out a medicinal meaning for oil are making too sharp a distinction between medicine and sacrament in the first-century mind.[19] While the point is well-taken, the Talmud certainly knows of the distinction, although it is not as sharply defined as it is in our own century.

It is worth noting that Irenaeus (*Haer.* I, 21, 3) knew of heretics who anoint their initiates with appropriate abracadabras and those who err by substituting anointing with oil and water in place of baptism.

3. Oil Was Used as a Psychological Reinforcement

In this interpretation the oil is 'a supplementary aid for awakening faith' in a suggestible mind, comparable to Isaiah's fig poultice (2 Kings 20:7) or Paul's handkerchief (Acts 19:12).[20] This viewpoint is fraught with problems as well. First, 2 Kings is vague on the point of whether or not Isaiah used a placebo, and Paul's use of cloths was as proof that the healing came from Paul's God. Second, neither Isaiah nor Paul recommended their tokens as a universal practice in the way that James does with oil. Finally, it is the elders who must pray in faith in this passage (14), not the patient.

4. Oil Was Used as a Symbol of Divine Favor

The interpretation which is here recommended is that anointing was neither medicine nor Extreme Unction, but rather a sign of God's healing presence. Anointing as the pouring or smearing of oil on the head was an ancient ritual in Israel. Prophets (Isa. 60:1), priests (Exod. 29:7), and kings (1 Sam. 10:1) were anointed when they were set apart unto God. Oil was a general symbol of God's special presence, election, and good favor.

The standard argument against our view goes that if James had been speaking of a religious-symbolic use of oil he would have used *chriō* ('anoint sacramentally') rather than *aleiphō* ('anoint').[21] It must be said first of all that such a rigid distinction comes from an idealism about language which was popular before the advent of modern linguistics. But even then, it is noteworthy that a master of the old school such as Richard C. Trench, does not rule out the possibility that *aleiphō* might refer to religious-symbolic anointing: *'Aleiphein* is used indiscriminately of all actual anointings, whether with oil or ointment; while *chriein* . . . is absolutely restricted to the anointing of the Son.'[22] Trench points out that in the LXX *aleiphein* is used of 'religious and symbolical anointings' twice (of priests in Exod. 40:13 and Num. 3:3; we should add Gen. 31:13), examples which disprove the 'secular' meaning of *aleiphō*. We might say that *chriō* is usually restricted to religious anointing, while *aleiphō* can refer to any anointing.

The discussion of whether *aleiphō* can denote a religious symbol becomes academic in that the word was used in Mark 6:13 to refer to miraculous healing accompanied by anointing. In James 5 the prayer of faith takes the place of an apostolic miracle and once again oil is deprived of any inherent healing properties.

An advantage to the view of oil as religious symbol is that we need not imagine the Twelve or the presbyters using oil as a body lotion. Even apart from the issue of propriety, it is impractical to picture the Twelve anointing multitudes in the open air and in the villages. They must have used the other method of anointing, which was carried on in the Early Church: that of pouring or rubbing the oil onto the head.

James confidently predicts the results of these actions:

The prayer offered in faith will rescue (*sōsei*) the sick;
The Lord will raise him up (from sickness);
If he has committed any sins, the Lord will forgive them.

There is clearly a spiritual side to the healing, that the Lord (not the medicine!) will forgive 'if he is in the state of having committed sins' (perfect periphrastic participle). In some cases, forgiveness and healing must go together. We gather that the elders will inquire about unrepentance before they pray (cf. John 5:14, 9:3; 1 Cor. 11:28–30). James knows that not all illness is caused directly by sin, but the possibility is real (notice the Future More Probable condition).[23]

James does not say whether or not the healing is instantaneous; he does say that it is forthcoming unless, presumably, there is some extenuating cause for the affliction. He does refer to the 'prayer of faith' in 15, which he commends in 1:6, 4:2–3, 5:16b–18. He contrasts this faith with double-mindedness both in 1:8 and 4:8, with 'doubt' in 1:6, and with praying with pleasure seeking in 4:3; James does not allow the possibility that a desire for health is a poor motive for prayer.[24] The context of James negates the opinion of Rendel Short,[25] viz., faith in James 5:15 and in 1 Corinthians 12:9 are the same thing, a kind of temporary supernatural endowment which is God's to give and not available when healing goes against God's will. Short labels any other prayer for healing 'false optimism'; he thus contradicts James' teaching about faith in James 1. The prayer of faith in 5:15 is surely a prayer in which the elders pray for healing and *believe that healing will result.*

James concludes this section in 16a with a general exhortation: 'Therefore, confess your sins to one another, and pray for one another, so that you may be healed.' James is moving to the daily life of the congregation (he switches from aorist jussives to present imperatives): if all Christians were to be admitting their sins to each other and praying for each other, the ultimate remedy of summoning the elders might be averted.[26]

In summary, we may glean from James this course of action:

1. The sick Christian should summon his or her own elders;

2. The elders should ask about past sins and urge repentance;

3. The elders should anoint (rub oil on the head) in the name of the Lord Jesus Christ;

4. The elders should pray for healing, believing that healing will be forthcoming.

Anointing with oil and praying for healing was practised for some time in Church history. In A.D. 416 Innocent I refers to James, and says that oil blessed by the bishop can be used by laypeople without a priest present.

In contrast to James 5:15 and the unequivocal promise of healing, the biblical record implies that God does not always heal: Trophimus is probably best known to us for having been 'left sick at Miletus' (2 Tim. 4:20). At the very least, all Christians before the Parousia will succumb to final illness and death. Christians are guaranteed final healing in the resurrection, and are also assured of God's concern to heal in this age.

In his discussion of James 5:15, Francis MacNutt helpfully lists no fewer than 'Eleven Reasons Why People Are Not Healed.'[27] James has already taken into account the possibility of God's discipline. Paul's experience in 2 Corinthians 12:7–9 points to sickness as a means of learning dependence upon God, if the 'thorn' is a physical ailment.[28]

According to James, the primary reason Christians are not healed is a lack of faith in prayer (MacNutt lists it first). A safe, generalized prayer for God to bless the sick runs directly counter to the prayer of faith. Unlike modern Christians, James does not immediately mitigate the possibility of healing in order to spare the feelings of the very sick or the unhealed. Faith always entails risk, or it is not faith. The unspoken assumption is that if God does not heal, it will be out of the ordinary.

Evangelicals should take heart from James 5 and not be pulled away from it because of appearances.[29] After all, anointing and praying are not the same as going to a faith healer, nor are we seeking healing along the lines of the 'natural laws' of non-Christian mystical healers. If anything, James 5 leads us away from charismatic healings, and there is no New Testament passage which connects anointing with miraculous healing after the Resurrection. Modern 'faith healers,' self-healers, and mystical healers do not urge their adherents to call for their own elders for anointing and prayer. Nor will we be sacerdotalists through using oil as a symbol. Nor will we be using a rite meant only for early Jewish Christians—such anointing is a part of the New Covenant, not of the Old.

My initial experiences with anointing came through serving as a Church elder at Stony Lane Baptist Church in Rhode Island. We taught that the sick Christian should initiate the process by asking for prayer, and also that the elders were responsible for reminding the congregation of that option. We did not rule out nor did we demand instantaneous healing. We discouraged people from throwing out their medicine or stopping their visits to the doctor. If healing did not come within a reasonable period of time, we did not ignore the physical symptoms and rationalize that it did come, yet invisibly. Healing in James is healing which can be seen, and not merely through the eye of faith; in such cases continued prayer is necessary.

Notes

[1] Cf. esp. Barron, *The Health and Wealth Gospel* (Downers Grove, Ill., 1987), for an excellent critique of the latter idea.

[2] See J. Cantinat, *Les Epîtres de Saint Jacques et de Saint Jude*, SB (Paris, 1973) 247. Cf. the attempt to read this in terms of spiritual weakness by Carl Armerding, ' "Is Any Among You Afflicted?" A study of James 5:13–20,' *BSac* 95, 1938, 195–201.

[3] Contra Cantinat, 248–49.

[4] Cf. Guthrie, *New Testament Introduction* (3rd. rev. ed.; Downers Grove, Ill., 1970) 761–64.

[5] Although note K. Seybold and U. B. Müller, *Krankheit und Heilung* (Stuttgart, 1978) 161, who assign a late date to James and conclude that the gifts of healings and miracles in 1 Corinthians 12:28 had become institutionalized in the presbyters. Calvin assumes that the charismatic gift is in view here; so do A. B. Simpson in *The Gospel of Healing* (London, 1915) and A. J. Gordon in *The Ministry of Healing* (2nd. ed.; Harrisburg, 1961), although they argue that the gift of healing is still available to the Church today.

[6] Note the frequent references to visiting the sick in the Babylonian Talmud (ed. I. Epstein): *b. B. Mes.* 30b; *b. Sabb.* 127a—'There are six things, the fruit of which man eats in this world, while the principal remains for him in the world to come, viz.: hospitality to wayfarers, visiting the sick,' etc.; in *b. Ned* 39b–40a, R. Akiba compares neglect of visiting the sick to the shedding of blood, since the visitor's prayers might have healed a dying man; there are guidelines for whether one should stand or sit with the sick (*b. Ned.* 39a) or when not to visit the sick (if the ailment is embarrassing—such as bowel trouble—or if it would be exacerbated by talking, *b. Ned.* 41a); note the concern about healing on the Sabbath, which seems to have been restricted to life-threatening ailments such as open wounds (*b. 'Abod. Zar.* 27b–28b); there are warnings against 'crying out' in prayer for the sick on the Sabbath, lest the rabbi be guilty of the work of healing (*b. Šabb.* 127a); note too that Polycarp thinks that good presbyters should 'care for all who are sick' (Pol. *Phil.* 6:1).

[7] Cf. Sophie Laws, *Epistle of James* (San Francisco, 1980) 227–29; C. L. Mitton, *Epistle of James* (London, 1966) 199; Peter Davids, *Epistle of James* (Grand Rapids, 1982) 193–94.

[8] Davids, 194.

[9] Schlier, *'aleiphō,'* *TDNT* I: 231.

[10] Cf. the *Midrash Rabba on Ecclesiastes*, trans. by A. Cohen (London, 1939). Dibelius and Greeven, *James* (Philadelphia, 1976) 252, assert without evidence that 'the whole procedure [in James 5] is an exorcism.' John Wilkinson, *Health and Healing* (Edinburgh, 1980) 148, shows that physical, not demonic, affliction is intended by *'astheneō.'*

[11] It seems clear that many modern writers plunder Ropes' (304–7) and Mayor's (170–73) commentaries on James for their selective references to anointing. Thus counseling authority Jay Adams can boldly claim that 'in fact, in biblical terms oil was used as the universal medicine . . . James did not write about ceremonial anointing at all.' Cf. Adams, *Competent to Counsel* (Grand Rapids, 1970) 107.

[12] So argue Cantinat, 249; Lenski, 664; Adams, 108; cf. esp. Wilkinson, 153ff.–he asserts that every method of modern healing is represented by some member of the Church today and that modern medical technology is thus the Church's equivalent for anointing.

[13] All Talmudic references are to *The Babylonian Talmud*, ed. by I. Epstein, 18 vol., London, 1961; they may be accessed by individual tractate.

[14] *Sōzō*, 'save,' is often used with non-soteriological meaning; note its use for physical healing in Matthew 9:21.

[15] Cf. Adams, 108.

[16] See Franz Mussner, *Der Jakobusbrief*, HTKNT: 13 (Freiburg, 1964) 220 and Davids, 193, who take a sacramental view of anointing on the basis of the 'eschatological oils' of Isaiah 61:3, *Adam and Eve* 36, and *Apoc. Mos.* 9:3. But the 'oil of gladness' in Isaiah 61:3 is clearly metaphorical; the 'oil of mercy' in *Adam and Eve* 36 (= *Apoc. Mos.* 9) is not stated to be eschatological, and it is interpreted in a Christian interpolation at *Adam and Eve* 42 to be a metaphor of salvation in Christ. Wilkinson, 150, is more to the point: neither official authority nor charisma is present; the elders pray as representatives of the congregation, which according to James 5:16 has the authority to pray for healing.

[17] Cf. Cantinat, 247.

[18] See Calvin and Mayor for comments on Extreme Unction.

[19] See Laws, 227.

[20] Mitton, 198-9.

[21] See Adams, 107.

[22] Trench, *Synonyms of the New Testament* (9th. ed.; London, 1988) 137. *Chriein* is so restricted in New Testament Greek, but the papyri show that *chriō* and *chrisis* were used of rubbing oil on animals (Moulton and Milligan, *Vocabulary of the NT*, 21, 693).

[23] See Wilkinson, 149, for a balanced picture of sin and sickness.

[24] Cf. Mussner, 224.

[25] Cf. R. Short, *The Bible and Modern Medicine* (London, 1953) 125.

[26] See Adams, 105–27.

[27] Fr. Francis MacNutt, *Healing* (Notre Dame, 1974) 248–61. It is unfortunate that Fr. MacNutt is heavily influenced by Agnes Sanford and the 'inner healing' movement, but he still provides much that is useful.

[28] But note that Paul prayed three times fully expecting God to remove the thorn (12:8), that it was by revelation that God showed him its purpose (12:9), and that Paul seems to believe that this was unusual and needed explanation.

[29] Cf. the unwarranted caution shown by the Reformed scholar A. W. Pink, *Divine Healing: Is It Scriptural?* (Swengel, Pa., 1952) 24–25; he reasons that it is permissible to anoint with oil, but that he would not want to 'dogmatize' about it. He also concludes that modern elders are not spiritual enough to carry out such faithful prayer. For a better-balanced Reformed viewpoint, note William Henry Anderson, Jr., *Christianity Today* 5, Jan. 30, 1961, 8–9.

THE MEANING OF "NATURE" IN ROMANS 1
AND ITS IMPLICATIONS FOR BIBLICAL PROSCRIPTIONS
OF HOMOSEXUAL BEHAVIOR

JAMES B. DEYOUNG
Professor of New Testament Language and Literature
Western Conservative Baptist Seminary, Portland

Article from *Journal of the Evangelical Theological Society*

In recent years various attempts have been made to give approval to homosexual nature or behavior on the basis of the Bible. Various passages of Scripture, including Romans 1, have been reinterpreted so that the traditional interpretation has been found incorrect or at least irrelevant for the modern age.

Part of this new approach to Romans 1 focuses on new ways of understanding the meaning of "nature" (*physis*) in verses 26–27. For some it is limited to "what is natural to me."[1] It is argued that Paul does not refer to those whose own nature or primary orientation is homosexual. Hence Paul condemns heterosexuals acting as homosexuals (perverts) in a context of idolatry and lust; he does not condemn true homosexuals, homosexuals born such (inverts), for practicing homosexuality. Boswell adds that it has nothing to do with natural law since this concept did not exist until many centuries after Paul.

Others believe that the foregoing distinction made between inversion and perversion regarding "nature" is legitimate for modern times but that Paul was unaware of it in his day. The Bible "knows nothing of inversion as an inherited trait, or inherent condition due to psychological or glandular causes, and consequently regards all homosexual practice as evidence of perversion."[2] Therefore Paul could hardly have made distinctions regarding perversion and inversion when these were unintelligible to him. Hence Paul is simply irrelevant or incomplete on the question of homosexuality.

Still another view holds that "nature" has nothing to do with Jewish views of the creation or with theories of natural law. It is a concept ultimately derived from Greek, not Jewish, sources.[3] The only model of homosexuality that Paul condemns is the current Greek one—namely, pederasty.[4] Hence Romans 1 has little or no relevance to the modern model of mutual adult-adult homosexuality.[5] There is no way of knowing whether Paul would oppose "the caring adult relationship of mutuality."[6]

The purpose of this article is to make a grammatical, historical, and contextual study of "nature." Its findings will then be related to the views expressed above to evaluate their merits.

I. The Linguistic Setting of *Physis*

It is necessary to consider first the possible meanings that *physis* may have in Romans 1:26–27.

1. *Greek usage.* The word *physis* is used profusely in secular Greek. Any citation of uses must necessarily be selective, but I believe that they are representative. The word has these meanings:[7] (1) origin, including birth and growth;[8] (2) the natural form[9] or constitution of a person, animal, or thing, including nature or character of a person; (3) the regular order of nature; (4) philosophically, nature as an originating power (parallel to *theos* among the stoics[10]), Nature personified, elementary substance (fire, water, air, earth[11]), the concrete idea of the creation; (5) creature or mankind; (6) kind, sort, species; (7) sex;[12] and (8) approximately equal to law (*nomos*).

In all these uses there is no suggestion that it has the meaning "what is natural to me" or "orientation." The closest approximation is category (2) above: "character, natural disposition, propensity."[13] Yet this usage is never associated with homosexuality. It points to what results from origin or growth and includes the instinct of animals.

In the third category occur examples of *kata physin* ("according to nature") and *para physin* ("contrary to nature"; cf. Rom. 1:26–27). Here is placed the well-known statement by Aristotle (*Politica* 1253): "Man is a political animal by nature" (*physei*).[14]

Gunther Harder basically follows the outline of LSJ in discussing the classical usage of *physis*.[15] He points out that early in Greek thought law and nature were distinguished as two different entities that determined one's life. Finally nature was "distinguished from the field of morals and ethics."[16]

Helmut Koester seeks to show how the concept of *physis* developed in two directions—one emphasizing origin, the other emphasizing being or substance.[17] Although he follows the general outline of the sources above, he makes important clarifications and additions. For example, one's tendency, quality, or character is called *physis* because this nature is a given and "not dependent on conscious direction or education."[18] Also he notes that Aristotle and Plato developed the two aspects of the idea of nature along the lines of either the true nature of things or the like origin of all being (universal nature).[19] It is this universal nature that was variously equated with deity, and the adjective *physikos* has the sense of "natural law."

In regard to the category of nature and ethics the Greeks, particularly the sophists, often viewed law and nature in antithesis.[20] Natural law was considered as consisting of two opposing spheres (nature and law) to which man is subject. "According to nature" means "normal," while "against nature" means "abnormal." These phrases in particular are used in ethical judgments, especially regarding sexual abnormality. Plato condemns pederasty and marriage between men as *para physin*.[21]

Koester's last category concerns nature as a cosmic and vital principle among the stoics. They sought to bridge the antithesis that had been growing in Greek thought. *Physis* becomes a universal divine principle. Man has received the *logos*, his own being, by nature. The goal of life is to attain in living to what corresponds to man's nature or essence. Common sense or reason enables man to know what is *kata physin* and what is *para physin*.[22]

Koester clearly shows the shortcoming of Greek thinking, for man is himself nature and in bondage. Man had to turn either inward (so stoicism) or outward away from the natural world (so gnosticism). Only in the Jewish and Christian belief in nature as the creation of God "did the concept of natural law become significant, since man could relate himself to the Creator and Lawgiver as the ultimate critical court."[23]

In the usage of the secular papyri at the time of the New Testament there occur only two senses of the word. These are (1) birth or physical origin and (2) innate properties or powers—what is derived from origin. *Physikos* means "natural, inward."[24]

2. *Jewish and Christian usage*. It is very significant that there is no Hebrew equivalent in the Old Testament for *physis*. The Jews did not have the Greek conception of nature due to two facts:[25] The Jews referred all existing things to creation or to the Creator God, and the Old Testament is primarily concerned with history, not philosophy and speculation.

In the noncanonical intertestamental literature the term occurs only in the LXX of the Wisdom of Solomon and in pseudepigraphical 3 and 4 Maccabees and the Testaments of the Twelve Patriarchs. The uses generally correspond to those found in classical Greek.[26] The adjective *physikos* does not occur at all in the LXX.

The term is used in the sense of endowment, character, and quality (4 Macc. 13:27; 16:3; Wis. 19:20). In Wisdom 13:1 men are described as "foolish by nature" (*mataioi physei*); they had no perception of God from his works of creation (13:2–5). Instead they worshiped God's works as their gods.[27]

Physis also occurs in the sense of human nature to which the law has been adapted ("we know that the Creator of the world, in giving us the law, conforms it to our nature," 4 Macc. 5:25). This (*kata physin*) is classical usage.[28]

Finally *physis*, it is claimed, is used of the regular order of nature, the creation. Here Harder apparently places two similar passages (4 Macc. 15:13, 25) where "nature" is linked with "parental love, filial affection, nurture, maternal affections" and with "parenthood, maternal love, and the torment of children." Yet it seems that these passages belong to the above category where "love for children" occurs (4 Macc. 16:3).[29]

Also in the last category belong references to "every mortal creature" (3

Macc. 3:29), "natures of animals" (Wis. 7:20), and "kinds" of human passions (4 Macc. 1:20). Again, however, this last reference may more appropriately be placed in the earlier category. Two references personify *physis* (4 Macc. 5:8–9) as the giver of good gifts.[30]

Another use from pseudepigraphical literature (*T. Naph.* 3:4–5) is especially important for the meaning of Romans 1:26–27, yet it is omitted by Harder. After affirming that God has "made all things good in their order" (2:7), the author notes that Gentiles "have forsaken the Lord and changed their order" (3:3). Then he writes (3:4–5):

> But ye shall not be so, my children, recognizing in the firmament, in the earth, and in the sea, and in all created things, the Lord who made all things, that ye become not as Sodom, which changed the order of nature. In like manner the Watchers also changed the order of their nature, whom the Lord cursed at the flood, on whose account he made the earth without inhabitants and fruitless.

Here the two uses of "the order of nature" (*taxis physis*) fit the first two categories above (character and human nature). The context includes references to creation made by God and asserts that the Lord is recognized there (cf. Rom. 1:18–23).

Physis occurs in other places in the Testaments in the sense of the "physical nature" of man (*T. Reub.* 3:1, 3) or "natural power" (*T. Dan.* 3:4–5). Anger "blinds one's eyes literally" (2:4).[31]

In summary, the literature of the apocrypha and pseudepigrapha supports concepts of *physis* quite similar to those of classical Greek. Two passages (Wis. 13:1 with homosexuality and Sodom in its contexts, and *T. Naph.* 3:4–5) have concepts very similar to those in Romans 1:19–27: "men being foolish by nature," and the sin of Sodom described as changing "the order of nature." Yet a clear identification of the physical creation as "nature" is lacking, in line with the Old Testament and contrary to Greek thinking. Harder seems inappropriately to suggest such usage by employing the final category above, and Koester fails to note this absence.

The writings of Philo and Josephus also provide additional insight into Jewish thinking about *physis*. Philo in particular makes a significant contribution in his extensive use of the word. Koester writes:

> As a central concept in his philosophy and his exposition of the Law, *physis* in Philo unites for the first time in Greek literature the elements in Old Testament and Greek thinking which were to be of decisive significance for the thought of the West: God and *natura creatrix*, creation and the natural world, natural law and divine demand.[32]

Philo adopts virtually all of the earlier Greek usages of *physis*, even using it of the creation.[33] Philo's special contribution is to combine the Greek (stoic) concept of nature with the Jewish (Old Testament) understanding of

God and the law. The *nomos physeōs* is always the Torah to which even God seems subject. The law follows nature, and nature ratifies law.

The phrases "contrary to nature" and "according to nature" occur frequently. For Philo sexual aberrations are a violation of natural law (*On Abraham* 135–36).[34] Philo also writes of the seven natural capacities of man as *kata physin chresis* (cf. *Mut. Nom.* 11–12): sexual potency, speech, and the five senses.

Josephus uses *physis* very frequently and reflects all of the common usage of the first century A.D. Like Philo he speaks of the "law of nature" and divine law.[35] Marital intercourse and childbirth correspond to the order of nature (*kata physin*), but sexual deviation is *para physin*.[36] In *Ant.* 1.200–1 he speaks of the "violence and outrage" of the Sodomites, and in *Ag. Ap.* 2.199 homosexuality deserves the death penalty. "No sexual connections" are lawful except the natural union of man and wife.

As in the New Testament *physis* occurs rarely (three times), and *physikos* does not occur at all in the apostolic fathers.[37] No doubt this is for the same reason as for the New Testament. The phrase "law of nature" is also very rare.

In certain apocryphal Acts and in the apologists frequency increases. The succeeding Church fathers use the term profusely.[38] Although all usages occur, those used for the creation or world are limited to a dozen or so.

II. The Historical Setting of *Physis*

Here it is necessary to consider the use of *physis* in its historical setting, especially as it pertains to homosexuality. We must also examine whether the term is limited to pederasty and whether that is virtually the only form known and practiced in Paul's day.

1. *Non-biblical sources.* Homosexuality seems to have existed more widely among the ancient Greeks than among any other people. The predominant form was pederasty.[39]

Plato, in the last work written before his death, implicitly and explicitly witnesses to the pervasiveness of homosexuality and advocates legislation to regulate it (*Laws* 636a–c; 835c; 836a–e; 838b–839b; 840de; 841de). There were laws against homosexuality in fifth-to-fourth-century Greece. In certain instances the death penalty was prescribed.[40] Plato treated homosexual love philosophically, and this seems to point to the existence of homosexual orientation.[41] Examples of lesbianism[42] as well as male adult-adult homosexuality are found.[43] The Greeks recognized the difference between what is natural and unnatural (cf. Plato *Laws* 636a–c; 836a–c; 838; 841de).[44] Greek religion gave significant support to homosexuality.[45]

What was the situation in Rome or Corinth at the time of Paul? The lexical research above shows that Philo and Josephus condemned homosexuality in general, not only pederasty, in the strongest of terms.[46]

In addition moral philosophers were questioning the merits of homosexuality in Paul's day.[47] Seneca condemns homosexual exploitation (*Moral Epistles* 47.7–8) that forces an adult slave to dress, be beardless, and behave as a woman. Plutarch speaks of homosexuality as "contrary to nature" (*Dialogue on Love* 751c–e; 752b–3). Finally Dio Chrysostom exposes the exploitative and lustful nature of homosexuality (*Discourse* 7.133, 135, 151–52; 21.6–10; 77/78.36).

Other evidence of the prevalence and form of homosexuality during Paul's day comes from Roman legislation. As early as 226 B.C. the *Lex Scantinia* penalized homosexual practices.[48] Cicero refers to subsequent application of it in 50 B.C., and other references are made to it by Suetonius (applied under Domitian), Juvenal and others (including Tertullian). The *Lex Julia de adulteriis coercendis* (about 17 B.C.), initially concerned with sexual offenses against a virgin or widow (*stuprum*), came to be applied to sexual acts committed with boys (third century) and then to homosexual acts between adults (fourth century). Justinian's *Codex* (sixth century) applied *Lex Julia* to homosexuality further[49] and set the legal tradition in Western civilization.

Another evidence of homosexuality comes from the poets, satirists, and historians of the day. Juvenal and Martial wrote of formal marriage unions of homosexuals. Historians and others viewed the second century B.C. as the turning point in Roman history. With military conquests achieved, Rome underwent "a moral crisis from which she never recovered."[50] It came about from the direct influx into Rome of "Asiatic luxury and Greek manners" that included homosexuality and other debauchery.[51]

2. *Sacred sources.* Throughout Scripture, adult homosexuality is assumed. This is apparent in the record of Sodom (Gen. 19; "men" of the city desired "men"), Gibeah (Judg. 19), and other condemnations of sodomy (Deut. 23:17–18; Lev. 18:22; 20:13). This is the case with the intertestamental literature also. Only in *T. Levi* 17:11 is pederasty specifically cited.

Throughout Scripture the condemnation is universal and absolute. It is never contemplated that one specific form of homosexuality is condemned while others are tolerated or accepted, whether this be homosexual rape (claimed for Gen. 19; Judg. 19), male prostitution (claimed for Deut. 23; 2 Kings 23:7; 1 Kings 14:24; 15:12; 22:46; Lev. 18; 20; 1 Cor. 6:9–11; 1 Tim. 1:8–10), pederasty (claimed for the New Testament, esp. Rom. 1:26–27), or perversion—that is, abandoning one's "natural" orientation for another (claimed for Rom. 1). In Paul the passive (*malakoi*) and active (*arsenokoitai*) partners are outside the kingdom of God (1 Cor. 6:9).

III. The New Testament Contextual Setting of *Physis*

In the New Testament the noun *physis* occurs fourteen times (eleven in Paul), the adjective three times (Rom. 1:26–27; 2 Pet. 2:12), the adverb once (Jude 10).

The non-Pauline uses are very few (five). The noun has the common Greek sense of "kind of beast" and "human nature" (James 3:7 twice) and "divine nature" (2 Pet. 1:4). In two places both the adverb (Jude 10) and the adjective (2 Pet. 2:12) refer to natural, irrational understanding comparable to that of beasts.

The setting of the word outside Romans offers few (four) instances (all involve the noun). It refers to the general order of nature—that is, what is fitting in regard to hairstyles (1 Cor. 11:14; there is no idea here of a divine Creator or creation). In Galatians 2:15 *physei Ioudaioi* refers to those being Jews in essence, in their true nature, by descent, just as Romans 2:27 refers to the "uncircumcision by nature," Gentiles essentially or in their true nature. In Galatians 4:8 the term means that those "not gods by nature" were not essentially deity; they had no divine quality or essence. In Ephesians 2:3 the word refers to the fallen nature of Jews (vv. 1–3). This usage has some bearing on the meaning in Romans 2, it seems.

In Romans outside of chapter 1 the noun refers to the Hellenistic-Jewish idea (as in Philo) of natural law (2:14), with the latter identifiable with the Mosaic law of the Old Testament.[52] The Gentiles possess a natural law that they obey naturally.

In Romans 2:27 Gentiles "by nature" refers to what Gentiles are essentially (see above on Gal. 2:15). Finally *physis* occurs in Romans 11:21, 24 in reference to the olive tree grown naturally (*kata physin*), with no artificial intervention (i.e., Israel). The Gentiles are a wild olive tree by nature (*kata physin*) and were grafted contrary to nature (*para physin*) into a cultivated olive tree (Israel).

With regard to Romans 1:26–27 the following considerations are necessary: the meaning of the words *physis* and *physikos*, the nature of the homosexuality involved, and the significance of the passage for the contemporary expression of homosexuality.

In light of the foregoing study of the Greek terms, for both the noun (which occurs in an adverbial prepositional phrase, "changed the natural use into the [use] contrary to nature") and the adjective (used twice) the meaning is the same. Koester remarks: "The stress on sexual faults corresponds to the so-called Noahic commandments of rabbinic Judaism but in both tenor and formulation it is in every way Greek in Paul, the idea being that of a violation of the natural order."[53]

Harder basically concurs. By way of Hellenistic Judaism this Greek (especially stoic) concept found a limited place in Christian thought. Paul's use points in two opposing directions: "It emphasizes the gap between Jews and non-Jews," and "it indicates what they have in common."[54]

If these observations are correct, then the view of those who see *physis* as meaning "what is natural to me" and thus try to justify inversion or orientation is wrong. Never does the term have such a meaning in Greek literature or biblical contexts.[55] If Plato could earlier write about Platonic homosexuality and orientation, his last work (*Laws*) gives no hint of this meaning. Even if it did, his *Laws* make it clear that homosexuality is something to be legislated as harmful to society and unnatural.

It is significant, however, that Paul avoids Greek formulations in the preceding verses. In 18–25 Paul avoids total use of *physis* to refer to the works of creation (as also in Acts 17), as is the pattern in the apocrypha and pseudepigrapha and the Old Testament (the latter never uses the term). The rest of the New Testament follows this pattern also.[56]

Now since Philo and Josephus use the term profusely in accord with Greek usage, it is clear that Paul is more a Hebraist or Biblicist than a Hellenist, even in Romans 1:26–27. Paul follows linguistically and theologically the Old Testament (Lev. 18:22; 20:13)[57] and the Jewish intertestamental literature. This is not accidental but "at least in part it is also a deliberate theological decision which rests on the fact that there is no place for 'natural theology' in the thinking of the New Testament."[58] Paul may also be following the lead of *T. Naph.* 3:4–5; *T. Asher* 7:1; *T. Benj.* 9:1; *T. Levi* 14:6; or *2 Enoch* 10:4–5; 34:1–3; or Wisdom of Solomon.

This means that *physis* refers to what is the constitution of man, his being, as derived from the Creator (Gen. 1–2). Note how the Creator and creation immediately precede in the context (Rom. 1:19–23). Plato and the Greeks, having no transcendent Creator and deifying nature itself, saw "natural" differently. But their terminology parallels Jewish-Christian thinking.

In regard to the nature of homosexuality, for Scroggs to claim that Paul "must have had, *could only have had*, pederasty in mind"[59] is untenable.

First, this assumes "that Greco-Roman culture decisively influenced New Testament statements about homosexuality" and that "Paul is dependent for his judgment that it is against nature ultimately on Greek, not Jewish sources . . . not on some doctrine of creation."[60] This overlooks the context and Paul's dependency on Old Testament concepts, as shown above.

Second, Paul's words themselves contradict this view and support a much more general idea of homosexuality, which would include adult-adult mutuality. Several terms bear this out.

Paul writes literally "males with males committing indecent acts"; he does not say "men with boys" (as Plato is capable of saying: *Laws* 836a–c). This phrase appears to be unique with Paul.

He compares ("likewise") lesbianism with male perversion. As lesbianism was usually between adults in mutuality, so the force of the comparative argues for male adult-adult mutuality.

The phrase "natural use" or "function" argues for activity or "relations" (NIV) of adults, not adult-child behavior, and not an orientation alone nor a Platonic relationship.

"Degrading passions" (v. 26) and "burned in their desire" argue that this is not Platonic nor morally neutral, whether referring to propensity or orientation or activity.

The terms "toward one another," "men with men," "in themselves" and "their error" all argue for adult reciprocal mutuality and mutual culpability, which would not characterize pederasty. As the error is mutual, so is the recompense.

The idea of "exchanged . . . abandoned the natural function" suggests that adult sexual relations are intended.

If the "model" of homosexuality makes a difference regarding acceptability or culpability, why is Scripture silent on the matter? Why is there no explicit debate over the matter in Philo or Josephus or among the Greeks? Even if one would grant that Philo and Josephus use the biblical accounts of adult homosexuality (Gen. 19) to condemn contemporary pederasty, does this not argue that they would view both as abhorrent? If the model here is pederasty, then Paul has no comment on bisexuality or male prostitution (both were common).

Scroggs's position suggests that the model of adult mutuality was unknown or little known in ancient times. Yet if it exists now, it certainly existed then. Man's nature has not changed, nor has the power of the gospel. Scroggs has no evidence that mutuality is more common today than it was then.

In regard to the matter of the relevance of the passage to contemporary society, the net effect of all the revisionist interpreters of Romans 1:26–27 is to make the passage irrelevant. Those who argue that homosexual inversion was unknown by Paul cannot escape the question: Was it then nonexistent? Since proponents must hold inversion to be universal for their view to be valid, it must either be included in Paul's terminology (and be condemned) or one rejects Paul as authoritative for contemporary man.[61] This must follow, for elsewhere he allows for no sexual expression except within a heterosexual, monogamous, permanent marriage (cf. Rom. 7:2–3; 1 Cor. 5–7; 2 Cor. 6; Eph. 5; Col. 3; 1 Thess. 4; 1 Tim. 3, 5; Titus 2; cf. Heb. 13:4).

For Scroggs to make the model of mutuality unknown to Paul, or not addressed by him, flies in the face of the examples Scroggs and others allow and other evidences above. To assert that one cannot know what Paul would have felt about this model is to totally reject his clear teaching elsewhere as to what constitutes acceptable sexual behavior. One could just as legitimately argue for such a model within incest, fornication, or adultery—as long as permanency, mutuality, etc., characterized it. This approach sets the end as adult mutuality and justifies any means to that end.

IV. Conclusion

The only model of sexual expression contemplated in Scripture is that which is patterned after the creation model of Genesus 1–2. This is the pattern that our Lord (Matt. 5; 19) and his disciples taught or commanded.

If it has been at least reasonably demonstrated that Paul opposes all forms of sexual expression between the same sex in Romans 1, then his judgments are, as Scroggs admits, "eternally valid."[62] Revisionist interpretations would do well to come under the authority of Scripture.

Notes

[1] J. Boswell, *Christianity, Social Tolerance and Homosexuality* (Chicago: Chicago University, 1980) 107–17; L. Scanzoni and V. R. Mollenkott, *Is the Homosexual My Neighbor?* (1978) 61–66.

[2] D. S. Bailey, *Homosexuality and the Western Christian Tradition* (London: Longmans, Green, 1955) 38.

[3] R. Scroggs, *The New Testament and Homosexuality* (Philadelphia: Fortress, 1983) 116–17.

[4] Ibid., 116–17, 122.

[5] Ibid., 122, 127–28.

[6] Ibid., 128–29.

[7] LSJ; E. A. Barber, *A Supplement* (Oxford: Oxford University, 1968) 149. Translations are either mine or are those of LCL.

[8] As in "the father by birth" (*kata physin*; Polybius *Histories* 3.9.6).

[9] As in "larger than man in appearance" (*kata physin*; Herodotus 8.38).

[10] So Marcus Aurelius: "All that is in tune with you, O Universe, is in tune with me . . . O Nature . . . All things come from you, subsist in you, go back to you" (4.23). Cf. Romans 11:36.

[11] Plato *Laws* 891c.

[12] Ibid., 770d; 944d; Sophocles *Trachiniae* 1062 ("a woman, being a female and not a male by nature") cf. Sophocles *Oedipus at Colonus* 445.

[13] See Polybius *Histories* 31.25.10 ("Scipio had good natural impulses toward the right").

[14] Aristotle goes on to discuss whether all slavery is against nature (*para physin; Politica* 1254).

[15] G. Harder, "Nature," in *New International Dictionary of New Testament Theology* (ed. C. Brown; Grand Rapids: Zondervan, 1976) 2. 656–58.

[16] Ibid., 658.

[17] H. Koester, *"Physis, physikos, physikōs," TDNT* 9 (1974) 251–66.

[18] Ibid., 253.

[19] Ibid., 256.

[20] Ibid., 261.

[21] Plato *Laws* 636a–b: "The gymnasia and common meals corrupt the pleasures of love which are natural not to man only but also natural to beasts"; 636c: "Pleasure in mating is due to nature (*kata physin*) when male unites with female, but contrary to nature (*para physin*) when male unites with male (*arrenōn*) or female with female (*thēleiōn*)." See also 836a–c; 838; 841d–e.

[22] Koester, *"Physis"* 263–66.

[23] Ibid., 266.

[24] MM 679.

[25] Harder, "Nature" 658.

[26] Ibid.

[27] This is obviously similar to Paul's words in Romans 1:19–23, esp. v. 21: Those who turned from honoring God as revealed in creation "became futile in their speculations" (*emataiōthēsan en tois dialogismois autōn*). Paul does not use *physis* in 1:19–23. In a parallel passage (Eph. 2:3) he describes lost mankind as we who "were by nature children of wrath." Interestingly, Wisdom refers to homosexuality in 14:26 ("confusion, change, of sex"), and the destruction of Sodom in 10:6–9, 19:13–17.

[28] Koester, *"Physis"* 266, reads 4 Maccabees 5:25, "according to (his) nature," as a reference

to God. Yet the placement of *hēmin* tends to support the reading of H. Anderson, which Harder also supports when he translates: "that the Creator of the world, as a Lawgiver, feels for us according to our nature" ("Nature" 658). It is a reference to human, not divine, nature. But by either view "nature" in the sense of the "constitution, essence" of someone is in view. See Anderson, "4 Maccabees," in *The Old Testament Pseudepigrapha* (ed. J. H. Charlesworth; Garden City: Doubleday, 1985) 2. 560.

[29] Harder, like Koester (*"Physis"* 267), puts these passages in the third category as referring to "the regular order of nature" evidently because of the presence of *genesis*, "creation" (translated as "filial affection" and "parenthood"), in both passages. Yet in the former passage (15:13) this represents a variant reading with few MSS supporting it; if *genesis*, it would be rendered "love of parents for offspring." Anderson, "4 Maccabees," prefers the reading *genesi*, dative plural of *genos*, "offspring," and renders it "filial affection" (hence practically identical to *genesis*). Other readings are *gennemasi* (practically the same as *genesi*) and *goneusi*, "love for parents." But the close proximity to 16:3 and the use of the same term in 16:3 (*philoteknias*) as 15:25 argue that these two passages belong to the first category above. The only place where nature is personified as a giver of good gifts is the speech of the pagan Antiochus IV (4 Macc. 5:8–9), following Greek usage.

[30] Most of the translations of these passages derive from Anderson, "4 Maccabees," or (for Wisdom) from E. J. Goodspeed, *The Apocrypha* (Chicago: Chicago University, 1938).

[31] The translation of H. C. Kee, "Testament of the Twelve Patriarchs," in *Pseudepigrapha* (ed. Charlesworth) 1. 808.

[32] Koester, *"Physis"* 267.

[33] Ibid., 267–69; Harder, "Nature" 658–59.

[34] The men of Sodom, Philo says, "threw off from their necks the law of nature and applied themselves to . . . forbidden forms of intercourse. Not only in their mad lust for women did they violate the marriages of their neighbors, but also men mounted males without respect for the sex nature which the active partner shares with the passive. . . . Then as little by little they accustomed those who were by nature men to submit to play the part of women, they saddled them with the formidable curse of a female disease" (*On Abraham* 135–36; see also 137 for *kata physin*).

[35] Harder, "Nature" 659. See Josephus *Ant.* 1.54; 2.292; 3.88; 4.8, 48; *J.W.* 1.544.

[36] See Josephus *Ant.* 1.322; 3.261, 275; *Ag. Ap.* 2.199 ("sodomy" = *pros arrenas arrenōn*); 2.273, 275.

[37] It is used of the sex of the hyena (corresponding to *genos*) in *Barn.* 10:7. In Ignatius it is used of the "true and proper nature" of Christians (Ign. *Eph.* 1:1; Ign. *Trall.* 1:1). The latter reference describes conscience as unstained "not according to use but according to nature" (*ou kata chrēsin alla kata physin*; cf. Rom. 1:26–27).

[38] *LPGL* 1494–1503. About eighteen columns are needed to cover the noun, adjective, and adverb. The church fathers are virtually united in their condemnation of homosexuality. See D. F. Wright, "Homosexuals or Prostitutes?" *VC* 38 (1984) 125–53, who effectively refutes Boswell and others who have raised doubts about this witness of the fathers, especially as based upon the word *arsenokoitai* (1 Cor. 6:9; 1 Tim. 1:10).

[39] According to P. E. Slater, *The Glory of Hera* (Boston: Beacon, 1968) 11, homosexuality was widespread and generally accepted among Greeks even though restricted by law. It rested on narcissism and took the forms of pederasty and male prostitution (34, 56–60, 74). It was intrinsically related to religion; the gods practiced pederasty (61). It probably receded in popularity after the fifth century B.C. (71).

[40] K. J. Dover, *Greek Homosexuality* (Cambridge: Harvard University, 1978) 13–27. Aeschines *Timarchus* 12 refers to three laws regulating pederasty and homosexual prostitution in Athens, even calling for the death penalty and prohibition from holding office. Plato *Symposium* 182a–184c records how pederasty is legally restricted in certain regions. See Scroggs, *Homosexuality* 49–52.

[41] As Dover, *Greek* 12, seems to admit. Note "inclination" in Plato (*Laws* 840d–e). See D. J.

Atkinson, *Homosexuals in the Christian Fellowship* 92–95. Scroggs, *Homosexuality* 52–53, dismisses Platonic love, the philosophical ideal, as a cover-up, yet he admits that inversion and perversion (if a valid distinction today) must have existed in the past as well (28, 32–34). See also Boswell, *Christianity* 81–87.

[42] Dover, *Greek* 171–73. See Plato *Laws* 636c; 839d. Scroggs admits some examples during Paul's time (*Homosexuality* 140–44), as does Boswell, *Christianity* 82–84.

[43] Dover, *Greek* 19–31, 37, 99. See Plato *Laws* 636a–c; 836a–c ("with men and boys as with women"). Even Scroggs (*Homosexuality* 32–34, 130) has difficulty trying to find only pederasty involved. See examples of adult mutuality and permanency in Boswell, *Christianity* 82–87.

[44] Dover, *Greek* 67–68, believes that the active partner is acting naturally and the passive one unnaturally. This is questionable and contradicted by Paul's use of "nature" and "natural" (Rom. 1:26–27).

[45] Even Dover acknowledges the critical role of religion in Greek homosexuality. Greek gods (e.g., Eros) were involved in homosexual relations. Plato (*Laws* 838e–839b) called for religious sanctions to sexual legislation. Finally Dover says that homosexuality developed more extensively among the Greeks than other peoples because the "Greeks neither inherited nor developed a belief that a divine power had revealed to mankind a code of laws for the regulation of sexual behavior; they had no religious institutions possessed of the authority to enforce sexual prohibitions" (*Greek* 63, 166, 203).

[46] Philo (*On Abraham* 26.133–36) cites homosexuality as unnatural and associated with the "curse of a female disease" at Sodom. He cannot be limited to pederasty, it seems (contra Scroggs, *Homosexuality* 88–91). Josephus refers to Sodom (*Ant.* 1.200–01; cf. 1.194–95) and reflects on the danger of homosexuality in his day (15.28–29). See also *Ag. Ap.* 2.199.

[47] See V. P. Furnish, *The Moral Teaching of Paul* (Nashville: Abingdon, 1979) 60–63.

[48] According to Bailey, *Homosexuality* 65–67. Also see V. L. Bullough, *Homosexuality: A History* (New York: Meridian, 1979) 31–32. Scroggs, *Homosexuality* 52, sides with Boswell's negative assessment of this and other early legislation (65–71), but Bailey argues well for its application to homosexuality.

[49] Other legislation came under the emperors Constantius and Constans (A.D. 342) against the passive sodomist, and the Theodosian Code (A.D. 390) called for the death of the active sodomite. See Bailey, *Homosexuality* 70–81.

[50] D. Earl, *The Moral and Political Tradition of Rome* (Ithaca: Cornell University, 1967) 17. See Bailey, *Homosexuality* 82–86, for examples of the homosexual literature of the era.

[51] Ibid., 18, 36. Livy *History of Rome* 39.6.7 placed the turning point at 187 B.C.; Polybius *Histories* 31.25.3–5 (cf. 6.57.5; Diodorus 31.26) placed it at 168; L. Calpurnius Piso put it at 154. The historian Sallust concurred in these assessments, as did the senators Cato the Censor and Scipio Aemilianus, who made strong speeches against the decline. At the same time (168) Antiochus IV was seeking to Hellenize Palestine, sparking the Maccabean revolt that cleansed the temple of idolatry in 165. What the Romans were not able to accomplish the Jews were able to do because of their faith in a transcendent God and his revealing a code of laws regulating sexual behavior, among other things.

[52] Koester, "*Physis*" 274. See also 1 Timothy 1:8–11, where the Mosaic law gives way to (natural?) law in general, and then this all is said to accord with the gospel.

[53] Ibid., 273. He has here in mind the Greek usage, especially in Plato, of *kata physin* and *para physin* for "normal, natural," and "abnormal, unnatural" (contra Scroggs, *Homosexuality* 114).

[54] Harder, "Nature" 661.

[55] One searches in vain for a commentator who gives *physis* this meaning. Even Scroggs doubts the validity of such a distinction or its presence here. See also Paul's use in Romans 11:21, 24.

[56] Harder, "Nature" 660–61. Note that the term never occurs in the more "Semitic" gospels (and never in John's and Luke's usage).

[57] Note how Paul coins *arsenokoitai* (1 Cor. 6:9–10; 1 Tim. 1:8–10) from Leviticus 18:22; 20:13.

[58] Koester, "*Physis*" 271.

[59] Scroggs, *Homosexuality* 122 (italics his). His exclusive model of pederasty seems to be a myth. He himself admits some texts have examples of permanency (30–31, 57–58), older adults (32–33), near equals in age (34). Indeed some younger men played the active partners over older men (33–34). His claim that today's culture emphasizes "the importance of equality and mutuality in all relationships" (36) is hardly believable. It is a myth for today's homosexual community where only 1 percent of homosexuals have had fewer than 8 lifetime partners, 75 percent of homosexual men report more than 30 partners, and the average homosexual has had 59 to 500 different sexual contacts, depending on the study used. Most AIDS victims have had more than 1000 sexual contacts. See R. Magnuson, *Are "Gay Rights Right?* (St. Paul: Berean League Fund, 1985) 68, 77–78.

[60] Scroggs, *Homosexuality* 16, 116–17. To say that no Greco-Roman text, nor Paul, seeks to explain why homosexuality is against nature (116) is to overlook the fact that both biblical (Lev. 18:22; 20:13) and nonbiblical (Plato *Laws* 636c) authors compare it to sex with women or with animals (*Laws* 836a–c). This implies a common point of comparison: the given nature of the creature involved. It could not be as subjective as each personal disposition, propensity, or orientation.

[61] As Scroggs, *Homosexuality* 124–25, acknowledges.

[62] Ibid., 125.

CHURCH HISTORY

Nathan O. Hatch, area editor

CHURCH HISTORY

NATHAN O. HATCH
Professor of History and
Vice President for Advanced Studies
University of Notre Dame

Introduction

Judged over two centuries, Jonathan Edwards stands forth as one of America's great original minds, one of the very few individuals whose depiction of reality has known enduring attraction. Even in modern America, with its churning secular currents, interest in Edwards remains strong among American intellectuals—theologians, literary scholars, historians, and philosophers. Over the last forty years, for instance, the number of Ph.D. dissertations on Jonathan Edwards has doubled every decade. The last two years has seen a new wave of significant publications on Edwards all attesting to the continuing allure of this eminent evangelical pastor and theologian.[1]

Yet the evangelical church, by and large, remains untouched by this engagement with Jonathan Edwards. It has failed to mine the rich veins that are found in the piety and the thought of this godly pastor. At a time when evangelicals are struggling for intellectual and ethical moorings, they would do well to reach back to recover insights more profound than those current today. In Edwards they can find a powerful voice for a substantive evangelical theology, for a God-centered view of the world, and for a Christian life of obedience and sacrifice. Edwards's analysis of religious experience brims with insight. Our cynical age needs to hear his arguments defending religious affections as the mainsprings of human behavior. At the same time, we need nothing more than his starkly realistic message that piety comes in godly and selfless forms as well as those that are devious and self-serving.

The following essays by Henry F. May and Mark A. Noll serve as a helpful introduction to the powerful intellectual legacy of Jonathan Edwards. Both were given at a conference on Edwards at Wheaton College in the fall of 1984 and were published in a volume of essays edited by Nathan O. Hatch and Harry S. Stout, *Jonathan Edwards and the American Experience* (Oxford University Press, 1988; paperback edition, 1989).

In May's essay, the keynote address of that conference, he unveils the intense dialogue that generations of Americans have sustained with the figure of Jonathan Edwards. In May's deft hands, the figure of Edwards becomes a superb index of how Americans have come to terms with those strands of stern Calvinism that are a central element in their historical identity. May is able to explain why Edwards has been taken so seriously by successive generations—from the veneration of the New Divinity theologians, to the disdain of Enlightenment thinkers such as John Adams, to the anguished rejection of Victorians such as Harriet Beecher Stowe and Samuel Clemens. Only a modern age of total war and holocaust has permitted America once again to gaze without flinching upon Edwards and his sober portrayal of reality and the necessity of divinely initiated grace.

In his essay "Jonathan Edwards and Nineteenth-century Theology," Mark Noll traces three major lines of Edwardsian descent, including the New Divinity, the "New Haven" theology emanating from Yale College, and the Presbyterian theology at Princeton Seminary. All of these traditions claimed Edwards as their progenitor and fought to retain his name in their theological speculations. In fact, Noll observes, each one of these traditions included important aspects of Edwards's thought, but none of them followed the master exactly. If Edwards did not survive intact in any one of those schools of thought, he did continue through the work of all three and exerted a formative influence on nineteenth-century theology.

Note

[1] These publications include Robert W. Jenson, *America's Theologian: A Recommendation of Jonathan Edwards* (Oxford University Press, 1988); Sang Hyun Lee, *The Philosophical Theology of Jonathan Edwards* (Princeton University Press, 1988); and the latest two volumes in the Yale Edition of the Works of Edwards: *A History of the Work of Redemption*, transcribed and edited by John F. Wilson (Yale University Press, 1989) and *Ethical Writings*, edited by Paul Ramsey (Yale University Press, 1989); also nearing completion in the Yale Edition are several volumes of Edwards's early sermons.

About the Area Editor

Nathan O. Hatch is Professor of History and Vice President for Advanced Studies at the University of Notre Dame. His recent book *The Democratization of American Christianity* (Yale University Press, 1989) was awarded the Albert C. Outler Prize in Ecumenical Church History by the American Society of Church History.

JONATHAN EDWARDS AND AMERICA

HENRY F. MAY
Margaret Byrne Professor Emeritus of History
University of California, Berkeley

Article from *Jonathan Edwards and the American Experience*

When I told a Berkeley friend that I had been asked to give a keynote speech for a conference on Jonathan Edwards, this friend, ever frank, asked the obvious question: "Why you? You don't know all that much about Edwards." He was of course quite right, I don't, and I realized this rather acutely when I saw the list of formidable Edwards experts who were going to be represented in this symposium. Then I thought, maybe that is *why* I am asked to do this. A keynote speech—a term borrowed from American politics—is not expected to be a profound scholarly inquiry. What is it supposed to do? It is supposed to help create an atmosphere of enthusiasm and unity, and perhaps to gloss over deep differences of opinion. Maybe this can't be done by people profoundly involved in passionate argument and can best be attempted by somebody distinctly on the periphery.

Aside from not knowing too much, I have one other qualification for this job. I have long found Edwards deeply interesting, sometime repellent, often attractive and moving. (And we all know the importance, in relation to real understanding, of lively affections.) When I first read as a graduate student that virtue consists in the disinterested love of being in general, my immediate response was not "how clever, how well put" but rather "how right, how beautiful." Long years later, after teaching a semester run-through of the history of American religion, I once offered to teach an undergraduate seminar on any topic we had covered. I prepared myself to deal with the churches and Vietnam, or the churches and civil rights. Instead, I got the most requests for a seminar on Edwards. Not very many requests of course—there were eight students. All had their special attitudes toward Edwards. At least three were part of the neo-evangelical movement that was flowering on the campuses in the wake of political movements of the sixties. (Incidentally, these were disappointed as they got to know Edwards better—he was not what they wanted him to be.) Of the others, one, the ablest, had a Catholic education, which meant—at that time—a solid grounding in philosophy and theology. At least one was an intelligent and articulate sceptic. We read most of the Edwards writing that was then generally accessible, and a lot of Edwards criticism from Oliver Wendell Holmes and Leslie Stephen through Parrington to—you guessed it—Perry Miller. We arrived at no consensus, and I think this was perhaps the course that I most enjoyed teaching at Berkeley.

More interesting than the question, "Why me?" is the question "Why you?" Why is it that Edwards has attracted not just a passing glance, but the devotion of years of hard work on the part of so many fine scholars? Is it because you believe him, love him, admire him? Is it because you find him complex and baffling, a perfectly engaging puzzle, a figure eternally subject to profound reinterpretation? Is it because he seems to some of you, as he did to Miller and others, to offer a key to the understanding of American culture? I suspect that all these and other powerful attractions helped to incline your wills in the direction of attending this conference.

It is an intriguing fact that, according to M. X. Lesser's massive Edwards bibliography, the number of dissertations on Edwards has doubled in each decade since 1940.[1] And the quality has gone up, as well as the volume. Yet, as with most interesting subjects, the more we know about Edwards, the harder he becomes to deal with. We have learned, for instance, that he did *not* develop on the far frontier isolated from European thought, that he was *not* suddenly changed in college by reading Locke, indeed that he was not really a Lockean. If you hear a noise, it is the crackling of burning lecture notes.

Who and what was Edwards *really*? Is it impossible to answer that question without the divine and spiritual light to which I claim no access. Since I am trained as a historian, all I can do is try to suggest, in most of the rest of this essay, what Edwards has meant to some kinds of Americans during the two centuries leading up to the present explosion of Edwards scholarship. I want to try to deal with motivation as well as understanding, to discuss the power of attraction and repulsion exerted by Edwards on several kinds of people in several historical periods. But before I do this I want to make it clear that I am not intending to patronize the past. Much as I admire the Edwards scholarship of today, I do not want to imply that in the past people saw Edwards through a mist of prejudice, and now we look at him in the clear light of objectivity. I assume that we all look at Edwards from where we are, and that this will always be so.

Most of us, in our first courses in historiography, heard a lot about the dangers of presentism. I agree that it is a disastrous mistake to push and kick one's subject matter so that it will fit into fashionable categories. This is clearly bad, and Edwards has suffered from it. But another kind of presentism gives most of its vitality to historical study, the kind that after rigorous discipline and close study of the sources asks the questions that arise from the most important concerns of the present. I think that the best Edwards scholarship has always done this. From each of the successive views of Edwards that I want briefly to present there is much to learn, about the preoccupations and assumptions of successive periods in intellectual history, but also about Edwards himself.

The first Edwards, of course, was that of his disciples. According to

Samuel Hopkins, perhaps his most devoted follower:

> President Edwards, in the esteem of all the judicious, who were well-acquainted with him, either personally, or by his writings, was one of the *greatest—best* and *most useful* of men, that have lived in this age. . . . And that this distinguished light has not shone in vain, there are a cloud of witnesses. . . . And there is reason to hope, that though now he is dead, he will yet speak for a great while yet to come, to the comfort and advantage of the church of Christ; that his publications will produce a yet greater harvest, as an addition to his joy and crown of rejoicing in the day of the Lord.[2]

How many ardent young men followed Edwards as closely as they could is a question much debated among recent scholars.[3] It seems clear that there were several hundred of these all-out Edwardsians, most of them intelligent, articulate, and poor. By the 1820s or 30s the New Divinity, developed directly from Edwards's theology, was being forced into rural strongholds in New England, where it long survived. Yet even in the centers of modified Calvinism, where Edwards's teachings were more and more modified to fit nineteenth-century optimism, Edwards was yet venerated by Congregationalist and Presbyterian divines. Timothy Dwight, one of the first of the long list of modifiers, called Edwards "that moral Newton, and that second Paul."[4] Lyman Beecher, the most powerful spokesman of nineteenth-century neo-Calvinism, made in his youth a statement he was never to retract: "I had read Edwards's Sermons. There's nothing comes within a thousand miles of them now."[5]

In a statement made by Edwards Amasa Park in 1839 one can hear the dying gasp of Edwardsian loyalty, struggling with the Genteel Tradition and losing:

> We bow before this father of our New England theology with the profoundest veneration. We read his precious volumes with awe in tears. We are so superstitious, that we almost fear to be called profane for lisping a word against the perfect balancing of his character. And yet we can not help wishing that he had been somewhat more of a brother and somewhat less of a champion. . . .
>
> We need and crave a theology, as sacred and spiritual as his, and moreover one that we can take with us into the flower-garden, and to the top of some goodly hill, and in a sail over a tasteful lake, and into the saloons of music, and to the galleries of the painter and the sculptor, and to the repasts of social joy, and to all those humanizing scenes where virtue holds her sway not merely as that generic and abstract duty of a "love to being in general," but also as the more familiar grace of a love to some beings in particular.[6]

Long before this, while the New Divinity was gaining its triumphs, even while Edwards was still alive, he was being rejected in several different ways by the protagonists of the Enlightenment. In New England from Charles Chauncy on, many took on the formidable task of refuting his arguments, and of showing that these were not only mistaken but immoral. The doctrine of necessity was crippling to the conscience. The idea of double predestination was an insult to the moral and benevolent God who established the law of nature and gave us the ability to know and follow it. To Ezra Stiles and John Witherspoon, practical men like most college presidents, the New Divinity was fanatical and obscurantist. To those who moved beyond liberal Christianity toward Enlightened scepticism, Edwards's whole subject matter was without interest. Nobody expressed this better than John Adams:

> Mr. Adams leaves to Homer and Virgil, to Tacitus and Quintilian, to Mahomet and Calvin, to Edwards and Priestly, or, if you will, to Milton's angels reasoning high in pandemonium, all their acute speculations about fate, destiny, foreknowledge, absolute necessity, and predestination. He thinks it problematical whether there is, or ever will be, more than one Being capable of understanding this vast subject.[7]

Quite different in spirit from this sort of eighteenth-century dismissal was the nineteenth-century revulsion against Edwards as a cruel monster, dangerous because of his great talents. Oliver Wendell Holmes expressed it well:

> It is impossible that people of ordinary sensibilities should have listened to his torturing discourses without becoming at last sick of hearing of infinite horrors and endless agonies.

Of Edwards's uncompromising insistence on the total depravity of unregenerate children Holmes asks:

> Is it possible that Edwards read the text mothers love so well, Suffer little *vipers* to come unto me, and forbid them not, for of such is the kingdom of God.[8]

Harriet Beecher Stowe described the effect of Edwardsian doctrines this way.

> It is a fact that the true tragedy of New England life, its deep, unutterable pathos, its endurances and its sufferings, all depended upon, and were woven into, this constant wrestling of thought with infinite problems which could not be avoided, and which saddened the day of almost everyone who grew up under it. . . .

> Thus was this system calculated, like a skillful engine of torture, to produce all the mental anguish of the most perfect sense of helplessness with the most torturing sense of responsibility.[9]

Mrs. Stowe's Hartford neighbor Samuel Clemens carried this revulsion much further. After reading *Freedom of the Will* Clemens wrote his minister:

> Continuously until near midnight I wallowed and reeked with Jonathan in

his insane debauch; rose immediately refreshed and fine at 10 this morning, but with a strange and haunting sense of having been on a three days' tear with a drunken lunatic. . . . All through the book is the glare of a resplendent intellect gone mad—a marvellous spectacle. No, not *all* through the book— the drunk does not come on till the last third, where what I take to be Calvinism and its God begins to show up and shine red and hideous in the glow from the fires of hell, their only right and proper adornment. By God I was ashamed to be in such company.[10]

It is not difficult to sympathize with these outraged Victorians. I agree with Holmes. To modify his statement slightly, if we can read the imprecatory sermons without horror, it is because of a failure of imagination. Consistent Calvinism is admired in recent times chiefly by people to whom it has never occurred that its doctrines might really describe the true state of affairs. If one is seriously to follow Edwards, recent scholarship has made clear, one must accept his doctrine of Hell not as a minor blemish on his intellectual system, but as essential to it.[11] One must accept as true his masterly descriptions of intolerable and interminable suffering. Still more difficult, to be a real Edwardsian one must come to terms with his insistence that God hates sinners and holds them in the utmost contempt. Once a human being has had his chance, and has not been able to accept it, God will never feel the slightest pity for him. If a person is saved, part of his duty will be to love all aspects of God forever, including his vindictive justice. Thus he will have to learn to rejoice in the rightness and beauty of eternal suffering for others. To be a real follower of Edwards, one must moreover come to terms with little Phoebe Bartlett, four years old, sure of her own salvation, sorry for her sisters, predicting their death, weeping over the sin of stealing plums but blaming her sister for talking her into it, and expressing plummy love for her minister, Mr. Edwards.

For many nineteenth-century Americans, especially in New England, it was not possible to pick and choose. They had been brought up to believe that Edwards's doctrines or something like them were saving truth. After this, to reject them meant a major emotional struggle, which left its marks. The life of Mrs. Stowe's family had been tragically affected by the preaching of a major Edwardsian. Holmes, writing to Mrs. Stowe about Calvinism, describes his upbringing in an image of almost Edwardsian power:

I have found myself like a nursery-tree, growing up with labels of this and that article of faith wired to my limbs. The labels have dropped off, but the wires are only buried in my flesh, which has grown over them. . . . I do not believe you or I can ever get the iron of Calvinism out of our souls.[12]

Clemens, not being a New Englander, had not had quite this sort of exposure to intellectual Calvinism. Yet many of his works, and still more clearly his marginal comments and letters, bear witness to his prolonged early exposure to the grim aspects of evangelical Protestantism, his fervent revulsion from it, and the fact that its ghost continued to haunt him. The Victorians who hated Calvinism took it and Edwards seriously, and we should take seriously their anguished rejection.

In the early twentieth century, instead of rebelling against Edwards, it became possible to patronize him. Countless writers portrayed him as a

talented but tragic figure, who could have been a great poet, a great philosopher, or a great scientist if he hadn't got mired in outworn theology. V. L.
Parrington's account, more balanced than one might expect, contains several pages of eloquent appreciation but ends in lament:

> The intellectual powers were his, the inspiration was lacking; like Cotton
> Mather before him, he was the unconscious victim of a decadent ideal and a
> petty environment. Cut off from fruitful intercourse with other thinkers,
> drawn away from the stimulating field of philosophy into the arid realm of
> theology, it was his fate to devote his noble gifts to the thankless task of
> reimprisoning the mind of New England within a system from which his
> nature and his powers summoned him to unshackle it. He was called to be a
> transcendental emancipator, but he remained a Calvinist.[13]

Rather similarly, Henry Bamford Parkes lamented in 1930 that Edwards
had abandoned his promising early pantheism for Calvinism.

> To have experienced those realities of human nature which are the founda-
> tion of Christianity, and yet to reject Calvinism, would have required, in a
> Connecticut schoolboy, in 1721, a wisdom, almost superhuman; but be-
> cause Edwards lacked that wisdom, his career is, in its hidden implications,
> the most tragic in American history. . . . The dark stream of Calvinism is but
> a tributary to the flood of American culture; Edwards merely carried to its
> extreme a tendency brought from Europe; in spite of his patriotism he was
> not really an American.[14]

It is harder for us to admire the progressive patronizers than to respect
the forthright rejecters of Victorian times. Patronizing Edwards, they remind
us of Edwards's own description of his own liberal contemporaries patronizing the great reformers of the sixteenth century:

> Indeed some of these new writers, at the same time that they have repre-
> sented the doctrines of these ancient and eminent divines as in the highest
> degree ridiculous, and contrary to common sense, in an ostentation of a
> very generous charity, have allowed that they were honest, well-meaning
> men; yea, it may be, some of them, as though it were in great condescension
> and compassion for them, have allowed that they did pretty well for the day
> in which they lived . . . living in the gloomy caves of superstition [they]
> fondly embraced, and demurely and zealously taught the most absurd, silly,
> and monstrous opinions, worthy of the greatest contempt of gentlemen
> possessed of that noble and generous freedom of thought, which happily
> prevail in this age of light and inquiry.[15]

This remains a sufficient putdown of liberal presentism. Yet I think one
should remember how hard it was in the early twentieth century to approve
any ideas that seemed to reject democratic progress. In a sense Parkes was
right: There was no place for Edwards in the rise of American civilization.
More recently Norman Fiering has warned us in a truly eloquent passage that
Edwards was almost alone in the eighteenth century in rejecting the idea of

the universal moral sense and the essential goodness of the common man. If we follow him in this we must realize that we are rejecting the most valuable heritage of the Enlightenment: "Only the two great wars of the twentieth century and the Holocaust have been able to shake into ruins, at least temporarily, the psychological optimism of the Shaftesbury-Hutcheson gospel of the innate goodness of man."[16]

It is out of the era of war and holocaust that the most powerful and interesting recent interpretation of Edwards has come: Edwards as a modern or postmodern intellectual. In 1949 Perry Miller presented him as one of the long and honorable line of American intellectuals who indicted utilitarian liberalism, complacency, and the profit motive, in a word (not Miller's), Babbittry. Edwards attacked the philistines, moreover, not in the name of transcendence but in behalf of "what seems rather a glorified naturalism."[17]

Miller has been well and thoroughly jumped on, by consistent naturalists, consistent theologians, and worst of all, by historians who convict him of either misreading or not reading some of the evidence. It is quite clear that Edwards was not any kind of naturalist.

Yet I think something is left of Edwards's modernity (asserted by others besides Miller) if only in terms of analogy. Edwards certainly was an enemy of complacency, and so are most important American writers, including of course Perry Miller. He is one of a long succession of American Jeremiahs, brooding over the grievous faults of their strange Israel. And there is something in Edwards's doctrine of moral necessity highly compatible with much modern thought. We are prevented from doing what we should do, even what we want to do, by our upbringing, our culture, our psychological formation—in short, our diseased will. It is understandable that Miller's *Edwards*, for all its many mistakes, sparked the revival of Edwards scholarship. It remains an interesting book, primarily because it was written by an interesting man.

In 1966 Alan Heimert, who might possibly be described as Miller's Samuel Hopkins, published his *Religion and the American Mind*.[18] With much learning and many exaggerations, Heimert associated Edwards and his followers with the American radical tradition from the Revolution on. One might say that where Miller had made Edwards an intellectual of the 1920s, his younger disciple made Edwards an intellectual of the 1930s. Heimert's book, partly because of a few unfortunate statements, called forth an extraordinary barrage of heavy artillery. And yet I don't think that Heimert was blown clear out of the water.

Edwards himself was not a social radical, not indeed directly interested in issues of social welfare, though Hopkins reports he was personally charitable to the poor. He was no precursor of Jeffersonian, still less of Jacksonian, democracy. He had nothing in common with the generally populist content of later American radicalism. He was in fact one of the greatest opponents of the theory that what is popular is right.

Yet it remains quite true that he offered no comfort to the wealthy and well-placed in their complacency, and that his closest followers were overwhelmingly among the radical supporters of the American Revolution. Heimert, even more clearly than other historians, shows us the reasons for this, the association of virtue, frugality, and sound doctrine with America—of decadence, luxury, and lukewarm religion with England.

There is even a useful analogy between the attraction of the New Divinity in the late eighteenth century and that of Marxism in the 1930s. Both attracted the young, the poor, and the intelligent. Both demanded total surrender and therefore appealed to those who wanted to give themselves completely to a cause. Both asserted that there was only one good force in the world, that from this only came all legitimacy, and that half-measures were evil. Survivors of the thirties find something familiar in the curse of Meroz invoked effectively against liberals.

One more major view of Edwards, related to that of Perry Miller but yet quite different, arose out of the successive revivals of religion in America, beginning with the neo-orthodox movement of the 30s, 40s, and 50s. Miller himself was friendly to this movement but outside it; he and others like him have been called "atheists for Niebuhr." The *theists* for Niebuhr saw a different Edwards, not a precursor of modern existentialism but a serious theologian in the tradition of Augustine and Calvin. It should be noted that Reinhold Niebuhr himself made very little use of Edwards and at one point disapproved his absolutist ethic as crippling to social responsibility.[19] His brother H. Richard Niebuhr, more interested than Reinhold in the study of the American religious past, listed Edwards's *Nature of True Virtue*, along with works by Pascal, Barth, Calvin, and others, among those books that had most influenced his own philosophy of life.[20]

As early as 1932, Joseph Haroutunian treated the history of New England theology as a long, tragic decline from Edwards's profundity, and announced in his preface that today's world could, *in its own way*, appreciate Calvinism better than it could the recent past:

> Whereas the language of Calvinism is in disrepute, the elements of good sense in Calvinism must always remain wherever there is good sense. . . . The optimism and the humanism of the nineteenth century have already lost their rational quality.
>
> It is probable that a revival of the "tragic sense of life," together with the wisdom and sobriety which grow out of it, should be forthcoming. It is necessary that men rediscover the truths once signified by the doctrines of divine sovereignty and divine grace, of predestination and election, of depravity and regeneration. . . .
>
> If the humanitarianism of Channing is modern, a post-modern mind is already in the making. Its spirit is as yet skeptical and "naturalistic." It believes itself to be in an alien world. In order to become religious, it must become reconciled with God.[21]

By 1966, when Conrad Cherry wrote his analysis of the theology of Edwards, the neo-orthodox movement had come and gone, leaving an important residue, at least in the study of the American past. This residue is quite apparent in Cherry's introduction:

> Whatever quarrel one may have with the specific features of the theologies of such thinkers as Karl Barth and Reinhold Niebuhr, they have, in diverse ways, reclaimed Augustinian and Calvinist categories in order to prick the contemporary conscience, wean man away from religious sentimentality, and throw him up against the hard reality of a God who judges as well as forgives. . . . the once deplorable doctrine of predestination symbolizes man's precarious situation in the presence of a God whose will cannot be reduced to our purposes.[22]

Writing from this perspective, Cherry totally rejects Miller's existentialist Edwards. Edwards did not reject either the Puritan past or covenant theology; he remained "first and last a Calvinist theologian," not neo-orthodox but essentially orthodox.

The mass revival of religion of the 1950s, often heartily disapproved of by neo-orthodox and other intellectuals, led to a reemphasis on Edwards as a critical revivalist. In 1959 John E. Smith, introducing Edwards's *Religious Affections* said that "our present religious situation enables us to understand him as perhaps never before. For we are falling or have fallen into some of the very pitfalls he sought to avoid; we are in a better position than any age since Edwards to understand the profundity of his contribution to theological thinking. . . . He has given us a means of exposing the pseudo religions of moralism, sentimentality, and social conformity." While legitimizing revival and "heart religion," Edwards, Smith points out, "failed to fall in with revivalism at two crucial points: He denied that the urgency of believing provides any criterion for the truth of religion or the sincerity of the believer, and he was unwilling to follow the pattern of most revivalists and set the religious spirit over against learning and intellect. For Edwards the Word must come in truth as well as in power."[23]

In the current revival of evangelical Protestantism, still another Edwards has been powerfully put before us—Edwards the serious and devoted student of the millennium. A long series of historians, clearly influenced by the new apocalyptic possibilities of the nuclear era, writing from both secular and religious points of view, have brought back to the surface a major part of Christian history long understated and explained away—the study of prophecy and the prediction of the last days. Starting with important hints from H. Richard Niebuhr, Edwards's millennial and apocalyptic thought has been thoroughly explored by a series of careful and insightful scholars including C. C. Goen and Stephen J. Stein.[24] Always eagerly searching the signs of the times for evidence of God's intentions, Edwards in his most optimistic moment in 1743 believed that he saw the millennium dawning in America.

In my opinion, the Edwards that emerges from scholars affected by recent religious movements, the Edwards who is primarily Calvinist, revivalist, and millenarian, is closer to the truth than Edwards the modern existentialist, so daringly and unforgettably presented by Perry Miller. It is valuable to have Edwards seen once more as a major figure in American religious as well as intellectual history. Yet a word of caution is necessary. The best theological students of Edwards know well, but some semipopular writers have forgotten, that Edwards is not really ancestral to any of the major kinds of nineteenth- or twentieth-century American religion. His millennial predictions about America have nothing in common with the foolish chauvinism of many nineteenth-century preachers. Destiny, to Edwards, was never really Manifest. He clearly disapproved the humanist and liberal tendency that has issued in the nearly secular humanitarianism of the mainline churches today. Populistic and uncritical revivalists, who have flourished in all periods, surely cannot claim as their ally the author of *Religious Affections*. Fundamentalists can have little commerce with a man who never feared that the discoveries of contemporary science could be in contradiction to religious truth. Dispensationalists are a long way from a man who thought that the worst trials promised by revelation were over and that the new day might already have dawned. What are most churchgoers to do with a man who, according to the best recent analysis, "explicitly denied the efficacy of petitionary prayer to bring about external change in the world"?[25]

Conclusion

I have tried so far to suggest a few of the main interpretations of Edwards—there are of course many others—that have succeeded each other in the past. It is time to ask where we are left. After this keynote, can the convention agree on a platform? On a few planks, I think.

First, I think we can agree that Edwards was somehow a great man, whether we admire him most as artist, psychologist, preacher, theologian, or philosopher. Second, I think we can probably agree on what was the starting point and motive of all his work: "To one cardinal principle Edwards was faithful—the conception of the majesty and sufficiency of God; and this polar idea provides the clue to both his philosophical and theological systems."[26] This was said not by Haroutunian or Cherry, not by any of the editors of the Yale edition, not by Norman Fiering, but by Vernon Louis Parrington, and it seems to me undeniable. Third, I think we can agree that Edwards, like all thinkers much worth studying, was fully of his own time and yet transcended it. He has had a great deal to say to people who loved and admired him, people who were horrified and haunted by him, people of many kinds of the eighteenth, nineteenth, and twentieth centuries. He seems both inexhaustible and impossible to pin down.

There are some other things on which I think we cannot and will not agree. First, is his work a massive, successful structure, or a majestic, instructive, and brilliant failure? There are many ways to ask this question. Can we understand the preacher who in one sermon tells his listeners to seek Christ: "You need not hesitate one moment, but may run to him and cast yourself upon him; you will certainly be graciously and meekly received by him,"[27] and in others makes it clear that nothing will avail unless one has been totally changed by the uncontrollable power of the Spirit? Probably there is no real inconsistency of doctrine here, but is there not an inconsistency in homiletic effect?

As for his theology, I am certainly not qualified to criticize it, but hope the theologians will tell me whether there is or is not a contradiction between believing, on the one hand, in a God that is both wholly other and wholly transcendent, and on the other hand, analyzing in detail his nature and intentions. Regarding Edwards's philosophy, Fiering, who regards him as a great and profound thinker, leaves the question of validity wide open: "A difficult question, and one we need not debate here, is whether Edwards's primary, objective, ontological foundation for virtue is philosophically or even theologically tenable." Regarding his effort to reconcile responsibility and predestination Fiering says, "It would be absurd to say that Edwards succeeded in dissolving this theological mystery (all of his solutions seem to be sophistical). . . ."[28]

Finally I come to what is for me the most difficult and interesting question of all. This is the question raised by James Hoopes: "Many modern scholars," says Hoopes, "have no idea what it feels like to perceive holiness [this seems to me a massive understatement], and those who do can no more describe the sensation to the rest of us than one can tell a man blind since birth what it feels like to see."[29] To bring together the affections, the understanding, and the will, Edwards has to rely on the sixth spiritual sense, "a Spiritual and Divine Light, immediately imparted to the soul by God, of a different nature from any that is obtained by natural means."[30] This supreme and crucial faculty is necessarily for unregenerate people, both indefinable and unverifiable. Perhaps Edwards's greatest achievement as a writer is that he comes close through his poetic powers to achieving the impossible. He almost manages to prove to the unilluminated the logical necessity of this supernatural illumination, and even to tell us what it is like.

This can be put in simpler terms arising out of the history of Edwards studies. Is it possible to have a fruitful discussion of a great religious thinker with the frank participation of believers, rejecters, and agnostics? This seems to me a question which a conference on this topic, in this place, needs to be faced head-on.

Notes

[1] M. X. Lesser, *Jonathan Edwards: A Reference Guide* (Boston, 1981) xli. This volume has

assisted me greatly in preparing the essay, reprinted in this volume.

[2] Samuel Hopkins, *The Life and Character of the Late Reverend Mr. Jonathan Edwards* (1765), reprinted in David Levin, ed., *Jonathan Edwards, a Profile* (New York, 1969) 1–2.

[3] The latest, and one of the best, contributions to this long debate is Joseph Conforti, *Samuel Hopkins and the New Divinity* (Grand Rapids, 1981). See especially 175–90.

[4] Timothy Dwight, *The Triumph of Infidelity*, quoted by Lesser, *Edwards*, 46.

[5] *The Autobiography of Lyman Beecher*, ed. Barbara M. Cross, 2 vols. (Cambridge, 1961) I, 46.

[6] E. A. Park, "The Duties of a Theologian," *American Biblical Repository* II, 4 (1840) 374.

[7] John Adams to John Taylor, 1814, reprinted in Adrienne Koch, ed., *The American Enlightenment* (New York, 1965) 222.

[8] Oliver Wendell Holmes, "Jonathan Edwards," in *Pages from an Old Volume of Life* (Boston, 1892) 393.

[9] Harriet Beecher Stowe, *Oldtown Folks*, ed., Henry F. May (Cambridge, Mass., 1966) 401.

[10] Clemens to the Reverend J. H. Twichell, February 1902, in A. B. Paine, *Mark Twain's Letters*, 2 vols. (New York, 1917) II, 719–20.

[11] See Norman Fiering, *Jonathan Edwards's Moral Thought and Its British Context* (Chapel Hill, 1981) 200–60.

[12] Holmes to Stowe, May 29, 1867, quoted in H. May, Introduction to *Oldtown Folks*, 29.

[13] V. L. Parrington, *Main Currents of American Thought*, 3 vols. (New York, 1927, 1930) I, 162–63.

[14] Henry Bamford Parkes, *Jonathan Edwards, The Fiery Puritan* (New York, 1930) 254.

[15] Jonathan Edwards, "Freedom of the Will," ed., Paul Ramsey (New Haven, 1967) 437.

[16] Fiering, *Edwards's Moral Thought*, 148.

[17] Perry Miller, *Jonathan Edwards* (New York, 1949) 276.

[18] Cambridge, 1966.

[19] Reinhold Niebuhr, *Moral Man and Immoral Society* (New York, 1960, 1st ed., 1932) 67.

[20] H. R. Niebuhr, "Ex Libris," *The Christian Century*, June 13, 1962, 754.

[21] Joseph Haroutunian, *Piety versus Moralism* (New York, 1932, paperback ed., New York, 1970) xxxii–xxxiii.

[22] Conrad Cherry, *The Theology of Jonathan Edwards* (New York, 1966) 6.

[23] John E. Smith, introduction to Edwards, *Religious Affections*, reprinted in Levin, ed., *Jonathan Edwards*, 211, 217.

[24] C. C. Goen, "Jonathan Edwards: A New Departure in Eschatology," *Church History* XXXVIII (1959) 25–40; Stephen J. Stein, introduction to Jonathan Edwards, *Apocalyptic Writings* (New Haven, 1977).

[25] Fiering, *Edwards's Moral Thought*, 97.

[26] Parrington, *Main Currents*, I, 152.

[27] Edwards, "The Excellency of Christ," in C. H. Faust and Thomas H. Johnson, *Jonathan Edwards, Representative Selections* (New York, 1925, paperback ed., 1962) 125.

[28] Fiering, *Edwards's Moral Thought*, 361, 292.

[29] James Hoopes, "Jonathan Edwards's Religious Psychology," *Journal of American History* LXIX (1982–83) 861.

[30] Edwards, "A Divine and Supernatural Light," in Faust and Johnson, eds., *Edwards*, 102.

JONATHAN EDWARDS AND
NINETEENTH-CENTURY THEOLOGY

MARK A. NOLL
Professor of History and Theological Studies
Wheaton College

Article from *Jonathan Edwards and the American Experience*

Jonathan Edwards appeared in several guises during the nineteenth century. For vast segments of the English-speaking world, and beyond, he was an honored figure from the annals of piety. To a sizable number of educated Americans, Edwards was not so much an inspiration to piety as an irreplaceable cultural artifact, viewed either as a Founding Father worthy of high honor or as an incubus to be shaken off. To a small number of post-Christian British intellectuals, Edwards was an intriguing philosophical curiosity. But for many Americans and Scots, as well as a curious few from England and Holland, Edwards still counted most as a theologian, as the author of doctrinal sermons, of treatises on *True Virtue, Original Sin, The History of Redemption*, and above all *Freedom of the Will*.[1]

An examination of Edwards's place in nineteenth-century theology must deal with two issues. The simpler, if more cumbersome, task is to chronicle the way in which Edwards commanded allegiance, provoked opposition, and precipitated controversy. The more complex is to assess the way in which Edwards's theology comported with the larger commitments of those who took notice of him.

If we define the nineteenth century, from an American perspective, as stretching from the Revolution to the First World War, we can trace three interrelated stories concerning Edwards during the period up to 1870.[2] The first concerns theologians who worked to dignify their own efforts by associating them with Edwards's name. This is often the story of conflict which arose when appropriators of Edwards encountered others who, with sometimes antithetical convictions, did the same. The second concerns those who found Edwards an impediment rather than an inspiration. It is the tale of efforts to rebut his arguments and overthrow his conclusions. The third concerns those who were not so much disputants about Edwards as developers of his insights.

During the last third of the century, Edwards became more clearly an anachronism. The reasons for this are found in the larger changes taking place in Western intellectual culture at that time. After describing Edwards's growing irrelevance as a theological force, the paper concludes with general

115

comments about the fate of Edwards's theology in the nineteenth century.

One final introductory word is required. This paper would have been impossible without the superb Edwards reference guide by M. X. Lesser, a work which, while ably assisted by other recent retrospectives, is now the *sine qua non* for serious reflection on Edwards in the nineteenth century. It is a model of industry for bibliographers, and a beacon for historians.[3]

The Struggle for Edwards's Mantle: Revival

Shortly after Charles Finney (1792–1875) began his famous evangelistic itinerations in 1824, he encountered the writings of Jonathan Edwards. And at least early in his career, Finney "often spoke of them with rapture."[4] Finney was especially encouraged that Edwards has defended evangelistic innovations. By the time Finney published his *Lectures on Revivals of Religion* in 1835, he had received stout blows from leaders of the older Calvinistic churches, who regarded his novel methods with a jaundiced eye. Against such critics, Finney paraded a long list of Christian worthies who had also forsaken traditions. Prominent in this list was "President Edwards," a "great man [who] was famous in his day for new measures." Specifically it was Edwards's refusal to baptize the children of unregenerate parents and his willingness to tolerate lay preachers that appealed to Finney as an anticipation of his own "new measures," like protracted meetings and the anxious bench. Each of these tactics broke convention to reach spirituality. But just as an "Old School" had opposed the colonial "New Light," so now other petty-minded naysayers obstructed means of "seeking out ways to do good and save souls."[5] With Edwards on his side, Finney possessed an unassailable precedent.

Almost as soon as Finney announced that he had discovered a new champion, however, his opponents rushed to retrieve Edwards for themselves. In the late 1820s and 1830s the conservative Congregational revivalist, Asahel Nettleton, his activistic colleague, Lyman Beecher, and Presbyterians Samuel Miller and Albert Dod led efforts to strip Finney of his Edwardsian pretentions.[6] Dod's criticism was the most sweeping. Finney's "use of the name of this great man" to defend his new measures was "to slander the dead." Finney might claim that Edwards sanctioned the widespread use of "lay exhortation," but this merely illustrated his "ignorance of Edwards's opinions and writings." To prove that point Dod quoted directly from the very works on revivals that Finney himself had cited, where "Edwards makes known, with all plainness his opposition to lay exhortation." Finney's "bold misrepresentation" of Edwards was merely one further "illustration of that unscrupulousness in the use of means for the attainment of his ends, which he too often manifests."[7]

It is significant that the first nineteenth-century struggle to claim

Edwards's mantle took place in connection with revival, for Edwards's relationship to the Awakening was a key to much of the controversy that followed. Finney and other Jacksonian evangelists valued Edwards for his place in the history of revival, even though they felt it necessary to set aside the specific convictions of his theology. New England Congregationalists, on the other hand, valued Edwards as a revivalist and perceived precisely in the exposition of revival his central theological contribution. By contrast, the more conservative, or Old School, Presbyterians valued Edwards's specifically theological pronouncements, but worried that these had been compromised by his revivalistic experiences. The Scots and the more romantic, or New School, Presbyterians had yet another perspective. To them it was important that Edwards combined the strictness of Old Calvinism with the experimental piety of revival.

The Struggle for Edwards's Mantle: "New" Theology versus "Old"

The dispute over Charles Finney's methods was only a curtain raiser as the main theological contention for Edwards, which pitted Old School Presbyterians against New England Congregationalists. This debate involved the three leading seminaries in the country—Andover, Yale, and Princeton—and many of the nation's finest intellects, including Yale's Nathaniel William Taylor, Andover's Edwards Amasa Park, and Princeton's Charles Hodge.[8] It was part of perhaps the most comprehensive American discussion at mid-century of the Great Questions concerning God, human nature, and the fate of civilization. To sum up a complicated picture, Princeton held sternly, if with some confusion, to traditional conceptions of human dependence and divine sovereignty. New England, while no less fervent in its faith, had begun to place greater confidence in human nature as defined by modern opinion. Because both parties felt that Jonathan Edwards had played a determinative role in defining Calvinism, the Enlightenment, and the American character, their contention for his mantle was a significant part of their more general controversy.

By mid-century the conservative Presbyterians and the mainstream New England Congregationalists had clearly diverged.[9] The Plan of Union, which had joined Presbyterians and Congregationalists in 1801 for the Christianizing of the frontier, came apart in 1837. The institutions of New England Congregationalism, like Andover and Yale, reflected an eclectic intellectual heritage made up of the mingled Puritan-Enlightenment assumptions of eighteenth-century Harvard and Yale, the more recent assumptions of philosophical Common Sense, a smattering of the nineteenth-century's new thought (at least as filtered through Coleridge), and the ideals of political freedom and ecclesiastical Independency. The institutions of the Old School Presbyterians, like Princeton Seminary and the College of New Jersey, defined their allegiances more simply as Scripture, the Reformed confessions, and Common Sense moral intuitions.

Attitudes toward Edwards were well in place before the polemics began. To New England, Jonathan Edwards was a treasured possession. Uniformly the Congregationalists held that he had established the course which they followed. Timothy Dwight, Edwards's grandson, a revered president of Edwards's alma mater (1795–1817), and the beloved mentor of Congregationalism's two great leaders in the first half of the century, the activist Beecher and the theologian N. W. Taylor, well illustrates this feeling of propriety. In a poetic flight of youthful fancy Dwight had called Edwards "that moral Newton, and that second Paul" who "in one little life, the gospel more/Disclos'd, than all earth's myriads kenn'd before."[10] Frank Hugh Foster, who composed the last full history of the New England theology, summed up nicely the Congregationalist attitude in the first half of the nineteenth century: "To agree with Edwards was still the high ambition of them all; and when they consciously disagreed, as did Taylor, they thought they were only expressing better Edwards's true meaning."[11]

Old School Presbyterians did not possess this same intimacy with Edwards, though they eventually came to make much of the fact that Edwards once expressed a preference for presbyterian polity over congregational.[12] Only Charles Hodge among leading Presbyterians expressed serious reservations about Edwards, and these were more than balanced by Hodge's general approval.

Although New England's bond to Edwards was closer than that of Princeton, it was nonetheless the Presbyterians who made the first contentious claims for Edwards's mantle. Presbyterian attention to Edwards arose within the context of church politics, especially the Presbyterian division into Old and New School denominations in 1837 and the reunion in the North of New and Old School in 1868. At issue was the extent to which New England's theological orientation and the specific ideas of Yale's N. W. Taylor had infected Presbyterians. In a word, Princeton abominated Taylor's theology and any other system in which they spied the barest trace of New Haven's errors. To Princeton it seemed especially galling that the New Haven and other faulty New England systems would continue to call themselves the descendents of Edwards who, the Old Schoolers felt, had taught pretty much what they did.

From the time of the Presbyterian division in 1837, Princeton authors wrote steadily about Edwards.[13] As they saw it, Edwards had too easily tolerated enthusiasm in the colonial Awakening; he had promoted eccentric views of a common humanity in his work on *Original Sin*; he had fostered unsound habits of metaphysical speculation; and his *Dissertation on the Nature of True Virtue* had been misguided in itself and a bad influence on later New England theology. Yet these were all relatively minor matters. In general, Edwards was a sterling example of an orthodox theologian who had distinguished himself in the "full and zealous maintenance of the old Calvin-istic doctrines." By contrast, later theologians in New England had aban-doned Edwards's dearest convictions and, drawing unwarranted conclusions from his foibles, promoted serious error. New England protestations about following Edwards were a sham. As one Princeton author asked pointedly in 1840, "Shall we not heed his counsels as well as revere his name?"[14]

These jabs had the inevitable consequence. New England responded to assert its claim to Edwards, and for twenty years the battle was joined. In the course of the exchange Princeton usually got the better of debate on the question of the will. Try as they might, New Englanders could not convinc-ingly link their belief in the will's "power to the contrary" with the arguments for moral necessity in Edwards's *Freedom of the Will.*[15] New England, on the other hand, showed that Princeton did not understand Edwards's ethical principles. Its theologians mounted a convincing case to demonstrate the continuity from Edwards's *True Virtue* to their more modern theories of benevolence.[16]

In the course of the debate three authors offered comprehensive inter-pretations of the Edwardsian heritage. The first of these was Andover's Edwards Amasa Park (1808–1900) who was goaded into action in 1851 after Charles Hodge had claimed that Park and his Congregationalist contempo-raries taught an "anti-Augustinian system" which contradicted the major positions of Edwards.[17]

Park responded with a prodigy of exegesis, tracing the continuities of theology in New England from Edwards to Park's own generation. In a very abridged summary, Park contended that New Englanders from Edwards onward believed: (1) that there is, strictly speaking, no sinful nature lying behind individual acts of sin—all sinfulness arises from the acts of evil themselves; (2) that, as a consequence, no guilt, or absolutely foreordained certainty to sin, passes down from Adam throughout the whole human race—guilt before God is not imputed from Adam but is each person's own responsibility; and (3) that by nature people have the power to do what God's law demands—there is no bondage of the will to the sinful inclinations of a sinful nature.[18]

Even in his own day, Park's effort to make Edwards conform with later New England views on free will, the voluntary character of sinfulness, and the rejection of imputation was not persuasive.[19] Edwards, in fact, did believe in the bondage of the will, he did believe in a sinful nature underlying sinful deeds, and he did hold to something like traditional views on the imputation of Adam's sin. In these regards, Hodge the interloper saw Edwards more clearly than Park the heir.

Park himself provided a clue as to why Princeton could regard his views as diverging so far from those of Edwards. Park's "scheme," as he put it, benefited from "the philosophy of Reid, Oswald, Campbell, Beattie, Stewart . . . *the philosophy of common sense.*" The great strength of this Scottish

contribution was "to develop 'the fundamental laws of human belief.' " Moreover, it "has aided our writers in shaping their faith according to those
ethical axioms, which so many fathers in the church have undervalued." The
result was that "the metaphysics of New England Theology . . . is the metaphysics of common sense."[20] So great was Edwards that Park could not give
him up, even if Edwards had denied Park's understanding of the natural and
universal moral sense. Yet so powerful had modern moral philosophy become that Park's only course was to read Edwards through the lenses which
it provided.

In addition, however, Park's account of New England Theology did properly spotlight a major Princeton misreading of Edwards. It had become
standard for Old School Presbyterians to treat Edwards's *Dissertation on the
Nature of True Virtue* as a badly flawed effort. On several occasions Princeton
had described this essay as a late and ill-conceived product of Edwards's pen
which encouraged Antinomianism, egotistic utilitarianism, revivalistic excess, and theological absurdities (e.g., Samuel Hopkins's "willingness to be
damned for the glory of God"). Park showed, by contrast, that *True Virtue*
was a mature product of Edwards's thought and that it lay at the heart of his
general theological concerns.[21] Park's efforts to translate this victory into a
defense of his substantive theological affirmations were not convincing, but
he did expose a persistent Princeton inability to grasp an important element
in Edwards's thought.

Park was fooling himself if he felt that his counterattack would silence
the Old School. In 1858, Princeton's Lyman Hotchkiss Atwater (1813–83)
offered the definitive Old School interpretation. Atwater was a Connecticut
Congregationalist who had been both a parishioner and student of N. W.
Taylor, but this early training had not taken, and he stood foursquare with
the Old School Presbyterians. From 1840 to 1868 Atwater was the major voice
in the *Princeton Review* defending Edwards and attacking the later New
England theologians. His review of theological history spared no tender
feelings in New England:

> Edwards held and devoted his labours to prove the doctrines commonly
> known as Old Calvinism, with the single exception theologically, that he
> taught Stapfer's scheme of the mediate imputation of Adam's sin; and with
> the further qualification, that he held an eccentric philosophical theory of
> the nature of virtue, as consisting wholly in love to being in general. . . .
> Neither of these peculiarities, however, was allowed to act upon or modify
> other parts of his theology. . . . We think it easy to show . . . that the distinc-
> tive features of this New Divinity, in all its successive forms, are utterly
> abhorrent to his entire system.[22]

Atwater surmised that New Englanders perceived such a connection only
because Jonathan Edwards, Jr., bore his father's name as he led succeeding
generations away from the elder Edwards's views.[23] In the course of his
account, Atwater paused to make explicit what had been implicit in Prince-

ton's earlier attacks on New England. If the Congregationalists succeeded in disposing of original sin and the imputation of Adam's guilt, the heart of Christianity was imperiled—"the whole doctrine of atonement and justification is implicated with that of imputation."[24] The battle for Edwards was part of a much larger struggle for faith itself.

In response to Atwater's Old School reading, Noah Porter (1811–92), professor of moral philosophy and metaphysics at Yale, a student of Taylor and also his son-in-law, shifted the grounds of debate. In 1861 Porter set out to vindicate N. W. Taylor as Edwards's legitimate heir and to disabuse Princeton of its errors concerning Congregationalist thought.[25] Unlike Park, however, Porter did not attempt to show that the *substance* of New England Theology had been carefully preserved from generation to generation. Rather he intended to show that Edwards's *spirit* had been the motivating force among the theologians who gathered under his name.

Porter first pointed out that, like Edwards, Taylor's "first so-called discoveries in theology were reached in the revivals of religion in which he was so earnest and fervent a laborer." He went on to suggest what the dogmaticians at Princeton had overlooked: that the "leading peculiarity which distinguished Edwards as a theologian, was, that he was a philosopher as well as a divine." Edwards was not content with "servilely copying the compromising philosophy" of the Westminster divines, but rather aspired to show the "unphilosophical" errors of his contemporaries. "The secret of Edwards's influence" was his willingness to contradict inherited authority, to strike out boldly for the truth. To Porter, the enduring Edwards was an Edwards of innovation: "He asserted principles in respect to philosophical theology, which excited and directed the minds of his so-called successors, and which, by right, entitle them to the appellation of Edwardsean—which made them what they were, bold, enterprising, logical, consistent thinkers."[26]

Porter was not concerned if bits and pieces of Edwards's inheritance had been rearranged as time went by. He conceded that contemporary New England theologians held to propositions that differed from Edwards's—that people possess a moral freedom to choose good or evil, that morality is a quality of action rather than enduring character, that neither guilt nor righteousness can fairly be imputed from one person to another, and that Jesus' death was a demonstration of God's moral government rather than a placation of divine wrath.[27] But these were trifles. Taylor's predilection for bold and independent inquiry, for refined philosophical reflection, was the key which marked him as Edwards's true successor.

According to Porter, Taylor's great accomplishment was to build a system logically from first principles of reason: "No teacher could possibly be more alive to the absolute necessity of intuitions, or more enforce the obligation to believe in and ascertain them as the necessary precondition of all logical deductions and all philosophy." This insignia routed Princeton and proved Taylor's right to speak as an Edwardsian. Taylor displayed his superiority especially in the clarity with which he perceived "first moral truths that are self-evident." Unlike the Old School Presbyterian, "who by shuffling statements and self-contradictory propositions and scholastic refinements and questionable interpretations, patches up a vindication of what he calls Orthodoxy," Taylor "used conscience and common sense to assail traditionary and fantastic speculations."[28] The final result was an advance for the Christian cause which paralleled the advance under Edwards.

The clash between Princeton and New England over Edwards continued until the late 1860s.[29] But the basic positions remained constant. Princeton held up Edwards as a great exponent of orthodox Calvinism, in spite of his lack of caution concerning revivals and religious experience and in spite of his foibles on virtue and unity with Adam.[30] By contrast, New Englanders held from first to last that Edwards belonged to them. To E. A. Park, the continuity resided in the dogmas, to Porter in the method.[31]

Several features of this struggle deserve special notice. First and most obvious was its testimony to the enduring theological stature of Edwards. Second, the nature of the struggle over Edwards testified to the presence of a philosophical revolution in America. Princeton, Yale, and Andover had become centers of Common Sense philosophy.[32] As such they accepted assumptions that were not only foreign to Edwards, but which he had largely opposed. To be sure, it made considerable difference which aspect of Common Sense prevailed at the various theological institutions in the nineteenth century. Princeton showed greatest fondness for the methodological aspects of Common Sense, Andover and Yale for the moral. And both Andover and Yale tinctured their Common Sense commitments with at least a modest infusion of Coleridgean romanticism, something which Princeton did not do until the arrival of James McCosh at the College of New Jersey in 1868.[33]

For Princeton, the Common Sense commitments altered the framework rather more than the substance of theology. In New England the deliverances of the moral sense became crucial principles of theology. In this regard, the investment in Common Sense moved New England further from Edwards's theology than it did Princeton.

Third, however, New England clearly perceived the intellectual spirit of Edwards more accurately than did Princeton. Edwards had indeed been an independent inquirer. As Samuel Hopkins put it in the first biography: Edwards "took his religious principles from the Bible, and not from any human system or body of divinity. Though his principles were *Calvinistic*, yet he called no man father. He thought and judged for himself, and was truly very much an original."[34] The New Englanders, especially Hopkins, Nathaniel Emmons, and Taylor, were also bold and original thinkers who likewise wished to be known as Calvinists while calling no man father. The Princeton Theology, on the other hand, defined itself as a conserving effort. It was willing to say "father" to a whole host of orthodox divines.

The protests of Yale and Andover against Princeton's reactionary intellect were valid. And in this *they* stood closer to Edwards.

The Rejection of Edwards

While Princeton struggled with Andover and Yale to lay claim to Edwards, a more diverse group of theologians attended to Edwards for different purposes. Charles Hodge, E. A. Park, and Noah Porter took Edwards's positive contribution for granted. These others called that assumption into question. During the nineteenth century at least forty-one substantial refutations of Edwards's major books appeared, ranging from Charles Chauncy's offended rejection of Edwards's *Original Sin* in 1785 to Lewis French Stearn's attack on the determinism of *Free Will* in 1890.[35] In between came a number of extended refutations (one reaching nearly a thousand pages), some carefully reasoned rebuttals, and a host of works marked more by wounded indignation than cautious reasoning. While most of Edwards's principal treatises came under attack, the *Freedom of the Will*—"the work," in Perry Miller's phrase, "through which his fame has been most widely spread abroad"—bore the brunt.[36]

The story of those who ventured into print against Edwards is an involved one, taking in Christians and skeptics; theologians from Scotland, England, and America; some who tried to separate the wheat from the chaff and some who consigned Edwards *en bloc* to oblivion. Yet the criticism, for all its variety, can be reduced to a very few themes.

The central objection was that Edwards's "iron network of philosophical necessity," though reflecting an intelligence of "gigantic power," led to conclusions which violated the commonly perceived morality of the universe.[37] To this central objection commentators added manifold protests concerning Edwards's use of logic, a number of complaints about the imprecision of his language, and a few counterarguments from the Bible. But the central point was the way in which Edwards's conclusions violated the moral conscience.

This theme dominated the attacks on Edwards's convictions about eternal damnation and the Adamic source of original sin. The same note predominated in protests against Edwards's beliefs about original sin, including his unusual assertion that all humanity participated in Adam's first sin. Such contentions, according to his critics, undercut the human sense of equity and cast aspersions on God's righteousness.

During the nineteenth century, however, Edwards's theological reputation did not rest primarily on his tracts concerning hell or original sin, but with his treatise on *Freedom of the Will*. Of Edwards's works, only the life of Brainerd appeared more often. At no time for a century and a half from its first publication in 1754 did more than fifteen years elapse between separate editions.[38] It was largely through this book that, in spite of Kantian philosophy, utopian republicanism, and the blooming of romanticism, Americans still took the first part of Samuel Johnson's famous epigram so seriously: "All theory is against the freedom of the will; all experience for it."[39] Henry Philip Tappan, sometime president of the University of Michigan, and author of the most extensive attack on Edwards's view of the will during the century, testified to the stature of this book in the introduction to his refutation:

> There is no work of higher authority among those who deny the self-determining power of the will; and none which on this subject has called forth more general admiration or acuteness of thought and logical subtlety. I believe there is a prevailing impression that Edwards must be fairly met in order to make any advance in an opposite argument.[40]

Arrayed against *Freedom of the Will* were at least twenty-nine serious nineteenth-century refutations.[41]

Tappan's effort was atypical in its judicious tone and its length, but not in its argument. In the first of three volumes Tappan exposed Edwards's logical fallacies, especially confusion over the nature of causation. He also demonstrated the inevitable drift of Edwards's theory to pantheism or atheism. The second volume undertook an elaborate discussion of consciousness, which provided the same kind of "knowledge of the phenomena of mind" as "of the phenomena of body." The deliverances of consciousness, so defined, demonstrated for Tappan the self-determining power of the will.[42] His third volume concluded the refutation by arguing for a tripartite division of the inner self into Will, Intellect, and Sensitivity. Tappan's faculty psychology was a typical device in the nineteenth century for attacking Edwards, for it allowed a separation of volitions from other actions and states. Needless to say, it was consciousness that revealed the presence of the faculties.

Nineteenth-century attacks on *Freedom of the Will* occasionally showed flashes of psychological wisdom. Rarely, however, did they penetrate to the levels of human insight or to the careful sifting of ordinary language which marked Edwards's treatise.[43] This is a judgment as applicable to Horace Bushnell, who opposed Edwards's "tricks of argument" with "the truth" of "consciousness," as to Charles Finney and Asa Mahan, whose works on the will carefully described the moral character of action but dismissed Edwards out of hand.[44]

The persistence of Edwards's nineteenth-century opponents in responding to his major works testified once again to his prominence in the theological arena. A consensus seemed to be growing, however, that reason, Scripture, and consciousness had finally dealt with Edwards, especially his arguments in *Freedom of the Will*. Yet whether because of doubts about these modern certainties, uneasiness about the security of their refutations, or respect for

Edwards himself, theologians until the last third of the century could not leave him alone.

The Fruitful Use of Edwards

Despite the chorus of dissent from his views, Edwards did not lack for defenders, proponents, and admirers throughout the nineteenth century. Besides those in the larger Calvinist family who contended with each other for the Edwardsian bequest, a number of others expressed admiration for his work. And Edwards still enjoyed a number of capable advocates. Jeremiah Day, president of Yale College during N. W. Taylor's tenure as professor of theology, authored two of the century's most perceptive defenses of Edwards on the will. Yet the comment of a favorable reviewer speaks as well for almost all of these productions. Day's work was a worthy effort, but it was "indispensible" only to those who did not have the patience to work through Edwards themselves.[45]

During the nineteenth century there were fewer successors to Edwards than admirers or proponents. If this is a tenable distinction, the category "successor" would include those who knew Edwards's work, respected it, and drew some inspiration from it. It would exclude those who used Edwards primarily for polemical purposes. And it would feature those who attempted to do theologically in their century what Edwards had done in his—that is, to exploit contemporary philosophy and sensibility on behalf of the traditional faith. Guardians of Edwards usually preserved either his creed, his piety, or his intellectual creativity. Successors attempted to preserve creed, piety, and creativity together.

In the United States, the New School Presbyterian Henry Boynton Smith (1815–77), longtime professor at Union Seminary in New York, came closest to being a successor of Edwards.[46] A mediator by temperament and conviction, Smith did not fear to draw resources from the Edwardsian tradition, from Old School Calvinism, and from nineteenth-century Europe. Yet his theology was consistently conservative. Smith had almost as much difficulty with N. W. Taylor's New Haven views as did Princeton. Theologically he differed from his American contemporaries by placing unusual stress on the person and work of Christ as the heart of the theology. Princeton, by contrast, regularly moved from authority—whether creedal or scriptural—and New England from consciousness, to Christ.

It would take us too far afield to examine the results of Smith's efforts to construct a theology with both Edwards's commitment to modern learning and his fidelity to historic Calvinism. But it is significant that in the programmatic exposition of his method, "The Relations of Faith and Philosophy," Smith singled out Edwards as one who saw "the necessity of bringing the subtlest researches of human reason into harmony with the truths which lie at the basis of all piety. . . . Intellect and faith acted together in him, distinct, yet as consentaneous as are the principle of life and the organic structure of our animal economy."[47] In his theology, Smith followed where Edwards had led. Neither philosophy without faith (which was Smith's harsh assessment of New Haven) nor faith without philosophy (his milder criticism of Princeton) provided for the nineteenth century what Edwards had offered to his.[48]

In only one other value did a significant number of nineteenth-century theologians appropriate Edwards as Henry B. Smith did. This was in Scotland, where Edwards had been famous before his death and where he continued to be widely read into the twentieth century. Scottish interest in Edwards was no mystery. Scotland shared a common Calvinistic heritage rooted in the English Reformation. Both New England and Scotland were cultural provinces of London, yet both resisted British alternatives to the older Calvinism, whether Latitudinarian Anglicanism or Arminian Methodism, well into the nineteenth century. Scotland was the home of that variety of the Enlightenment which Americans domesticated for themselves, and regular cultural interchange went on throughout the eighteenth and nineteenth centuries.[49]

Edwards's own history was interwoven with Scotland as well. He appears to have given serious, if not prolonged, consideration to Scottish offers for clerical employment after his dismissal from Northampton. Edwards also enjoyed the epistolary friendship of several Scottish clergymen. And many Scots remembered that Edwards's *Humble Attempt to Promote Explicit Agreement and Visible Union of God's People, in Extraordinary Prayer, for the Revival of Religion and the Advancement of Christ's Kingdom on Earth* (1747) was a response to a memorial with the same goal from Scotland.[50]

To be sure, Edwards had his Scottish detractors as well, but these only echoed the negations to be heard in North America. Much more interesting were those who made use of Edwards for positive purposes. The two most conspicuous of these were Thomas Chalmers (1780–1847), Scotland's greatest divine during the first half of the nineteenth century, and John McLeod Campbell (1800–1872), its most creative nineteenth-century theologian. They were thinkers who shared a common respect for Edwards, made a common criticism of his works, and yet developed his insights in very different ways.

Edwards's impact on Thomas Chalmers was especially profound. Chalmers had been a young ministerial student, with a predilection for "Moderate" spirituality and a fondness for William Godwin, when he encountered Edwards's *Freedom of the Will* in 1796. The result was electric. As an elderly man Chalmers recalled that there was "no book of human composition which I more strenuously recommend than his Treatise on the Will—read by me forty-seven years ago, with a conviction that has never since faltered, and which has helped me more than any other uninspired book, to find my way through all that might otherwise have proved baffling and transcendental and mysterious in the peculiarities of Calvinism."[51] Edwards's lasting bequest to Chalmers was twofold: He gave Chalmers a sense of how God's omnipotence was manifest in every aspect of creation, and he greatly impressed Chalmers by embodying both intellectual acuity and spiritual fervor. Chalmers eagerly took up the phraseology of an American correspondent when he wrote in 1821 that Edwards was "perhaps, the most wondrous example, in modern times, of one who stood richly gifted both in natural and spiritual discernment."[52]

For all their respect, the Scottish theologians had a common criticism of Edwards. Chalmers expressed it indirectly when writing about his adolescent encounter with *Freedom of the Will*:

> I remember when a student of Divinity, and long ere I could relish evangelical sentiment, I spent nearly a twelve-month in a sort of mental elysium, and the one idea which ministered to my soul all its rapture was the magnificence of the Godhead, and the universal subordination of all things to the one great purpose for which He evolved and was supporting creation. I should like to be so inspired over again, but with such a view of the Deity as coalesced and was in harmony with the doctrine of the New Testament.[53]

This indirect criticism became more pointed in John McLeod Campbell. Campbell remains an important figure in the history of the Kirk because of a spectacular theological trial in 1831, which led to his being dismissed from the ministry, and because of the creativity of *The Nature of the Atonement* (1856), the book which summed up his heterodox views. A good part of Campbell's *Atonement* carries on a dialogue with Edwards, particularly in an effort to render Edwards's conception of Christ's redeeming work more human.[54] Built into Campbell's constructive theology, therefore, is an answer to the criticisms raised by Chalmers.

These two Scottish theologians were not descendents of Edwards, like the New Englanders, nor were they his advocates, like the Princetonians. They were rather those who attempted more generally for theology in their age what Edwards had desired in his. They esteemed the Calvinist heritage and wished to preserve it as more than a merely spiritual legacy. Yet they wanted also to respond to the world in which they lived with proper appreciation of the insights which could improve their Calvinism.

For Chalmers this meant adjusting the Scottish Realism of the eighteenth century to the demands of religious experience, leavening his natural theology with a sense of the limits of apologetics, and urging the Kirk to respond to the altered social conditions of early industrial Scotland. Chalmers, himself an able mathematician, was the leader in his day of practical godliness. He sought a faith which could be at home in the furthest reaches of contemporary science. He sought a theology with room for careful reason and unbounded response to grace. And he looked for a church which could use its resources to relieve practical suffering. When these aspirations failed in the established church, Chalmers became the leader of the famous Disruption of 1837 which created the Free Church of Scotland.[55]

For Campbell, following Edwards's course meant exchanging the older views of a legal, penal atonement for an ethical, subjective one. Campbell's theology arose from a practical need. Several of his most faithful parishioners felt trapped by the fear that they were not of the elect, and others seemed to pursue good works only in order to win safety for themselves. In response, Campbell began to reassess the nature of Jesus' death for sinners. Was it true, as the Kirk held, that Christ died only for the elect? Did his death not rather suggest the possible reconciliation between God and all humanity? Was it not possible to think of Christ's sacrifice as a kind of supererogation of suffering which opened the way to God? In working out his positive answer to these questions, Campbell made specific use of a suggestion Edwards had raised in a treatise on *The Necessity and Reasonableness of the Christian Doctrine of Satisfaction for Sin* (published with the collected works in the nineteenth century). There Edwards suggested that for the greatness of evil "either an equivalent punishment or an equivalent sorrow and repentance" must exist. Although Edwards had not considered the second possibility, Campbell took it seriously and argued that the atonement is best explained by the infinite nature of Jesus' sorrow for sin. This solution pushed Edwards's Calvinism out of its own orbit, away from an objective to a subjective view of the atonement. And it certainly took the enormity of sin less seriously than had Edwards. Yet Campbell still manifested a remarkably fruitful effort to put Edwards to use in a situation where the problem was not, as for Edwards, waking the unconcerned to their spiritual need, but assuring the faithful of the certainty of God's love.[56]

Whether Chalmers and Campbell were as successful as Edwards in their theological efforts is not at issue here. What is clear is that these Scottish theologians had read Edwards with profit. They, along with H. B. Smith, did not try to duplicate his work or to dignify their innovations by associating them with his name. They rather drew together piety, learning, and doctrine to make the effort Edwards had made, which was to give each of these elements its proper attention in an integrated exposition of theology. They were, in this sense, Edwards's most faithful disciples in the nineteenth century.

The Irrelevance of Edwards as Theologian

While published commentary on Edwards continued to build throughout the nineteenth century, specifically theological interaction declined dramatically after the Civil War. Publication of Edwards's works also faltered at mid-century before falling off rapidly toward the end of the period. In the first quarter of the twentieth century, fewer editions of his works combined were published than the number of editions of *Freedom of the Will* alone which had appeared in New York by itself during the third quarter of the nineteenth century. Theological commentary followed a similar curve. Fewer theologians felt it necessary to refute Edwards; the first major effort of this sort was published in 1890. No serious defense of Edwards appeared after 1865. Periodicals and books teemed with genealogical, filiopietistic, antiquarian, historical, and even literary and philosophical assessments. But as a theologian, Edwards was becoming irrelevant.[57]

The reasons for Edwards's theological eclipse at the end of the nineteenth century are patent. Edwards lived in a world which assumed the existence of God pretty much as defined by the Protestant reformers, which assumed that the Bible could provide authoritative teaching for all, which assumed that theological discussion deserved a prominent place in the culture, and which assumed that sophisticated intellectual labors were compatible with piety. Some of these assumptions weakened in the hundred years after Edwards's death. But they still were close to the center of American civilization. None of them, however, survived in intellectual circles at the end of the nineteenth century. In spite of Edwards's efforts, which had helped keep alive the agenda of that earlier world, his questions were no longer those of America's dominant intellectuals.

This did not mean that the cultural arbiters had lost their respect for Edwards. Some very learned people even held to a Calvinism similar to his. Yet even for these ones Edwards had become a fossil.

A trio of works published in 1908 encapsulates the situation. The Congregational church historian, Williston Walker, lauded Edwards in his volume *Great Men of the Christian Church* as "the ablest theologian and most powerful thinker that colonial New England ever produced." To Walker, however, Edwards's significance lay mostly in his inspiration for the modern missionary movement.[58] The country's first historian of American philosophy, I. Woodbridge Riley, claimed to find "the real Jonathan Edwards" not in the "sulphurous" Calvinist, but in a "philosopher of feelings, a fervent exponent of the dialect of the heart." By making this distinction Riley continued a tradition that extended back at least thirty years to the time when Moses Coit Tyler, in his *History of American Literature*, had distinguished between the enduring Edwards of artistic imagery, who missed his true calling by becoming a minister, and the constricted Puritan thinker.[59] The third assessment came from the modernist theologian, George A. Gordon, who defined Edwards's place in "The Collapse of the New England Theology." Gordon was full of praise for Edwards's intellect, "a mind of singular openness and of unceasing movement." Yet in very short compass he wrote off the lasting significance of the New England Theology—Hopkins, Dwight, Taylor, and Park, as well as Edwards—because of its immature views on Scripture, human freedom, divine morality, world religions, and proper humanism.[60] The one thing which bound these disparate assessments together was the absence of serious theological interaction. All treated Edwards as a major figure. None paid attention to his theology.

This disposition prevailed widely at the turn of the century. A conservative like Princeton Seminary's B. B. Warfield could still praise Edwards for his unremitting labors in defense of a system that was "simply Calvinism." He could speak much as Hodge and Atwater had a generation before of Edwards's substantial identity with "the doctrines of the Calvinistic schoolmen" and use that judgement to trace the defalcations which followed in New England.[61] But Warfield, who was busy defending conservative theology against modern enemies, appears to have made no use of Edwards's ideas as such. Edwards was an honored figure in Calvinist history, but no longer a resource.

By the end of the century Edwards had become the subject of doctoral dissertations and articles in professional journals. The bicentennial of his birth in 1903 was the occasion of a raft of publications. Historians, like Frank Hugh Foster in his still useful *Genetic History of the New England Theology*, were able to put Edwards into a chronological framework. But the vast majority of those who paid attention to Edwards treated him as a person without a word for the present, or translated his contribution into terms which Edwards would not have understood. One of the best late-century studies of Edwards, the life by the romantic Episcopalian A. V. G. Allen, exemplified and furthered this trend. To Allen, Edwards was important precisely in spite of his theology:

> The divine revelation, as it came through him as its vehicle, was associated with much that was untrue. If we can make allowance for the human equation in his teaching, for the reasoning which however solid or true was based upon false premises, if we can look at the negative side of his theology as the local and transitory element of his time, there will then remain an imperishable element which points to the reality of the divine existence, and of the relevation of God to the world, as no external evidence can do. Indeed, it is only by exposing what was false or distorted in his theology that the real man stands forth in the grandeur of his proportions.[62]

By the end of the century, critics in a salvage operation had begun to track the path from Edwards to Emerson.[63] On this journey there was no room for his theology.

Edwards and Nineteenth-Century Theology

"The marvel," as Henry May once put it, "is that [Edwards] affected American culture as deeply as he did."[64] There are no immediately obvious reasons why Edwards's theology should survive through the nineteenth century. Thomas Chalmers and Henry B. Smith may have moved in directions similar to Edwards's. Theologians like the Princetonians may have preserved the letter of his major convictions. And the more adverturesome New Englanders certainly aspired to Edwards's metaphysical accomplishments. Yet the tide everywhere in the century was running the other way. Where Edwards preserved intellectual unity, the nineteenth-century mind was falling in two. Where Edwards distrusted the self, the self became the originator of truth in the century after his death. And where Edwards tightly circumscribed the deliverances of the unregenerate consciousness, the nineteenth century made universal consciousness the one unquestioned oracle.

Edwards's thought was always in pursuit of unity. In the most famous instances, as H. B. Smith saw clearly, Edwards gave himself to "the reconciliation of divine sovereignty with the consciousness of freedom [*Freedom of the Will*] . . . [and] the radical identity of virtue and religion [*The Nature of True Virtue*]."[65] Already in Edwards's own day, however, American thought was dividing against itself. On the one hand, Americans became the champions of freedom and self-determination. On the other, they pursued the certainties of law, whether Baconian and positivistic or organic and romantic. Henry Philip Tappan, Edwards's most persistent nineteenth-century opponent, illustrates this later bifurcation. Although Tappan devoted three volumes to disposing of *Freedom of the Will*, yet when he became president of the University of Michigan in 1852, he imported a Prussian model of education which aimed at the discovery of predictable necessities for the moral and physical worlds alike.[66] At the end of the century, precisely when American intellectuals were swarming to discover the necessary regularities of the new social sciences, A. V. G. Allen interpreted Edwards's "denial of the freedom of the human will" as an "awful conception of humanity and its destiny."[67] The difference was that Edwards's determinism and his freedom were unified as functions of his theism, while the determinism of the nineteenth century was a function of nature and its freedom a function of the transcendental self. Edwards may not have succeeded in his effort to gather the entire universe under God's majesty. But his consistent efforts in that direction set him apart from the intellectual polarities which followed.

Again, Edwards lived before it grew fashionable to bestow great trust upon the self, yet in the nineteenth century no principle was more firmly in place. The myths of the American Revolution pointed in this direction, the deliverances of Scottish moral philosophy took it for granted, the newer Kantianism agreed, and prominent varieties of piety—whether Schleiermacher's reliance upon a sense of dependence or Wesley's upon experience—began at the same place. The Great Awakening had taught Edwards to distrust the self's deliverances, to beware the great capacity for self-delusion.[68] In the nineteenth century this caution was overridden. In its place came the conviction that the self was where the journey to knowledge and spiritual fulfillment began.

This attitude toward the self underlay the overwhelming confidence in the revelatory character of consciousness. Over and over in the nineteenth century, the attack on Edwards returned to his inadequacy with respect to modern sensitivities. His system, to cite just one of the many expressions of this complaint, was simply "contrary to the common consciousness and experiences of mankind."[69] No one expressed this opinion with greater force than Oliver Wendell Holmes, a Unitarian who also spoke for those more theologically conservative than himself. In an essay from 1880, Holmes praised Edwards's character and logical abilities. But he had no sympathy for Edwards's ideas. Edwards did not really belong to the civilized history of New England. "His whole system," rather, "had too much of the character of the savage people by whom the wilderness had recently been tenanted." It belonged more to Scotland or New Jersey, "where the Scotch theological thistle has always flourished." The reasons for his disapproval had everything to do with consciousness, with genteel perceptions of the world:

> Edwards's system seems, in the light of to-day, to the last degree barbaric, mechanical, materialist, pessimistic. If he had lived a hundred years later, and breathed the air of freedom, he could not have written with such old-world barbarism. . . . The truth is that [his] whole system of beliefs . . . is gently fading out of enlightened human intelligence.[70]

Edwards's assessment of consciousness had been much more complicated. He learned a great deal from Locke, Hutcheson, and other theoreticians of the mind. But his fundamental difference from those who followed was that he restricted himself, in D. H. Meyer's phrase, to using "the language of morality . . . the language of Lockean psychology" in order "to reestablish the truths of faith."[71] In the nineteenth century it became much more common to use the substance of moral sentiment to recast the truths of faith. In whatever form it took—simplistic Baconianism, sophisticated Scottish ethics, or the new romantic idealism—the nineteenth-century appeal to consciousness left Edwards far behind. The difference between Edwards and the nineteenth century on this score fully justifies the recent arguments of Norman Fiering, David Laurence, and Harold Simonson concerning the immense distance which separated Edwards's perceptions from the common sensical, the Emersonian, and the romantic conceptions that followed.[72]

All this having been said, the question does not go away. How was it that Edwards remained so important throughout the nineteenth century? How did it come about that he continued as a full partner in the theological enterprise for more than a century after his death?

To these questions there are historical answers. In spite of their uneasiness about his ethics and his metaphysics, the handful of Americans predisposed toward Calvinism found Edwards's majestic vision of divine sovereignty irreplacable. In spite of his determinism, the much larger number of American Protestants recognized that his theology reflected a depth of piety which demanded attention. And in spite of the whole overlay of theology, numerous intellectuals still realized that Edwards's profundity of thought required at least some account.

Yet it may not be inappropriate, in conclusion, to suggest the sort of theological reasons with which Edwards himself may have felt more at home. In this view, Edwards survived not because he anticipated the norms of nineteenth-century intellectual discourse, but because he was their foil.

Perry Miller once again provides a key. His essay, "From Edwards to Emerson," with its unbalanced, if evocative account of intellectual descent from the Northampton minister to the Concord sage, may have put later scholars off the track of Edwards's fundamental significance. His book on Edwards may be full of mistaken philosophical judgments. But Miller still could put his finger on reasons for Edwards's survival by recognizing that "there come periods, either through disaster or self-knowledge, when applied science and Benjamin Franklin's *The Way to Wealth*" are not enough.[73] Since Edwards wrote for such situations, and since they have been, in fact, the general fate of humanity through the ages, and the special lot of even intellectuals in the twentieth century, our culture could not be rid of him.

Edwards greatly influenced the first part of the nineteenth century, in spite of the axioms which governed theological discourse in that period. He possessed enough staying power to survive the last part of the century, when theologians were convinced that the world really had become a better place. And so in the twentieth century he could be resurrected when holocausts and meaninglessness once more intruded into the common consciousness. The final reason may well be that while others preached self-reliance or sang the song of the self, Edwards drove nearer the truth—that nothing can be saved without confronting its own damnation, that freedom is found within necessity, that the way to gain one's life is to lose it.

Notes

[1] For an excellent overview of reactions to Edwards during the nineteenth century, see M. X. Lesser, *Jonathan Edwards: A Reference Guide* (Boston, 1981). Further references to this work are noted by year and enumerated title for that year, e.g., Lesser 1845.1. All information concerning the publication of Edwards's works is from Thomas H. Johnson, *The Printed Writings of Jonathan Edwards, 1703–58: A Bibliography* (Princeton, 1940).

[2] Henry May, *The Enlightenment in America* (New York, 1976), and *The End of American Innocence: A Study of the First Years of Our Own Time, 1912–17* (New York, 1959), nicely define the beginning and end of this cultural entity.

[3] The value of Lesser's guide (full citation in note 1) is enhanced by a fine introductory essay tracing reactions to Edwards since the publication of his first works. Other valuable introductions include Daniel B. Shea, "Jonathan Edwards: The First Two Hundred Years," *Journal of American Studies* 14 (1980), 181–97; Nancy Manspeaker, *Jonathan Edwards: Bibliographical Synopses* (New York, 1981); and Donald Louis Weber, "The Image of Jonathan Edwards in American Culture" (Ph.D. dissertation, Columbia University, 1978).

[4] S. C. Aiken to Lyman Beecher, Apr. 20, 1827, in *The Autobiography of Lyman Beecher*, ed. Barbara M. Cross (Cambridge, Mass. 1961), II, 67.

[5] Charles G. Finney, *Lectures on Revivals of Religion*, 2nd ed. (New York, 1835), 241–42.

[6] *Letters of the Rev. Dr. Beecher and Rev. Mr. Nettleton, on the "New Measures" in Conducting Revivals of Religion* (New York, 1828), 14, 20, 29. Samuel Miller to W. B. Sprague, Mar. 8, 1832, in Sprague, *Lectures on Revivals of Religion* (London, 1959; orig. 1832), 24–25, 28–30, 41–42 of separately numbered Appendix. Similar comments from Miller are also found in his biography, *Life of Jonathan Edwards*, in *The Library of American Biography*, ed. Jared Sparks (New York, 1849; orig. 1837), 193.

[7] Albert Dod, "Finney's Lectures," *Princeton Review* 7 (Oct. 1835), 657–58.

[8] In 1840, Andover had 153 students and 5 faculty, Yale 72 students and 4 faculty, Princeton 110 students and 4 faculty. The only other seminaries of comparable size were the New School Presbyterian Seminary in New York (90 students, 5 faculty) and the General Theological Seminary of the Episcopal Church, also in New York (74 students, 5 faculty); figures from Robert Baird, *Religion in the United States of America* (New York, 1969; orig. 1844), 368–69. Bruce Kuklick's *Churchmen and Philosophers: From Jonathan Edwards to John Dewey* (New Haven, 1985), redresses neglect by treating the theological discussions at mid-century as serious intellectual endeavors. Basic information on these figures may be found in Sidney Earl Mead, *Nathaniel William Taylor 1786–1858: A Connecticut Liberal* (Chicago, 1942); Anthony C. Cecil, Jr., *The Theological Development of Edwards Amasa Park: Last of the "Consistent Calvinists"* (Missoula, Mont., 1974); and Archibald A. Hodge, *The Life of Charles Hodge* (New York, 1969; orig. 1881).

[9] Various aspects of this disengagement are treated in George M. Marsden, *The Evangelical Mind and the New School Presbyterian Experience: A Case Study of Thought and Theology in Nineteenth-Century America* (New Haven, 1970), 7–87; Sydney E. Ahlstrom, *A Religious History of the American People* (New Haven 1972), 456–69; and Fred J. Hood, *Reformed America: The Middle and Southern States, 1783–1837* (University of Alabama, 1980), 178–85.

[10] Timothy Dwight, "The Triumph of Infidelity" (1788), in *The Connecticut Wits*, ed. Vernon Louis Parrington (New York, 1969), 260.

[11] Frank Hugh Foster, *A Genetic History of the New England Theology* (New York, 1962; orig. 1907), 369.

[12] See, for example, Miller, *Life of Edwards*, 118–19.

[13] Miller, *Life of Edwards* (1837); J. W. Alexander and A. B. Dod, "Transcendentalism," *Princeton Review* 11 (Jan. 1839), 38–43; Charles Hodge, *The Constitutional History of the Presbyterian Church in the United States of America* (Philadelphia, 1851; orig. 1840), II, 39–101; Anonymous, "The Law of Human Progress," *Princeton Review* 18 (Jan. 1846), 26; Anonymous, "Short Notices," *Princeton Review*, 27 (Oct. 1855), 701–2.

[14] Miller, *Life of Edwards*, 245; Lyman Atwater, "The Power of Contrary Choice," *Princeton Review* 12 (Oct. 1840), 549.

[15] For debate over free will, see Atwater, "The Power of Contrary Choice," *Princeton Review* 12 (Oct. 1840), 532–49; Atwater, "Dr. Edwards's Works," *Princeton Review* 15 (Jan. 1843), 57, 64; Atwater, "Modern Explanations of the Doctrine of Inability," *Princeton Review* 26 (Apr. 1854), 236–46; and Atwater, "Whedon and Hazard on the Will," *Princeton Review* 36 (Oct. 1864), 679–703. Congregationalist responses are found in Edward Beecher, "The Works of Samuel Hopkins," *Bibliotheca Sacra* 10 (Jan. 1853), 76–80; and Edwards Amasa Park, "New England Theology," *Bibliotheca Sacra* 9 (Jan. 1852), 170–220.

[16] Princeton misreadings of *The Nature of True Virtue* are found in Miller, *Life of Edwards*, 241–44; Archibald Alexander, *Outlines of Moral Science* (New York, 1852); Atwater, "Outlines of Moral Science by Archibald Alexander," *Princeton Review* 25 (Jan. 1853), 19–23; and Hodge, *Systematic Theology* (Grand Rapids, Mich., 1979; orig. 1872–73), I, 432–34. Convincing replies came from Beecher, "The Works of Samuel Hopkins," *Bibliotheca Sacra* 10 (Jan. 1853), 77–78; Anonymous, "Dr. Alexander's Moral Science," *Bibliotheca Sacra* 10 (Apr. 1853), 390–414; and Anonymous, "President Edwards's Dissertation on the Nature of True Virtue," *Bibliotheca Sacra* 10 (Oct. 1853), 705–38.

[17] Hodge, "Professor Park and the Princeton Review," *Princeton Review* 23 (Oct. 1851), as

reprinted in *Essays and Reviews* (New York, 1857), 631-32.

[18] Park, "New England Theology," *Bibliotheca Sacra* 9 (Jan. 1852), 174–75.

[19] One Episcopalian reviewer, for example, passed off Park's entire effort as simply a modern manifestation of Pelagianism. Anonymous, "New England Theology," *Church Review* 5 (Oct. 1852), 352. A Congregationalist, Parsons Cooke, had this conclusion about Park's reading of theological history: "We have rarely met with an instance, in which so distinguished an author as Edwards has met with so much injustice at the hand of a commentator." Cooke, "Edwards on the Atonement," *American Theological Review* 11 (Feb. 1860), 118. A review more favorable to Park is R. P. S., "The Andover and Princeton Theologies," *Christian Examiner and Religious Miscellany* 52 (May 1852), 309–35.

[20] Park, "New England Theology," 191–92. Foster, *Genetic History*, 472–76, puts Park's reliance upon Common Sense moral philosophy into broader context.

[21] A representative statement of Park's argument is in "New England Theology," 196–97.

[22] Atwater, "Jonathan Edwards and the Successive Forms of New Divinity," *Princeton Review* 30 (Oct. 1858), 589. "Stapfer's scheme" refers to Edwards's belief that all humanity sinned in Adam at the Fall; see *The Works of Jonathan Edwards: Original Sin*, ed. Clyde A. Holbrook (New Haven, 1970), 392n.

[23] Atwater, "Jonathan Edwards," 602, 613. On the emergence of a more utilitarian ethic and a governmental theory of the atonement in Jonathan Edwards's son, see Robert L. Ferm, *Jonathan Edwards the Younger 1745–1801* (Grand Rapids, Mich., 1976), 114–33.

[24] Atwater, "Jonathan Edwards,," 617.

[25] Noah Porter, "The Princeton Review on Dr. Taylor and the Edwardean Theology," *New Englander* 18 (Aug. 1860), 726–73.

[26] Ibid., 731–32, 737, 739.

[27] Ibid., 744.

[28] Ibid., 770–71, 743, 744, 772.

[29] The last exchange again involved strife over N. W. Taylor. See Charles Hodge, "Presbyterian Reunion," *Princeton Review* 40 (Jan. 1868), 52–83; George Park Fisher, "The Princeton Review on the Theology of Dr. N. W. Taylor," *New Englander* 27 (Apr. 1868), 284–348; Fisher, "The Augustinian and the Federal Theories of Original Sin Compared," *New Englander* 27 (June 1868), 468–516, with reference to Edwards on 507; Timothy Dwight, "Princeton Exegesis: A Review of Dr. Hodge's Commentary on Romans V. 12–19," *New Englander* 27 (July 1868), 551–603; Lyman Atwater, "Professor Fisher on the Princeton Review and Dr. Taylor's Theology," *Princeton Review* 40 (July 1868), 368–97; and Fisher, "Dr. N. W. Taylor's Theology: A Rejoinder to the Princeton Review," *New Englander* 27 (Oct. 1868), 740–63.

[30] A late statement of this position is Atwater, "The Great Awakening of 1740," *Presbyterian Quarterly and Princeton Review* 5 (Oct. 1876), 685–89.

[31] For late statements, see Park, "Jonathan Edwards," in *Cyclopedia of Biblical, Theological, and Ecclesiastical Literature*, ed. John McClintock and James Strong (New York, 1882; orig. 1870), III, 63–67; and Noah Porter, "Philosophy in Great Britain and America," Appendix I in *History of Philosophy from Thales to the Present Time*, by Friedrich Ueberweg (New York, 1874), II, 443–48, Lesser 1874.3.

[32] I have developed at greater length the discussion in this paragraph and reviewed some of the important literature on this subject in "Common Sense Traditions and American Evangelical Thought," *American Quarterly* 37 (Summer 1985), 216–38.

[33] On McCosh's fondness for Edwards, which did not, however, make him a complete disciple, see J. David Hoeveler, Jr., *James McCosh and the Scottish Intellectual Tradition: From Glasgow to Princeton* (Princeton, 1981), 53–54.

[34] Samuel Hopkins, "The Life and Character of the Late Reverend Mr. Jonathan Edwards," in *Jonathan Edwards: A Profile*, ed. David Levin (New York, 1969), 41.

[35] Charles Chauncy, *Five Dissertations on the Scripture Account of the Fall; and its Consequences* (London, 1785), 191–99, 260–64, Lesser 1785.1. Lewis French Stearns, *The Evidence of Christian Experience* (New York, 1890), 84–87 and passim, Lesser 1890.10.

[36] Perry Miller, "General Editor's Note," *The Works of Jonathan Edwards: Freedom of the Will*, ed. Paul Ramsey (New Haven, 1957), vii.

[37] Fisher, "The Philosophy of Jonathan Edwards," *North American Review*, 128 (1879), 300; Albert Taylor Bledsoe, *An Examination of President Edwards's Inquiry into the Freedom of the Will* (Philadelphia, 1845), Lesser 1845.2.

[38] Publication data are from Johnson, *Printed Works of Edwards.*

[39] James Boswell, *The Life of Samuel Johnson*, Library of English Classics (London, 1922), II, 464.

[40] Henry Philip Tappan, *A Review of Edwards's "Inquiry into the Freedom of the Will* (New York, 1839), xi.

[41] See Lesser, *Jonathan Edwards.*

[42] Tappan, *The Doctrine of the Will, Determined by An Appeal to Consciousness* (New York, 1840), 8. The third book was *The Doctrine of the Will, Applied to Moral Agency and Responsibility* (New York, 1841).

[43] This judgment is based on a rapid perusal of a handful of nineteenth-century works and on the extracts in Lesser, *Jonathan Edwards*, and Manspeaker, *Jonathan Edwards*. See Paul Ramsey, "Introduction," in *Freedom of Will*, 10 n. 3, for a better-informed judgment which comes to roughly the same conclusion.

[44] Horace Bushnell, *Nature and the Supernatural* . . . (New York, 1858), 48, 49; Charles Grandison Finney, *Lectures on Systematic Theology*, ed. J. H. Fairchild (New York, n.d.; orig. 1878), 323; Asa Mahan, *Doctrine of the Will* (New York, 1845), 10.

[45] Anonymous, "A Review of *An Examination of President Edwards's Inquiry on the Freedom of Will*, by Jeremiah Day," *American Biblical Repository*, 2nd ser., 5 (Apr. 1841), 500–4, Lesser 1841.1. The two works by Day are described in Lesser under 1838.1 and 1841.3.

[46] On Smith, see Marsden, *Evangelical Mind and New School Presbyterian Experience*, 157–81; and Richard A. Muller, "Henry Boynton Smith: Christocentric Theologian," *Journal of Presbyterian History*, 61 (Winter 1983), 429–44.

[47] Smith, *Faith and Philosophy: Discourses and Essays* (Edinburgh, 1878), 59–61, 90.

[48] This formulation of Smith's concerns is from Marsden, *Evangelical Mind and New School Presbyterian Experience*, 163.

[49] On the status of America and Scotland in relation to London, see John Clive and Bernard Bailyn, "England's Cultural Provinces: Scotland and America," *William and Mary Quarterly*, 3rd ser., 11 (1954), 200–13. The nature of cultural exchange is nicely illustrated by L. H. Butterfield, *John Witherspoon Comes to America* (Princeton, 1953).

[50] On Edwards's extensive correspondence with one notable Scottish divine, see Henry Moncrieff Wellwood, *Account of the Life and Writings of John Erskine* (Edinburgh, 1818), 196–225; and on Edwards's brief contemplation of a Scottish pastorate, ibid., 514–15.

[51] Chalmers to William B. Sprague, *Annals of the American Pulpit* (New York, 1854), I, 334.

[52] Chalmers, *The Christian and Civic Economy of Large Towns* (Glasgow, 1821), I, 318. Chalmers here paraphrases what an American correspondent had written concerning Edwards only shortly before: Henry Hollock (from Savannah) to Chalmers, Sept. 11, 1818, in Thomas Chalmers Papers, New College, University of Edinburgh. (This reference is courtesy of Professor Robert Calhoon of the University of North Carolina at Greensboro.) For a full account of Chalmers's intellectual and social efforts, see Stewart J. Brown, *Thomas Chalmers and the Godly Commonwealth in Scotland* (London, 1982), with specific reference to the influence of Edwards, 14–15.

[53] Quoted in William Hanna, *Memoirs of the Life and Writings of Thomas Chalmers* (Edinburgh, 1851), I, 17.

[54] John McLeod Campbell, *The Nature of the Atonement and Its Relation to Remission of Sins and Eternal Life* (London, 1959; orig. 1856), 51–75. A helpful recent treatment of this work is Brian Gerrish, in *Tradition and the Modern World: Reformed Theology in the Nineteenth Century* (Chicago, 1978), 71–97. For general context, see J. H. S. Burleigh, *A Church History of Scotland* (London, 1960), 331–32.

[55] See Burleigh, *Church History of Scotland*, 313ff.; Brown, *Thomas Chalmers and the Godly Commonwealth*; and for theological assessment, two essays by Daniel F. Rice, "Natural Theology and the Scottish Philosophy in the Thought of Thomas Chalmers," *Scottish Journal of Theology* 24 (Feb. 1971), 23–46, and "An Attempt at Systematic Reconstruction in the Theology of Thomas Chalmers," *Church History* 48 (June 1979), 174–88.

[56] Campbell, *The Nature of the Atonement*, 137. I am indebted to Professor David Wells of Gordon-Conwell Theological Seminary for helpful explanation of Campbell's theology.

[57] See Lesser, *Jonathan Edwards*, and Johnson, *Printed Works of Edwards*, there were only 18 reprintings of Edwards's major works in the period 1876–1925 (compare 76 for 1826–75), while the number of secondary works on Edwards totaled 372 in the period 1876–1925 (compare 232 for 1826–75).

[58] Williston Walker, *Great Men of the Christian Church* (Chicago, 1908), 339–53, Lesser 1908.3.

[59] I. Woodbridge Riley, "The Real Jonathan Edwards," *Open Court* 22 (Dec. 1908), 705–15, Lesser 1908.2; and Moses Coit Tyler, *A History of American Literature* (New York, 1878), II, 177–92, Lesser 1878.7.

[60] George A. Gordon, *Humanism in New England Theology* (Boston, 1920), 12; this is an expanded version of "The Collapse of the New England Theology," *Harvard Theological Review*, 1 (Apr. 1908), 127–68, Lesser 1908.1.

[61] Warfield, "Edwards and the New England Theology," *Encyclopedia of Religion and Ethics*, ed. James Hastings (New York, 1912), V, 221–27; reprinted in *The Works of Benjamin B. Warfield* (Grand Rapids, Mich., 1981; orig. 1932), IX, 528, 531–38.

[62] Alexander V. G. Allen, *Jonathan Edwards* (New York, 1975; orig. 1889), 386–87.

[63] Allen, *Jonathan Edwards*, 68, where Allen cites Edwards's sermon *Divine and Supernatural Light* as proto-Emersonian. The first effort Lesser records to identify a link between Edwards and Emerson came in 1880 (Mrs. John T. Sargent, ed., *Sketches and Reminiscences of the Radical Club of Chestnut Street, Boston* [Boston, 1880], 362–75, Lesser 1880.9), sixty years before Perry Miller's famous essay, "From Edwards to Emerson," *New England Quarterly* 13 (Dec. 1940), 589–617.

[64] May, *The Enlightenment in America*, 50.

[65] Henry B. Smith, *Faith and Philosophy*, 16.

[66] See Charles M. Perry, *Henry Philip Tappan: Philosopher and University President* (Ann Arbor, Mich., 1933), 212–48; and Alan Creutz, "The Prussian System and Practical Training: The Educational Philosophies of the University of Michigan's First Two Presidents," *Michigan History* 65 (Jan./Feb. 1981), 32–39.

[67] Allen, *Jonathan Edwards*, 73.

[68] See Norman Fiering, *Jonathan Edwards's Moral Thought and Its British Context* (Chapel Hill, N.C., 1981), 174: "The deepest lesson he took from the Great Awakening may have been a renewed appreciation of the labyrinth of the human heart."

[69] George B. Cheever, "Review of Professor Tappan's Works on the Will," *American Biblical Repository*, 2nd ser., 7 (Apr. 1842), 422.

[70] Oliver Wendell Holmes, "Jonathan Edwards," in *Papers from an Old Volume of Life*, in *The Works of Oliver Wendell Holmes* (Boston, 1892; orig. 1880), VIII, 392, 394, 395, 398. Although he was a champion of free will, Holmes could not resist ascribing Edwards's theological views to his "ill-health," ibid., 396–98.

[71] Donald H. Meyer, *The Democratic Enlightenment* (New York, 1976), 28.

[72] Fiering, *Jonathan Edwards's Moral Thought*; David Laurence, "Moral Philosophy and New England Literary History: Reflections on Norman Fiering," *Early American Literature* 18 (Fall 1983), 187–214; and Harold P. Simonson, "Typology, Imagination, and Jonathan Edwards," in *Radical Discontinuities: American Romanticism and Christian Consciousness* (Rutherford, N.J., 1983), 19–43.

[73] Perry Miller, *Jonathan Edwards* (New York, 1949), xiii.

SYSTEMATIC THEOLOGY

David F. Wells, area editor

SYSTEMATIC THEOLOGY

DAVID F. WELLS
Andrew Mutch Professor of Historical and Systematic Theology
Gordon-Conwell Theological Seminary

Introduction

While I was poring over the essays written during this last year, I became aware of an argument that was going on in my own mind. On the one side were voices that insisted that essays should be chosen strictly on their technical merit. On the other side were those who claimed to know what would and would not "fly" in the evangelical world. It is not easy to find accord between those who were arguing because the two sides have been moving steadily apart in recent years. One side of the evangelical movement may write off what is technically excellent as "boring" or "irrelevant"; the other side of the evangelical world may dismiss what sells like hotcakes as "trivial" and "superficial." This chasm is now wide and deep, and few there are who know how to span it. I hope, however, that readers will be able to see in the selected essays that they possess both technical merit and contemporary relevance.

Christopher Lasch's essay is, as a matter of fact, an interloper since it appeared not in 1988 but in 1989. The reason for bending the rules and allowing for its including now, rather than waiting until next year, is that it is a contemporary analysis, and those are best read when the ink is still drying!

The theological task is many-sided, but few would dispute that its main task, at least within the evangelical world, is to bring the unchanging truth of God's Word into our changing contemporary world. Lasch's essay helps us in the last part of this journey. He writes poignantly of how his own outlook has changed over the last three decades and, in the process, provides us with cultural analysis that is trenchant. His argument is that the political (and sometimes religious) "Left" and "Right" now often sound similar because the "Right" has borrowed what used to be the centerpiece of the "Left's" vision of America, namely the hope in progress. This addiction to progress is diminishing our natural resources not to mention those of the human psyche. The reservoir of our spirituality is drained. The dream of progress and those allured by it are alike exhausted. Lasch offers us some new light on our current situation, and his essay is a model of the kind of reflection that we should be bringing to our world.

Vern Poythress's essay explores what he says is a typically Reformed interest: namely, the intrusion of sin into the process of understanding God's Word. This interest is, indeed, typically Reformed. Inasmuch, however, as sin intrudes not only into Reformed minds, but into all minds, it would be a happy day when his interest became a typically evangelical interest!

The significance of Poythress's study needs to be spelled out; some will automatically apply his thesis in its wider context, but others may not see this possibility as readily. The opinion has grown steadily in their scholarly guild over the last century that biblical interpretation is a "science," a technique that yields tamper-free conclusions as science is supposed to do. The interpreter is imagined to be a disinterested observer at the side of the biblical text, one who has no prior investment in the outcome of the investigation. He or she simply asks ruthless questions and then fearlessly follows the truth wherever it may lead! If a competitor can show that an interpreter was not as free of "bias" as the outward appearance indicated, then the exegetical conclusions immediately fall under the cloud of suspicion.

The philosophical naivety of those suppositions is quite remarkable. Indeed, while many biblical scholars, evangelicals among them, have been marching off in lock step in that direction, they have met numerous contemporary philosophers marching in exactly the opposite direction, but such is the degree of specialization in modern academia that few seem to have noticed what is happening.

The important point here is that everyone has presuppositions. Every interpreter brings with him or her a whole internal world made up of prior knowledge, experience, learning, perception—a personality shaped in a certain way, a particular culture with its own patterns of thought and assumptions and, what Poythress notes, sin. To think of the interpreter as a disinterested scientist in a white coat, bending over the biblical text, uninvolved in the outcome of the finding, is about as far from reality as one can be anthropologically, philosophically, and theologically.

One wonders whether evangelical interpreters in homes and churches are any more aware than those in the professional guild of how sin works through our culture and our minds to skew the reading of Scripture. One does not have to look far to find Scripture being used as a sanctuary for what is flagrantly wrong, or a justification for what, to anyone else, is obvious self-interest. Perhaps worse still, it is used simply as a trigger to release a flow of "feelings" about life that are considered more interesting than what Scripture itself actually says. No interpreter, whether in or out of the guild, should assume his or her immunity from sin in the process of interpreting but should, instead, be looking for Christ's redemption in it.

These essays are addressing matters vital to evangelical spirituality: how we read the Scriptures, how we live, and how we live in this particular world. In each of these spheres, we need to know the redemption that we have in Christ.

About the Area Editor

David F. Wells (B.D., London University, England; Th.M., Trinity Evangelical Divinity School; Ph.D., University of Manchester, England) is Andrew Mutch Professor of Historical and Systematic Theology at Gordon-Conwell Theological Seminary. Born in what is now Zimbabwe, he studied initially at the University of Cape Town, where he became a Christian. He is a member of the Lausanne Committee for World Evangelization and serves on its theology working group. He was general editor and co-author of *Eerdmans Handbook to Christianity in America* (1983) and *Reformed Theology in America: A History of Its Modern Development* (1985). His recent books include *God and Evangelist: The Role of the Holy Spirit in Bringing Men and Women to Faith* (1987) and *The Person of Christ: A Biblical and Historical Analysis of the Incarnation* (1984).

THE OBSOLESCENCE OF LEFT & RIGHT

CHRISTOPHER LASCH
Watson Professor of History
University of Rochester

Article from *New Oxford Review*

The unexpected resurgence of the political right, not only in the United States but throughout much of the Western world, has thrown the left into confusion and called into question all its old assumptions about the future: that the course of history favored the left; that the right would never recover from the defeats it suffered during the era of liberal and social democratic ascendancy; that some form of socialism, at the very least a more vigorous form of the welfare state, would soon replace free-market capitalism. Who would have predicted twenty-five years ago that, as the twentieth century approached its end, it would be the left that was everywhere in retreat?

But the characteristic mood of the times, a baffled sense of drift, is by no means confined to people on the left. The unanticipated success of the right has not restored moral order and collective purpose to Western nations, least of all to the U.S. The new right came to power with a mandate not just to free the market from bureaucratic interference but to halt the slide into apathy, hedonism, and moral chaos. It has not lived up to expectations. Spiritual disrepair, the perception of which furnished much of the popular animus against liberalism, is just as evident today as it was in the 1970s.

Conservative contributors to a recent symposium on the state of American conservatism report widespread "discouragement" with the accomplishments of the Reagan revolution, so called. Like liberals, conservatives suffer from "demoralization" and "malaise." According to George Panichas, the "crisis of modernity" remains unresolved by a "sham conservatism" that merely sanctions the unbridled pursuit of worldly success. Clyde Wilson writes that the "everyday virtues of honesty, loyalty, manners, work, and restraint" are more "attenuated" than ever. In the early 1960s it was still "possible to take for granted that the social fabric of the West ... was relatively intact." Under Reagan, however, it continued to unravel.

Ritual deference to "traditional values" cannot hide the right's commitment to progress, unlimited economic growth, and acquisitive individualism. Conservatives Paul Gottfried and Thomas Fleming point out that the goal of "unlimited material opportunity and social improvement" plays a much larger part in contemporary conservatism than a defense of tradition. "Skepticism about progress," once the hallmark of conservative intellectuals, has all but disappeared. "Political differences between right and left have by now been largely reduced to disagreements over policies designed to achieve comparable ... goals." The ideological distinctions between liberalism and conservatism have been increasingly obscure. The old categories no longer define the lines of political debate.

Limits: The Forbidden Topic

The uselessness of the old labels and the need for a reorientation of political ideas are now beginning to be acknowledged. A few years ago, in a book heralded as the manifesto of a resurgent liberalism, Paul Tsongas, then a senator from Massachusetts, called for liberals to become more conservative on economic issues and more radical on "social issues" like gay rights, feminism, and abortion. Bernard Avishai of MIT, writing in *Dissent*, replied that Tsongas "got it backward" and that the left needed to combine economic radicalism with cultural conservatism. Such statements testify to a growing awareness of the need to rethink conventional positions. They still owe too much, however, to the old terms of debate. We need to press the point more vigorously and to ask whether the left and right have not come to share so many of the same underlying convictions; including a belief in the desirability and inevitability of technical and economic development, that the conflict between them, shrill and acrimonious as it is, no longer speaks to the central issues of American politics.

A sign of the times: both left and right, with equal vehemence, repudiate the charge of "pessimism." Neither side has any use for "doomsayers." Neither wants to admit that our society has taken a wrong turn, lost its way, and needs to recover a sense of purpose and direction. Neither addresses the overriding issue of limits, so threatening to those who wish to appear optimistic at all times. The fact remains: The earth's finite resources will not support an indefinite expansion of industrial civilization. The right proposes, in effect, to maintain our rigorous standard of living, as it has been maintained in the past, at the expense of the rest of the world (increasingly at the expense of our own minorities as well). This program is self-defeating, not only because it will produce environmental effects from which even the rich cannot escape but because it will widen the gap between rich and poor nations, generate more and more violent movements of insurrection and terrorism against the West, and bring about a deterioration of the world's political climate as threatening as the deterioration of its physical climate.

But the historical program of the left has become equally self-defeating. The attempt to extend Western standards of living to the rest of the world will lead even more quickly to the exhaustion of nonrenewable resources, and irreversible pollution of the earth's atmosphere, and the destruction of the ecological system on which human life depends. "Let us imagine," writes

Rudolph Bahro, a leading spokesman for the West German Greens, "what it would mean if the raw material and energy consumption of our society were extended to the 4.5 billion people living today, or to the 10–15 billion there will probably be tomorrow. It is readily apparent that the planet can only support such volumes of production . . . for a short time to come."

These considerations refute conventional optimism (though the real despair lies in a refusal to confront them at all), and both the right and left therefore prefer to talk about something else—for example, to exchange accusations of fascism and socialism. But the ritual deployment of these familiar slogans, together with their rhetorical inflation, far beyond the point where they retain analytical value, merely provides one more indication of the emptiness of recent political debate. For the left, fascism now includes everything to the right of liberalism or social democracy, including such disparate configurations as the Ayatollah Khomeini's Iran, the opposition to the Sandinista regime in Nicaragua, and Reaganism itself. For the right, Communism (or "creeping socialism") embraces everything to the left of, and including, the New Deal. Not only have these terms lost their meaning through reckless expansion, but they no longer describe historical alternatives at the end of the twentieth century.

It ought to be clear by now that neither fascism nor socialism represents the wave of the future. The sorry history of "actually existing socialism" (i.e., Communism), the fiasco of the Cultural Revolution in China and the sharp reaction against it, the waning prestige of the Soviet Union, and the decline of socialist movements in the West indicate that socialism's moment has come and gone. As for fascism, it cannot be regarded as a generic configuration at all, and certainly not as the final stage of capitalist decay. Nor does the looser concept of totalitarianism provide an acceptable substitute. The history of the twentieth century suggests that totalitarian regimes are highly unstable, evolving toward some type of bureaucratic rule that fits neither the classic fascist nor the socialist model. None of this means that the future will be safe for democracy, only that the danger to democracy comes less from totalitarian or collectivist movements abroad than from the erosion of its psychological, cultural, and spiritual foundations from within.

The Making of a Malcontent

My own faith in the explanatory power of the old ideologies began to waver in the mid-1970s, when my study of the family led me to question the left's program of sexual liberation, careers for women, and professional child care. Until then I had always identified myself with the left. I grew up in the tradition of Midwestern progressivism, overlaid by the liberalism of the New Deal. I believed in the Tennessee Valley Authority, the CIO, and the United Nations. In the bitter debates about foreign policy that began to divide liberals in the late 1940s and 1950s, I sided with those who advocated continued efforts to reach an accommodation with the Soviet Union. I shared my parents' regret that Franklin Roosevelt's overtures to the Russians had been abandoned by his successors—unwisely and prematurely abandoned, it seemed to us. Harry Truman was no hero in my parents' circle. It seemed obvious to them that his policy of containment, his constant warnings against appeasement, and his ill-advised attempt to co-opt the internal security issue (which only whetted the appetite for tougher measures against domestic "subversion") had not made Americans any safer in the world. On the contrary, the world seemed to become more and more dangerous every day.

The mass media have tried to idealize the 1950s, in retrospect, as an age of innocence. They did not seem that way to me or to most of my contemporaries. A chronic state of international emergency led to the erosion of civil liberties at home and the militarization of American life. Under Joseph McCarthy, anti-Communism reached a feverish pitch of intensity; nor did McCarthy's fall widen the boundaries of permissible debate. Critics of containment, like Walter Lippman and George Kennan (after 1955), found it difficult to get a hearing, and their plea for "disengagement" from the cold war made no impression, so far as my friends and I could see, on American policy. We felt more and more helpless in a world dominated by two huge military establishments, both of them girding themselves for some apocalyptic confrontation and seemingly impervious to the promptings of humanity or even to a realistic assessment of their own national interests.

The rapidly unfolding events of the early 1960s pushed me further to the left. Unlike many of my Harvard classmates, I did not welcome John Kennedy's election or the resulting Cambridge-White House connection. Kennedy's foreign policy—and the international scene continued to dominate my political reactions at this time—seemed even more reckless than Truman's. I was not impressed by the "best and brightest," having had some acquaintance with their kind. To me, the migration of Harvard to Washington meant the political ascendancy of Route 128, home of the high-tech industries that were springing up on the periphery of Boston. This vast suburban sprawl, founded on the union of brains and military power, furnished visible evidence of the military-industrial complex, as Eisenhower called it.

Eisenhower's farewell address stirred me far more deeply than Kennedy's inaugural, with its call to get America moving again. The former became one of my reference points in the politics of the early 1960s, along with Dwight Macdonald's article on the 1960 election explaining why he did not plan to vote for either candidate. That article led me in turn to Macdonald's political memoir of the 1930s and 1940s, a slashing, witty, and moving indictment of the warfare state. I began to read other social critics who spoke to my sense of foreboding, to the feeling that we Americans had somehow entrusted our destiny to an implacable war machine that ground on almost wholly independent of human intervention, mindlessly going about its business of destruction.

The writings that gave shape and direction to my thinking in the early 1960s—Randolph Bourne's war essays, C. Wright Mills's *The Power Elite*, William Appleman Williams's *The Tragedy of American Diplomacy*, John Kenneth Galbraith's *The Affluent Society*, Paul Goodman's *Growing Up Absurd*, Herbert Marcuse's *Eros and Civilization*, Norman O. Brown's *Life against Death*—contained certain common themes, I now see: the pathology of domination; the growing influence of organizations (economic as well as military) that operate without regard to any rational objectives except their own self-aggrandizement; the powerlessness of individuals in the face of these gigantic agglomerations and the arrogance of those ostensibly in charge of them.

The Vietnam War confirmed this impression of implacable, irresistible power. When the State Department's "truth squad" rolled into Iowa City (I was there teaching at the University of Iowa), with orders to correct the dangerous errors spread by academic opponents of the war, I got a small taste of our government's sensitivity to public opinion. I stood up to contest the official justification of American policy, only to be told by one of our helpful public servants to "sit down and shut up." I took heart, however, from the growing opposition to the war, from the formation of a new left, and from the student movement's attempt to explain the connection between the war and the bureaucratization of academic life. Industry's growing dependency on the most advanced technology had drawn the "multiversity" into the military-industrial complex; but while this development had undoubtedly had a deplorable effect on scholarship and teaching, it opened a small window of hope, since a campaign against secret military research—so flagrantly at odds with the academic ethic of publication and open discussion—might disrupt the flow of classified information from the corporations to the Pentagon. Such was the rather wistful reasoning that encouraged some of us to see academic reform, eminently desirable in its own right, as something more than a purely academic affair—as a strategic move against the military-industrial machine at its most vulnerable point.

This strategy assumed that the university, deeply compromised by its entanglement with the corporations, the military, and the state, nevertheless honored the ideal of a community of scholars and was therefore open to pressure mounted in the name of that ideal. It soon became clear, however, that the student movement took a different view of the university, one that indiscriminately condemned all institutions and equated "liberation" with anarchic personal freedom. As the new left degenerated into revolutionary histrionics, its spokesmen—clownish media freaks like Jerry Rubin and Abbie Hoffman, seekers of "existential" authenticity like Tom Hayden, connoisseurs of confrontation like Mark Rudd—obviously found it more and more difficult to distinguish between power and authority. My own reading and experience had convinced me that American society suffered from the collapse of legitimate authority and that those who ran our institutions, to the degree to which they had lost public confidence, had to rely on bribery, manipulations, intimidation, and secret surveillance. Work had become a disagreeable routine, voting a meaningless ritual, military service something to be avoided at all cost. The attempt to enlist public confidence in government had given way to the search for "credibility." Authorities in almost every realm had forfeited public trust; but the only way to counter the resulting cynicism, it seemed to me, was to reform our institutions so as to make them worthy of trust, not to play on the cynicism by insisting that it was impossible to trust anyone over 30.

The fact of being over 30 myself no doubt colored my perception of these matters. My generation—those of us who hadn't sold out to the New Frontier—found ourselves caught in the middle of a struggle in which generational issues rapidly overshadowed issues of class and race. The young militants denounced us as enemies of the revolution, by virtue of our having jobs, families, and positions of responsibility (however severely circumscribed by the realities of bureaucratic power), while our elders—the old social democratic, anti-Communist left, well on its way to neoconservatism by this time—lectured us on our ingratitude to the society that had favored us with every advantage and given us tenured positions in its universities. We ourselves regarded our criticism of American society, of the university in particular, as an act of loyalty, designed to restore public confidence in authority. The old social democrats saw it, however, as willful and calculated subversion, another instance of the "treason of the intellectuals"—if anything, more reprehensible than the rebellion of the *enragés*, which could be excused as an excess of youthful idealism.

My growing dislike of the new left did not imply any break with the historic traditions of the left, which I held in higher regard the more I came to understand them. The trouble with the new left, it seemed to me, lay precisely in its ignorance of the earlier history of the left—which did not prevent it from recapitulating the most unattractive features of that history: rampant sectarianism, an obsession with ideological purity, sentimentalization of outcast groups. By the late 1960s I thought of myself as a socialist, attended meetings of the Socialist Scholars Conference, and took part in several abortive attempts to launch a journal of socialist opinion.

Somewhat belatedly, I ploughed through the works of Marx and Engels. I read Gramsci and Lukacs, the founders of "Western Marxism." I immersed myself in the work of the Frankfurt School—Horkheimer, Adorno, Marcuse. Their synthesis of Marx and Freud—to whom I had been introduced in the first place by Marcuse and Brown, who wanted to put psychoanalysis at the service of social theory—struck me as enormously fruitful, providing Marxism with a serious theory of culture. The tradition of English Marxism, as articulated by Raymond Williams and E. P. Thompson, appealed to me for something of the same reason. It repudiated economic determinism and the mechanistic distinction between economic "base" and cultural "superstructure." It showed that class consciousness is the product of historical experience, not a simple reflection of economic interest. The work of Williams and Thompson also showed how Marxism could absorb the insights of cultural conservatives and provide a sympathetic account, not just of the economic hardships imposed by capitalism, but of the way in which capitalism thwarted the need for joy in work, stable connections, family life, a sense of place, and a sense of historical continuity.

In the last 1960s and early 1970s, Marxism, with the many refinements and modifications introduced by those who rejected the positivistic, mechanistic side of Marxism, seemed indispensable to me for a whole variety of reasons. It provided a left-wing corrective to the anti-intellectualism of the new left—its cult of action (preferably violent, "existentially authentic" action), its contempt for the autonomy of thought, its terrible habit of judging ideas only by their immediate contribution to the revolution. Marxists took the long view and preached patience: the gradual preparation of a new culture. Marxism explained a great many things, it seemed, that could not be explained in any other way, including the aggressive foreign policy that had troubled me for so long. In the late 1950s I had listened attentively to Kennan, Lippmann, and other "realists," who argued that the worst features of American policy originated in misplaced moral fervor. Vietnam convinced me, however—as it convinced so many others—that American imperialism grew out of the structural requirements of capitalism itself, which continued to rest on colonial exploitation. Those who rejected the economic determinism often associated with Marxism nevertheless took it as an essential principle of social analysis that a society's institutions had to be understood as expressions of its underlying structure, of the characteristic configuration of its productive forces in particular.

But in my case the attraction of Marxism lay not only in its ability to provide a general explanatory framework but in its more specific insights into the "devastated realm of the spirit," in Gramsci's wonderful phrase. In this connection, I was much taken by the Marxist critique of mass culture. Here the ideas of the Frankfurt School appeared to coincide with ideas advanced by American socialists associated in the 1930s with *Partisan Review* and later with *Politics, Commentary, and Dissent*. These native critics, notably Dwight Macdonald and Irving Howe, had condemned Stalinism, partly on the grounds that it subjected culture (as it subjected everything else) to the requirements of official dogma. Having defended artistic and intellectual independence against *Kulturbolshewismus* in the 1930s, they went on, in the 1940s and 1950s, to defend it against the very different but no less insidious distortions imposed by the market. The reduction of art to a commodity, they argued, had the same effect on culture that mass production had on material objects: standardization, the destruction of craftsmanship, and a proliferation of meretricious goods designed for immediate obsolescence. The critics of mass culture, as I read them, were not primarily concerned with the debasement of popular taste; nor were they arguing that mass culture served as a source of the "false consciousness" that lulled the masses into acceptance of their miserable condition. No, they were on the track of something ominous: the transformation of fame into celebrity; the replacement of events by images and pseudo-events; and the replacement of authoritative moral judgment by "inside-dopesterism," which appealed to the fear of being left behind by changing fashions, the need to know what insiders were saying, and the hunger for the latest scandal or medical breakthrough or public opinion poll or market survey.

The critique of mass culture provided further evidence that our society was no longer governed by a moral consensus. What held it together was "credibility"; and the Watergate affair, coming hard on the heels of the Vietnam War—itself largely motivated by the need to maintain American credibility in the eyes of the world—seemed to indicate not merely that our public officials no longer cared about the truth but that they had lost even the capacity to distinguish it from falsehood. All that mattered was the particular version of unreality the public would be induced to "buy." If "disinformation," as it later came to be called, proved eminently marketable, it was because information itself was in pitifully short supply. Disinformation monopolized the airwaves. It was not that Americans had become stupid or credulous but that they had no institutional alternative to the consumption of lies. Their only available defense was to turn off the television set, cancel subscriptions to newspapers and periodicals, and stay away from the polls on election day. More and more people in fact availed themselves of these options, to judge by declining newspaper sales, lower and lower ratings for political events, and the shrinkage of the electorate. But public opinion polls now made it possible, in effect, to dispense with the electorate by allowing an infinitesimal but allegedly representative sample of the population to determine the outcome of elections in advance.

The Land of Opportunity: A Parent's View

The topics to which I turned in the mid-seventies—the changing pattern of family life and long-term changes in personality structure—grew out of a belief that social order no longer required the informed consent of citizens; that every form of authority, including parental authority, was in serious decline; that children now grew up without effective parental supervision or guidance, under the tutelage of the mass media and the helping professions; and that such a radical shift in the pattern of "socialization," as the sociologists called it, could be expected to have important effects on personality, the most disturbing of which would presumably be a weakening of the capacity for independent judgment, initiative, and self-discipline, on which democracy had always been understood to depend.

Such were the theoretical concerns, if I can dignify them with that name, that informed my studies in culture and personality; but those studies also grew more deeply out of my experience as a husband and father. Like so many of those born in the Depression, my wife and I married early, with the intention of raising a large family. We were part of the postwar "retreat to domesticity," as it is so glibly referred to today. No doubt we hoped to find some kind of shelter in the midst of general insecurity, but this formulation hardly does justice to our hopes and expectations, which included much more than refuge from the never-ending international emergency. In a world dominated by suspicion and mistrust, a renewal of the capacity for loyalty and devotion had to begin, it seemed, at the most elementary level with families and friends. My generation invested personal relations with an intensity they could hardly support, as it turned out; but our passionate interest in each others' lives cannot very well be described as a form of emotional retreat. We tried to recreate in the circle of our friends the intensity of a common purpose, which could no longer be found in politics or the work place.

We wanted our children to grow up in a kind of extended family, or at least with an abundance of "significant others." A house full of people, a crowded table, four-hand music at the piano, nonstop conversation and cooking, baseball games and swimming in the afternoon, long walks after dinner, a poker game or *Diplomacy* or charades in the evening, all these activities mixing children and adults—that was our idea of a well-ordered household and a well-ordered education. We had no great confidence in the schools; we knew that if our children were to acquire any of the things we set store by—joy in learning, eagerness for experience, and capacity for love and friendship—they would have to learn the better part of it at home. For that very reason, however, home was not to be thought of simply as the "nuclear family." Its hospitality would have to extend far and wide, stretching its emotional resources (and its financial resources as well, in my own case) to the limit.

None of this was thought out self-consciously as a pedagogical program, and it would have destroyed trust and spontaneity if it had been; but some such feelings helped shape the way we lived, along with much else that was not thought out but purely impulsive. Like all parents, we gave our young less than they deserved. At least, however, we did not set out to raise a generation of perfect children, as many middle-aged parents are trying to do today; nor did we undertake to equip them with all the advantages required by the prevailing standards of worldly achievement. Our failure to educate them for success was the one way in which we did not fail them—our one unambiguous success. Not that this was deliberate either; it was only gradually that it became clear to me that none of my own children, having been raised not for upward mobility but for honest work, could reasonably hope for any conventional kind of success, which was no longer to be had on such terms. The "best and brightest" were those who knew how to exploit institutions for their own advantage and make exceptions for themselves instead of playing by the rules. Raw ambition counted more heavily, in the distribution of worldly rewards, than devoted service to a calling—an old story, perhaps, except that now it was complicated by the further consideration that most of the available jobs and careers did not inspire devoted service in the first place.

Politics, law, teaching, medicine, architecture, journalism, the ministry—they were all too deeply compromised by an exaggerated concern for the "bottom line" to attract people who wished simply to practice a craft or, having attracted them by some chance, to retain their ardent loyalty in the face of experiences making for discouragement and cynicism. If this was true of the professions, it was also true—it hardly needs to be said—of factory work and even of the various crafts and trades. At every level of American society, it was becoming harder and harder for people to find work that self-respecting men and women could throw themselves into with enthusiasm. The degradation of work represented the most fundamental sense in which institutions no longer commanded public confidence. It was the most important source of the "crisis of authority," so widely deplored but so little understood. The authority conferred by a calling, with all its moral and spiritual overtones, could hardly flourish in a society in which the practice of a calling had given way to a particularly vicious kind of careerism, symbolized unmistakably in the 1980s by the rise of the yuppie.

The unexpectedly rigorous business of bringing up children exposed me, as it necessarily exposes almost any parent, to our "child-centered" society's icy indifference to everything that makes it possible for children to flourish and grow up into responsible adults. To see the modern world from the point of view of a parent is to see it in the worst possible light.

This perspective unmistakably reveals the unwholesomeness, not to put it more strongly, of our way of life: our obsession with sex, violence, and the pornography of "making it" and "scoring" sexually; our addictive dependence on drugs and "entertainment"; our impatience with anything that limits our sovereign freedom of choice, especially with the constraints of marital and familial ties; our preference for "nonbinding commitments"; our third-rate educational system; our third-rate morality; our refusal to draw a distinction between right and wrong, lest we "impose" our morality on others and thus invite others to "impose" their morality on us; our reluctance to make moral judgments or be judged morally; our indifference to the needs of future generations, as evidenced by our willingness to saddle them with a huge national debt, an overgrown arsenal of destruction, and a deteriorating environment; our inhospitable attitude to newcomers conceived in our midst: our unstated assumption, institutionalized in the national policy on abortion, that only those children born for success ought to be allowed to be born at all.

Having come to see America in this way, I could understand why the family issue had come to play such a large part in the politics of the 1970s and 1980s, and why so many Democrats had drifted away from their party. Liberalism now meant sexual freedom, women's rights, gay rights, denunciation of the family as the seat of all oppression, denunciation of "patriarchy," denunciation of "working-class authoritarianism." Even when liberals began to understand the depths of disaffection among formerly Democratic voters and tardily tried to present themselves as friends of the family, they had nothing better to offer than a "national policy on families"—more welfare service, more day care centers, more social workers and guidance counselors and child development experts. None of these proposals addressed the moral collapse that troubled so many people—troubled even liberals, although they refused to admit it publicly. Liberals and social democrats showed their true colors when they belatedly and awkwardly pronounced the family a "legitimate object of concern," their words dripping with condescension.

The Party of the Future and Its Quarrel with "Middle America"

It was not just condescension, however, but a remarkably tenacious belief in progress that made it so hard for people on the left to listen to those who told them things were falling apart. That kind of talk had always been the stock in trade—hadn't it?—of those who could not bear to face the future, pined for the good old days, and suffered from a "failure of nerve." The controversies in which I found myself embroiled after the publication of my *Haven in a Heartless World* and *The Culture of Narcissism* gave me a better understanding of the left's quarrel with America. If people on the left felt themselves estranged from America, it was because, in their eyes, most Americans refused to accept the future. Instead they clung to backward, provincial habits of thought that prevented them from changing with the times. Those in the know understood that what "cultural pessimists" and "doomsayers" mistook for moral collapse represented merely a transitional stage in the unfolding process of "modernization." If only everyone could be made to see things so clearly! The transition to a "postindustrial" society and a "postmodern" culture naturally caused all sorts of readjustments and dislocations, but the inevitable supersession of older ways, however painful in its side effects, had to be accepted as the price of progress.

Nor was it only material progress that lay ahead. To my surprise, I found that my friends on the left—those who had not by this time written me off as "part of the problem," who still regarded me, in spite of all evidence to the contrary, as potentially salvageable—still believed in moral as well as in material progress. They cited the abolition of slavery and the emancipation of women as indisputable evidence that the ideal of universal brotherhood was closer to realization than ever before. Its realization was chiefly impeded, it seemed, by the persistence of tribal loyalties rooted in the patriarchal stage of social development. The ties of kinship, nationality, and ethnic identity had to give way to "more inclusive identities," as Erik Erikson used to say—to an appreciation of the underlying unity of all mankind. Family feeling, clannishness, and patriotism—admirable enough, perhaps, in earlier days—could not be allowed to stand in the way of the global civilization that was arriving just in time to save the human race from the self-destructive consequences of its old habits of national rivalry and war.

The left's quarrel was with the backward, benighted, or simply misguided opponents of progress whose blind resistance might prevent the future from arriving on schedule. It was the belief in progress that explained the left's curious mixture of complacency and paranoia. Confidence in being on the winning side of history made progressive people unbearably smug and superior, but they felt isolated and beleaguered in their own country, since it was so much less progressive than they were. After all, the political culture of the U.S. remained notoriously backward—no labor party, no socialist tradition, no great capital city like London or Paris, where politicians and civil servants mingled with artists and intellectuals and encountered advanced ideas in cafes and drawing rooms. In America the divorce between Washington and New York; and the culture of Washington itself, for that matter, seemed light-years ahead of the vast hinterland beyond the Appalachians—the land of the Yahoo, the John Birch Society, and the Ku Klux Klan.

By the late 1970s and early 1980s, I no longer had much confidence either in the accuracy of this bird's-eye view of America or in the progressive view of the future with which it was so closely associated. "Middle Americans" had good reason, it seemed to me, to worry about the family and the future their children were going to inherit. My study of the family suggested a broader conclusion: that the capacity for loyalty is stretched too thin when it tries to attach itself to the hypothetical solidarity of the whole human race. It needs to attach itself to specific people and places, not to an abstract ideal of universal human rights. We love particular men and women, not humanity in general. The dream of universal brotherhood, because it rests on the sentimental fiction that men and women are all the same, cannot survive the discovery that they differ. Love, on the other hand—flesh-and-blood love, as opposed to a vague, watery humanitarianism—is attached to complementary differences, not to sameness. A feminist, protesting against the excessive attention paid to sexual differences, urges people to enlarge their "narrow views of men and women," adding that whereas "our biological differences are self-evident, our human similarities are exciting." On the contrary, it is our biological differences that excite us. That progressive men and women have lost sight of this obvious point suggests that they are dangerously out of touch not just with "Middle America" but with common sense.

Once you reject the view of historical progress that means so much to people on the left, their sense of themselves as the party of the future, together with their fear of being overwhelmed by America's backward culture, becomes an object of historical curiosity, not the axiomatic premise from which political understanding necessarily proceeds. As I began to study the matter, I found that the left's fear of America went back a long way, at least as far back as the late 1930s, when the New Deal suffered a series of setbacks from which it never quite recovered. It persisted, this uneasiness, even during the long period of liberal ascendancy that followed the Second World War. The conviction that most Americans remained politically incorrigible—ultranationalist in foreign policy, racist in their dealings with blacks and other minorities, authoritarian in their attitudes toward women and children—helps explain why liberals relied so heavily on the courts and the federal bureaucracy to engineer reforms that might have failed to command popular support if they had been openly debated. The big liberal victories—desegregation, affirmative action, legislative reapportionment, legalized abortion—were won largely in the courts, not in Congress, in state legislatures, or at the polls. Instead of seeking to create a popular consensus behind these reforms, liberals pursued their objectives by indirect methods, fearing that popular attitudes remained unreconstructed. The trauma of McCarthyism, the long and bitter resistance to desegregation in the South, and the continued resistance to federal spending (unless it could be justified on military grounds) all seemed to confirm liberals in the belief that the ordinary American had never been a liberal and was unlikely to become one.

The "Promised Land" of the New Right

The use of undemocratic means to achieve democratic goals aligned liberalism more and more closely with blacks, women, and other minorities and divided it from the constituencies that united behind Roosevelt and Truman. Advocating ideals of individualism, social mobility, and self-realization that come closest to fulfillment in the professional classes, liberals defended the underdog with an upper-middle-class accent. Sooner or later, these policies were bound to generate a "backlash against the theoreticians and bureaucrats in national government," as George Wallace put it. By 1968, when Wallace's strong showing among working-class voters in the North foreshadowed a new political alignment, Americans were "fed up," in his words, "with strutting pseudo-intellectuals lording over them, writing guidelines, . . . telling them they have not got sense enough to know what is best for their children or sense enough to run their own schools and hospitals and local domestic institutions."

Twelve years later, the working-class revolt against liberalism helped bring the new right to power under Reagan. But Reagan's defense of "traditional values," it turned out, did not amount to much. As governor of California, Reagan deplored the "wave of hedonism" that had rolled over the country and pleaded for a "spiritual rebirth, a rededication to the moral precepts which guided us for so much of our past." In the campaign of 1980, however, he ridiculed Jimmy Carter for saying very much the same thing. The theme of "spiritual rebirth" gave way to Reagan's characteristic strategy of evasion and denial. There was nothing wrong with America after all—nothing that could not be cured by discrediting those who claimed to find something wrong. Criticism of "hedonism" gave way to a crusade against pessimism, as if the chief threat to "traditional values" came from those who sold America short. A self-proclaimed conservative, Reagan had no more use than people on the left for "nay-sayers" and "prophets of doom," as he called them. When he denounced those who falsely claimed that America suffered from a spiritual "malaise," he echoed the main theme of Ted Kennedy's unsuccessful campaign in the 1980 primaries. If Reagan succeeded where Kennedy failed, perhaps it was because he managed to create the impression that moral regeneration could be achieved painlessly through the power of positive thinking, whereas Kennedy relied on the usual array of federal programs.

"Don't let anyone tell you that America's best days are behind her," Reagan said, "that the American spirit has been vanquished. We've seen it triumph too often in our own lives to stop believing in it now." Swept into office by the accumulated anger and resentment of the "forgotten middle class," Reagan interpreted his election as a demand for reassurance. "One of my dreams," he said, "is to help Americans rise above pessimism by renewing their belief in themselves." The "traditional values" celebrated by Reagan—boosterism, rugged individualism, a willingness to resort to force (against weaker opponents) on the slightest provocation—had very little to do with tradition. They summed up the code of the cowboy, the man in flight from his ancestors, from his immediate family, and from everything that tied him down and limited his freedom of movement. Reagan played on the desire for order, continuity, responsibility, and discipline, but his program contained nothing that would satisfy that desire. On the contrary, his program aimed to promote economic growth and unregulated business enterprise, the very forces that have undermined genuinely traditional values. A movement calling itself conservative might have been expected to associate itself with the demand for limits, not only on economic growth but on the conquest of space and the ungodly ambition to acquire godlike powers over our natural environment. Reaganites, however, condemned the demand for limits as another counsel of doom. "Free enterprises," according to Burton Pines, a new-right ideologue, "insist that the economy can indeed expand and as it does so, all society's members can . . . increase their wealth."

These words crudely express the essence of the belief in progress that has dominated Anglo-American politics for the last two centuries. The idea of progress, contrary to received opinion, owes its appeal not to its millennial vision of the future but to the seemingly more realistic expectation that the expansion of productive forces can continue indefinitely. The history of liberalism—which includes a great deal that passes for conservatism as well—consists of variations on this underlying theme.

That "optimism" and "pessimism" still remain the favorite categories of political debate indicates that the theme of progress is not yet played out. In the impending age of limits, however, it sounds increasingly hollow. We can begin to hear discordant voices, which always accompanied the celebration of progress as a kind of counterpoint but were usually drowned out by the principal voices. A closer study of the score—the history of progressive ideology and its critics—will bring to the surface a more complicated texture, a richer and darker mixture of harmonies, not always euphonious by any means, than we have been accustomed to hear. It is the darker voices especially that speak to us now, not because they speak in tones of despair but because they help us to distinguish mere "optimism" from hope and thus give us the courage to confront the mounting difficulties that threaten to overwhelm us.

CHRIST THE ONLY SAVIOR OF INTERPRETATION

VERN SHERIDAN POYTHRESS
Professor of New Testament Interpretation
Westminster Theological Seminary

Article from *Westminster Theological Journal*

The *Westminster Theological Journal* has long provided a platform for creatively investigating implications of Reformed theology. In this article, I endeavor to continue the tradition by sketching some implications of Reformed soteriology for biblical hermeneutics.

Since human interpretation is corrupted by sin, it no less than other human activities stands in need of redemption. Interpretive sins no less than other sins can find a remedy only in the sacrifice of Christ (Acts 4:12). Hence we must affirm that Christ is the Savior of interpretation. We acknowledge this truth indirectly whenever we speak of the indispensable work of the Holy Spirit in illumining to us the message of Scripture (1 Cor. 2:14–16). Yet this work of the Holy Spirit can never be independent of the work of Christ in dying and rising in order to save us. Hence it is worthwhile to make explicit ways in which Christ redeems our human interpretation, as one aspect of his redemption of the total creation (Rom. 8:18; Col. 1:20).[1]

We are accustomed to thinking of biblical interpretation as Christocentric. Biblical theologians correctly observe that the NT use of the OT is consistently Christ-centered in character (note Luke 24:25–27, 44–49). "No matter how many promises God has made, they are 'Yes' in Christ" (2 Cor. 1:20). Certainly this conviction should affect our hermeneutical procedure: We ought to come to any particular passage of the Bible asking the question of how the passage speaks about Christ. In a real sense, Christ is the central content of the Bible's message.

But Christ is the center of interpretation in at least two more senses besides this familiar one. First, he is the Lord of interpretation. As the omnipotent God and the eternal Word he is not only the author and speaker of Scripture, but also the creator, the providential ruler, and the standard for every step in every person's interaction with the Bible.[2]

Second, Christ is our redeemer with respect to interpretive sinfulness. He is the substitute, sin-bearer, and purifier for our interpretive rebellion. On this second point I propose to concentrate. For convenience, I will employ the categories and perspectives developed in my earlier article on God's lordship.[3]

161

1. Christ as Savior in relation to divine authority, control, and presence

All human interpretation takes place in subjection to God's authority, control, and presence. But sin perverts interpretation because sinners hate this subjection to God. Our sin corrupts our relationship to God and thereby calls forth God's judgement. We remain under God's authority (Deut. 32:39), but in sin we seek to set up our own rival, counterfeit authorities. We remain under God's control (Prov. 21:1), but in sin we seek to hide ourselves from him. Hence God's authority impinges on us as judicial condemnation; God's control operates on us to punish and destroy us; God's presence in blessing is withdrawn, and he is present in cursing as an enemy to war against us and terrify us (e.g., Deut. 28:15–68).

Christ saves us from our desperate lostness. He is the eternal God who has God's own authority, control, and presence to save us. He becomes man, subjecting himself to our misery, and takes away our lostness by bearing it himself on the cross. We can explain Christ's work in terms of reconciliation to God's authority, control, and presence. Christ reconciles God's authority to us by bearing judicial condemnation. By his vindication in the resurrection we receive God's authoritative pronouncement that we are justified.

Next, Christ reconciles God's control to us by utterly submitting to God, dying in weakness and desolation. Therefore we are not destroyed but made alive by God's power at work in Christ's resurrection.

Finally, Christ reconciles God's presence to us by being alienated from God's presence, forsaken by God (Matt. 27:46). Through Christ's resurrection and ascension we ascend to the heavenly places with him (Eph. 2:6).

In sum, in the cross and the resurrection Christ definitively reasserts God's authority, control, and presence over a fallen world. He asserts God's utter goodness by blessing and saving in the midst of the wickedness of the people who crucify him. He asserts God's utter control over evil by fulfilling the prophecies of the OT. In addition, his own predictions are fulfilled in the very midst of the worst crime of human history (Acts 2:23; 4:26–28). He asserts God's assured presence to the end of time by manifesting his glory to the world in the resurrection, the foundational act that has power to fill the world with God's glory.

Hence Christ's life, death, and resurrection bear directly on every human act of interpretation. First, every step and every act of interpretation takes place in the context of standards, whose ultimate reference point is divine authority. Only through the effect of Christ's work do we receive approval from his standards. Second, every act of interpretation takes place under the control of God. And only through the effect of Christ's work does God's control renew us rather than destroy us. Moreover, only through Christ do we subjectively cease to have the sinful impulses to replace God's authority with our counterfeits, to throw over the bonds of God's control, and to hide from God's presence. Third, every act of interpretation takes place before the presence of God. Only through the effect of Christ's work does God become our friend, and the blessed intimacy of his presence is reestablished.

These conclusions about the implications of Christ's work apply preeminently in the case of interpretation of the Bible. When we are interpreting the Bible, we are interpreting God's own speech to us, so that the influence of our sin is most prominent. Hence only through Christ can we come to interpret the Bible rightly. But the implications also hold in the case of interpretation of all human communication. Human communication derives from people who are made in God's image. As God's image, human authors have limited but real authority, control, and presence. Hence we are able to say analogous things concerning divine and human communication. Moreover, love of God and love of neighbor go together. Hatred of God is the ultimate source of all human enmity. Sin will therefore affect interpretation of human writings in a manner analogous to the effect on divine writing in the Bible.[4]

To many people these claims must seem unbelievable. Surely the situation is not that bad, they say. We have only to look around us. Many non-Christians achieve creditable and valuable interpretations of human writings and of the Bible as well. To this complacency there are several replies.

First, the subtlety of a sin does not imply its triviality. Some of the worst sins—hypocrisy, for example—are the most subtle. What to the human eye may seem like a tiny, almost undetectable deviation from ethical perfection may be a symptom of raging wickedness in the heart (see Matt. 5:21–42).

Second, no sinner, however violent and fanatical, escapes God (Ps. 139:7–12; Heb. 4:12–13; Acts 17:28). The inescapable knowledge of God (Rom. 1:20) causes people in spite of themselves to acknowledge truth— sometimes a truth that a Christian has overlooked and can profit from.

Third, the sacrifice of Christ causes benefits to flow even to those who are not saved. The Bible nowhere speaks directly of these broader benefits, but we can produce an indirect argument. The promise made to Noah concerning the preservation of the world is a response to Noah's sacrificial offering (Gen. 8:20–22). The sacrificial offering can have no ultimate value before God unless it faintly points forward to the efficacious sacrifice of Christ. Moreover, the preservation of the world in a broad sense involves the good gifts that God gives to unbelievers such as in Acts 14:17. Hence all good things that unbelievers temporarily enjoy in this life flow from the goodness of God in Christ. We could also argue simply from general principle. When God restrains his judgement against those who deserve it (Luke 13:1–5), it must be because he has found a way to be merciful for a time, and that mercy can harmonize with perfect holiness only because of Christ's suffering. From these arguments we conclude that we owe the achievements of unbelieving interpretation to the broader implications of the work of Christ.[5]

Fourth, no one can fully assess how much the practice of interpretation in the Western world is still living on "borrowed capital" from the Christian world view of its past. What may happen once this capital is consumed? From where will the culture obtain standards for interpretation? Though a few voices of warning and despair are raised, most secularists do not realize the abyss of interpretive arbitrariness and demonic deception into which they may gradually slip. If one looks at consumerist propaganda, Nazi propaganda, and Communist propaganda, one gets some foretaste. But abysses of Hinduism, sadism, occultism, Satanism, and animism lurk beyond.

The exalted character of human beings as the image of God becomes their terrible curse when they apostasize. In a horrible way they do become like God, knowing good and evil (Gen. 3:22). That is, human beings who are sinners continue to image God, but now in a horrible way. They pretend to determine good and evil by their own standards, just as God determines good and evil by the standards of his own divine being. Moreover, human beings exercise a dominion that is an image of God's dominion. In this dominion their own idolatrous determination rules themselves and all their works. Once they repudiate God, they have no anchorage except in the overwhelming judgement of God making them slaves to Satan (1 John 5:19). They are capable of indefinite degeneration and destruction, limited by the bounds of hell. We do not dream of what is possible for human perversity to do in interpretation.

2. Christ as Savior of the self, the law, and the world

Now let us consider how Christ accomplishes the salvation of various aspects of interpretation. Every act of interpretation is simultaneously interpretation of oneself, interpretation of the law or standard, and interpretation of the world.[6]

It is easy to see how Christ is the Savior of the self. Christ provides the forgiveness of our sins and the Father translates us from the kingdom of Satan into Christ's kingdom (Col. 1:13). We are renewed in the image of Christ and made sons of God (Rom. 8:29; Gal. 4:5). All interpretation is in a sense necessarily interpretation of one's own thoughts and impressions. How is this interpretation changed by Christ? Having died and risen with Christ, we are new people whose own thoughts and impressions have been subject to death and resurrection. They are the same yet not the same, for they have been judged, what is sinful has been crucified (Gal. 5:24), and they have undergone renewal by the resurrection power of Christ.

Christ is also the Savior of the law. First of all we may speak of the law in an objective sense, that is, the standard of God governing our activity of interpretation. Christ comes into the world as the truth, as the very embodiment of God's standard. But people reject this truth. The truth of God is crucified. Christ's crucifixion is thus the archetypical accomplishment of that crucifixion of God's truth to which we all incline in our sin. But then Christ is raised. Thus the truth of God is vindicated and established. Christ releases us from condemnation for having crucified God's truth in our previous interpretation (justification). Christ also brings us into real (though imperfect) conformity with God's standard (sanctification). We begin to conform our interpretive acts to God's norms instead of violating them.

Second, we may consider the law from the point of view of what the interpreter actually knows. Interpreters in fellowship with Christ come to know Christ's purity, and hence have a renewed knowledge of the purity required of them in interpretation. Knowing Christ the truth, they are open to the knowledge of the subordinate truths of the text. Through the power of Christ's death they daily come alive to God in celebrating the wisdom of God's law.

Next, Christ is the Savior of the world. Sinners desire to be like God, and this desire inclines them to sovereignly dictate the facts, including the facts that confront us in the interpretation. Christ in submitting himself to the facts of this earthly existence accomplishes the healing of our desires to set aside the facts. Moreover, as we have observed, the broader benefits of Christ's sacrifice include the preservation of the world and the giving of gifts even to unbelievers. We are provided with the resources of textual copying, lexicons, and historical information through the benefits of Christ.

In the previous article on lordship I argued that non-Christian interpretation tends to create idols and thereby produce tensions between law, world, and self.[7] Rationalism, empiricism, and subjectivism in interpretation arise from an idolatrous absolutization of law, world, and self, respectively. Against this background, we can simply say that Christ came to save us from these idolatries. Let us make explicit the meaning of his salvation.

Christ was crucified because of the Pharisees' idolization of law, their human standard of tradition, but by his death the power of idolized law was broken, and even what was temporary in character in the Mosaic law was abolished (Eph. 2:15). The law henceforth must always be the "law of Christ" (1 Cor. 9:21). Even in the OT the law was never a rationalized abstraction. But since the resurrection and ascension of Christ his law and standard is inseparable from the personal presence of Christ and the historical facts of his incarnation and life in the world.

Christ was crucified because of the empiricist pragmatism at work in Pilate's concern to keep intact Roman peace and order and his own position (Luke 23:1–25). But now we must live in the light of the supremely empirical facts of the crucifixion and the resurrection of Christ. These are not bare facts or neutral facts, but facts inseparable from the plan of God and the abiding presence of the crucified and resurrected Christ who now rules over all the empirical kingdoms of the world. Moreover, a thoroughgoing attention to facts includes attention to the fact of the certainty of the coming judgement of Christ. Only what is done in service to Christ will stand the "pragmatic" test of judgement by fire.

Christ was crucified because of the subjective emotivism of the crowds who were stirred up to demand his crucifixion and the release of Barabbas. As a result, Christ demonstrated on the cross the supreme subjective depth of his love for us. His love is not mere unbridled subjectivity, but obedience to the Father and to his plan. As the risen one Christ pours out his love and demands of us a love that is not a contentless gush of woozy feeling, but obedience to his law, his commandments, and his person (John 14:15–24).

All non-Christian accounts of hermeneutics necessarily fail at this point. In failing to acknowledge God as the source of law, world, and self, they open themselves to idolatry and so contribute to the deepest hermeneutical difficulties and alienations rather than solving them. Non-Christians examining hermeneutics may be admirably sensitive to human weakness and perversion in many respects. Frequently, it seems, they have achieved much greater intellectual penetration than Christians. But by refusing to call human corruption sin, they obscure its roots. In addition, they are blind to the only remedy. Growth in autonomous hermeneutical self-consciousness and sophistication never reveals the radical character of sin or its remedy, but only spreads the cancer of sinful pride. Human beings who have made themselves like gods (Gen. 3:22) cannot rectify their mistake, because their gods control their interpretation. Only the foolishness of the cross can save.

3. Christ as Savior of meaning, personal fellowship, and worldly application

The word of God in Scripture expresses propositional meaning, confronts us with the presence of the person of God himself, and exercises control over us and over the world. In fact, these three functions of Scripture each characterize the whole of Scripture; they are perspectives on one another. But they become a curse to us rather than a blessing apart from the work of Christ.

First, the propositional meaning of Scripture is a witness against us (Deut. 31:26–29). Its truthfulness witnesses to our untruth; its statements of fact witness against our denial or contradiction of facts; its pure ethics witnesses against our failures and compromises. We do not wish to come to the light, lest our deeds should be exposed (John 3:19–20). In conformity with the intrinsically fissiparous character of evil, rebellion against truth takes many forms. Some of us may hypocritically acknowledge the truth in the hope that we will conceal our lack of obedience and conformity. Others may try to destroy meaning altogether. And truly there is no meaning apart from God's creation, or apart from his wisdom and plan that has decreed each fact and assigned to each thing its role. Hence modern people feel the malaise of what seems to be a meaningless world, a meaningless self, and empty or meaningless standards. Christ came as the truth to save us from our propensity to untruth. He came as the way and the life to save us from our meaninglessness and evaporating morals. He was crucified and so underwent an "absurd" destruction. He descended into the meaninglessness of the absence of the Father. We too will descend into the meaninglessness of hell, or else find our meaning in the life of another, in the resurrection of Christ's reign.

In the beginning Adam and Eve found meaning in all the world through their fellowship with God. All the world contained facts ordained by God for their blessing. They had no need of reconciliation from sin. But now, when we are sinners, we will not find the secret of any meaning at all in the world except if our hatred of the glory of God is removed through Christ's substitution.

Next, the word of God confronts us with God's presence, the presence of personal fellowship. But we can never experience his presence in neutral fashion. We are either a friend of God or an enemy. We are made uncomfortable and we grow in hatred, or we are made admirers and we grow in love. God came to earth and became supremely present to us in Jesus Christ. In Christ's crucifixion the world expressed its hatred of God's presence and declared its enmity. Echoing this supreme hatred, unbelievers in interpreting Scripture react in fundamentally the same way. But Christ's crucifixion also means the salvation of the world. Christ overcomes enmity with God and establishes friendship, because he has born God's enmity and wrath on the cross. He has suffered God's abandonment and hatred (Matt. 27:46), in order that in Christ we might be indwelt by the Father and the Son.

These facts apply to the interpretation of Scripture. Christ by the power of his death takes on himself the enmity of God, and opens the way for God to come to us as we interpret Scripture as our divine lover and friend. Christ by the power of his resurrection brings us into heaven as we interpret Scripture, and we meet God in person without dying.

Next, the word of God controls us. God's word hardens us, darkens us, and announces our death when we hear in unbelief (Isa. 6:9–10; Mark 4:11–12; 2 Cor. 2:15–16). By God's prophetic word Christ was put to death, and the world became dark (Luke 23:44), in order that through Christ's resurrection the message of the gospel might come as a power of life (2 Cor. 2:5–6; 4:6). When we are united to Christ, we experience the word of God as gospel, as saving life, because Christ's own resurrection life is not only announced but imparted (John 15:7–8, 10).

4. Christ as Savior of author, discourse, and audience

To interpret responsibly, we must pay attention to author, discourse, and audience. That is, we must attend to the particularities of the discourse we are interpreting, we must bear in mind that the discourse expressed the intention of a particular author, and we must bear in mind that the author intended to address a particular audience in a particular situation to persuade, motivate, or command them. The same sequence of words can mean different things if used by a different author in a different situation.

Christ comes as the light of the world to restore and renew our interpretation of authors, discourses, and audiences. Though all these areas are linked, let us consider each separately.

First, Christ is the Savior of our interpretation of authors. His saving power preeminently affects our knowledge of God, the divine author of Scripture and the source of all general revelation. Only through Christ is our knowledge of God renewed. "No one knows who the Son is except the Father, and no one knows who the Father is except the Son and those to whom the Son chooses to reveal him" (Luke 10:21). Our knowledge comes supremely through Christ's death and resurrection. "When you have lifted up the Son of Man, then you will know who I am and that I do nothing on my own but speak just what the Father has taught me" (John 8:28). Since all interpretation must continually adjust itself to what an author is likely to have meant, all interpretation of the Bible, and subordinately all interpretation of general revelation, must adjust itself in the light of the Son's revelation of the Father on the cross. In the light of the cross and the resurrection we understand the seriousness of God's assertions of his justice, his holiness, his power, his mercy, and his love. Thus, only through the cross do we really understand what Scripture says as the speech of this God who has revealed himself in Christ.

Christ also renews our knowledge of human authors, including not only the human authors of the books of the Bible but authors of uninspired writings. To see how, we must first appreciate some of the difficulties. All interpretation of authors presupposes a knowledge of human nature. We must know something about the similarity of other human beings to ourselves, in order to have confidence that they are talking about experiences and insights in terms with which we are familiar. We must share at some level common institutions of marriage, family, work, and religious cult, a sense of right and wrong, of justice and injustice. But we must also be aware of the possibility of deep differences between different human beings, lest we simply project our own ideas onto another person. We must know something of differences among male and female, young and old, wise and foolish, worshipers of Yahweh or of Krishna or of Mammon, participants in an industrial technological culture, a nomadic culture, an agricultural tribal culture, or an ancient city culture. We must know what human beings are like in their depths. But how do we obtain knowledge of human nature? Are its depths to be revealed by psychoanalysis, or existentialism, or biblical teaching about the Creation and Fall? How do we know what is possible here, when people do not necessarily know themselves? How do we make judgements about human intention, if such intention includes not only the differences of human beings but the depths of the unconscious?

We may naively suppose that there is agreement among thinking people about these matters. But why should we ignore the controversies in philosophical hermeneutics that touch on the nature of human beings? Why should we ignore the kind of perversion of understanding human nature that arises in behaviorism, or in Communism, or in Hitler, or in Marquis de Sade, or in the Pharaoh who opposed Moses? People with ideologies like these interpret virtually all human communication in a manner globally different from what we approve. Who is to say what human nature is?

People who no longer acknowledge their creatureliness and who bury their sin are self-deceived and perverted in knowledge of human nature. They cannot rescue themselves, neither can they even define themselves or find the meaning of humanity. There is no way back to unfallen Adam. Even the Bible gives us only a small amount of information about Adam. We can renew our knowledge of human nature only by anchoring ourselves in what human nature will be, through the man Jesus Christ. As perfect man, his knowledge of himself and of human nature is unperverted. Through him we see that now, after the Fall, our purpose as human beings is to serve God through the renewal that comes from his death and resurrection. The destiny of human nature is to worship God in being conformed to the image of his Son (Rom. 8:29). Such worship reaches a climax when we receive a body in the likeness of the man from heaven (1 Cor. 15:49). Only in union with Christ's death and resurrection do we any longer understand what human beings are. The implicit intention of every Christian author must be to promote the reflection of the glory of Christ in us. The implicit intention of every non-Christian author must be to suppress the light (John 3:19–20). Thus, only through Christ can we understand authorial intention.

Second, Christ is the Savior of our interpretation of discourses. Self-centeredness tempts us to overwhelm texts and read into them what we want, rather than respect their objective factuality. We make a god of our own desires. Even the ancient textual copyists were tempted by their own desires to "improve" on the text. This impulse needs redemption through crucifixion of the flesh (Gal. 5:24). In addition, as I have already argued, the whole idea of meaningfulness presupposes a context of God-given order, including the orderly structure of human language. Some instances of modern deconstructionist interpretation make it plain that stable meaning can disappear when the presence of God is denied.

How, then, do we find a remedy for the abuses of human language and discourse? Such abuse is remedied by the abuse that was suffered by Christ the Word. From the beginning to the end of his life he was misunderstood (John 1:10–11; 3:4; 4:11; 6:52, 66; 12:37–40; Matt. 27:47). The destructive power of human language was typified in the accusations and taunts about the "King of the Jews" during Jesus' crucifixion. Such destructive power is remedied in part by the fact that the gospel records place those taunts in the new narrative context of the resurrection, in which they speak better than they knew. The gospel records cause even those words to serve the purposes of God.

Third, Christ is the Savior of our interpretation of audiences and their situations. As we have observed, our interpretation is influenced by our understanding of the intended audience and their situation. As before, interpretation of the audience presupposes knowledge of human nature. But now the most prominent issues concern the profitability of discourses and the responsibilities of audiences. Our evaluations must be based on the standards of God and God's goal for human existence. Christ as the man from heaven is both our standard and our goal.

Not only the persons of the audience, but the situation of the audience, and what the audience is to do with the situation, depend on knowledge imparted through Christ. We must know what is the proper goal for the situation. Our interpretation thus depends on our vision of the new Jerusalem as the final situation, and the light of the Lamb as the defining component of that situation (Rev. 21:22–23).[8]

5. Christ as Savior of the dynamics of interpretation

Let us see how the framework developed above can explicate the process of interpretation in a particular case. Let us suppose that Sally (a Christian) is studying Psalm 23:1a, "The Lord is my shepherd." Sally grows in understanding of the content of the passage by integrating it with the surrounding literary context and the context of general revelational facts about shepherds and sheep. In doing so, Sally overcomes not only ignorance characterizing all finite creatures, but sinfulness resisting facts. Sally may have sinful pride that causes her to think that there is nothing to be learned about shepherds or sheep, or that there is nothing to be learned about a passage like this one that is already familiar, or that there is nothing to be learned from a passage from the "inferior" revelation of the OT. She may have a distorted otherworldliness that makes her think that shepherds and sheep are not worthy of attention, or that makes her think that it is not worthwhile asking about the applications of this passage to mundane affairs like her use of money and her attitude toward her work. God overcomes the sinfulness of her pride by the humiliation of Christ in his death, and overcomes her false form of otherworldliness by the worldliness of Christ's death and tangibility of his resurrection body.

We may also view the same process as a process of understanding God. Through Christ's salvation Sally grows in understanding the God who speaks Psalm 23:1a. Suppose that previously Sally had thought of God only as a teacher, or only as a helper in immediate difficulty. These inadequate thoughts had caused a truncated interpretation of the implications of Psalm 23:1a. The effect sprang partly from sinful blindness that caused her to retreat from the full-orbed impact of God's fellowship. As Sally reads, Christ overcomes her misconceptions by removal of fear and retreat, because he himself suffered ultimate "retreat" from God in his death.

Next, the same process is a process in which Sally grows in understanding herself. Through sinfulness she has resisted the humiliation involved in being compared to sheep, or resisted the truth about the incompetence of sheep to look after themselves. She has desired to be autonomous and so resisted the implications about comfort, guidance, and nourishment in the psalm. Christ gives her true self-knowledge because in the cross he shows the deep dimensions of Sally's sin and in the resurrection he gives her the confidence to look at her sin without shrinking, because of the promise of new life. And so Sally puts to death her former resistance.

Much of this process may take place without Sally consciously being aware of all the ways in which the work of Christ is implicated in her growth. But Sally's subjective consciousness is not the only measure of what is going on. In view of God's holiness, the seriousness of God's curse on sin, and the frightfulness of God's giving people over to evil (Rom. 1:18–32), we know that Christ's work must be the objective basis by which Sally overcomes sin at any point in her life. It is so even when Sally is not self-consciously aware that she is overcoming sin, much less self-consciously aware of how and why she does so.

6. Christ as Savior of the hermeneutical circle

As I observed in my earlier article, Sally's growth in understanding involves several instances of hermeneutical circles.[9] Her understanding of any one passage (Ps. 23:1a) is affected by the surrounding passages (Psalm 23 as a whole; the Book of Psalms; the Bible as a whole); her understanding of God is affected by her previous understanding of God; her understanding of herself is affected by her previous understanding of herself; and all these influence one another. We who are analyzing Sally are ourselves like her. Our self-conscious hermeneutical reflection is still one more circular influence. Hence our sinfulness in each aspect also contributes to the continuation of sinfulness in all the aspects. The radical nature of human depravity means that sin contaminates every aspect of human life. The hermeneutical circle simply traces ways in which such contamination operates.

In this situation, hermeneutical self-consciousness can be an instrument that we use to discover, criticize, and root out sin. But it can be so only if our own self-consciousness is purified by the work of Christ. In other words, our hermeneutical reflection must itself be an instance of "working out our own salvation in fear and trembling, because God is at work in us both to will and to act according to his good purpose" (Phil. 2:12–13). On the other hand, hermeneutical self-consciousness can easily become a way of saving ourselves instead of believing in God's salvation. Then it becomes a curse. From this curse as well Christ came to save us. Christ in his death suffered the destruction of his own understanding (Matt. 27:46) in order that in his resurrection he might communicate to us perfect wisdom (Luke 24:45). Christ's cry of dereliction in Matthew 27:46 is so deep that it is not exhaustively analyzable. But we can say that Christ's suffering included great intellectual and emotional distress, not merely physical pain. As a man he ceased to understand himself, because in his intellectual agony he did not comprehensively understand the action of God toward him. By contrast, in his resurrection he perfectly understands himself, because out of the fullness of messianic accomplishment and wisdom he communicates what all the Scriptures say about him (Luke 24:44–45). Christ undergoes, as it were, a hermeneutical death and resurrection with respect to his understanding of himself and the OT, in order that we may be saved from our hermeneutical sin.

7. Conclusion

The fundamental implication of these reflections is similar to that of my earlier reflections of God's lordship in interpretation. Just as there is no metaphysical interpretive standpoint free of the lordship of God, and just as no moment in interpretation escapes his exhaustive mastery, so no human standpoint is free of the conflict of sin and redemption, and no moment in interpretation escapes the penetrating influence of our relation to Christ's life, death, and resurrection. There is no neutrality. There is no "objectivity" even in the sense of which Enlightenment rationalism dreams. The only ultimate objectivity is also an exhaustively personal subjectivity, namely the eternal objective fact of intra-Trinitarian communion in truth, power, and personal fellowship. The only finite replicas of such objectivity are never to be found in the realm of the lie (John 8:44), but in the freedom of the sons of God. As we are subjectively indwelt by the Spirit of truth, we bow before God's majestic wisdom and drink our fill of the water of life flowing from the throne of the Lamb. Only through this deeply subjective experience do we have unfettered access to objective truth. All interpretation present and future is controlled by these realities.

Notes

[1] I assume that the Bible consistently teaches not universal salvation but salvation of the cosmos—that is, a total world-system and a renewed human race united in Jesus Christ. This salvation includes the aspect of purification that takes place when God finally and eternally cuts off unclean individuals (Rev. 21:8, 27; 2 Thess. 1:8–10). See Benjamin B. Warfield, "God's Immeasurable Love," in *The Savior of the World* (reprint; Cherry Hill, NJ: Mack 1972) 69–87.

[2] I have explored some implications of this lordship in an earlier article, Vern Sheridan Poythress, "God's Lordship in Interpretation," *WTJ* 50 (1988) 27–64.

[3] Ibid.

[4] In terms of older categories of systematic theology, I am simply reasserting the doctrine of

total (radical) depravity.

[5] Here I am simply applying the Reformed doctrine of common grace to the question of human interpretation. See, for example, the penetrating discussion of Cornelius Van Til, *The Defense of the Faith* (Philadelphia: Presbyterian and Reformed, 1955) 155–78; id., *Common Grace* (Philadelphia: Presbyterian and Reformed, 1947).

[6] See Poythress, "God's Lordship in Interpretation," 34–39.

[7] Ibid., 37–39.

[8] From within the liberal/modernist tradition, the emphasis on the importance of history and its goal is especially prominent in the writings of Pannenberg. See., e.g., Wolfhart Pannenberg, *Theology and the Kingdom of God* (Philadelphia: Westminster, 1969); id., *Human Nature, Election, and History* (Philadelphia: Westminster, 1977); id., *Basic Questions in Theology* (3 vols.; Philadelphia: SCM, 1970–73).

[9] Poythress, "God's Lordship in Interpretation," 54–63.

ETHICS/SPIRITUAL LIFE

Donald G. Bloesch, area editor

ETHICS/SPIRITUAL LIFE

DONALD G. BLOESCH
Professor of Theology
University of Dubuque Theological Seminary

Introduction

The articles selected for this section of the book are designed to introduce the reader to some salient issues in ethics and spirituality. As will become apparent, these selections do not necessarily reflect my views, but their significance for the contemporary church is obvious.

Of particular interest is Don Zinger's "Are Grace and Virtue Compatible?" which examines two options in ethics today—the virtue or character ethics of Stanley Hauerwas, a Methodist, and an ethics of grace, as we find it in the Lutheran theologian Gilbert Meilaender. Both these options are to be contrasted with consequentialist ethics and deontological ethics, which appeals to universal principles for ethical guidance. Zinger poses a pertinent question: Can a virtue-character ethic exist in harmony with a theology of grace? From Meilaender's perspective, the answer must be a resounding no. Confessing Lutherans will readily detect an inevitable works-righteousness in an ethic that sets out to cultivate virtue in imitation of Christ. According to Meilaender, virtue comes not from disciplined habits of character but from the liberation of the sinner by divine grace.

Zinger wishes to explore the possibility of incorporating a virtue-character ethic within an evangelical ethics of grace. He astutely recognizes that to appeal to grace without sounding the call to costly discipleship is to sell out the gospel.

Instead of combining disparate types of ethics, however, I suggest that we look at an ethics of the divine commandment, which is based on the paradoxical unity of gospel and law, and which is found in Calvin and Barth. Grace does not undercut the moral imperative but empowers us to fulfill this imperative. In the framework of this type of ethics it is more appropriate to speak of obedience than of virtue.

Howard Rice's contribution, "Feasting and Fasting in the Reformed Tradition," has far-reaching ecumenical implication, for he pleads for a return to the discipline of fasting in the churches of the Reformation. Rice reminds us that Calvin believed that the good things of the world are not simply to be used but to be enjoyed. Calvin broke decisively with the body-mind dualism that is a product of Manichaeism and Neo-Platonism. Yet, Calvin and the

Puritans were also alert to the dangers in an immoderate and indiscriminate use of the gifts of life. These blessings are not to be enjoyed at the expense of our neighbor in need. Indeed, the gifts we have are to be distributed for our neighbor's benefit.

Rice proposes fasting as a worthwhile spiritual discipline for the church today. Its theological basis lies not in contempt for the body but in the need to subdue bodily appetite in order to enhance prayer and sensitize one to the crying needs of the impoverished peoples of the world. He makes a convincing case that our social outreach is incomplete if we concentrate exclusively on freeing people from degrading physical conditions without at the same time bringing people the hope of freedom from the passions of the flesh that can sap spiritual vitality.

Bruce Demarest and Charles Raup touch on several important issues in their thoughtful essay, "Recovering the Heart of Christian Spirituality." They remind us that Protestantism suffers from the scourges of both intellectualism, in which Christianity is practically equated with a world view, and moralism, in which faith is reduced to ethical achievements. They make an impassioned plea to unite our conceptual knowledge of God with experiential knowledge if we are to make progress in the spiritual life. They rightly contend that churches are not satisfying the spiritual hunger of our age, which accounts for the rising interest in Eastern religions and the emerging New Age movement. They boldly call us to learn from the spiritual heritages of Roman Catholicism and Eastern Orthodoxy and be willing to adopt disciplines foreign to our own traditions but capable of enhancing spiritual life.

While there is some wisdom in their recommendations, we should take care not to fall into practices that stand in contradiction to the clear witness of the biblical prophets and apostles and the Protestant Reformers. Can centering prayer, in which we empty ourselves of all thoughts, be reconciled with the biblical idea of prayer as the pouring out of the soul before God? Is there not a danger that the reverent repetition of spiritually meaningful words, which the authors advocate, may all too easily degenerate into the vain repetition of ritual prayer, which has been so widespread in Catholic and Orthodox (and now New Age) circles? I wholeheartedly agree that we should respectfully listen to our brothers and sisters in the older Christian traditions, for they have much to teach us. Yet we must not confuse biblical, prophetic prayer with mystical prayer, which has its source in the Greek mystery religions and Neo-Platonism rather than in Holy Scripture.

Writing from a Catholic perspective, Monika Hellwig questions some of the attitudes and practices of her church in her provocative essay, "In Spirit and in Truth: A Catholic Perspective on the Holy Spirit." She decries the tendency, so conspicuous in pre-Vatican II Catholicism, to domesticate the Holy Spirit by binding the Spirit to the offices and rites of the church. Spirit should not be subordinate to structure, but structure should be opened to the wind of the Spirit. Whereas in the traditional Catholic view a crucial role of the Spirit is to guarantee the infallibility of church teaching, she suggests that the primary role of the Spirit is to bring renewal to persons, structures, and nations. She deftly criticizes Roman Catholic conservatives for trying to control the work of the Spirit, but she lauds Pope John XXIII and the Second Vatican Council for presenting a challenging vision of the freedom of the Spirit.

Although keenly aware of the flaws in Catholic traditionalism, Hellwig needs to be equally alert to the dangers in the new Catholicism: sundering the unity of Spirit and Word and viewing revolutionary movements in society as vehicles of the Spirit. Making clear that the pivotal question is "where to look for the guidance of the Holy Spirit," she concludes that the Spirit is working in base communities, revolutionary liberation movements, and the cry of the oppressed for justice. She sees promise in "the reemergence of prophecy in new, often communal forms."

Despite her solid contribution to an important discussion, Hellwig can be faulted for blurring the lines between the work of redemption, which is God's work alone, and human efforts and strategies for liberation. Although the latter may have their inspiration and genesis in the message of the kingdom, the kingdom of God must not be confounded with movements of social reform. The kingdom is God's own creation, and for it we must wait and pray. Only the Spirit of God can bring about "a corporate transformation of the human situation," but we can bear witness to the Spirit's work in our words and deeds and demonstrate its reality in our personal lives.

A more solidly biblical orientation is to be found in Albert Outler's "A Focus on the Holy Spirit: Spirit and Spirituality in John Wesley." Outler takes Wesley as a model of true spirituality, who bore potent witness to the power and reality of the Holy Spirit in his life, work, and thought. Wesley admirably united the pneumatological and the ethical, constantly looking for a synthesis of spirituality and social reform. For him, authentic spirituality was "a daily growth in pure and holy religion." His pilgrimage was "from a dedicated perfectionist who seldom succeeded to a wayfarer of the Spirit who seldom failed." Interestingly, Outler describes Wesley's Aldersgate experience as "less the reconstruction of Wesley's basic doctrines of God-in-Christ than an unexpected discovery of their power and effects."

Acutely conscious of the qualitative gulf between New Age spirituality with its emphasis on self-fulfillment and evangelical spirituality with its call to lose ourselves in the service of Christ's kingdom, Outler wisely urges biblical Christians to look to Wesley for guidance in realizing true spirituality in our time. My one criticism is that his essay smacks slightly of a Wesleyan triumphalism. Does not Wesley's emphasis on Christian perfection need to be held in tension with the Reformers' emphasis on justification by the alien righteousness of Christ and on the Christian's constant need for the forgiveness of sins? Wesley, of course, made a prominent place for justification, but he was sometimes inclined to regard sanctification as a still higher salvation.

Here is not the place to give a comparative analysis of different Christian theologies, but I fundamentally agree with Outler's positive assessment of Wesley and certainly include him as one of the fathers of the church universal.

From these essays one may justifiably conclude that both a rationalist objectivism and an experientialist subjectivism are challenging the Christian faith today. We need a theology that unites Word and Spirit in order to lay a sound basis for the life of discipleship. We need a theological vision that will bring together spiritual discipline and ethical obedience. Is not such a vision given in the gospel and the law revealed to us in Holy Scripture?

About the Area Editor

Donald G. Bloesch (B.D., Chicago Theological Seminary; Ph.D., University of Chicago; D.D., Doane College) is Professor of Theology at the University of Dubuque Theological Seminary. Before joining the faculty in 1957, he had a pastorate for three years in a United Church of Christ in the Chicago area. In the spring semester of 1982 he was Visiting Professor of Religion at the School of Religion, University of Iowa, Iowa City. A past president of the American Theological Society (Midwest division), he is active in that society and the Karl Barth Society. He has done post-doctoral work at the Universities of Oxford, Basel, and Tübingen. He has received fellowships from the World Council of Churches, the American Association of Theological Schools, and the Institute for Advanced Christian Studies. He is author (or editor) of twenty-five books in theology and spirituality and over 250 articles and book reviews. His most recent books are *Freedom for Obedience* (Harper & Row, 1987) and *Theological Notebook* Vol. I (Helmers and Howard, 1989).

ARE GRACE AND VIRTUE COMPATIBLE?

DON H. ZINGER
Professor of Religion
Grand View College, Des Moines

Article from *Lent*

With a credit card billing came a little memo in striking calligraphy: "Character is not an inheritance; each person must build it for himself." This is only one expression of the pervasiveness of the concern for character and virtue in various elements of our culture. This interest in a virtue or character ethic is matched in philosophical and theological circles by a revival of an ethical theory in which character traits or virtues are seen as the basic moral characteristics that allow us to flourish as authentically human. This was the theory at the root of the medieval synthesis of faith and reason, so vehemently attacked by Luther. As one reads the Visa dictum above, that attack is no surprise.

If character is something each person builds, how can this ethic be compatible with a theology of grace, which presents us Christ as a sheer undeserved gift? On the other hand, is grace destructive of the root of moral endeavor? I propose to examine two Christian ethicists for insights. One is Stanley Hauerwas of Duke University; the other is Gilbert Meilaender, a Lutheran. My conclusion: a cautious positive note on further exploration of such a Christian virtue-character ethic, more along the lines of Meilaender than Hauerwas, along with strong warning signals from Luther.

First, some background on ethical theory: in modern thought, there are two basic approaches to making ethical decisions. One is the Consequentialist claim that it is only the results of an act which determines its ethical value. Surely there is much of this in Christian ethics, such as Jesus' saying, "By their fruits you shall know them."

At the same time there is a strong element of the second type of ethical position in Christian ethics. This school of thought, the Deontological approach, is the position that inherent in duty or in the act itself are qualities that determine the rightness or wrongness of the act. From this basis comes the pattern of biblical obligatory principles, rules and laws.

There are problems with both approaches that we leave for others to point out. Here let us simply note that either has difficulty standing without the other, so a third approach, standard in ancient Greece and in the Roman Catholic tradition, is increasingly attractive. This virtue or character ethic holds that the person, the moral agent, is crucial. Priority is given to the question, "What kind of person am I and to what community do I belong?" In the first two positions, characteristic of modernity, that question seems less central. In modernity we ask either "What results am I looking for?" or "Out of which principle am I directed?" With virtue-character in the forefront, priority is given to the self and to virtues and vices which allow the self, the moral agent, to flourish or to wither. Then, secondarily, there occurs analysis of consequences of acts, obligatory duties, etc. It is not my purpose here to further analyze these three basic ethical positions. Rather I ask of the third one, the virtue-character ethic, whether it can live in harmony with an evangelical sense of grace, of the gratuitous gift of the Gospel?

Can Virtue Come from Grace?

Luther was a harsh critic of the virtue ethic of his day. He saw it as a wedge for works righteousness, squeezing righteousness out of one's own spiritual resources. Luther saw the Christian life as a pilgrimage from the baptism of a justified, forgiven sinner, which results in the daily deaths and resurrections of a sinner yet saint. What we do depends on what we are. Here Luther agrees with the virtue ethic. Yet what we are is seen by God as an alien righteousness won for us by the sacrificial death of Christ. Doing good depends on being seen by God as good, but that good is Christ's and not our own doing. We act in spite of our estrangement and because of our justification, which is the gift of forgiveness.

But is it possible, on the one hand, that in reality the Christian has the roots of moral striving cut? Can grace be seen as destructive to morality? Christians from Paul to Bonhoeffer have pondered this. And on the other hand, is it destructive of grace to live out an examined life of virtue, disciplining one's life in a pattern called character? Can a virtue ethic lead us to climbing the ladder of moralism and legalism to hand ourselves proudly to the Judge?

A Contemporary Approach Strong on Virtue Yet Tenuous on Grace: Stanley Hauerwas

The work of Stanley Hauerwas, a Methodist, reveals the possible pitfall of a virtue ethic, seen from a Lutheran stance. Taking the cue from a story-narrative theology, Hauerwas sees a Christian life that enfleshes the biblical stories, shaping our character in forms of faith, love, courage, patience, and especially peacemaking. At once the appealing strength of a virtue ethic is evident. Hauerwas of course supremely looks to the story of Jesus Christ. The Story is closer to the heart of theology than an abstract discourse on principles and rules. So we are formed as persons, as moral agents. Our lives are given pattern. The person yields a motif, as we live out the intentionality, the metaphor of the community we represent, the people who imitate Jesus. This is an ethic of imitation, especially of the suffering love and peacemaking of Jesus.

Just as the cross here seems more revelatory of suffering love than of atonement, so it is no surprise that justification takes a back seat to sanctification in Hauerwas's work. We cannot slavishly imitate Christ's life, but we can participate in the community of suffering love and apply that to contemporary issues. Hauerwas is nobly appealing to the Christian conscience. His appeal to peacemaking and other virtues is a glaring mirror of the occasions we live out of "cheap grace." However, the problem with the thought of Hauerwas is the lack of roots for sanctification in the sheer gift of Christ, that is, in justification by grace. As Hauerwas puts it, "But justification is only another way of talking about sanctification." Thus he points to our transformation by initiation into the community of the cross and resurrection.[1]

Has Lutheranism become only a highly organized "tradition" that makes mildly good people? If so, Hauerwas deserves our attention. Or, on the other hand, can one be Christian with the nobility of virtue, yet without the fountainhead of grace? Hauerwas seems to yield a kingdom ethic, but one which is a kingdom of virtuous lives. Luther would indeed see such a virtue ethic as an opening for a moralism hostile to grace. Is there another approach?

Virtue Flowing from Grace: Gilbert Meilaender

Gilbert Meilaender calls for the Christian to look to the source of our virtues in grace. Whether it be love or gentleness or gratitude, the fountainhead is the mercy of Christ, not, as in the traditional virtue ethic, an elaborate fostering, nurturing, developmental process. In this view virtue comes not from disciplined habits of character but from the liberation of the sinner by Christ. One cannot spray fruit in order to make the tree well. The person must be virtuous. The person in Christ is so. "Only the divine initiative can create a virtuous self."[2] This depends on a passivity before God, not a developmental human effort.

In case of a charge of his being too simple or too radical, Meilaender would reply in terms of the doctrine of *simul justus et peccator* and in view of the believer's pilgrimage toward the Consummation, the Eschaton, the absolute future of God. (Meilaender needs to spell out this defense in a less sketchy fashion.) His conclusion is that character is a gift and not something we simply work at. He does not rule out moral education, but he thinks it is "safe only when we gather to worship, when we continually return to hear the Word."[3] Here at the point of analyzing our moral growth, of seeing parish life as nurturing the moral life, Meilaender needs to defend his position more fully. Is this simply an excellent restatement of Luther's theology or is there something new about moral education that Meilaender has to offer? Is grace simply incompatible with moral education? How would the faith development theory of J. Fowler be harmonious with his position? We wait for more analysis here.

Concluding Reflections

1. I assume, though I have not argued it above, that America and in some sense Western civilization is in a moral crisis and needs the antidote of some type of virtue-character ethic to take us beyond the acidity of individualism.

2. The advantage of Christian virtue ethic over other forms of the account of the Christian life is that it addresses the prior question of what kind of person I am and to what people do I belong, rather than getting hung up on absolutes and norms, principles and commands. Such an ethic is also the proper grounding for reflection on the ethics of consequentialism on the one hand, and of a deontological approach on the other hand.

3. Meilaender's position has the strength of resisting moralism and legalism in the name of grace. The priority of the first commandment as the fountain of grace in Luther's Large Catechism might lead one in the same direction as Meilaender.

4. Whether that life of grace can be understood and lived by us without such moralism and legalism is the danger signal sent up by Luther's classic Evangelical position. Luther could be blunt. "Properly speaking, the gospel demands no work of us to become holy and redeemed. Indeed it damns such works and requires of us only that we trust in Christ. . . ." In his confrontation with Cardinal Contarini, Luther objected that even verbally insisting that justification *must* lead to good works is a crack in the door to legalism and moralism.

5. To take the way of Hauerwas is to sell out grace. However, refashioned in a context of grace, Hauerwas would be taken seriously as showing what Christian virtues in authentic Christian community may be like. His writing sparkles with vividness and power.

6. To take grace without seeing it as costly grace is to sell out the gospel. Our time needs an account of the Christian life that portrays it as spontaneous and yet examined, as Spirit given and yet given to virtues that have full human grounding and do not seem to come out of the blue of intuition. Christian ethical theory in our day needs the stimulus of a virtue-character position, if such an account can avoid moralism and legalism, if indeed parish life can be a focus of moral education, rooted in grace.

Christians in our parishes need to know where their goodness lies. Teaching traditional values will not save us, nor will chummy suburban Christianity, certainly not slushy grace. What is needed is a life rooted in grace, that is in the Christ, nourished in the Word.

Notes

[1] Stanley Hauerwas, *The Peaceable Kingdom, a Primer in Christian Ethics* (Notre Dame University Press, 1983), p. 94.

[2] Gilbert Meilaender, *The Theory and Practice of Virtue* (Notre Dame University Press, 1984), p. 114. His most recent book: *The Limits of Love: Some Theological Explorations* (University Park and London: Pennsylvania State University Press, 1987).

[3] Ibid., p. 126.

FEASTING AND FASTING IN THE REFORMED TRADITION

HOWARD L. RICE
Professor of Ministry and Chaplain
San Francisco Theological Seminary

Article from *Pacific Theological Review*

When I was growing up, I believed that one of the many differences between Catholics and Protestants was that they fasted and we did not. Furthermore, we Protestants took some malicious delight in the difference, tempting our Catholic friends on Fridays with hamburgers and secretly laughing at what we believed to be the folly of their refusal to violate their arbitrary rules. We feasted while they fasted.

Feasting and fasting are alike in that both have to do with our attitude toward and our use of the gifts of the material world. Both feasting and fasting are integral to every religion; there is nothing unique in the Christian tradition about the fact that both feasting and fasting have been practiced throughout its history. Yet every religious tradition has its own way of understanding the central meaning of both feasting and fasting as expressions of a basic attitude toward the material world. Our spirituality or piety (I use the terms synonymously) is the pattern by which we shape our lives in response to our experience of God's grace. John Calvin defines piety as "that union of reverence and love of God, which a knowledge of [God's] benefits causes."[1] We all practice a piety of some kind, and its form is determined by our attitude toward the world.

Within traditional Christianity there is a wide diversity of understandings about the material world, from the rejection of the world as evil to be avoided at all costs to the attitude that God gives material prosperity as a reward for goodness and that one should acquire and enjoy material possessions to the utmost. At different times in history and among people of different social class, this variety takes particular shape. It is not an accident, for example, that people who have prospered tend to ascribe their wealth to a benevolent God and to view their possessions as a sign of God's particular favor toward them.

Paul expressed both the dilemma and the potential of our relationship with the material world when he wrote to the Philippians, "I know how to be abased, and I know how to abound; in any and all circumstances I have learned the secret of facing plenty and hunger, abundance and want."[2] Paul hints that dealing with plenty and abundance may be as difficult as dealing with want and hunger; both require assistance from the one "who strengthens" us. Both have to be learned. Because of their intimate connection, those who do not know what it is like to be in want do not know how to deal with plenty. Those who do not know how to fast do not know how to feast.

In a materialistic society, how do we as Christians face abundance and plenty? Because most of us live in abundance in contrast to much of the rest of the world, we cannot avoid the issue of our attitude toward our prosperity. How do we respond to the evangelists of abundance who proclaim that God rewards the faithful with riches? Do they tempt us to believe we deserve them? Can we learn how to abound when we know that others are starving? Our feasting is often marked by a concerted effort to forget about the way food is distributed unevenly in our world. Conscientious Christians sometimes have a hard time enjoying a feast. It may be that only a recovery of the discipline of fasting can bring the necessary balance into our lives which will make us able to feast with joy and delight.

The Reformed tradition provides a historical rootage which can be of assistance to us in understanding our own situation. The Reformed tradition developed among people who were the middle class of the time and flourished among those who were generally neither the landed aristocracy nor the peasant poor. Its social placement had much to do with its attitude toward the world, and it may thus give us guidance as we struggle with how it is we can be faithful as rich Christians in a world of want.

No text in Scripture has posed the problem of our relation to the material world more sharply than Romans, in which Paul declares, "to set the mind on the flesh is death, but to set the mind on the Spirit is life and peace."[3] This has been read and continues to be read as a denunciation of the material world as if that world is opposed to the domain of God. A world of the spirit, in this view, is free from the body, escapes the temptations of the flesh, and is enabled by the power of a disembodied risen Christ to avoid contamination with the stuff of this world. In his commentary on this passage, Calvin rejects body/spirit dualism by his definition of Paul's terms: "the term flesh includes all that human beings retain from their natural character," but "spirit, on the other hand, is called the renewing of our corrupt nature, while God reforms us."[4] These definitions establish a perspective on the material world that does not fall into the dichotomy of a bad material world and a good nonmaterial, spiritual world. For Calvin, sin expresses itself in the totality of human life, thinking, feeling, acting, politics, economics, and piety. He rejects the notion that sin came into the world by sensual temptation and insists that "unbelief has opened the door to ambition, but ambition has proved the parent of rebellion."[5]

Because he rejects body/mind dualism, Calvin can celebrate the glory and beauty of nature as God's gift to human beings. "It is no small honor that God, for our sakes, has so magnificently adorned the world, in order that we may not only be spectators of this beauteous theater, but also enjoy the multiplied abundance and variety of good things which are presented to us in it."[6] This good creation is intended for human use as a promise by God of "a liberal abundance, which should leave nothing wanting to a sweet and pleasant life."[7]

This goodness of life includes human sexuality, which Calvin declared to be ordained by God for human salvation.[8] He wrote that, "conjugal intercourse is a thing that is pure, honorable and holy."[9] He takes issue with Paul's admonition that "it is better to marry than to be aflame with passion,"[10] saying "there is not strictly a comparison here, inasmuch as lawful marriage is honorable in all things. . . . The apostle . . . has made use of a customary form of expression, though not strictly accurate."[11] The joy of sexuality is for men and women equally. Calvin calls it an "error of some who think that the woman was formed only for the sake of propagation."[12]

The glories of the created order go beyond our need for survival. Calvin described God's provision of food as "meant not only for necessity but also for delight and good cheer." The same applies to clothing and other parts of creation. "In grasses, trees, and fruits, apart from their various uses, there is a beauty of appearance and pleasantness of odor"[13] which are meant to be enjoyed. "Hath the Lord clothed the flowers with the great beauty that greets our eyes, the sweetness of smell that is wafted upon our nostrils, and yet will it be unlawful for our eyes to be affected by that beauty, or our sense of smell by the sweetness of that odor? What? Did he not so distinguish colors as to make some more lovely than others? What? Did he not endow gold and silver, ivory and marble, with a loveliness that renders them more precious than other metals or stones? Did he not, in short, render many things attractive to us, apart from the necessary uses?"[14]

When we feast, we enjoy God's good provision and celebrate our gratitude to God. Calvin declares that we must count the blessings of life "among those gifts of divine generosity which are not at all to be rejected."[15] The Second Helvetic Confession explicitly approves those feast days which celebrate the memory of the Lord's nativity, circumcision, passion, resurrection, and ascension.[16] The Westminster Confession mentions days of thanksgivings upon special occasions.[17] It does not, however, identify these days, since the influence of Puritanism had led to the rejection of the traditional church year.

Puritans were not overly solemn and world-denying. They held public feasts or thanksgiving after a good harvest, a military success, or some other event which they interpreted as a blessing from God.[18] The Puritans appreciated the gifts of food and drink, knew how to enjoy feasts, and celebrated the joys of sex. In the early seventeenth century, Lewis Bayly, an Anglican Calvinist, whose book *The Practice of Piety* became a Puritan classic, describes feasting as "a solemn Thanksgiving (appointed by Authority) to be rendered unto God on some special Day; for some extraordinary Blessings or Deliverances received. . . . Such Feasts are to be celebrated by a publick rehearsal of those special Benefits by spiritual Psalms and Dances, by mutual feasting, and sending Presents every man to his neighbor, and by giving Gifts to the Poor."[19] This summary is as close as anyone has come to describing a really good feast. It includes song and dance, the delight of eating, gift giving, and remembering the poor.

Yet there is danger in immoderate and indiscriminate use of the gifts of life. Understanding our natural tendency to hang on to material gifts, Calvin warns, "We know how far enticements prevail to deceive us, especially when we are treated daintily; and experience shows us how difficult it is to be moderate when all is affluence around us, for luxury follows immediately upon plenty. . . . The virtue of abstinence is rarely exercised when there is an abundance of provisions."[20] Calvin seeks to provide a middle ground against two extremes: "The righteous will manage their domestic affairs with prudence and discernment so that they will be neither too lavish nor sordidly parsimonious, but in everything they will study to combine frugality with economy, without giving way to luxury."[21] He sums up the proper use of all our possessions in this way: "All the gifts we possess have been bestowed by God and entrusted to us on condition that they be distributed for our neighbors' benefit."[22]

Reformed piety is frequently characterized as a this-worldly asceticism because of the seriousness of its effort to avoid overindulgence while at the same time being thankful for God's good gifts.

Feasting without fasting can dangerously increase our natural tendency to greed and blinding self-indulgence. Calvin defines fasting "not simply as restraint and abstemiousness in food, but as something else. Throughout its course, the life of the Godly indeed ought to be tempered with frugality and sobriety, so that as far as possible it bears some resemblance to a fast."[23] Fasting thus becomes a metaphor for the Christian life itself, for the effort to avoid entanglement with luxury and the risk of being co-opted by our possessions into such fear of losing what we have that we compromise our faithfulness.

Likewise for Howard Thurman the metaphor of fasting applies to the whole of Christian commitment. "This is a living world; life is alive, and as expressions of life we, too, are alive and sustained by the characteristic vitality of life itself. God is the source of the vitality, the life, of all living things. . . . What is true for our bodies is also true for mind and spirit. At these levels God is immediately available to us if the door is opened . . . the door is opened by yielding to Him that nerve center where we feel consent or the withholding of it most centrally."[24] Thurman maintains that to offer to God what is most important to us is to become energized by God's living Spirit.

For Calvin also, sacrifice and commitment are intimately connected: "Where is your thanksgiving if you so gorge yourself with banqueting or wine that you either become stupid or are rendered useless for the duties of piety and of your calling? Where is your recognition of God if your flesh boiling over with excessive abundance into vile lusts infects the mind with its impurity so that you cannot discern anything that is right and honorable? Where is our gratefulness toward God for our clothing if in the sumptuousness of our apparel we both admire ourselves and despise others, if with its elegance and glitter we prepare ourselves for shameless conduct? Where is our recognition of God if our minds be fixed upon the splendor of our apparel?"[25]

Fasting is not just a metaphor for the Christian life. It is a specific devotional practice, which Calvin describes as "temporary in character, when we withdraw something from the normal regimen of living, either for one day or for a definite time, and pledge ourselves to a tighter and more severe restraint in diet than ordinarily."[26] Bayly calls such fasting a "help to further us the better to worship God."[27]

Calvin and Bayly speak of fasting as having three objectives. First, "we use it to weaken and subdue the flesh that it may not act wantonly,"[28] to which Bayly adds the cautionary note that we do not fast "to weaken our Bodies, as that we are made unfit to do the necessary Duties of our Calling."[29] Remembering that Calvin and other Reformed theologians insisted that the flesh does not mean the same thing as body, and that spirit is not something disembodied from the world, we can understand the Second Helvetic Confession's definition of the purpose of fasting: "Now, the more seriously the Church of Christ condemns surfeiting, drunkenness, and all kinds of lust and intemperance, so much the more strongly does it commend to us Christian fasting. For fasting is nothing else than the abstinence and moderation of the godly, and a discipline, care and chastisement of our flesh undertaken as a necessity for a time being, whereby we are humbled before God, and we deprive the flesh of its fuel so that it may the more willingly and easily obey the Spirit."[30]

Fasting is not a sign of hatred for the body, nor a belief that by punishing the body the soul will be somehow purified. Rather it is letting go of an otherwise good thing as a sign of our desire to avoid the idolatry of possessions.

Second, we fast "that we may be better prepared for prayers and holy meditations,"[31] or in Bayly's words, "that we may more devoutly contemplate God's Holy Will, and fervently pour forth our souls unto him by Prayer."[32] Although fasting serves other purposes, its main purpose is to enhance prayer. Calvin wrote that Paul and Barnabas fasted "to render themselves more eager and more unencumbered for prayer. Surely we experience this: with a full stomach our mind is not so lifted up to God that it can be drawn to prayer with a serious and ardent affection and persevere in it."[33] He describes Anna, who served God with fasting and prayers, as a woman who "in this way trained herself to sustained prayer."[34] Emily Herman, the early-twentieth-century British mystic and Presbyterian contemporary of Evelyn Underhill, captured Calvin's meaning: "We are slowly coming back to the stern truth that only the pure can see either the beauty of heaven or the beauty of earth, and that purity, in all but a few rarely endowed souls, cannot be gained or kept without a stern and frequently painful discipline. We are coming to realize once more that ecstasy of spirit can only be had at the expense of ecstasy of sense; that one cannot be drunk with wine and filled with the Spirit at the same time."[35]

Third, we fast "that it may be a testimony of our self-abasement before God when we wish to confess our guilt."[36] Fasting can thus be called a "serious Humiliation and judging of ourselves" so that we become reconciled to God as "friends and children."[37]

Confessional fasting can be either public or private, but public fasting is for the purpose of confessing corporate guilt and is a communal sign of repentance. Bayly describes a public fast as having the purpose either of removing a public calamity or of obtaining a public blessing.[38] The Puritans practiced such public fastings regularly, especially in the spring, when seeds were in the ground. Spring was also a time of privation, as the store of winter food supplies was being exhausted. It is no coincidence that this spring fast of the Puritans corresponded with the Catholic observance of Lent.[39]

Despite insistence upon the centrality of fasting, the custom gradually fell into disuse. Jonathan Edwards was concerned about the disregard for fasting by ministers in his time. He compared fasting with private prayer: Fasting "is a duty recommended by our Savior to his followers, just in like manner as secret prayer is . . . though I do not suppose that secret fasting is to be practiced in a stated manner, and steady course, as secret prayer, yet it seems to me, it is a duty that all professing Christians should practice and frequently practice."[40] Since Edwards' time, fasting has been rejected by most Reformed Protestants. This rejection seems to have coincided with their rapid ascent on the ladder of material success. The more possessions we have, the more difficult the discipline of fasting becomes.

Even private fasting is not purely individualistic, but has a close relationship to works of mercy and charity. Bayly makes this clear by defining the good works on fast days as either "works of piety to God or the works of Charity." These works of charity include "forgiving wrongs, remitting debts to the poor that are not well able to pay; but especially in giving alms to the poor, that want relief and sustenance. Else we shall under pretence of Godliness, practice Miserableness; those, who will pinch their own bellies, to defraud their labouring servants of their due Allowance."[41] He thus insists, "Be sure to give at least so much to the poor on thy fasting-day, as thou wouldst have spent in thine own diet, if thou hadst not fasted on that Day."[42]

Emily Herman sums up a theology of the body which provides grounding for the practice of fasting. "Our social gospel is incomplete. It does not embrace the full Christian doctrine of the body. That men cannot rise to their full spiritual destiny while living under degrading physical conditions is only one half of the truth about the body. . . . The other half of the truth is that no man who neglects bodily discipline—whether he be a well paid artisan gorging himself with coarse food, or an aristocrat of culture choosing his refined physical pleasures with artistic restraint—can enter the kingdom which God has prepared."[43]

A recovery of the practice of fasting among Reformed Christians today might help deepen a sense of identity with the have-nots of the world, with those people whose hunger is, in part, caused by our over-consumption. If Americans ate less beef, the land that is used for raising beef for export could be used by many Third World nations to feed their own people. Fasting might provide us with a discipline for putting materialism in perspective by teaching us to distinguish what we need from what we have come to believe that we need. It might enhance our respect for the environment by making us aware of how our consumption increases hazards to earth or depletes needed scarce materials. It might strengthen and deepen our prayers. It might also provide us with critical distance from our dominant materialistic culture. Dorothee Soelle says, "The very act of appropriating anything into one's own pattern of living and consuming is in itself an act of standing somewhat apart from the outer world which is so deeply ingrained in us."[44]

A recovery of fasting might also enable us to reclaim the centrality of our most important feast, the sacrament of Holy Communion. Although Reformed Christians have tended to observe the sacrament infrequently, they nevertheless observed it in conjunction with preparatory fasting. Among the Scots, the Thursday before Communion Sunday was known as the Fast Day, and was observed as a day of personal self-examination and prayer, often concluding with a service of public prayer in the evening.[45] The practice of preparatory services and fasting persisted among American Presbyterians until quite recently and produced an attitude of reverential expectation for the sacrament which is commonly missing today.

Feasting upon the bread and wine is a way of being grasped by the experience of the Holy in the material elements. It is a central way of expressing our relationship with the created world. Calvin made explicit the connection between being mysteriously fed at the Lord's Supper and eating the physical elements: "Our souls are fed by the flesh and blood of Christ in the same way that bread and wine keep and sustain physical life."[46] The Reformed confessions also emphasize the significance of Holy Communion as a connection between the physical and the spiritual in the life of Christians. The Scots Confession declares: "The faithful, in the right use of the Lord's Table, do so eat the body and drink the blood of the Lord Jesus that he remains in them and they in him; they are so made flesh of his flesh and bone of his bone that as the eternal Godhood was given to the flesh of Christ Jesus, which by nature was corruptible and mortal, life and immortality, so the eating and drinking of the flesh and blood of Christ Jesus does the like for us."[47]

This and other Reformed confessions also interpret, more or less accurately, the importance of appreciating the sacramental feast as a mystery. "Though it seems an incredible thing that the flesh of Christ, while at such a distance from us in respect of space, should be food for us, let us remember how far the secret virtue of the Holy Spirit surpasses all our conceptions, and how foolish it is to wish to measure its immensity by our feeble capacity."[48] He can say "from the substance of his flesh Christ breathes life into our souls—indeed, pours forth his very life into us—even though Christ's flesh itself does not enter into us."[49]

The attempt to rationalize the experience of the holy in the physical has often prevailed among Reformed Protestants and has reduced the meaning of the sacrament to a visual aid to help us remember. Just as fasting produces a readiness for prayer that cannot be explained, so participation in the Lord's Supper produces a sense of Christ's presence that cannot be explained.

Calvin refuses to rationalize what he calls the "mystical blessing" which we receive because "the Lord's body was once for all so sacrificed for us that we may now feed upon it, and by feeding feel in ourselves the working of that unique sacrifice; and that his blood was once so shed for us in order to be our perpetual drink."[50] Despite his effort to explain the presence of Christ in the Sacrament, he finally declares, "I shall not be ashamed to confess that it is a secret too lofty for either my mind to comprehend or my words to declare. And, to speak more plainly, I rather experience than understand it."[51]

Just as both fasting and feasting have profoundly corporate implications, so the Lord's Supper is not simply a means to achieve personal enjoyment or to benefit us spiritually. It always points us to our relationship with others. Calvin speaks about the unity among believers to which the sacrament testified. Because the bread "is made of many grains so mixed together that one cannot be distinguished from another, so it is fitting that in the same way we should be joined and bound together by such great agreement of minds that no sort of disagreement or division may intrude."[52] As we share together, we discover with new power that all who are bound together in Christ are members of his body. Calvin urges us all to treat all these as members of our body, to cherish, protect, and help them as those with whom we share Christ's body.[53]

A recovery of the traditional Reformed emphases in the Eucharist might enable us to discover with new power that we are members of a community rather than solitary individuals. It could enhance our sense of the value of material things which become bearers of the holy both in the sacrament and throughout our lives. It could, if practiced more regularly, deepen our sense of mystical union with the incarnate one and free us from our slavery to rationalism.

Any genuine recovery of Reformed piety must involve our attitude toward the material world. Our tradition has much to teach us that can assist us in the struggle to be faithful in the middle of our affluence by recalling us to the importance of fasting and feasting. Fasting, whether from food or from other things that have become too important for us, is a way of becoming free from the idolatry of things. It is also a way of discovering the importance of sharing with others in a world of tremendous need. As we fast in our own personal lives, we may discover the connection between fasting and politics. Rich nations may need to learn the discipline of fasting as much as rich individuals. Then, as we fast, we can also rediscover the centrality of feasting, especially the feast of the Lord's Supper, in which we discover through elements as common as bread and wine that we are brought into Christ's risen presence.

Notes

[1] John Calvin, *The Institutes of the Christian Religion*, John McNeil, ed., Westminster Press, Philadelphia, 1960, I,II,1.

[2] Philippians 4:12 (RSV).

[3] Romans 8:6.

[4] Calvin, *Commentary on the Epistles of Paul the Apostle to the Romans and to the Thessalonians*, trans. Ross MacKenzie, Eerdmans, Grand Rapids, 1961, Romans 8:35, p. 186.

[6] Calvin, *Commentaries on the First Book of Moses Called Genesis*, trans. John King, Baker Book House, Grand Rapids, 1948, vol. 1, Genesis 3:6, p. 153.

[7] Calvin, *Commentary on the Book of Psalms*, trans. James Anderson, Baker Book House, Grand Rapids, 1948, vol. 4, Psalm 104:31, p. 169.

[7] Calvin, *Commentary on Genesis*, vol. 1, Genesis 1:30, p. 100.

[8] Calvin, *Commentary on Genesis*, vol. 1, Genesis 2:18, p. 129.

[9] Calvin, *Commentary on the Epistles of Paul the Apostle to the Corinthians*, trans. John Pringle, Baker Book House, Grand Rapids, vol. 1, 1 Corinthians 7:6, p. 231.

[10] Calvin, *Commentary on Corinthians*, 1 Corinthians 7:9, p. 235.

[11] Ibid.

[12] Calvin, *Commentary on Genesis*, vol. 1, Genesis 2:18, p. 131.

[13] Calvin, *Institutes*, III,X,2.

[14] Ibid.

[15] *Institutes*, III,IX,3.

[16] *The Book of Confessions*, Presbyterian Church (U.S.A.), The Office of the General Assembly, New York and Atlanta, 1983, 5.226.

[17] *Confessions*, 6.116.

[18] Charles Hambrick-Stowe, *The Practice of Piety*, University of North Carolina Press, Chapel Hill, 1982, p. 100.

[19] Lewis Bayly, *The Practice of Piety*, printed for Daniel Midwinter at the Three Crowns in St. Paul's Churchyard, London, 1714, pp. 228–29.

[20] Calvin, *Commentary on the Book of Daniel*, trans. Thomas Myers, Baker Book House, Grand Rapids, 1948, Daniel 1:8, vol. 1, p. 97.

[21] Calvin, *Commentary on the Book of Psalms*, vol. 4, Psalm 112:5, p. 69.

[22] Calvin, *Institutes*, III,V,5.

[23] *Institutes*, IV,XIII,18.

[24] Howard Thurman, *Disciplines of the Spirit*, Harper & Row, New York, 1963, p. 21.

[25] Calvin, *Institutes*, III,X,3.

[26] *Institutes*, IV,XII,18.

[27] Lewis Bayly, *The Practice of Piety*, p. 295.

[28] *Institutes*, IV,XII,15.

[29] Bayly, *The Practice of Piety*, p. 295.

[30] *The Book of Confessions*, 5.227.

[31] Calvin, *Institutes*, IV,XII,15.

[32] Bayly, *The Practice of Piety*, p. 295.

[33] *Institutes*, IV,XII,16.

[34] Ibid.

[35] Emily Herman, *The Meaning and Value of Mysticism*, George H. Doran, New York, 1925, p. 105.

[36] Calvin, *Institutes*, IV,XII,15.

[37] Bayly, *The Practice of Piety*, p. 296.

[38] *Piety*, p. 297.

[39] Charles Hambrick-Stowe, *The Practice of Piety*, p. 102.

[40] Jonathan Edwards, "Thoughts on the Revival of Religion in New England, 1741," in *Edwards on Revival*, Dunning and Spaulding, New York, 1832, p. 401.

[41] Bayly, *The Practice of Piety*, p. 291.

[42] *Piety*, p. 292.

[43] Emily Herman, *Creative Prayer*, Harper and Brothers, New York, 1934, p. 141.

[44] Dorothee Soelle, *Death by Bread Alone*, Fortress Press, Philadelphia, 1975, p. 73.

[45] Evelyn Underhill, *Worship*, Crossroad, New York, 1982, p. 293.

[46] Calvin, *Institutes*, IV,XVII,10.

[47] *The Book of Confessions*, 3.21.

[48] *Institutes*, IV,XVII,10.

[49] *Institutes*, IV,XVII,32.

[50] *Institutes*, IV,XVII,1.

[51] *Institutes*, IV,XVII,32.

[52] *Institutes*, IV,XVII,38.

[53] *Institutes*, IV,XVII,40.

Some evangelicals identify Christianity with a formally correct theology or a coherent world view. A few even define the person, as image of God, exclusively as the power of a rational mind![1] Christendom furthermore suffers the scourge of *moralism* when it believes that ethical achievements, apart from a vital relation to God, constitute the heart of the Christian life. Not uncommon in conservative circles is the belief that a Christian attains mature spirituality by legalistically adhering to a set of rules or a code of conduct. M. Kelsey sums up the present state of affairs with the following astute observation: "In Protestantism, God became a theological idea known by inference rather than a reality known by experience."[2]

II. The Problem of an Undernourished Heart

Surely the Christian faith requires sturdy intellectual foundations. Who God is and what He has done for humankind in Christ constitute the non-negotiable foundation of true spirituality. Similarly the Christian faith embraces right moral action. Good works, as the letter of James emphasizes, represent the inevitable fruit of a heart that is properly related to God. However, conceptual knowledge of God and good works must be joined with an experiential knowledge of God nurtured in an atmosphere of faith and commitment. C. Jung, who was not an evangelical Christian, observed that the religion of many professing Christians was largely intellectual, lacking in vital experience of God. Jung concluded that as a result of this imbalance many Christians were spiritually and emotionally ill. Persons created in the image of God are not adequately nourished by a faith that is primarily intellectual or moralistic. For example, the mere thought of food will not satisfy a hungry person. Nothing short of actual partaking of food will suffice. So it is that Christians hunger and thirst for a participation in God that strikes a chord of reality in their total, lived experience. Believers need personally to discover and relate to the God who not only engages their minds, but who also lovingly reveals himself to their hearts.

The contemporary rush of Christians to psychotherapists suggests that many believers, some of whom have been saved for decades, have deep-seated needs that are not being met. The Christian therapist assists the broken and hurting individual to come into a healing relationship with God, with himself and with others. Significant numbers of Christians in our day need to bring their head knowledge of God into the heart in the form of a total experience that fulfills them as renewed image-bearers of God. Human spiritual hunger must be satisfied. People who do not engage the true and living God in a fulfilling, lived experience are vulnerable to transcendent experiences offered by Eastern religions, the New Age Movement, Satanism, or hallucinogenic drugs. Thus, some fault for the contemporary drift to the East and to the cults may lie at the doorstep of the church with its intellectual and legalistic approach to the Gospel. Evangelicalism tionalistic and moralistic modes is a church still i

III. Heart Intimacy with G

During the last two decades many Roman Catholic tants outside the Pentecostal tradition have eagerly renewal movements. This phenomenon cannot be in the exotic or offbeat. Nor can it be viewed as a mindless experience for theology. Rather the co "charismatic" renewal movements testifies to a sigi porary Christendom. Neither the intellectualism and ism nor the ritualism of Catholicism satisfies the hui relationship with Christ. Christians of all stripes hi offers—and that is a living, experiential intimacy wit

Consider a few biblical examples. The first hun communed with God in Eden (Gen. 3:8). The patriarch ous personal encounters with the Lord (Gen. 12:3; 13:4 with God in human form at Peniel (Gen. 32:30). Mo personally when called to lead Israel out of Egypt (Exo many persons had life-transforming encounters with numerous incidents of intimate experiential contact Holy Spirit (Acts 2:4; 4:31; 6:10). In the epistles Paul exp yearning for experiential intimacy with Christ. Notev 3:10: "I want to know Christ and the power of his i fellowship of sharing in his sufferings, becoming like hin yearning for an intimate experience with Christ is not contemporary Christians. But we note a significant diff that his intimate relationship with Christ would be increa to discover an experiential intimacy that has been lost.

How can we recover the lost heart of Christian spirit of "devotions" is a natural place for evangelical Protesta customary "devotions" should give pride of place to the *intimacy* with God. In general, a person achieves intimacy and by being completely open and available to another. voice of God and by opening the heart to him, the Chris experiential intimacy with Christ. The desired intimacy enhanced by employing helpful spiritual disciplines th openness and availability to God.

First, Christians can heighten their ability to listen in discipline of reverent quiet. God in wisdom has chose children by quiet promptings and whispers (1 Kings 19:1 ness of heart is necessary to detect the voice of God (Hab.

relationship with God himself. In this way, prayer, which many people perceive to be a tedious duty, becomes a glorious feast of spiritual communion and communication.

IV. Conclusion

By advancing these proposals we do not advocate the formation of another (evangelical) renewal movement. We do, however, urge a renewal of the biblical practice of heart-intimacy with God by encouraging evangelical Christians to utilize time-honored and edifying spiritual disciplines. We concur with R. Lovelace, who writes, "We need to listen carefully to other kinds of Christians. Mainline Protestants, Roman Catholics, and Orthodox believers have preserved biblical values that we lack."[7] Through spiritual disciplines such as the above, true Christians whatever their tradition can realize daily intimacy with the living and loving God. Then like the apostle Paul we can commit ourselves not to rekindling the flame that has been lost, but to cultivating passionately what we possess—a deep, experiential intimacy with Jesus Christ. By so recovering authentic Christian spirituality the believer will joyfully discover that head, hands, and heart unite as a powerful force for God in a dry and thirsty land.

Notes

[1] See G. H. Clark, who argues that "the distinction between truth and falsehood . . . is the basic element in the image of God." *The Biblical Doctrine of Man* (Jefferson, Mich.: The Trinity Foundation, 1984) 25.

[2] M. T. Kelsey, *Christo-Psychology* (New York: Crossroad, 1982) 11.

[3] For a complete discussion of the positive role of quietness in facilitating personal experience of God, see M. T. Kelsey, *The Other Side of Silence: A Guide to Christian Meditation* (New York: Paulist, 1976).

[4] M. B. Pennington, *Centering Prayer: Renewing an Ancient Christian Prayer Form* (Garden City, NY: Image Books, 1982) 86–87. Pennington's book is the most helpful on the subject of prayer of quiet or centering prayer.

[5] D. G. Bloesch, "Prayer," *Evangelical Dictionary of Theology*, ed. Walter A. Elwell (Grand Rapids: Baker, 1984) 867.

[6] See Arthur Green, ed., *Jewish Spirituality*, 2 vols. (New York: Crossroad, 1987) l.xix.

[7] R. F. Lovelace, "Evangelical Spirituality: A Church Historian's Perspective," *JETS*, 31 (1988) 35. Lovelace observes that attention to renewal practices in the long history of mainline Christianity is important, because for most of our history "evangelicals did not even have a category of spiritual theology, as Roman Catholics did." Ibid., 25.

IN SPIRIT AND IN TRUTH
A CATHOLIC PERSPECTIVE ON THE HOLY SPIRIT

MONIKA K. HELLWIG
Professor of Theology
Georgetown University

Article from *Quarterly Review*

The Second Vatican Council was a watershed in official Catholic theology and a vindication of previously suspect theological explorations among Roman Catholic scholars. Much of what was officially recognized in the council was a long-term response to the insights and challenges of the sixteenth-century reformers and their followers. However, much was also a direct response to contemporary experience and understanding. Not least among the important shifts in understanding has been the Catholic sense of the Holy Spirit at work in the world and among believers. This has always been an important theme, but it has not always been viewed in the same way.

The basic points concerning the doctrine of the Holy Spirit are fixed: the Triune God, known to Christians as the transcendent creator and sustainer, expressed historically in the Word that is Jesus Christ, immanent in the human community as a sharing of the love between the Father and the Son; a history of sin and salvation in which the Spirit is active as the source of prophetic discernment and action; the Spirit of God as breathed forth by Jesus to his followers in a new and unique way in his death and resurrection; and the continuing life and mission of the community of believers as the essential life of the Spirit, which heals, strengthens, and builds community; and finally, the indwelling of the Holy Spirit as the essence of grace. These fixed points provide a frame of reference and a language of interpretation for Catholic discourse about the divine dimension of Christian life and experience for individuals and communities.

This frame of reference is built up from scriptural modes of expression that are common to all the Christian traditions. But Catholic theology throughout the centuries has also consciously followed the imagery, language, and thought patterns of the church fathers, thereby setting up traditional interpretations that may be at variance with modern scholarly interpretations of the original biblical text. In particular, the association of the Holy Spirit with sacramental efficacy and with the rulings of hierarchic church authority has emerged from continuous reflection upon historical experience.

Although Catholic piety and theology at no time denied the prophetic experience of the Holy Spirit, it must be admitted that until the Second Vatican Council there was a certain tendency to attempt to domesticate the power of the Spirit, and to see that power as operating almost exclusively through official ecclesiastical channels. Thus it has been understood that the Holy Spirit guided the writers of the various books of Holy Scripture and also guided the community of believers in establishing the canon. The Holy Spirit has also been understood as the guiding principle in the process of tradition, guaranteeing the inerrancy of definitive hierarchic teachings in which the process of tradition culminates. It has been taught that the Spirit is conferred upon the faithful in the sacraments, that is, by baptism, confirmation, and ordination, all of which are permanent in nature and confer certain powers.

Thus Catholic piety acknowledges that the Holy Spirit is the source of gifts or charisms by which the church is built up and fulfills its tasks. But there has been a certain tendency to institutionalize charisms in theory and practice, identifying them with the role of ordained officeholders in the church. It is this tendency to arrogate the workings of the Spirit to established institutional patterns that has been persistently questioned in modern times.[1]

There has been, however, a complementary aspect in liturgy and spirituality to balance the institutionalizing tendency. The feast of Pentecost is traditionally preceded by a novena (that is, a nine-day series of special prayers) for the coming of the Holy Spirit into the hearts of the faithful, bringing the "gifts" and "fruits" of the Spirit. The gifts are enumerated as seven (from Isa. 11:2 as rendered in Jerome's Latin translation, the Vulgate): wisdom, understanding, knowledge, counsel, fortitude, piety, and the fear of the Lord. Medieval theology gave extensive definition and content to these gifts, which are explained quite elaborately. Thomas Aquinas, for instance, sees them as effects and manifestations of divine salvation working in the souls of the faithful.[2] Tradition also enumerates twelve "fruits" of the Holy Spirit (compiled from a blending of various Pauline and Johannine texts in the New Testament): charity, joy, peace, patience, kindness, goodness, long-suffering, humility, fidelity, modesty, continence, and chastity. These are taken to be palpable evidence of a spirit-filled community or individual life.

Within the liturgy itself, prayers to the Holy Spirit are formulated officially in several hymns, notably the hymn for vespers, "Veni Creator Spiritus" ("Come, Creator Spirit"); the hymn for matins, "Jam Christus Astra Ascenderat" ("Christ Has Now Ascended to the Stars"); the sequence at the Eucharist, "Veni Sancte Spiritus" ("Come, Holy Spirit"); and a long series of shorter texts, such as antiphons, versicles, and responsories—all for the feast of Pentecost alone. However, the theme of Pentecost is also echoed in various ways in the liturgy for the rest of the year, and the whole liturgy for the sacrament of confirmation is built upon it. Moreover, popular piety, taking its cue from liturgical formulations, included many types of prayers and hymns to the Holy Spirit, asking for wisdom and seeking guidance in particular decisions. Several communities of vowed religious have been and are dedicated to the Holy Spirit.

The Impact of the Second Vatican Council

It is probably difficult, if not impossible, for Christians of other churches to realize the tremendous impact the Second Vatican Council has in the Catholic church and community. It is no exaggeration to say that from the Council of Trent in Reformation times through the First Vatican Council in the late nineteenth century and up to the eve of the Second Vatican Council in the early 1960s, the official attitudes of the institutional Catholic church were defensive—doggedly repeating the old formulae of faith and moral teaching against Protestants, Enlightenment rationalists, modern technology, political democracy, some of the findings of science and many of the best thinkers within the Catholic community. Although individual Catholics could be far more open, it did seem that the central authority in Rome was constantly fighting a rearguard action to prevent the progress of the modern world. With the election of Pope John XXIII everything changed in radical and unexpected ways, although Pope John himself might have been surprised at such a turn of events and certainly considered himself conservative in the long run.

The difference that Pope John XXIII made in calling the council was due quite clearly to his attitude on the Holy Spirit. He once remarked that he understood his role as Pope to be not a matter of telling the church what the Holy Spirit was saying, but instead looking around and discerning in the lives of Christian people what the Spirit was already doing in the church. There was a great simplicity and humility about him, and he was ready to learn not only from the Catholic community but from all Christians—and even from non-Christians of good will. When asked why he called the council, he said that his desire was to open the windows and let a lot of fresh air into the Vatican. At that council, for the first time in the history of the church, there was great representation from the Third World, giving perspective from a wide variety of cultures and historical experiences. Also, for the first time since the schism of the eleventh century that divided East from West, and since the schisms of the sixteenth century that divided the churches of North and South in the West, observers from the churches of the East and the Protestant churches were invited to the council, and were constantly drawn into informal exchange with the Bishops and their advisers.

From such exchanges, and from the voices that came from many parts of the world, there arose a very different sense of the Catholic church. The documents that were drawn up at that council expressed this different sense. Indeed many people at that time were speaking about the council as a new Pentecost, with the Spirit sweeping church authorities along with a boldness and freshness of outlook that they themselves had not dreamed of until they were gathered together praying for the guidance of the Spirit on behalf of the whole church. What happened was a far greater openness to the world, to other Christians, to one another within the church. That led to a new approach to old questions about Scripture and tradition, such as the nature of the church and its role in the world, the participation of the laity in church affairs, and the ministry of the priesthood.

Some people both inside and outside the Catholic church have wondered seriously whether the new openness that began twenty-five years ago with the Second Vatican Council can possibly continue in the present pontificate. They have noticed that there is a far more heavy-handed intervention from Rome in the affairs of the local churches, that a distinctly more conservative type of bishop is now appointed whenever there is a vacancy, that there have been moves from Rome to restrict women to their roles in pre-council times, and that ecumenism and social action appear to be suspect before Roman authority.

There is no doubt that all these things have happened. Yet a return to the pre-Vatican II church is not really possible. The changes that have been made in the liturgy alone would be sufficient to guarantee that the effects of the council will continue to grow. Those liturgical changes include a far more extensive use of Scripture and frequent commentary on Scripture readings, a reshaping of the rites so that their meaning is much clearer, and the regular use of the vernacular language of each country rather than Latin in public worship. Because the laity have more active participation in the liturgy, they have gradually come to think of their role in the ordinary life and action of the church in a more active way also. And because there has been extensive consultation on various issues before the synod of bishops (which since the council now meets from time to time in Rome), the laity have recovered their sense of involvement in the discernment processes and decisions of the church. Combined with the more creative interest of the church in public and social issues of justice and peace, there is a renewed sense of what it means to be the church in the world. This progress is not easily reversed, even during a very conservative pontificate.

An overview of Catholic piety before Vatican II suggests that the action of the Holy Spirit in the community of believers was seen mainly in two ways: the public guidance of the institutional church in its hierarchy, laws, and teachings, and the private guidance of individual Christians in living a good and devout life within that church. It was in the aftermath of Vatican II that the prophetic element came once more to the fore, and this is due in large measure to explicit teaching on the role of the Holy Spirit that was incorporated into the documents of the council. It is true that many of these explicit references to the Holy Spirit have to do with apostolic succession, the role of bishops, the ministry of ordained priests, the teaching office of the church, and so forth.[3] Yet there is also a definite shift of emphasis toward a broader, more ecumenical and prophetic understanding.

Thus *Lumen gentium*, the *Dogmatic Constitution on the Church*,[4] speaks of all Christians (and not only Catholics) as joined by the bond of the Holy Spirit that is active among them with sanctifying power because they are baptized and because they are believers (*Documents*, pp. 33–34, 36–37). Moreover, this text envisages the bond as one that moves Christians to play a role in the conversion of the world so that it becomes the temple of the Holy Spirit. *Unitatis Redintegratio*, the *Decree on Ecumenism*, repeatedly points out that ecumenism is not our initiative, but that of the Holy Spirit, whose gifts are poured out on Christians of all denominations, drawing them together in the communion of redemption (*Documents*, pp. 343–66). *Dignitatis Humanae*, the *Declaration on Religious Freedom*, links the workings of the Holy Spirit with the need to acknowledge that faith is by invitation and not by command (*Documents*, p. 696).

Apostolicam Actuositatem, the *Decree on the Apostolate of the Laity*, clearly states that the inspiration and power of the Holy Spirit has awakened the Catholic laity to sense their vocation as Christians in a world that is in great need of redemption (*Documents*, p. 494). This theme is developed at great length throughout the document *Gaudium et Spes*, the *Pastoral Constitution on the Church in the Modern World*, which admits that selfless service for others in temporal affairs is also among the varied gifts of the Spirit (for example, see *Documents*, p. 226). The characteristic offering that the Christian faith can make to the public welfare of the community is discernment—that gift of the Holy Spirit that seeks out concrete situations to work toward human salvation (*Documents*, p. 213). This discernment is applied very explicitly in the document to matters of social justice and peace among nations and races (*Documents*, p. 227–28).

Prophecy, Liberation, and the Holy Spirit

This pattern of thought in the documents of Vatican II has led to a new impetus in the Catholic laity toward "basic Christian communities," serious ecumenical encounters, deep involvement in peace movements, and toward bold steps in liberation theology, spirituality, and activity in pursuit of social justice. There is a newly reemerging theme in spirituality behind this, and it is the notion of discernment. Spiritual discernment is, of course, a biblical idea. Scripture is full of the awareness that we must constantly discern whether our actions, attitudes, inclinations, and preferences are motivated by the Spirit of God or are driven by the spirit of Satan the tempter, that is by a spirit of rebellion, self-centeredness, greed, lust for power, and so forth. But it is probably true to say that the life of the churches encouraged a bold and prophetic kind of discernment in the first three centuries that suffered a setback with the Constantinian establishment and never really recovered during the subsequent centuries of Christendom—and that has for the most part been seen as highly improper since the Enlightenment. It would seem to be this bold and prophetic kind of discernment that is returning openly and widely in our times.

Among Catholics, such a sense of personal and communal discernment has been widely fostered by the renewed vigor of the Ignatian retreats. These are retreats built around the *Spiritual Exercises* of St. Ignatius of Loyola, spiritual guide and teacher of the Catholic Reformation and founder of the Jesuits.[5] These retreats are constructed to coax the retreatant step by step to see and judge everything in the light of the mysteries of faith, and to become introspectively aware of the movement of different "spirits." The aim of the training is to become sensitive to the inspiration and guidance of the Holy Spirit in one's life, and to follow it with confidence and courage. People who have been formed in this way are likely to be loyal church members but they will not be so dependent on detailed and constant directives from authority. They are unlikely to be legalistic or timid. In most cases they will think more critically and more creatively about their own situation and options and about the situations and problems of communities. In working with communities they will tend to respect the discernment of others, and therefore they will be inclined to seek consensus and communal discernment processes.

All this, of course, tends to the kind of association in faith that has come to be designated "basic Christian community." It involves active and creative participation of all in prayerfully discerning what is good and bad, possible and impossible in a situation, and in planning and executing what the Christian community will do about it. There is a built-in prophetic or critical aspect to such basic Christian communities because they usually meditate on the Scriptures together and because they try to see the situations in which they live by the light of the gospel. This means that they often see a stark discrepancy between what is preached and what is done, or between the gospel and church practice, as well as the discrepancies they see between the world of God's creating and the world as we know it. All this lifts the individual's awareness of and attention to the guidance of the Holy Spirit out of the realm of purely private concerns into that of public or societal issues. This is supported in Catholic basic communities by the underlying doctrinal position that the redemption is a corporate transformation of the human situation, geared not only to the saving of souls out of the world, but to the saving of the world, that is of the human situation in all its aspects, relationships, structures, and systems.

Such a thrust in contemporary spirituality could not be without conflict. It is a movement that questions established patterns of social control and of political and economic organization and policy. It is a movement that also challenges dearly held, though erroneous, identifications of religious faith with national, racial, and class loyalties. It touches and questions traditional ideas about spirituality and religious authority, about who has the right and duty to interpret revelation, about the privacy of faith, the identification of the *status quo* with the divine will, and many such sensitive topics. This is the basis for the pervasive and resilient phenomenon of "liberation theology" and its underlying Christian social praxis.[6] It should be no matter of surprise or consternation that this new movement in theology has on the one hand been a widely and comprehensively ecumenical one, and on the other hand been polarizing and conflictual within denominations, most notably within Catholicism. A prophetic movement is generally conflictual; if it were not so there would be no need for a prophet stance.

However, there is more here than the ordinary experience of the prophet or the prophetic movement. Some of the more conservative circles within Catholicism—whether lay, clerical, or hierarchic—cling to the understanding that the gifts and guidance of the Holy Spirit are expressed in charisms for governance and teaching of the community that are bestowed upon the official leaders of the church, and charisms for individually holy (but rather passive) lives which are bestowed on Christians who do not hold office in the church. Many such more conservative Catholics also have a persistent sense that it is proper to draw an analogy from this for secular affairs: the proper guidance is given to the office holders, not to protesting groups who agitate for peace, nuclear disarmament, and for social justice in racial and economic matters. So strongly are they convinced of this that they would even apply the principle to the bishops, as with the joint pastorals on race relations, nuclear disarmament, and the American economy. There is a deep struggle in the Catholic church of the United States over this. It is at root a conflict between the orthodox understanding of the guiding role of the Holy Spirit in the Church and the implications of the statements on that topic in the documents of the Second Vatican Council. Pneumatology and ecclesiology are very closely intertwined (as indeed they usually are) in this debate over a critical and far-reaching shift in perception of the existential meaning of the gospel of Jesus Christ and of the life of his Holy Spirit that he bequeathed to us.

It is true, of course, that formal academic courses in theology still discuss the classic issues. Seminary professors and others demonstrate that the Holy Spirit is equal and coeternal with the Father and Son. They discuss the procession of the Divine Persons and the problem with the vocabulary of "persons" in speaking of the divine. They continue to deal with the matter of the "*filioque*" as with the issue of the *epiklesis*. They set out the scholastic interpretations and elaborations of the "gifts" of the Spirit, and the traditional teaching about the Spirit as the soul of the Church indwelling in the community and the individual baptized believers. They discuss the special role of the Spirit in confirmation and ordination, and in the role of Bishops and of the teaching office of the Church.[7]

All this is still subject matter for formal theological discussion in Catholic circles, but the substantive issue for the community of Catholic believers and for the Church's practical policies is the reemergence of prophecy in new, often communal forms that are frequently of consequence in the secular world. The substantive issue, in other words, is where to look for the guidance of the Holy Spirit. The remaining vestiges of the triumphalist "Christendom" mentality suggest that in the Church and in a Christian country this guidance of the Spirit has long been securely institutionalized, so that a prophetic voice should be extremely rare. But the vistas reopened by Vatican II—on Scripture and on the mode of Christian life and thought of the early patristic era—suggest that prophecy be seen instead as the ordinary communal and individual mode of life of Christians in the course of history as the Spirit works in Church and world, readying the human situation for the full realization of the Reign of God. The Christendom mode is predominantly a static one in which the voice of the Holy Spirit has been duly recorded and is regularly played back for succeeding generations. The mode revived by Vatican II is dynamic and vital, necessarily allowing for differences in perception and for trial and error and for conflict. But it is perhaps especially in this mode that true faith in the immanent working of the Holy Spirit in Church and world is realized.

Notes

[1] The influential texts of the church fathers on the Holy Spirit have been gathered very conveniently by J. Patout Burns and Gerald M. Fagin, *The Holy Spirit*, vol. 6 of Message of the Fathers of the Church, ed. Thomas Halton (Wilmington, Del.: Michael Glazier).

[2] For a fuller discussion of this see Yves Congar, *The Meaning of Tradition* (New York: Hawthorne, 1964), especially chapter two; and Karl Rahner, *The Dynamic Element in the Church* (London: Burns & Oates, 1964), chapters two and three.

[3] The issue of the presence of the Holy Spirit in the structure of the church recurs repeatedly in the volumes of *Concilium* and in the writings of the Latin American "liberation theologians." For a succinct statement of the problem see Roger Haight, *An Alternative Vision* (New York: Paulist Press, 1985).

[4] This and all references to Vatican II documents are taken from Walter M. Abbott, ed., *The Documents of Vatican II* (New York: America Press, 1966).

[5] See David Fleming, *The Spiritual Exercises of St. Ignatius* (St. Louis: Institute of Jesuit Sources, 1978), for both literal and interpretative translations of the text of the notes left by St. Ignatius of Loyola and the living tradition of the Exercises.

[6] For an overview of this movement see Haight, *Alternative Vision, passim.*

[7] See, for example, Michael Schmaus, "Holy Spirit," in *Sacramentum Mundi*, ed. Karl Rahner, et al. (New York: Herder, 1969), vol. 3, pp. 53–61.

A FOCUS ON THE HOLY SPIRIT:
SPIRIT AND SPIRITUALITY IN JOHN WESLEY

ALBERT C. OUTLER
Professor Emeritus
Perkins School of Theology

Article from *Quarterly Review*

"And I believe in the Holy Ghost, the Lord and Giver of Life, Who proceedeth from the Father and the Son; who with the Father and the Son is worshipped and glorified, Who spake by the Prophets."[1]

Any attempted focus on the Holy Spirit is bound to be blurred. The terms for "spirit," in many languages (*ruach, pneuma, spiritus, Geist, esprit*, etc.) point beyond precise denotations. But they also point "behind" self-consciousness, and they point "toward" the radical ineffability of such terms as "soul," "selfhood," "psyche"—whether in reference to the human mystery or to the Encompassing Holy in which [or in whom] we live and move and have our being. Something of this sort seems presupposed in St. Paul's address to the Athenians in Acts 17:23–31. Pneumatological reflection on this aura of human awareness of Holy Spirit has therefore to be an exercise in discernment, and a tricky one, because it can be no more than groping along a pathway between the quicksands of credulity on one side, and the thickets of superstition and magic on the other.

Neither "transcendence" nor "immanence" is a biblical term, but the paradox of their dialectical integration is a biblical commonplace. Phrases like "the Spirit of God" are derivative metaphors from familiar things connoting spontaneity, like breath or wind; they go on to include such elusive realities as life itself (e.g., "the breath of life"). They were then extended to such matters as *human dispositions* (e.g., the "poor in spirit"). On their other side, they point to God's prevenient initiatives in human affairs and history, and here their emphasis is on the *spontaneity* of divine action, whether from beyond or within. Within perspectives such as these, the biblical people felt comfortable with a wide range of anthropo*morphisms*, with a myriad of anthropomorphic images, similitudes, and analogs. At the same time, they were horrified by various anthropo*centrisms*, for there they could see the sort of over-reaching self-centeredness that distorts the primal human vision of transcendence. The original temptation was an attractive promise that our finite limits can be surpassed (as in our contemporary slogans: "you can have it *all*"; "your world should have no bounds"). Thus it is that *idolatry* was and still continues as the archetypal sin of pride-in-action—forbidden by the *First* Commandment.

The ontic pair of human happiness and tragedy have always lived together in the mysterious paradoxes of divine-human interaction. This is reflected in later explorations (as in Origen's theses about an "original righteousness and happiness," or in St. Augustine's opening "confession" ("Thou has made us *for thyself* "),[2] with its implication that the natural inclination of the human heart is harmony and peace, not in ourselves but in God. And these are echoes of a New Testament idea: viz. that humanity is designed for "life in the Spirit" (Gal. 5:25 and 2 Pet. 1:4), *because* it is, first and last, God's special project, and above all, a *divine gift.*

It is remarkable how carefully the biblical references to "Spirit" and "Holy Spirit," "God," and "Spirit of Christ" manage to avoid what came later to be called modalism on the one side, and sheer mystification on the other—yet with never an attempted conceptualization that ever pretended to be definitive. One thing is clear, however: in all true spirituality there is a deep moral taproot; the *gifts* of the Spirit (1 Cor. 12:1–13) are correlated with the *fruits* of the Spirit (as in Gal. 5:22–25).

It is a commonplace that in Christianity's emergence (or expulsion) from its Jewish matrix in the later decades of the first Christian century, and with its hazardous ventures into the hellenistic world, a language about the Holy Spirit's continuing presence and agency in human life and in the newborn church passed into the formulae of Christian worship. It helped to differentiate the new Christian sect from the other *thiasoi* ("mystery religions") in the Greco-Roman world with which Christianity was unavoidably associated (and at times confused). The point here, however, is that all of this happened without a fully realized pneumatological doctrine that we know of. The earliest approach to such a formulation appears in St. Irenaeus (in his *Demonstration of the Apostolic Preaching*, I, 1:6). But notice how much pneumatological preunderstanding is taken for granted, as if already lodged in devout Christian consciousness by the seventh decade of the second Christian century:

> And the third article is the Holy Spirit, through whom the prophets prophesied and the patriarchs were taught . . . and the just were led in the paths of righteousness—and whose power in these last times has been poured forth upon humanity over all the earth, renewing men and women to God. Therefore from the baptism of our rebirth comes these three articles, granting us rebirth unto God the Father, through his Son, by the Holy Spirit. . . . So, without the Spirit, there is no hearing the Word of God, and without the Son there is no approaching the Father—for the Son is the knowledge of the Father, and knowledge of the Son is through the Holy Spirit. . . .

The early creeds affirmed "Holy Spirit" by title (another instance of how much could be taken for granted). But it was not until the Spirit's full deity was *denied* by the Pneumatomacheans in the mid-fourth century that a major theologian thought it worthwhile to explain it at some length (unless

Athanasians' *Epistles to Serapion* may be counted as explanations). This reasoned refutation of tritheism comes from St. Gregory of Nyssa—along with a summary trinitarian formulary:

> It is not possible to confess that Jesus is Lord except by the inspiration of the Holy Spirit. Therefore, Father, Son, and Holy Spirit are to be known only in a perfect Trinity, in closest interaction and unity, before all creation. . . . [3]

It was in this climate (ca. A.D. 375) that the drafters of the Constantinopolitan revision of 381 were able to flesh out the cryptic ending of the original Nicene Ecthesis of 325 ("And in the Holy Spirit") with the fuller phrasings that have stood ever since, in "The Creed Commonly Called Nicene."

> . . . the Lord and Giver of Life who proceeds from the Father, who with the Father and the Son is worshipped and glorified, who spoke through the prophets. . . .

St. Augustine was looking both backward and forward with his lament (ca. A.D. 393) over the neglect of pneumatology (as a doctrine) by the theologians:

> Wise and spiritual men have written many books about the Father and the Son. . . .

> With respect to the Holy Spirit, however, there has not been as yet, on the part of learned men and competent interpreters of the Scriptures, a discussion that is full enough or careful enough, to make it possible for us to obtain an intelligent conception of what constitutes the Spirit's special individuality (*proprium*) in virtue of which it is the case that we cannot speak of him either as Son or Father but only Holy Spirit—excepting that they predicate the Spirit as the Gift of God and that we cannot believe that God's Gift is inferior to himself.[4]

Some of the obvious reasons for this underemphasis upon pneumatology are instructive. On the one side, there has been the tilt toward various sorts of "domestication" of the Holy Spirit in Holy Church. This goes back as far as Simon Magus, and always it has tended to link Spirit too closely with the institutional Church. Eastern Orthodoxy resisted this domestication more successfully than the Latin West—which is one of the reasons for the Protestant preference for the correlation of Spirit and Church in an opposite domestication: Holy Spirit in Holy Scripture. This produced new patterns of authority, with a new guild of certified interpreters of Scripture, with an acknowledged authority "rightly to divide the word of Truth." On the fringes of both traditions, of course, were the champions of "the free Spirit"—from Montanus to Joachim and the Fraticelli, to the Anabaptist "spirituals," to the English Quakers and German pietists and French quietists, down to our current charismatics. But this godly motley have an appalling track record of disruption and fanaticism. St. Paul had forewarned against this (in 1 Cor. 14), but St. Paul has not always been heeded by those with disparate causes that rested on other grounds.

The intent of so impressionistic a prelude as this, thus far, has been to call attention to the fact that, in the history of Christian doctrine, theologians with a special interest in the person and work of the Holy Spirit are something of a rarity. Moreover, even at the level of genius (e.g., St. Bonaventura and Cardinal Nicholas of Cusa) such men and women have drawn down suspicion upon themselves of obscurantism at best or fanaticism at worst. And there has been a tendency toward "enthusiasm," always aimed at lifting the level of spirituality in the church, but, almost as often, spreading abroad the image of a spiritual *elite* whose versions of spiritual superiority have offended other Christians, who themselves find much comfort in deploring "spiritual pride."[5] There is, therefore, no question of even a thumbnail sketch of the hopelessly heterogeneous tradition of "Christian Spirituality." The literature is unmanageable and the story interminable.[6]

It may, however, be allowable for us to pick out an arbitrarily chosen sample of "a focus on the Holy Spirit" that has had an importance of its own and, maybe, a continuing relevance. Moreover, in this particular collection of essays in pneumatology, it may not be inappropriate to select John Wesley for a closer look at an exemplary correlation of "Spirit and Spirituality."

Wesley was neither foremost nor hindmost in the tradition he represented, but he is interesting all the same. Any suspicion of Methodist triumphalism can always be allayed by a quick glance at the bibliographical subject heading of "pneumatology," and the Methodist presence (or absence) in it. But there is a better warrant for a brief summary of Wesley's focus on the Holy Spirit: that is, his persistent concern for a *trinitarian* doctrine of the Holy Spirit—a concern that appealed to Scripture tradition and to rational argument for his vivid experience of the radical difference between nominal orthodoxy and fruitful Christian spirituality.[7] This is to suggest that Wesley's pneumatology begins with an awareness of the religious and ethical import of a valid integration of Christology, soteriology, and pneumatology; the vital linkage between theo-logy, Christo-logy, and pneumato-logy held together by a consistent emphasis on prevenience of all grace, a habituated awareness of the Holy Spirit as the Giver of all Grace.[8]

John Wesley's pneumatology has many interesting aspects (and none of them can be spelled out fully here). It gathered up into itself an attempted balance between spirituality and ethics. It seeks the excitements of the free Spirit without abandoning the stabilities of a life ordered by a numinous sense of existence (*coram Deo*). It allows for the paradox of instant exaltations and the processes of Christian maturation (toward what Wesley called "the plerophory [fullness] of faith").

John Wesley's Britain was working its way through a bad case of burnout (political, cultural, religious) even in a time of exciting colonial adventures and of opening horizons in science and new technology.[9] The intellectual excitements of the age were being generated by the impulses of the Enlightenment. But the state-church was suffering from exhaustion after two centuries of nearly fruitless turmoil from the harrowings of the Tudor "Reformation," the holy war between Puritans and royalists, the blood-baths of the Civil War, the hysterics of the Commonwealth, the debilitations of Restoration, Old Dissent and the new deism.

Wesley's first three decades reflect the sort of fruitless devotion that left him deeply discontent. His first "conversion" in 1725—to a lifelong dedication to God, which was never repudiated or outgrown—was not "life-giving." The second (an illuminist experience, in 1727) reinforced his mystical impulses and his Puritan habits of self-examination.[10] There are obvious parallels between the "singularities" of the Oxford Methodists and other patterns of an asceticism-within-the-world with which Protestant rigorism had sought to replace the monastic flight from the world.[11]

Wesley's most famous experience on May 24, 1738 ("Aldersgate") has long since achieved an iconic status in Wesleyan hagiography. But it is still worth noticing that Aldersgate was not the transformation of an irreligious man into a man of faith ("an almost Christian" into an "altogether Christian"). Nor was it a triumph of Moravian pietism (the Moravians themselves were quick to deny this). It was not the last of his conversions.[12] It was not even the beginning of the Methodist Revival. And yet one is blind not to see it as a decisive turning point in Wesley's entire life and work, as a reorientation of his sense of mission and a more fruitful harvest in it. Aldersgate was less the reconstruction of Wesley's basic doctrines of God-in-Christ than an unexpected discovery of their power and effects. And its focus was the "internal witness of the Holy Spirit," (as in Rom. 8 and Eph. 2:5, 8–10). Whatever psychological account one may prefer, the theological import of Aldersgate was largely *pneumatological.*

Its story has already been better told by Wesley (in that long *Journal* entry for May 24, *et seq.*) than by any of his biographers thus far. Most of them have ignored the remarkable sequence of lections in the round of his daily prayers for the day—from 2 Peter 1:34 at matins (with its stress on divine-human "participation"), followed by a congruent emphasis in the anthem for vespers at St. Paul's (Ps. 130, *Book of Common Prayer*). The actual "Aldersgate experience" came at a reluctant compline and was far less subjective than tradition has it.

Typically, the emphasis has been on Wesley's "warmed heart." But Wesley understood enough of his tightly reined temperament to add a crucial adverb: a *"strangely* warmed" heart. The active verbs in his narration (e.g., *"I felt"*) are misread unless the verbs in the passive voice (e.g., warm*ed*) are stressed even more. Otherwise, the sense of the divine initiative in the whole affair is distorted into something more like a "peak experience" than a providential climax. "I felt my heart strangely warm*ed*"; "An assurance *was given* me. . . ."

Methodist sentimentalists have overstressed Wesley's *feelings* (as so often he did himself, but not here). But Aldersgate and its subsequent developments make more sense if the stress falls on the sheer *givenness* of the assurance of *pardon* (a synonym for "justification"). Thus, the Aldersgate experience was Wesley's personal appropriation of the familiar promises of Romans 8:10–17, 26–28. Nor did it bring an instant comprehension. It took five subsequent decades for his Christian self-understanding to grow and mature. May 24, 1738, was the dramatic turning point in an extraordinary career, from a dedicated perfectionist who seldom succeeded to a wayfarer of the Spirit who seldom failed (at least not in his reliance upon God's upholding Providence).

He had been brought up in a particular tradition of will-mysticism by a mother who was a closet theologian in her own right (and a highly competent one into the bargain!).[13] This heritage continued with him (with altered valences) throughout his life.[14] Before Aldersgate and the early flush of the Revival, his mystical quest had combined with other obsessions to bring him to despair, to bitter complaints against "the mystic writers."[15]

It is remarkable that Aldersgate recedes from sight so quickly in subsequent autobiographical accounts; the reasons for this are not altogether clear. What remains—and has not yet been studied in requisite depth—are the pneumatological overtones which develop into a sort of theme and variations throughout the corpus and provide a ground-tone in Wesley's version of the *ordo salutis*. In a series of sermons published in 1746–48 he began to sort out the dynamics of his doctrine of grace (prevenient in all its modes—repentance, justifying faith, assurance, regeneration, sanctification) in a perspective that is explicitly pneumatological and implicitly trinitarian. In "The Witness of the Spirit," Discourse I (1746), the emphasis is on

> the testimony of the Spirit as an inward impression on the soul, whereby the Spirit of God directly "witnesses to my spirit that I am a child of God" [assurance and reconciliation]. This "Spirit" not only worketh in us every manner of thing that is good but also shines upon his own work and clearly shows us what he hath wrought.[16] (I, 8, 10)

Twenty years later, in a revised version under the same text and title, Wesley defends this notion of "perceptible inspiration" against all critics, adding a heightened emphasis on the correlation of the Spirit's witness and its genuine fruit: "inward and outward holiness. . . . " "Holiness" is for Wesley, of course, another term for "true religion, . . . the love of God, and of neighbour." Pneumatology, therefore, is never merely spiritual without an ethical imperative, or *vise versa*. Personal holiness and social holiness are never disjoined—and their order never reversed.

> Let us never rest in any supposed testimony of the Spirit which is separate
> from the fruit of it. . . . Let us never rest in any supposed "fruit of the Spirit"
> without the [objective] witness [to filiation]. ("The Witness of the Spirit,"
> Discourse II, V. 3–4)

Wesley's refutation of the charges of enthusiasm (as in his sermon No. 37
"On the Nature of Enthusiasm") is to join his critics in rejecting fanaticism,
spiritual pride, and all their congeners. Thus, he can stress the "*fruits* of the
Spirit" that depend upon persuasion, insight, conviction (Gal. 5:24).

> How many impute things to the Holy Spirit, or expect things from him,
> without any rational or scriptural ground! Such are they who imagine that
> they do or shall receive "particular directions" from God, not only in points
> of importance, but in things of no moment, the most trifling circumstances
> of life. Whereas, in these cases, God has given us our own reason for a guide,
> though never excluding the "secret assistance" of his Spirit.[17]

Authentic spirituality is "*a daily growth* in pure and holy religion. . ."[18]

In Wesley's religious epistemology, God-*in-se* is unknowable and ineffa-
ble. God-language, even when logical in form, is apophatic in function. What
we "know" of God is what God reveals to us: in and through his "works" (in
creation and nature); in and through the law and the prophets; in and
through Jesus Christ, as the divine *eikon* (Col. 1:15) and *character* (Heb. 1:3).
Moreover, it is God as Holy Spirit who is the revealer of all these revelations.
As Holy Spirit, God is "Lord and Life-Giver." The operation of the Holy Spirit
in regeneration is so radical as to move Wesley to vivid hyperbole:

> When [the new-born Christian] is born of God, born of the Spirit, how is the
> manner of his existence changed! His whole soul is now *sensible* of God. . . .
> The Spirit or breath of God is immediately inspired, breathed into the new-
> born soul, and the same breath which comes from, returns to God. As it is
> continually received by *faith*, so it is continually rendered back by *love* in
> prayer and praise and thanksgiving. . . . And by this new kind of *spiritual
> respiration*, spiritual life is not only sustained but increased day by day. . . .
> The eyes of the understanding are opened. . . .[19]

The eyes of faith now *see*, "third ears" are now *opened*. "All the spiritual
senses being now *opened*, faith has a clear intercourse with the invisible
world. . . . He who is born of the Spirit, dwelling in love, dwelleth in God and
God in him."

From the images of birth and perception, he moves on to metaphors of
growth and maturation:

> The [enlivened person] feels in his heart the mighty working of the Spirit of
> God . . . ; he is inwardly sensible of the graces which the Spirit of God works
> in his heart. . . . By the use of these, he is daily increasing in the knowledge of
> God, of Jesus Christ whom he hath sent, and of all the things pertaining to his
> inward kingdom. And now he may properly be said *to live*. . . . God is

continually breathing, as it were, upon his soul and his soul is breathing unto God. Grace is descending into his heart, and prayer and praise ascending to heaven. And by this intercourse between God and man, this fellowship with the Father and the Son, as by a kind of *spiritual respiration*, the life of God in the soul is sustained and the child of God *grows up*, till he comes "to the full measure of the stature of Christ."[20]

Rhetoric of this sort is readily distorted when it is psychologized or sentimentalized. The workings of God as Spirit are more deeply inward than self-consciousness can reach; it is prevenient and objective, beyond manipulation. A precondition of valid worship is "the realization that God—the Spirit and the Father of the spirits of all flesh—should discover *himself* to your spirit, which is itself a breath of God—*divinae particula aurae* (a particle of the divine aura)."[21]

It is important to note this antidote to obscurantism and its context, specifically its equal emphasis upon the rationality and ethical concerns of authentic spirituality:

How does the Spirit of God "lead" his children to this or that particular action. . . . Do you imagine it is by "blind impulse" only? By "moving" you to do it, you know not why? No, he leads us by our "eye" at least as much as by our "hand". . . . For example, here is a man ready to perish with hunger. How am I led "by the Spirit" to relieve him? First, by "convincing" me that it is his will that I should and, secondly, by his filling my heart with love toward him. . . . This is the plain, rational account of the ordinary leading of the Spirit. . . . Now where this is, there is no dead form, neither can there be. . . . All that is said and done is full of God, full of spirit and life and power.[22]

Once one begins to look for them, such gyroscopic balances turn up in almost every part of John Wesley's prose—and throughout Charles Wesley's verse as well.

After the Revival's energies came to be relatively self-sustaining, practical and theoretical questions about Christian maturation began to loom larger than before. These brought with them a shift, not *away* from justification and regeneration, but *toward* the wider horizons of growth and development. This included the tricky business of differentiating between what Gordon Rupp called Wesley's "pessimism of nature" and his "optimism of grace." He took as much as he could from the prophets of the new doctrine of progress; he denied outright their secularistic premises.[23] In rhetoric and action, he looked more and more to a synthesis of spirituality and social reform (as in his "poor relief" and his anti-slavery crusade). Reform became the social analog to his soteriological image of "restoration of the divine image."

The Holy Spirit is the giver of all spiritual life: of righteousness, peace and joy in the Holy Ghost—of holiness *and* happiness—by the restoration of that image of God wherein we are created. . . . [which always includes a communal imperative].[24]

In a paired sermon, "On the Omnipresence of God" (Aug. 12, 1788), Wesley sought to turn traditional abstractions about immanence into vivid metaphors of God's active presence, in and through the Holy Spirit:

> The great God, the eternal, almighty Spirit, is as unbounded in his presence as in his duration and power. . . . God acts . . . throughout the whole compass of creation, by sustaining all things, without which everything would sink into its primitive nothing, by governing all, every minute superintending everything . . . strongly and sweetly influencing all, and yet without destroying the liberty of his rational creatures. . . . (I, 2, II, 1)

> In order to attain to these glorious ends spare no pains to preserve always a deep, a continual, a lively, and a joyful, sense of his gracious presence (i.e., *coram Deo*). (III, 6)

Notice the absence here of modalism, tri-theism, or spiritual*ism*. As the whole context will show, here is a conscious attempt at a trinitarian doctrine of the Holy Spirit. In his last published sermon but one—No. 120, "On the Unity of the Divine Being"—notice Wesley's unacknowledged fidelity to *orthodox* Christian teaching (here and elsewhere, in the tradition of *"Christian* Platonism")

> True religion is right tempers toward God and man. It is, in two words, gratitude and benevolence. . . . It is the loving God with all our hearts and our neighbors as ourselves. . . .

> This begins when we begin to know God by the teaching of his own Spirit. As soon as the Father of spirits reveals the Son in our hearts and the Son reveals the Father, the love of God is shed abroad in our hearts. Then, and not until then, are we truly happy. We are happy first in the consciousness of God's favour, which is better than life itself; then, in all the heavenly tempers which he hath wrought in us by his Spirit. Again, [we are happy] in the testimony of his Spirit that all our [good] works please him, and lastly, in the testimony *of our own spirits* that, "in simplicity and godly sincerity we have had our conversation in the world."[25] Standing fast in this liberty wherewith Christ hath made them free, real Christians "rejoice ever more, pray without ceasing and in everything give thanks." And their happiness still increases as they grow up into the measure of the stature of the fullness of Christ. (16–17)

Christianity is that religion which stand or falls by its profession of faith in one God: Lord and creator, Lord and Savior, Lord and Giver of Life. This selfsame God has disclosed himself in Jesus (and made him to be both Lord and Christ). Moreover, as Holy Spirit, God has "saved" Jesus from being lost or distorted in history's limbo or obscured in the mist of timeless truths. Any separate focus on tri-unity confounds the uniqueness of Christian truth: "unitarianism," "Christo-monism," "spiritual*ism*." Pneumatology is especially vulnerable to the seductions of anthropo*centrism* (usually in one or another form of credulousness, fanaticism, antinomianism, self-righteous-ness, pantheism, superstition). In both the biblical revelation and in the Christian tradition, there is an unwearied struggle to conserve the balance and wholeness of God's mystery and self-disclosure. John Wesley was one of those who joined in this struggle in his time and circumstance.

The prospect of contemporary Christianity is grimly problematic. None of its past epochs can serve it well any longer as a norm or paradigm, least of all its notorious mesalliances with Western secularisms and their current debilitations ("the ambiguity of the modern scientific consciousness, the loss of Western political and spiritual dominance, the death of the Western deity of progress . . . ; this situation is therefore, quite new . . .").[26] The nineteenth-century sense of Western "dominance" and "cultural superior-ity" has been numbed; in more recent times, the human prospect around the globe has been diminished. Concurrently, the clamors of the wretched of the earth can no longer be ignored, even though much of the trendy rhetoric in praise of Christian social activism has been scarcely more than that—trendy rhetoric.

The visionaries and passionaries of our time, in their myriad clamant causes, sound more and more like "enthusiasts" in Wesley's pejorative sense (i.e., benevolent souls who will good ends without being prepared to identify and accept the necessary means, or the primal motives, that could convert their good will into effective action). More and more the options between "The New Age" or human self-realization[27] and the New Age of God's rule and *his* righteousness stand opposed—and the crux of the matter seems, once more, the ancient choice between the Tempter's Promise ("you shall be as gods") and the Promise of the Paraclete ("when he, the Spirit of Truth, is come, he will guide you into *all* truth." John 15:26–27; 16:13). There is a non-negotiable difference between the idealized human potential as the prescrip-tion for a human ethical agenda (as in Feuerbach), and the biblical vision of the *humanum* restored in and for its primal design—by its Designer. For this latter possibility, it is the power and grace of God in Christ that can bring us to that finally realized Rule of God (*apocatastasis*) foreseen in Acts 3:21 and 1 Corinthians 15:24–28. Betimes, come weal or woe, it is our privilege to live in the assurance that "the grace of our Lord Jesus Christ, the love of God and the communion of the Holy Spirit" really *is* with us and the whole People of God, *always.*

Notes

[1] "The Creed commonly called Nicene," Article III, as in the Book of Common Prayer of the Church of England (1662), in the Order for Holy Communion.

[2] *Confessions* I,i.

[3] Gregory of Nyssa, "On the Holy Spirit; Against the Followers of Macedonius, N-PNF1 2nd Series 5, 319 ff.); see also his essay, "On Not Three Gods, to Abladius." Ibid., p. 331–36.

[4] *On Faith and the Creed*, Ch. IX, 18, 19, 20.

[5] As in Ronald A. Knox, *Enthusiasm: A Chapter in the History of Religion* (Oxford: Clarendon Press, 1950), who *defines* his subject as "a chronic tendency in church history reflected in the 'clique,' where an excess of charity threatens unity—, . . . an *elite*, of Christian men and (more importantly, women) who are trying to live a less worldly life than their neighbors, to be more attentive to the guidance (directly felt, they would tell you) of the Holy Spirit," p. 1.

[6] Samples of what could be done in special cases, however, can be seen in Henri Bremand's brilliant *Literary History of Religious Thought in France* or in the ponderous beginnings of the current multivolumed project of *World Spirituality*, edited by Ewert Cousins.

[7] A remarkable current inquiry into this ancient problematic may be seen in Fr. Kilian McDonnell, OSB, "A Trinitarian Doctrine of the Holy Spirit," in *Theological Studies*, vol. 46, 1985, pp. 191–227. Here is a challenging and substantive program for what has become an urgent desideratum: an updated pneumatology that includes historical perspective along with the opening horizons of a postmodern and global age. One would not wish to claim that Wesley achieved what Fr. McDonnell is calling for—only that he understood some of the same issues and worked at them in something of the same spirit.

[8] See the quite remarkable, even if somewhat difficult, essay of Fr. David Coffey, *Grace: The Gift of the Holy Spirit* (Manly: Catholic Institute of Sydney, 1979).

[9] It still puzzles cultural historians that the Industrial Revolution began in Britain; cf. Fernand Braudel, *Civilization and Capitalism, 15th–18th Century*, vol. 2, 330–48; vol. 3, 536–38, 555–88.

[10] See, for example, the minute daily and hourly records of his attention to the vicissitudes of his spiritual states in R. H. Heitzenrater's newly-edited diaries in *The Works of John Wesley*, vol. 5, 1988.

[11] Cf. Heitzenrater, *op. cit.*; the Curnock edition of *John Wesley's Journal*, vol. I, 79–105; and the Frank Baker edition of *The Works of John Wesley*, "Letters," 1980, 141–551.

[12] Cf. *Journal*, Jan. 4, 1739.

[13] See for example her letters to him at Oxford, in *Letters I*, Frank Baker, ed., *The Works of John Wesley*, vol. 25, pp. 167–68, 178–80, 183–85, 382–83.

[14] Jean Orcibal, "The Theological Originality of John Wesley and Continental Spirituality," in *A History of the Methodist Church in Great Britain* (London: Epworth Press, 1965), edited by Rupert Davies and Gordon Rupp, vol. 1, pp. 81–113.

[15] Cf. his poignant memoir of the Georgia fiasco (in Henry Moore's *Life*, I, 342) and his attack on William Law, in Baker's edition of the *Letters*, II, 25, 540–42, 546–48.

[16] The human reaction of faith to grace is conscious (joy): "the soul as intimately and evidently perceives when it loves, delights and rejoices in God" (I, 11).

[17] "On the Nature of Enthusiasm," 20.

[18] Ibid., 39.

[19] Sermon 19, "The Great Privilege of Those That Are Born of God," I: 7–10.

[20] Sermon 45, "The New Birth," II: 4–5.

[21] *A Farther Appeal to Men of Reason and Religion*, Part II, III.

[22] Ibid., Part II, III: 9.

[23] For a brilliant summation of these premises, see Carl L. Becker, *The Heavenly City of the Eighteenth Century Philosophers* (New Haven: Yale University Press, 1932), especially pp. 102–3.

[24] Sermon 110, "The Discoveries of Faith," June 11, 1788, 7.

[25] 2 Cor. 1:12, where *anestraphemen* means something like "lifestyle."

[26] Langdon Gilkey, *Society and the Sacred* (New York: Crossroad Press, 1981), p. 13.

[27] As in *The 1988 Guide to New Age Living* and the bi-monthly *New Age Journal*.

PRACTICAL THEOLOGY: PASTORAL PSYCHOLOGY AND COUNSELING

David G. Benner, area editor

PASTORAL PSYCHOLOGY AND COUNSELING

DAVID G. BENNER
Professor of Psychology
Redeemer College, Ancaster, Ontario

Introduction

Something interesting has occurred this past year in journals relating psychology to Christian faith and ministry. The two articles included in this section were among a considerable number published on the topic of spirituality. They are particularly noteworthy because a Protestant perspective on spirituality has in the past appeared infrequently in pastoral psychology journals. While Catholic writers have often written on spirituality from a psychological perspective, Protestants have generally neglected the topic.

Not surprisingly, the term *spirituality* is used differently by those who seem to be discovering (or rediscovering) this lost jewel, and perhaps its variant usages is why Protestants have been mistrustful of it. Because most authors make no attempt to define it, the concept of spirituality has suffered ambiguity.

The following articles present two ways in which Christian authors are attempting to bring a psychological perspective to the topic of spirituality. The first article, by Daniel Helminiak, uses Erich Fromm's understanding of personality as a springboard for examining spirituality as a characteristic of the personality that seeks perfection. The author traces this quest for perfection through other major personality theorists. While this component of personality has not usually been understood in religious terms, he argues that the quest for perfection can readily support a distinctive Christian understanding of spirituality.

The second article, by D. Louise Mebane and Charles R. Ridley, presents a contrasting perspective on perfectionism. They identify this spiritual quest for perfection as a reflection of counterfeit spirituality. Applying the organizational theory concept of role-sending, Mebane and Ridley explore the methods in which pastors communicate an expectation of perfectionism to their congregations and how those in the congregation take on this role. After outlining the negative consequences of parishioners who adopt the perfectionist role, they recommend ways to eliminate the perfectionist syndrome from Christian life.

These articles do not present the last psychological word on spirituality. They do, however, advance the understanding of the psychology of spirituality from Protestant perspectives, and it is to be hoped they will inspire other Protestant authors to contribute to this area of scholarship.

About the Area Editor

David G. Benner (M.A., York University; Ph.D., York University) is Professor of Psychology at Redeemer College in Ancaster, Ontario. He is editor of *Baker Encyclopedia of Psychology* (1985). Other recent books include *Christian Counseling and Psychotherapy* (1987) and *Psychotherapy and the Spiritual Quest* (1988). His most recent book, coedited with LeRoy Aden, is *Counseling and the Human Predicament: A Study of Sin, Guilt, and Forgiveness* (1989).

SPIRITUAL CONCERNS IN ERICH FROMM

DANIEL A. HELMINIAK
Director for Spiritual Growth and Pastoral Counselor
Omega Point Counseling Center, Austin, Texas

Article from *Journal of Psychology and Theology*

This article summarizes Erich Fromm's understanding of human nature and pinpoints his account of the human tendency ever to seek further perfection: biological dichotomy results in contradictions that produce existential needs whose various resolutions determine passions and strivings, which are incessant and inherently unquenchable. Though not wholly unambiguous, his position is basically correct. Empirical evidence and logical argument support it. It presupposes a spiritual component in human nature that strives toward what is objectively correct and truly worthwhile, and so it is not only useful as a secular transformation of many traditionally religious concerns but is also open to easy theist and, ultimately, Christian interpretation. Here is the basis for an account of spirituality that cuts across cultures and religions. Fromm's account of the matter squares well with the more detailed and profound analysis of dynamic human consciousness—"spirit"—presented by Bernard J. F. Lonergan (1957, 1972) and used by Daniel Helminiak (1987) to provide a technical nontheist definition of spiritual development.

It is generally taken for granted in Western civilization that spirituality has to do with God and religion. Yet such emphasis on religion results in a plurality of differing and sometimes opposing views. This fact is obvious within the diversity of the Christian traditions, even without consideration of the still more diverse spiritual traditions in other world religions. Nonetheless, beneath the differences, one might discern basic similarities. Indeed, on this shrinking planet, the hope for a peaceful and united world civilization seems dim unless there emerges an understanding of a spirituality common to all people simply because all are human.

Can one maintain an adequate treatment of spirituality apart from theism? Could treatment of the spiritual be safely removed from the care of the religions and be placed within the purview of the human sciences? Is it possible to propose an adequate account of spirituality on the basis of the human as such, an account that is fully open to theist and Christian expansion though God and Christ do not feature explicitly in the account? Some strands of thought within mainstream Western psychology do suggest such a possibility. In view of the current tensions within and among our churches and in our world, it behooves us to search out these strands and to examine them with the utmost urgency and rigor. The position of Erich Fromm represents one such strand.

Salvatore Maddi (1980) categorizes the personality theory of Erich Fromm—along with those of Alfred Adler, Robert W. White, Gordon Allport, Albert Ellis, and several existential psychologists—under the perfection version of the fulfillment model of personality. The fulfillment model proposes that there is an inner force in the human and that the unfolding of this force results in all human development. The perfection version of this model emphasizes the personal drive to compensate for genetic or functional weaknesses and so ever to transcend oneself. The goal is attainment of all that one could be, not simply the actualization of all that one already somehow is. This version of the model envisages unlimited human fulfillment.

Maddi's perfection-fulfillment model is strikingly similar to aspects of Helminiak's (1987b) account of spiritual development. This account presupposes an intrinsic principle of authentic self-transcendence, defined by Bernard Lonergan (1957, 1972) as constitutive of the human. Lonergan speaks of this principle as dynamic human consciousness and articulates it in terms of four "levels" (or focuses that human conscious capacity may take).

> There is the *empirical* level on which we sense, perceive, imagine, feel, speak, move. There is an *intellectual* level on which we inquire, come to understand, express what we have understood, work out the presuppositions and implications of our expression. There is the *rational* level on which we reflect, marshall the evidence, pass judgment on the truth or falsity, certainty or probability, of a statement. There is the *responsible* level on which we are concerned with ourselves, our own operations, our goals, and so deliberate about possible courses of action, evaluate them, decide, and carry out our decisions. (Lonergan, 1972, p. 9)

This intrinsic human principle is dynamic because it spontaneously prompts one to ever further attentive awareness, intelligent understanding, reasonable judgment, and responsible decision. Its ultimate goal is all that there is to be known and loved. It will rest satisfied only in the fullness of what is actually true and really worthwhile.

According to Lonergan's analysis, that four-level structure is inherent in human consciousness. It follows that that structure also has normative implications for human activity. So, as a parallel to the four levels of consciousness, there arise four "transcendental precepts": "Be attentive, Be intelligent, Be reasonable, Be responsible" (Lonergan, 1972, pp. 20, 302). To the extent that one follows these precepts, one is authentic (Helminiak, 1984b; Lonergan, 1972). Thus, "authenticity" is given a technical meaning, free from the subjective whim or the affective preference often associated with this term in contemporary usage.

Although these acts—awareness, understanding, judgment, and decision—occur in an embodied organism, in themselves they are neither spatial nor temporal. Accordingly, they may be called spiritual (Helminiak, 1982a, 1984a; Lonergan, 1957), and Lonergan occasionally refers to this dynamic principle as "human spirit" (e.g., 1957, p. 519; 1972, p. 302). Were one to faithfully follow this principle, which *per se* is open to all that is, one would advance toward the furthest possible human development. This advance could legitimately be termed spiritual development because it results from that inherent spiritual principle.

This account of spiritual development rests on a kind of phenomenological analysis of the human itself; its basis is philosophic. It prescinds from consideration of any ultimate transcendent such as God. Thus, on the one hand, it represents a nontheological account of spiritual development. On the other hand, it also entails a redefinition of human psychology, for it insists on explicit acknowledgment of the specifically human: spiritual acts of dynamic human consciousness.

The similarity between Maddi's (1980) perfection-fulfillment model and that notion of spiritual development provokes the question, "From where did those psychological theorists derive their notions of an inner tendency toward unlimited perfection?" This article answers this question in the case of Erich Fromm and so presents another bit of evidence that supports the possibility of a universally valid, objectively sound, yet nontheist account of spirituality. A first section will summarize Fromm's understanding of human nature and its existential exigencies. Fromm's position on the focal issue will then already be clear. A second section will recount the empirical or quasi-empirical evidence for Fromm's position. A final section will show how, in a wholly humanistic context that presumes a broad (nontheist) sense of the term "religion," Fromm expressly treats spiritual issues, calls for a more adequate notion of human psychology, and so advances a position similar in many ways to Lonergan's and Helminiak's. Some criticism of Fromm's position, necessary because of the delicacy of the present enterprise, will be included there.

Fromm's Understanding of the Human Situation

In two of his works, *Man for Himself* (1947) and *The Anatomy of Human Destructiveness* (1973), Fromm presents a basically unchanged treatise on human nature. In Fromm's stark and poignant phrase, the human is "the freak of the universe" (1947, p. 40; 1973, p. 225). Situating humankind within the evolutionary order of life, this fact is the heart of the matter. From it follows all the peculiarity and the driving motivation in the human. Fromm's understanding may be summarized as follows.

In the evolution of life, the human appears where determination by instinct is at a minimum and possible adaptation is at a maximum. The relative lack of instincts and the emergence of self-awareness, reason, and imagination fix an insurmountable dichotomy in the human. Still rooted in and limited by the natural, humans must nonetheless determine their own life's conditions on a sociobiological and historical basis. There is no escaping this exigency. All the driving power, all motivation, arises from the need to resolve contradictions inherent in the human situation. Existential needs demand the construction of frames of orientation and devotion—religious systems. Within these arise the passions and strivings that explain so much of human behavior. Environmental and sociological factors significantly determine the form of these passions and strivings, and constellations of passions and strivings constitute human character. Different kinds of character are different ways that basic human striving may be expressed. Then, character does for humans what instincts do for animals. For better or worse, people act according to their character.

In brief, biological dichotomy results in contradictions that produce existential needs whose various resolutions determine passions and strivings. Since these passions and strivings are ultimately grounded in the biological dichotomy that defines the human, they are incessant and inherently unquenchable. Here, then, in Fromm's theory, is the basis for the core tendency toward ongoing perfection in the human. Elaboration is possible.

Fromm (1947) does not hesitate to insist that "there is a human nature characteristic of the human species" (p. 20). One must specify this human nature before one can speak coherently about human behavior and personality. Human nature is specified by considerations of its biological and mental determinants. Two evolutionary factors, according to Fromm (1973), indicate the emergence of the human: (a) "the ever-decreasing determination of behavior by instincts" and (b) "the growth of the brain, and particularly of the neo-cortex" (p. 223). The combination of these two factors results in a new phenomenon. The novelty is not instrumental intelligence, for lower animals are able in varying degrees to use tools to achieve their ends. *Self-awareness* is the critical, distinguishing factor in the human. "Man is the only animal who not only knows but who also knows that he knows" (p. 225). The human being alone has "*reason*, the capacity to use his thinking to *understand* objectively—i.e., to know the nature of things as they are in themselves, and not only as means for his satisfaction" (p. 225). "Self-awareness, reason, and imagination have disrupted the 'harmony' which characterizes animal existence. Their emergence has made man into an anomaly, into the freak of the universe" (Fromm, 1947, p. 40).

The "disharmony" in the human situation is clarified by comparison with the animal situation.

> Man is the only animal for whom his own existence is a problem that he has to solve and from which he cannot escape. . . . He cannot go back to the prehuman state of harmony with nature, and he does not know where he will arrive if he goes forward. Man's existential contradiction results in a state of constant disequilibrium. This disequilibrium distinguishes him from the

animal, which lives, as it were, in harmony with nature . . . it has its specific ecological niche to which its physical and mental qualities have been adapted by the process of evolution. (Fromm, 1973, p. 225)

The disharmony in the human situation makes humans into an anomaly. To the human biological dichotomy there correspond existential contradictions. Fromm (1973) is emphatic in stating that these constitute human nature: "I propose that man's nature cannot be defined in terms of a specific quality, such as love, hate, reason, good or evil, but only terms of fundamental *contradictions* that characterize human existence and have their root in the biological dichotomy between missing instincts and self-awareness" (p. 226). In his earlier work Fromm (1947, pp. 41–43) discusses these specific existential contradictions: the opposition between life and a death that is an unalterable fact, known as such, and ultimately unrationalizable; the tension between immense human potential and the finiteness of human life, that is, the known difference between what one could accomplish and what one does accomplish; and the conflict between being irreducibly unique and aware of that uniqueness while at the same time being dependent for one's happiness on one's fellow human beings. In Fromm's later treatment the distinction between biological dichotomy and existential contradictions is not highlighted. There, in words repeated virtually verbatim in these two publications twenty-six years apart, only a poetic and poignant presentation of the human being's lot occurs:

He is part of nature, subject to her physical laws and unable to change them, yet he transcends the rest of nature. He is set apart while being a part; he is homeless, yet chained to the home he shares with all creatures. Cast into this world at an accidental place and time, he is forced out of it, again accidentally. Being aware of himself, he realizes his powerlessness and the limitations of his existence. He visualizes his own end: death. Never is he free from the dichotomy of his existence: he cannot rid himself of his mind, even if he should want to; he cannot rid himself of his body as long as he is alive—and his body makes him want to be alive. (Fromm, 1947, p. 40; 1973, p. 225)

"The disharmony in man's existence generates needs which far transcend those of his animal origin" (Fromm, 1947, p. 46). Fromm (1973) calls these needs existential "because they are rooted in the very conditions of human existence. They are shared by all men" (p. 226). In specifying these needs, Fromm hopes to delineate "primary human experience" (p. 228). Conceiving the human in light of evolutionary history, Fromm attempts "a 'reconstruction' of man's mind as it may have been at the beginning of prehistory" (p. 227). Fromm's concern is to explicate human nature. Thus, he is proposing something akin to Carl Jung's archetypes. But to find a link among all humankind, Fromm needs no appeal to some mystical collective unconscious. His appeal is rather to the issues confronting every human being simply because each one is human. If similarities in the psychic structuring of human experience occur, that is because all humans share the same human nature, the same inevitable dichotomies, and the same existential needs (pp. 230–239).

Basic among these existential needs is the need to make sense of life. That is, there is the need to restore unity by a comprehensive thought system. But since the human being "is an entity endowed with a body as well as a mind he has to react to the dichotomy of his existence not only in thinking but also in the process of living, in his feelings and actions. . . . Devotion to an aim, or an idea, or a power transcending man such as God, is an expression of this need for completeness in the process of living" (Fromm, 1947, p. 48).

Existential needs result in human passions. It is the function of the passions to satisfy the existential needs. With this understanding Fromm argues strenuously against the position of Freud and Lorenz, who attempt to link all human behavior to instincts, that is, biological needs. According to Fromm (1973), it is passions that make one human: "As von Holbach, the philosopher of the French Enlightenment once said: *'Un homme sans passions et desires cesserait d'etre un homme.'* ('A man without passions or desires would cease to be a man.')" (p. 8). Human passions, "the striving to love, to be free, as well as the drive to destroy, to torture, to control, and to submit" (p. 7) cannot be explained reductionistically. Passions are "man's attempt to make sense out of life and to experience the optimum of intensity and strength he can (or believes he can) achieve under the circumstances" (p. 9). Fromm sees the multiple passions that motivate human behavior as expressions of the biological and existential dichotomy that characterizes the human as such.

So the argument comes full circle, consistently, coherently. Fromm (1947) is deliberate in his position. He gives a clearly stated answer to the question: What is the source of the drive to perfection in the human? Relentless human striving is rooted in the dichotomous nature of the freak of the universe.

> Reason, man's blessing, is also a curse: *it forces him to cope everlastingly* with the task of solving an insoluble dichotomy. . . . Man is the only animal for whom his own existence is a problem which he has to solve and from which he cannot escape. He cannot go back to the prehuman state of harmony with nature; he must proceed to develop his reason *until he becomes master of nature, and of himself.*

> The emergence of reason has created *a dichotomy* within man which *forces him to strive everlastingly for new solutions.* The dynamism of his history is intrinsic to the existence of *reason which causes him to develop* and, through it, to create a world of his own in which he can feel at home with himself and with his fellow men. *Every stage he reaches leaves him discontented* and perplexed, and this very perplexity urges him to move toward new solutions. There is no innate "drive for progress" in man; *it is the contradiction in his existence that makes him proceed* on the way he set out. . . . *He is impelled to go forward and with everlasting effort to make the unknown known* by filling in with answers the blank spaces of his knowledge. . . . *He is driven to overcome this inner split, tormented by a craving for*

"absoluteness," for another kind of harmony which can lift the curse by which he was separated from nature, from his fellow men, and from himself. (pp. 40–41, emphases added)

It is one of the peculiar qualities of *the human mind* that, *when confronted with a contradiction*, it *cannot remain passive.* It is set in motion with the aim of resolving the contradiction. *All human progress is due to this fact.* (p. 44, emphases added)

The Evidence for Fromm's Position

Fromm (1947) is well aware that he is proposing a particular understanding of human nature. His is "an anthropologico-philosophical concept of human existence" (p. 45). He does not expect to validate his position through simple observation or measurement of that human nature. Still, human nature

is a theoretical construction which can be inferred from empirical study of the behavior of man. In this respect, the science of man in constructing a "model of human nature" is no different from other sciences which operate with concepts of entities based on, or controlled by, inferences from observed data and not directly observable themselves. (p. 24)

This understanding of science is certainly correct (cf. Campbell & Bickhard, 1986).

Then what data on human behavior does Fromm advance to support his understanding of human nature? Arguing for the adequacy of a humanistic ethics in *Man for Himself* (1947), Fromm opposes both the ethics of authoritarian religions, which claim divine revelation as their legitimation, and post-Enlightenment relativism, which suggests there is no common human nature. The latter discussion is apropos here. The former will be treated in the next section.

If there is a fixed human nature of some kind, then human nature cannot be completely malleable. That it is not, Fromm (1947) argues decisively. First, if human nature were infinitely malleable, the human being "would be only the puppet of social arrangements and not—as he has proved to be in history—an agent whose intrinsic properties react strenuously against the powerful pressure of unfavorable social and cultural patterns" (p. 21). Secondly, if the human were completely malleable, there could be no psychology or anthropology. "Since the special manifestations of man would be nothing but the stamp which social patterns put on him, there could only be one science of man, comparative sociology" (p. 22). Finally, if human beings were completely malleable, there would be no history; the human race would have reached an evolutionary dead end. For, on the one hand, if humans adapted to their environments by changing their nature and so becoming fit to live under one set of conditions, they "would have reached a blind alley of specialization which is the fate of every animal species, thus precluding history. If, on the other hand, man could adapt himself to all conditions without fighting those which are against his nature, he would have no history either" (p. 23).

Fromm's strongest evidence on this issue is human history and the ongoing adaptation of the human race. The evidence is general. The argument falls into the category *patet ex experientia* (it is obvious from experience). Such argument does not usually make a strong case, yet Fromm's case seems to be beyond reasonable doubt, and one would be hard pressed to refute its logic. Although Fromm's evidence does not support his particular understanding of human nature, it does suggest that human nature is of some particular form. Ironically, the form most suggested by the evidence is radical adaptability. However, the adaptability suggested is not the infinite malleability that Fromm refutes. It is, rather, a capacity to adapt again and again, each time for the continued well-being of the organism. Such adaptability could well be called learning ability. This conclusion, implicit in Fromm's position, would indeed support the particular understanding of human nature that he proposes.

On a second front, in *The Anatomy of Human Destructiveness* (1973) Fromm argues against an instinct explanation of human motivation, as advocated by Freud and Lorenz. Instinct is understood as a biological drive serving physiological needs. Fromm asserts flatly that "man suffers severely when he is reduced to the level of a feeding and propagating machine, even if he has all the security he wants" (pp. 7–8). Fromm provides ample evidence for his assertion, citing many now classic studies. The case against a reductionist instinct explanation of human behavior is closed, and the case has been won (cf. Eagle, 1984, pp. 6–16; Maddi, 1980, pp. 268–277). Fromm highlights the implausibility of the case for instinct with this comment: "People have committed suicide because of their failure to realize their passions for love, power, fame, revenge. Cases of suicide because of a lack of sexual satisfaction are virtually nonexistent" (p. 8).

Fromm has argued well to discredit other supposed understandings of human nature: infinite malleability or no real nature at all, and biological instinctual reductionism. He is harder pressed to provide positive support for his own notion of human nature. Fromm (1947) may rely on experiences in his psychoanalytic practice and conclude that "problems of ethics can not be omitted from the study of personality, either theoretically or therapeutically" (p. xiii). He may be "increasingly impressed by . . . the strength of the strivings for happiness and health, which are part of the natural equipment of man" (p. x). But the therapeutic session is notorious for producing the results that the therapist expects (cf. Eagle, 1984, pp. 154–163). Echoing von Holbach, Fromm may also insist that "the most striking feature in human behavior is the tremendous intensity of passions and strivings which man displays" (p. 45). But such personal impressions and common assertions do not constitute scientific evidence.

I think that Fromm's notion of human nature in general is correct, so despite its weakness I am impressed by his argument. However, more than mere personal preference is involved here. Fromm's argument can easily be strengthened to the point of logical invulnerability. His most impressive positive appeal is to the salience of human passions. Once again, the evidence offered is common experience: *patet ex experientia*. It is this common experience that impresses me. Still, even if not so impressed, no one could object to Fromm's conclusion without confirming that conclusion in the very act of objecting. Any objection, unless it be sheer raving, must turn on meaningful interpretation, accuracy of judgment, and commitment to some values: orientation and devotion, the very issues at the heart of Fromm's notion of human nature (cf. Lonergan, 1957; 1972). Unfortunately, Fromm does not present this further logical argument, yet it is implicit in his overall presentation. Certainly, then, Fromm's argument is compelling. His conclusion about human nature, inferred from observable human behavior, is as reasonable and at least as well supported as any other position available.

Fromm's Position as Religious or Spiritual

As already noted, according to Fromm, the existential need for "frames of orientation and devotion" and the various such frames that people construct, wholesome or destructive, serve a "religious" function. If Fromm (1947) avoids the term "religious," he does use the term "spiritual" to identify his concern in contrast to Freud's narrowly constructed "homo psychologicus":

> The progress of psychology lies not in the direction of divorcing an alleged "natural" from an alleged "spiritual" realm and of focusing attention on the former, but in the return to the great tradition of humanistic ethics which looked at man in his physicospiritual totality, believing that man's aim is to be *himself* and that the condition for attaining this goal is that man be *for himself*. (p. 7)

Later Fromm notes, "The very best but also the most satanic manifestations of man's mind are expressions not of his flesh but of his 'idealism' of his *spirit*" (p. 50, emphasis added).

Not just in words, but also in substance, Fromm's concern is the spiritual in the human. His articulation of the issue is not as detailed nor as precise as Lonergan's (1957, 1972) analysis of dynamic human consciousness, human spirit. Most glaringly, Fromm's analysis of what he globally calls "reason" lacks explicit indication of an ethical component; there is no reference to what Lonergan calls the fourth level of consciousness, the level of responsible decision making. Nonetheless, Fromm does relate ethical concerns to the trio that for him is determinative of the human: self-awareness, reason, and imagination. Fromm (1947) insists, "Valid ethical norms can be formed by man's reason and by it alone" (p. 6). Indeed, the whole of *Man for Himself* (1947) is dedicated to this proposition. Moreover, because in modern Western civilization "mental" tends merely to mean "logical," the term "imagination" serves to speak about insight and creativity and does not refer simply to the production of internal images (cf. Helminiak, 1986b, pp. 280–281, note 12). Given these clarifications, Fromm's trio appears to refer to that same human reality, dynamic consciousness, human spirit, that Lonergan treats.

Furthermore, Fromm's presentation of the "spiritual" in human nature exhibits the same three characteristics as the (a) *intrinsic* principle of (b) *authentic* (c) *self-transcendence*, on the basis of which Helminiak (1987) argues that human development *is* spiritual development. First, Fromm rejects the notion that ethical concerns derive only from something transcendent to human beings. Rather, such concerns emerge from something inherent in the human. That one must be virtuous means that one must act in accord with one's own nature.

> Aristotle uses virtue to mean "excellence"—excellence of the activity by which the potentialities peculiar to man are realized. "Virtue" is used, e.g., by Paracelsus as synonymous with the individual characteristics of each thing—that is, its peculiarity. . . . Man's virtue . . . is that precise set of qualities which is characteristic of the human species, while each person's virtue is his unique individuality. He is "virtuous" if he unfolds his "virtue." (Fromm, 1947, p. 13)

So " 'good' is what is good for man and 'evil' is what is detrimental to man; the *sole criterion of ethical value being man's welfare*" (p. 13). Or again,

> to love one's neighbor is not a phenomenon *transcending* man; it is something inherent in and *radiating from* him. Love is not a higher power which descends upon man nor a duty which is imposed upon him; it is his own power by which he relates himself to the world and makes it truly his. (p. 14)

Obviously, then, Fromm holds that concern for what one ought to do and be arises from an intrinsic principle.

Second, as noted above, Lonergan (1972) provides a refined understanding of human authenticity, specified by the four transcendental precepts. Fromm's concern is for human authenticity in this same sense, for he advocates pursuit of what is objectively true and good in itself. So Fromm argues correctly that insistence on an inherent human source of ethical norms does not lead to amorality. The purpose of *Man for Himself* (1947) is

> to show that our knowledge of human nature does not lead to ethical relativism but, on the contrary, to the conviction that the source of norms for ethical conduct are to be found in man's nature itself; that moral norms are based on man's inherent qualities, and that their violation results in mental and emotional disintegration. (p. 7)

Fromm insists, "The principle that good is what is *good for man* does not imply that man's nature is such that egoism and isolation are good for him . . . man finds his fulfillment and happiness only in relatedness to and solidarity with his fellow men" (p. 14).

Third, then, according to Fromm, the inherent tendencies of human nature toward what is objectively right and good imply self-transcendence. They oppose egoism and isolation and call for relatedness and solidarity. To go out of and beyond oneself, to love one's neighbor, is an inherent power. Love of neighbor *radiates from* humankind.

If spiritual development is determined by an *intrinsic* principle of *authentic self-transcendence* and if Fromm, in his own way, describes such a principle in the human being, then Fromm is advocating an understanding of human nature as spiritual in its essential distinctiveness.

Such an understanding is accurate. Moreover, it is sorely needed and, for my part, most welcome in our day. In a secular culture such an understanding can advocate concern for values in secular terms. Indeed, Fromm's position is an alternative to the still prevalent secular positions that his works opposed: biological, reductionistic instinctivism, and ethical relativism. And his position is a valuable alternative also to the other position that he opposed: authoritarian religion.

Undoubtedly, the apparent antireligious theme throughout Fromm's thought (1942; 1947, pp. 8–14; 1950) and his emphatic option for humanism have precluded appreciation for his work among many institutionally affiliated religious people. Yet, as is obvious in the present analysis, Fromm's basic position firmly advocates many of the same concerns that, by understood mandate, the religions in our society supposedly foster. His opposition is not to religion as such, as any fair reading of his works must make obvious. He rightly opposes only religion that oppresses valid human freedoms and restricts authentic human growth—as do most institutionalized religions in one way or another! And there's the rub. Still jealous of their self-appropriated divine authority in many areas, even the more sane religions continue to make little impact on the chaos of intellectual agnosticism and ethical relativism in contemporary society. The message that would more likely meet the present secular needs is substantially the one articulated by Fromm a generation ago. Though merely humanist in itself, this message is not opposed to theism or to Christianity; it opens up onto them (Helminiak, 1982b, 1986a, 1987a, 1987b).

Intimations of such an understanding are discernible even in Paul's writings. In Romans 2:14–15, Paul notes that, "When the Gentiles who have not the law do by nature what the law requires, they are a law to themselves," for "what the law requires is written on their hearts." In Philippians 4:8–9, Paul seems to exhort basic human goodness, yet he knows that this relates one to God: "Whatever is true, whatever is honorable, whatever is just, whatever is pure, whatever is lovely, whatever is gracious, if there is any excellence, if there is anything worthy of praise, think about these things. What you have learned and received and heard and seen in me, do; and the God of peace will be with you."

Ironically, many religiously affiliated people interested in spirituality look to Carl Jung as the arch-guru among psychologists (cf., for example, Brewi & Brennan, 1982; Grant, Thompson, & Clarke, 1983; Thompson, 1982). Yet Jung's position is inherently and dangerously ambiguous on those very spiritual issues on which Fromm is clear. Jung

> recognized that psychology and psychotherapy are bound up with the philosophical and moral problems of man. But while this recognition is exceedingly important in itself, Jung's philosophical orientation led only to a reaction against Freud and not to a philosophically oriented psychology going beyond Freud. To Jung "the unconscious" and the myth have become new sources of revelation, supposed to be superior to rational thought just because of their nonrational origin. . . . In his eclectic admiration for any religion Jung has relinquished [the] search for the truth in his theory. Any system, if it is only nonrational, any myth or symbol, to him is of equal value. He is a relativist with regard to religion—the negative but not the opposite of rational relativism which he so ardently combats. (Fromm, 1947, pp. viii–ix)

If, unlike Fromm, Jung often refers to God and to Christ, in his system these are archetypes of the psyche, not objective realities as in theism and Christianity. Jung's position on God, Christ, and the problem of evil is seriously flawed (Doran, 1979). In contrast, while Fromm opposes (authoritarian) religion and hardly uses the term "spiritual," the substance of his humanist position, as this analysis shows, is in the mainstream of Western religious concerns and classical philosophy.

Yet Fromm's position is a psychological one. So he challenges the field of psychology as well. Fromm developed a position that opposed the two dominant psychological schools of his age: orthodox psychoanalysis and behaviorism. The present analysis makes it clear why Fromm's and similar positions were deemed the Third Force in psychology: humanistic psychology (cf. Misiak & Sexton, 1973). His understanding of human nature demands that psychology take into account questions of human meaning and of moral value—orientation and devotion—overlooked in those other approaches. Fromm's position squares well with what Doran (1977) calls "authentic psycho-therapy" (p. 216) and with what Helminiak (1986a, 1987a, 1987b) calls psychology within the philosophic, in contrast to the merely positivist, viewpoint. Thus, Fromm envisages a conception of psychology that is adequate to the human conceived as intrinsically spiritual. By the same token, Fromm proposes a safe and sound basis for a nontheist account of spirituality.

Nonetheless, Fromm's position is not altogether without ambiguities and flaws. If his position is to be supportive of a possible scientific (i.e., psychological, not theological) account of spirituality, the ambiguities must be clarified and the flaws corrected. There is too much at stake to gloss over subtleties.

What is the precise nature of Fromm's supposed dichotomy at the heart of the human situation? According to one account, the dichotomy is between the decreased determination by instincts and the growth of the neo-cortex (Fromm, 1973, p. 223). In another place there is the "dichotomy between missing instincts and self-awareness" (p. 226). And in still another place, cited in the third long quote of this article, the dichotomy is between body and mind (p. 225). That these three statements of the basic human dichotomy are not immediately identical is obvious. Still, discussing the issue further would hardly be profitable. As is sufficiently clear, the bulk of Fromm's argument casts humans in contrast to other animals because of the capacity to think. And the key "dichotomy" in the human is between biological, organic rootedness on the one hand, and the capacity and necessity to determine the meaning and structure of one's life on the other. Such a general answer to this first question may stand, for the following consideration will more surely get to the heart of the matter.

Fromm's all so clearly stated answer to the question, "What is the source of the drive to perfection in the human?" contains a consistent ambiguity. Close reading of the fourth long quote above (Fromm, 1947, pp. 40–41, 44) reveals that two driving forces are unwittingly named. First, reason itself is the driving force. It continually demands further answers, further understanding, futher coherence. It intimates an absoluteness that unifies all. It cannot remain passive in the face of inconsistencies. But second, the dichotomy within the human, the inner split, is the driving force because that dichotomy demands to be overcome. Well, then, is it the dichotomy in human nature or the nature of reason itself that forces humans to strive everlastingly?

Some of Fromm's statements suggest it is reason's very inquisitiveness, its incessant questioning, its demands for complete and coherent explanation, that drives humans ever onward. But if this is the case, why is reason styled a curse? Others of Fromm's statements suggest it is only because of the dichotomy—between physical organism and intellectual responsibility—that humans continue to strive.

But one wonders if the word "dichotomy" is not too strong. One wonders if only this exaggerated description (and not the incessantly inquisitive nature of reason) elicits the name "curse." A further realization encourages this line of speculation: Fromm too easily associates existential "contradictions" with biological "dichotomy" when, as is likely, he uses the term "contradiction" in the Hegelian and Marxian sense to mean simply an inconsistency, a disequilibrium, a mismatch between one's mental concepts and environmental realities. Then the "contradictions"—and perhaps even that imposing dichotomy?—suggest simply questions to be answered rather than opposites to be reconciled. It may be reason's incessant curiosity, and not some dichotomy at all, that explains the incessant striving.

The question can be phrased otherwise. Does the dichotomy in human existence constitute the enduring human problem to be solved, or is it the vast and elusive universe that needs to be ever further understood? In the former case the source of human striving is a supposed human dichotomy; in the latter, merely the marvel of human reason. But which is it? There is no answer to this question in Fromm's statements on the issue.

In fact, the bulk of Fromm's statements point to reason as the source of human striving. I would agree with this solution, though I prefer to speak of Lonergan's more broadly explicated "dynamic consciousness" (Lonergan, 1957, pp. 4ff; 1972, pp. 7ff) in place of "reason." But if this is really Fromm's answer, his extensive analysis of evolutionary history and of the emergence of the human into stark biological dichotomy needs to be significantly refined—a major theoretical undertaking. The flaw in Fromm's position is serious.

I would agree that reason—dynamic human consciousness—is the source of human striving because appeal to reason would resolve the issue. In contrast, positing a radical dichotomy in the human creates more problems. Such an explanation depreciates, rather than appreciates, the distinctively human: it implies a radical self-rejection, for the biological remains always in opposition to the reasonable. And such an explanation suggests intrinsic self-contradiction: the only reasoning creature in nature is supposedly constitutionally absurd, an irrational; so attainment of the goal of dynamic consciousness, coherent explanation and loving embrace all that there is to be known and loved, is precluded by the very nature of the agent alone qualified to pursue that goal. This position degenerates to one of absolute existential absurdity, and talk of reason is ultimately a joke. So the notion of an inherent dichotomy in the human cannot be correct.

Besides, the evolutionary emergence of reason need not be seen to create a dichotomy. Other explanations are available. The ancient Hebrew account suggests that not the human spiritual potential itself but the *misuse* of that potential is the source of the experienced dichotomies in humans. Genesis 3 deals with sin, not with the emergence of reason (Maly, 1968, paragraphs 26–29). The latter interpretation of the "Fall"—suggested by Fromm's calling reason a "curse" (1942, pp. 33–35; 1947, p. 40) and humanity's "lost paradise, the unity with nature" (1947, p. 41, but also see p. 12)—is simply untrue to the text.

Or again, the emergence of reason in history certainly raises painful existential questions for humans, and the tension between the soaring of the mind and the denseness of the body does demand attention: "The spirit is willing, but the flesh is weak" (Mark 14:38). But questions and tensions are hardly dichotomies. Dualistic opposition between body and mind is not a necessary conclusion. Plato conceived the human situation as one to be lived in an "in between" stance, in the *Metaxy* (Voegelin, 1974). Truly human experience occurs in that moment of understanding between the already understood and conceptualized, on the one hand, and the newly emerging understanding and conceptualization, on the other. The Metaxy is a dynamic point between the concrete world and the ideal world, between matter and mind. The tension between the two is creative and fruitful. "Dichotomous" misdescribes the reality. Not intrinsic dichotomy but dynamic human consciousness explains the incessant human drive toward perfection.

Fromm's understanding of human nature is not without ambiguity and even outright flaw. Yet the main thrust of his presentation seems to be correct. Humans seek everlastingly to transcend themselves because to do so is the distinctive characteristic of the nature that sets them apart from other animals. Acknowledgment of this intrinsically human dynamism toward authentic self-transcendence provides a basis for a revised conception of human psychology and, by the same token, for an adequate nontheist account of human spirituality.

Conclusion

This article has summarized Erich Fromm's understanding of human nature and pinpointed his account of the human tendency ever to seek further perfection. Though not wholly unambiguous, his position is basically correct. Empirical evidence and logical argument support it. It allows for a spiritual component in human nature and so is useful as a secular formulation of many traditionally religious issues. Fromm, the avowed humanist and harsh critic of religions, makes a valuable contribution to the psychological study of spirituality. That is, he provides the basis for an authentic spirituality that cuts across cultures and religions. When that contribution is appreciated more widely and crystallized in a more generally accepted form, Fromm will have made his contribution also to that task toward which he dedicated so much of his energy: peaceful and wholesome life on this planet—the kind of life that believers know is open to eternal fulfillment in God and Christ.

References

Brewi, B., & Brennan, A. (1982). *Mid-life: Psychological and spiritual perspectives.* New York: Crossroad.

Campbell, R. L., & Bickhard, M. H. (1986). *Knowing levels and developmental stages.* New York: Karger.

Doran, R. M. (1977). *Subject and the psyche: Ricoeur, Jung, and the search for foundations.* Washington, DC: University Press of America.

Doran, R. M. (1979). Jungian psychology and Christian spirituality (Parts I, II, & III). *Review for*

Religious, 38, 497–510, 742–752, 857–866.

Eagle, M. N. (1984). *Recent developments in psychoanalysis.* New York: McGraw-Hill.

Fromm, E. (1942). *Escape from freedom.* New York: Rinehart & Co.

Fromm, E. (1947). *Man for himself: An inquiry into the psychology of ethics.* New York: Rinehart & Co.

Fromm, E. (1950). *Psychoanalysis and religion.* New York: Bantam.

Fromm, E. (1973). *The anatomy of human destructiveness.* New York: Holt, Rinehart & Winston.

Grant, W. H., Thompson, M., & Clarke, T. E. (1983). *From image to likeness: A Jungian path in the gospel journey.* New York: Paulist.

Helminiak, D. A. (1982a). How is meditation prayer? *Review for Religious, 41,* 774–782.

Helminiak, D. A. (1982b). Where do we stand as Christians? The challenge of Western science and Eastern religions. *Spiritual Life, 28,* 195–209.

Helminiak, D. A. (1984a). Consciousness as a subject matter. *Journal for the Theory of Social Behavior, 14,* 211–230.

Helminiak, D. A. (1984b). Neurology, psychology, and extraordinary religious experiences. *Journal of Religion and Health, 23,* 33–46.

Helminiak, D. A. (1986a). Four viewpoints on the human: A conceptual schema for interdisciplinary studies (Part one). *The Heythrop Journal, 27,* 420–437.

Helminiak, D. A. (1986b). *The same Jesus: A contemporary Christology.* Chicago: Loyola University Press.

Helminiak, D. A. (1987a). Four viewpoints on the human: A conceptual schema for interdisciplinary studies (Part two). *The Heythrop Journal, 28,* 1–15.

Helminiak, D. A. (1987b). *Spiritual development: An interdisciplinary study.* Chicago: Loyola University Press.

Lonergan, B. J. F. (1957). *Insight: A study of human understanding.* New York: Philosophical Library.

Lonergan, B. J. F. (1972). *Method in theology.* New York: Herder & Herder.

Maddi, S. R. (1980). *Personality theories: A comparative analysis.* Homewood, IL: Dorsey.

Maly, E. H. (1968). Genesis. In R. E. Brown, J. A. Fitzmyer, & R. E. Murphy (Eds.), *The Jerome biblical commentary* (Vol. 1, pp. 7–46). Englewood Cliffs, NJ: Prentice-Hall.

Misiak, H., & Sexton, V. A. (1973). *Phenomenological, existential, and humanistic psychologies: A historical survey.* New York: Grune & Stratton.

Thompson, H. (1982). *Journey toward wholeness: A Jungian model of adult spiritual growth.*

New York: Paulist.

Voegelin, E. (1974). Reason: The classic experience. *The Southern Review, 10*, 237–264.

THE ROLE-SENDING OF PERFECTIONISM: OVERCOMING COUNTERFEIT SPIRITUALITY

D. LOUISE MEBANE
Doctoral Student in Clinical Psychology
CHARLES R. RIDLEY
Associate Professor of Psychology
Graduate School of Psychology
Fuller Theological Seminary

Article from *Journal of Psychology and Theology*

Roles are a set of recurrent or patterned behaviors expected of people occupying a particular position (Graen, 1976; Katz & Kahn, 1978). For example, an enlisted soldier is expected to salute a military officer. Furthermore, saluting behavior occurs every time the soldier is in the presence of an officer. Roles are a necessary and inevitable function of social systems.

Role-sending (or role-making) is the process by which the expectations of one person or a group of people are transmitted to a focal person in order to elicit a particular set of behaviors (Graen, 1976; Katz & Kahn, 1978). The concept originated in organizational psychology theory. For every role that is sent, a role is received, consisting of the receiver's perceptions and cognitions of the transmitted expectations (Katz & Kahn, 1978). This latter process is referred to as role-taking.

The purpose of this article is to discuss role-sending in the church. Particular attention is given to how church leaders, especially pastors, send roles to their congregations. Among the many roles sent, the expectation of perfectionism is a frequent case in point. The perfection role or perfectionism, we propose, is actually counterfeit spirituality and poses deleterious consequences for wholesome Christian living, and as the Persian mystic, Rumi, once said, "Counterfeits exist because there is such a thing as real gold."

To accomplish its objective, this article is organized into four major sections. The first section examines the dynamics of role-sending with its multi-faceted dimensions. The second section is a discussion of role-sending in the church with specific emphasis on the sending of expectations of perfection by pastors. The third section describes some of the adverse by-products associated with the role of perfection, and the fourth section prescribes recommendations to resolve this problem of faulty role-sending.

The Dynamics of Role-Sending

Role-sending and role-taking interact dynamically to form a role episode (Katz & Kahn, 1978). A role episode is comprised of four components: (a) *role expectations*, which are the evaluative standards applied to the focal person's behavior; (b) *sent-role*, which consists of communication based upon the sender's expectations in attempting to influence and shape the focal person's behavior; (c) *received role*, which is the focal person's perception of the role-sendings and includes the reflective role expectations that focal persons "send" to themselves; and (d) *role behavior*, which is the actual behavior as response to the complex of information or sent role. The role episode is depicted in Figure 1.

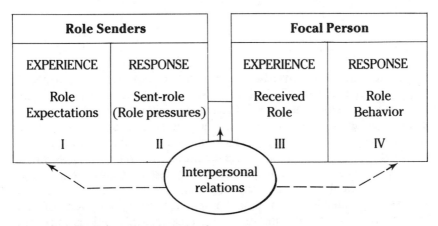

Figure 1. A model of the role episode.

Note: From *The Social Psychology of Organizations* (2nd ed.) by Daniel Katz and Robert L. Kahn. Copyright © 1978, by John Wiley & Sons, Inc. Reprinted by permission of John Wiley & Sons, Inc.

The example of military saluting illustrates the components of a role episode. Evaluative standards are the ratings with accompanying rewards or penalties. The expectation is initially communicated in the form of a command. The reflective expectation is the soldier's internalized belief in saluting without the need for a verbal command. Consistent saluting of an officer is the actual role behavior.

The person who holds the role expectation is referrred to as a role sender. The focal person, whose behavior is being influenced, is also called the role receiver. These terms imply that role expectations involve both verbal and nonverbal communication (Smith, 1973). The role episode always involves reciprocal expectations of both sender and receiver (Thompson & Van Houten, 1970). Therefore, to some extent, all participants in an organization send and receive roles.

Role expectations and sent roles are concerned with the motivations, cognitions, and behaviors of the sender as a member of the role set. On the other hand, the received role and role behavior are concerned with the cognitions, motivations, and behavior of the focal person. These concepts underscore the complex and dynamic nature of the role episode which is an ongoing and interdependent cyclical process (Katz & Kahn, 1978).

In formal organizations, roles are more a function of the role episode than of individuals' unique personality characteristics. Individuals representing a wide spectrum of personalities can be observed enacting the same role behavior. Using the military illustration, all soldiers engage in saluting despite their various temperaments. This demonstrates the tremendous impact of social system dynamics in maintaining role behavior.

There are several kinds of role-sending messages, including direct instructions, information about rewards and penalties contingent on role performance, and evaluations of present performance in relation to role expectations. The statements of role-sending may be given in specific behavioral terms (i.e., "You must always salute in the presence of an officer"), or the statements may be indirect, inferring the expectations (i.e., "Soldiers who fail to salute an officer get disciplined").

The role episode involves more than the transmission of information regarding the role sender's expectations. Role expectations are perhaps more correctly described as "role pressures" (Smith, 1973). In actuality, the sender is trying to influence the receiver to conform to his or her behavioral expectations. Attempts by the sender to gain compliance are implied by the consequences of reward or sanctions contingent upon the role behavior. The focal person's ensuing behavior is feedback to the role sender regarding the impact of his or her message. Compliance is rewarded, while noncompliance is sanctioned. This completes the role-sending episode. If the behavior is not acceptable to the role sender, another episode may be initiated to further seek the receiver's compliance.

Other salient dimensions of role-sending messages are *sign*—prescriptive (preferred behaviors) or proscriptive (behaviors to be avoided); *magnitude*—strength of the influence attempt; *specificity*—extent to which the role expectations are made concrete and detailed; *range*—conditions under which compliance is intended; and *intensity*—extent to which the focal person has freedom of choice in compliance or noncompliance (Gross, Mason, & McEachern, 1958).

The magnitude and intensity of role influences are of particular interest and may vary considerably both within and between role sets. For example, role influence attempts may be balanced (A influences B approximately as much as B influences A) or imbalanced (A influences B more than B influences A). In addition, these attempts may be intentional or unintentional, and conscious or unconscious. Therefore, it is not uncommon for senders to be relatively unaware of their influence attempts on focal persons (Kahn, Wolfe, Quinn, Snoek, & Rosenthal, 1964). Finally, magnitude and intensity depend upon the importance of the issues to the sender and the subsequent resistance encountered.

In any case, most organizations typically have a few individuals who emerge as the more dominant role senders. Regardless of the intentionality of the sender, role pressures have significant consequences for the receiver, and these consequences may be healthy or unhealthy depending upon the behavioral expectation and the response.

Role-Sending in the Church

One of the responsibilities of the church as a social system is to influence the way people develop standards for living. These standards include prescriptions and proscriptions about patterned and motivated behavior. Essentially, the church has a role-sending function. As previously indicated, all participants in an organization send roles. Church members are no exception. For example, roles can be sent from the pastor to the congregation, elders to pastor, Sunday school instructors to class members, and parents to Sunday school instructors and vice versa.

Most often, pastors are the dominant role senders because of their unique position and ordained authority. The pastor most consistently sends powerful role expectations. These may be sent formally or informally. Perhaps the most potent formal expectations are conveyed via weekly sermons and homily to the focal persons in the congregation. Seymour (1983) states, "Throughout the history of the church an essential task of the pastoral office has been the teaching of Christian faith and lifestyle" (p. 6).

Role-sending in the church typically originates in the conversion message. Rambo (1982) has provided helpful insight, drawing upon Murphey's description of the conversion process:

> The conversion process begins with the individual's accumulation of experience and knowledge. Over time, potential converts translate their knowledge of the world into personal terms related to their individual identities. In Christian-oriented groups, this personal understanding of life tends to emerge as a sense that one has sinned and is therefore in jeopardy of damnation. Next comes an acknowledgment by the potential convert that he or she deserves the wrath of God. Desperation and a sense of helplessness flourish in this psychological environment of self-condemnation.

> Again in Christian terms, during this difficult time the individual receives the message of the liberating grace of God in Jesus Christ; in other traditions, the message is similar, appearing as a panacea to all the troubles of the self-identified sinner. Thus, the pattern, with varying content, is this: the

person goes from mere knowledge to an experience of personal failure in life, and the growing intensity of that experience leads to a deep sense of being lost. Upon accepting the saving message, the convert experiences a sense of deliverance. Then he or she undertakes the long process of sanctification—that is, modification of the entire life-style. (p. 97)

The aforementioned psychological set predisposes the convert to acquiesce to faulty role-sending. With an utter sense of damnation, the convert is rendered vulnerable to any life-changing message, especially one that emphasizes clear behavioral expectations. In role-sending terms, the role episode has tremendous magnitude because it is a powerful influence attempt. It is also highly intense because the converts view themselves as having limited choice in the selection of their role behavior.

In addition, the sent role may be highly specific. To illustrate, Rambo (1982) has described the impact of a charismatic leader (pastor) as a role model:

The leader shows the convert, both explicitly and implicitly, how to act, think, and feel in order to begin to achieve the transformation that is the goal of the conversion experience. Typically, modeling is unconscious, but in some situations the convert is admonished explicitly to feel and act like the leader, even to the point of using the same mannerisms, gestures, words, and so on. The implication is that the leader's power is related to his or her behavior and that it is therefore valuable for the recruit to emulate the leader in the hope of reaping spiritual benefits. (p. 102)

This is precisely where faulty role-sending originates. The major thesis of this article is that often an unrealistic and unbiblical message of how to live the "Christian life" is sent in the church. If pastors intend for their behavior to be modeled, it is understandable that only their best behaviors and accomplishments are openly displayed. The outcome is that pastoral perfection is modeled to imperfect parishioners.

The potent message sent is "you need to be a perfect Christian." The attending assumption is the need to be completely successful or competent especially in overcoming all personal struggles and limitations. Tjosvold's (1983) research on the concept of "social face" is relevant. Social face is the positive image a person wants to project. Disconfirmation or loss of face is generally followed by attempts to restore "face."

A notorious social face in the church is the need to appear perfect. Christians often hide their personal struggles and temptations from other people and often deceive themselves as well. They do so because they equate perfection with spirituality. Therefore, they make every attempt to avoid appearing imperfect, which, in their view, is tantamount to being unspiritual.

In many cases, the congregation also sends messages that the pastor needs to be perfect. Clergy have additional impossible demands of universal expertise placed upon them. According to the "pedestal effect," they are expected to be paragons of Christian virtue and experts in every endeavor

(Blackbird & Wright, 1985). They also have been described as "believer-saints" (Smith, 1973). To fall short in any aspect of ministry is to become vulnerable to criticism, despite outstanding performance in other areas (Jud, Mills, & Walters, 1970).

Bowers (1963) has demonstrated how clergy have internalized saintly expectations for themselves. As a psychiatrist, she has treated numerous members of the Catholic clergy. She stated that priests are revered hierarchically just below God and nearly equal to Christ with powers that defy human imagination. Although Bowers's case illustrations are derived from the Catholic priesthood, we believe that her observations also are applicable to Protestant clergy. In fact, she insists that denominational differences do not limit this "burden of the ideal self-image."

Our experience has shown that some pastors have a proclivity for expecting perfection of members in their congregations. They appeal to explicit behavioral standards as the solution to spiritual deficiency. Their implicit expectation of perfectionism is perhaps even more potent. Ironically, pastors themselves have a need to be invulnerable to the very people from whom they expect perfection.

Consequences of Perfectionism

Perfection in the sense of errorlessness or flawlessness is a human impossibility. To use the Latin phrase, *errare humanum est,* to err is human. Moreover, the tremendous emphasis on human perfection is theologically untenable (Brown, 1986; Warfield, 1958). Assuming that human personality is an integrated whole, demands for perfection often backfire, resulting in deleterious psychological and spiritual consequences. Among the more serious by-products are fear, hypocrisy, and legalism.

Fear
Perfectionists live with inordinate fear. Fear is an anticipation of impending danger and comparative helplessness (Solomon, 1983). The motivational dynamic underlying fear is self-protection. The behavioral consequence of fear is avoidance or escape.

Perfectionists expend considerable energy in avoiding fear-evoking stimuli. They do so regardless of whether or not the feared stimuli are actually harmful. In some cases, as in a needle injection by a physician, the fear-evoking stimulus is painful but not harmful. In other cases, as in a fire that rages out of control, the fear-evoking stimulus is both painful and harmful.

Fear is a natural human emotion and is not itself sin (Morosco, 1973). However, fear in the perfectionist can lead to counterfeit spirituality. This powerful emotion frequently results in inappropriate avoidance behavior. People often avoid painful situations or events, claiming it as evidence of authentic spirituality. In reality, the avoidance is anxious self-protection.

A pastor who avoids taking a minority position on a controversial issue may illustrate the point. Because of the need to appear perfect, the pastor may fear a loss of credibility. One could argue that a more healthy response would be for the pastor to take an unpopular stand, despite the accompanying criticism.

Hypocrisy

Hypocrisy is a pretense of virtue and piety that actually does not exist. In the New Testament, hypocrisy connotes either the idea of play-acting or unprincipled action (Hubbard, 1984). Play-acting, in particular, appears problematic for perfectionists. They place a premium on flawless external behavior. The motivational dynamic underlying hypocrisy is insincerity and duplicity. The behavioral consequence of hypocrisy is inconsistency.

The hypocrite has a discrepancy between behavior and motives. Deceit occurs when overt behavior is intended to disguise or misrepresent a person's true motives. Thus, two people can engage in identical behaviors but with different motives behind their actions. On the other hand, unidentical behaviors may be initiated from similar motives. The essential note of concern is the unpretentious representation of one's motive through behavior.

The case of the pastor who avoids controversy is again illustrative. The pastor's actual behavior implies commitment to the majority position. In reality, the behavior misrepresents the pastor's true conviction—support for the minority position. The pastor, then, is insincere and unauthentic. Of course, if the pastor agrees with the majority position, then there is no discrepancy. On the other hand, evidence of inconsistency would be reflected in the pastor's casting support for the other position if majority opinion had swayed in that direction.

A major problem with all forms of inconsistency is the unawareness of it on the part of those people involved. Often, an objective observer is needed to point out the inconsistency (Guthrie, 1981). Many perfectionists in the church are unaware of their hypocrisy because there may be no corporate challenge to their inconsistency.

Legalism

Legalism is strong reliance on an overly rigid adherence to rules governing behavior (Macquarrie, 1987; Maring, 1979). It includes behavioral prescriptions and proscriptions. The motivational dynamic behind legalism is approval-seeking. The behavioral consequence of legalism is conditionality such that the criteria for acceptance (of self and others) is based upon human performance. Weisinger and Lobsenz (1981) have captured this problem:

> The need to be perfect places a person in a self-destructive double bind. If

one fails to meet the unrealistic expectation, one is failed; but if one does meet it, one feels no glow of achievement for one has only done what was expected. There is no objective way to measure effort or improvement, no chance to relish success, no reason to build up one's self-image. (p. 273)

The problem of legalism in the perfectionist is noted by the tendency to evaluate experiences in a dichotomous manner (Burns, 1980). Perfectionists view behavior completely in black and white terms without any consideration for shades of grey. Any deviation from the legalists' perfectionistic standards would automatically categorize them as unspiritual.

We would like to add the observation that perfectionism leads to an upward redefinition of performance standards. When perfectionists meet a standard of behavior, they paradoxically discover that their performance falls short of the next higher level of performance. This results in endless attempts to gain unattainable approval.

Once the illustrative pastor gets beyond the prevailing controversy, other equally compelling, approval-seeking situations arise. However, success at each subsequent achievement fails to produce the desired sustaining approval. Thus, success turns into failure, and the pastor's recourse is to initiate new approval-seeking behavior.

Perfectionism with its accompanying legalism is inadequate to achieve God's approval. The assumption underlying legalism is that people have within themselves the capacity to obtain God's approval. Legalism is unbiblical because God's approval is never predicated upon human performance. "It is made still plainer that no one is justified in God's sight by obeying the Law" (Gal. 3:11). Human behavior should occur as faithful obedience in light of God's grace and unconditional love. It should not occur as legalistic attempts to gain God's approval.

Recommendations

Perfectionism is counterfeit spirituality. It is a contradiction to authentic Christian living. Furthermore, it produces several debilitating by-products, namely, fear, hypocrisy, and legalism. As illustrated, these by-products have both spiritual and psychological ramifications. Two major recommendations are made to remedy this problem.

Embrace Valid Theology
Invalid theology is a major source of the problem. Role-sending in many churches tends only to emphasize behavioral expectations. Conspicuously absent in the message, however, is an emphasis on grace and forgiveness. There is a seeming paradox; we are imperfect beings who are called to be perfect. On this subject, Brandsma (1982) has stated:

Yet God's standards continue to be unfaltering ("Be ye perfect"). This situation is irreconcilable and was until "in the fullness of time" God acted in a historical context to forgive through and indicate his righteousness in the Christ events. The incarnation and resurrection remain great mysteries in many aspects, but one meaning of God's action is quite clear—we are forgiven. (p. 45)

Unfortunately, the message taught and modeled is mendacious. There is a need to explicate more adequately Christian perfection.[1] For example, the statement by Jesus, "Be ye perfect" (Matt. 5:48), is a contrast to the legalistic piety of the scribes and Pharisees. The imperative is not restricted to moral perfection in the sense of ethical sinlessness or legal perfection in the sense of keeping the "whole law" (Guelich, 1982; Rondelle, 1971). Certainly, God's standards are high, though his grace is more than adequate to help meet those standards. Christian perfection refers to a qualitative relationship with God and other people.

Another Scripture used to support an incorrect view of Christian perfection is 1 John 3:9 (cf. 5:18): "No one born of God commits sins; for God's nature abides in him, and he cannot sin because he is born of God." However, the statement is an assurance of being born of God, not assurance of the believers' sinless perfection (Brown, 1986).

Christian perfection is a holy and wholehearted embracing of God, reflected in charitable, merciful, repenting, and forgiving conduct. The conduct is the effect rather than the cause of this qualitative standing. According to Jesus, perfection is righteousness that exceeds the scribes and Pharisees (Matt. 5:20). These religious leaders perfectly obeyed the "letter" of the law but imperfectly fulfilled the "spirit" of the law. They were religious but not spiritual.

A quote from Seamands's (1981) popular writing is useful: "Perfectionism is a counterfeit for Christian perfection, holiness, sanctification, or the Spirit-filled life. Instead of making us holy persons and integrated personalities—this is, whole persons in Christ—perfectionism leaves us spiritual Pharisees and emotional neurotics" (p. 78).

A past and present pitfall in the church is the attempt to gain God's favor through religious practice. Any standard of human behavior or performance is inadequate to achieve God's approval. God's approval is found in the redemptive indicative—the perfect forgiveness of sins (Rondelle, 1971). It is freely given without regard to human merit and despite human demerit. This is the essence of the gospel—unmerited favor.

Perfectionists need a redefinition of God (Stoop, 1987). They need to view God as more than a judge. Human attempts to achieve God's approval disregard the reality of the grace of God (Gal. 2:21), making Christ's death a mockery. The good news is that people do not have to perform to gain God's approval. God's approval is based upon redemption in Christ.

The Heidelberg Catechism (1962) represents this theological emphasis. At the outset, the seriousness of sin is underscored. Subsequently, the theme of grace is developed as the prescription for sin. Thus, this ecumenical Protestant document recognizes that authentic spirituality accounts for the human condition.

Role Modification

Role modification is an intentional intervention to change flawed role behavior. With regards to the perfection role, changes in both the pastor and church members generally will be required. Because of their emotional investment, many people will initially resist change.

Role modification begins with a role appraisal. The appraisal determines the necessity for role modification. It includes two parts: (a) clarification of the sent expectations, which should be based upon the theological correction; and (b) a comparison of the role sender's expectations (of self and others) with his or her perceptions of the observed role behavior.

Realistically, pastors should model their full humanity with all its imperfections and failures as well as accomplishments humbly achieved through God's grace. Imperfection must be openly acknowledged and accepted. Authenticity and honesty must be modeled along with healthy striving toward self-improvement.[2]

Role modification in the church allows the freedom to question, negotiate and, if appropriate, modify motivated and patterned behavior. This is not a proposition for rewriting the Bible or pushing moral standards to their limits. In fact, Romans 6:1–2 sums up the solution: "What shall we say then? Shall we go on sinning so that grace may increase? By no means! We die to sin."

If congregations are given the freedom to ask and struggle with tough questions, half the problem is solved. The other half of the problem concerns the validity of the message sent. Pastors need to be careful about teaching behavior in "black and white" terms. They need to teach biblical standards without either being legalistic or dispensing "cheap grace" (Bonhoeffer, 1963). They must recognize that teaching people to internalize Christian values is the greater challenge. Unless pastors teach correct biblical principles, many church members will adopt unauthentic behavioral patterns. This will result in performance according to the pastor's perfectionistic expectations.

Conclusion

Some pastors are inclined to have an unrealistic need to appear perfect. In turn, they are inclined to send expectations of perfection to their congregations. Vulnerable congregational members are psychologically predisposed to adopt the pastor's unrealistic role expectations.

The expectations of perfection are psychologically and theologically untenable. Psychologically, perfectionism is an unachievable human goal. Theologically, perfectionism is a counterfeit to true spirituality. Attempts to achieve perfection produce unhealthy personal consequences.

The church needs a biblical corrective to faulty role-sending. Pastors should evaluate critically their theology and the messages they send to their congregations. They should emphasize that Christianity encompasses both law (that is, instruction rather than legalism) and grace. All Christians should recognize that authentic spirituality increases rather than decreases their freedom. They also should recognize that in freedom comes greater vulnerability and responsibility.

Valid theology will provide the guiding principles for all Christians to uniquely live out their spirituality. Within that context, Christians will feel free to ask and struggle with the tough questions of personal application. Out of honest struggling will come wholeness and healthiness. Christians additionally will be encouraged by authentic pastoral models.

We conclude with a challenge from the apostle Paul. "For freedom, Christ has set us free; stand fast therefore, and do not submit again to a yoke of slavery" (Gal. 5:1).

Notes

[1] For critical discussions of Christian perfection, refer to Flew (1934) and Toon (1983).

[2] For excellent discussions on authentic living and spirituality refer to Duncombe (1969), McMinn (1988), and Peck (1978). In Peck, see the section, "Discipline."

References

Blackbird, T., & Wright, P. (1985). Pastor's friendships, part 1: Project overview and an exploration of the pedestal effect. *Journal of Psychology and Theology, 13*, 274–283.

Bonhoeffer, D. (1963). *The cost of discipleship*. New York: Macmillan.

Bowers, M. (1963). *Conflicts of the clergy: A psychodynamic study with case histories*. New York: Thomas Nelson & Sons.

Brandsma, J. M. (1982). Forgiveness: A dynamic theological and therapeutic analysis. *Pastoral Psychology, 31*, 40–50.

Brown, C. (1986). Person of Christ. In G. W. Bromiley (Ed.), *The international standard Bible encyclopedia* (Vol. 3) (pp. 781–801). Grand Rapids: Eerdmans.

Burns, D. D. (1980, November). The perfectionist's script for self-defeat. *Psychology Today*, 34–52.

Duncombe, D. C. (1969). *The shape of the Christian life*. Nashville: Abingdon.

Flew, R. N. (1934). *The idea of perfection in Christian theology: A historical study of the Christian idea for the present life.* London: Oxford University Press.

Graen, G. (1976). Role-making processes in organizations. In M. D. Dunnette (Ed.), *Handbook of industrial and organizational psychology* (pp. 1201–45). Chicago: Rand McNally.

Gross, N., Mason, W., & McEachern, A. W. (1958). *Explorations in role analysis: Studies of the school superintendency role*. New York: Wiley.

Guelich, R. (1982). *The sermon on the mount: A foundation for understanding.* Waco, TX: Word.

The Heidelberg Catechism. (1962). New York: United Church Press.

Hubbard, D. A. (1984). Hypocrisy. In W. A. Elwell (Ed.), *Evangelical dictionary of theology* (p. 539). Grand Rapids: Baker.

Jud, G., Mills, E., & Walters, G. (1970). *Ex-pastors: Why men leave the parish ministry.* Philadelphia: Pilgrim.

Kahn, R., Wolfe, D., Quinn, R., Snoek, J., & Rosenthal, R. A. (1964). *Organizational stress: Studies in role conflict and ambiguity.* Malabar, FL: Krieger.

Katz, E., & Kahn, R. L. (1978). *The social psychology of organizations.* New York: Wiley.

Macquarrie, J. (1987). Legalism. In J. F. Childress & J. Macquarrie (Eds.), *The Westminster dictionary of Christian ethics* (p. 347). Philadelphia: Westminster.

Maring, N. H. (1979). Legalism. In P. K. Meagher, T. C. O'Brien, & C. M. Aherne (Eds.), *Encyclopedic dictionary of religion* (Vol. 2) (pp. 2084–85). Washington, DC: Corpus.

McMinn, M. R. (1988). *Your hidden self.* Grand Rapids: Baker.

Morosco, R. E. (1973). Theological implications of fear. *Journal of Psychology and Theology, 1* (2), 43–50.

Peck, M. S. (1978). *The road less traveled: A new psychology of love, traditional values and spiritual growth.* New York: Simon and Schuster.

Rambo, L. (1982). Charisma and conversion. *Pastoral Psychology, 31,* 96–108.

Rondelle, H. (1971). *Perfection and perfectionism: A dogmatic-ethical study of biblical perfection and phenomenal perfectionism.* Berrien Springs, MI: Andrews University Press.

Seamands, D. (1981). *Healing for damaged emotions.* Wheaton, IL: Victor.

Seymour, J. L. (1983). Teaching as religious leadership: Rethinking the pastoral role. *Quarterly Review, 3,* 6–17.

Smith, D. P. (1973). *Clergy in the cross-fire: Coping with role conflicts in the ministry.* Philadelphia: Westminster.

Solomon, R. C. (1983). *The passions.* Notre Dame, IN: University of Notre Dame Press.

Stoop, D. (1987). *Living with a perfectionist.* Nashville: Thomas Nelson.

Thompson, J., & Van Houten, D. (1970). *The behavioral sciences: An interpretation.* Reading, MA: Addison-Wesley.

Tjosvold, D. (1983). Social face in conflict: A critique. *International Journal of Group Tensions, 13,* 49–64.

Toon, P. (1983). *Justification and sanctification.* Westchester, IL: Crossway.

Warfield, B. B. (1958). *Perfectionism.* Grand Rapids: Baker.

Weisinger, H., & Lobsenz, N. (1981). *Nobody's perfect.* New York: Warner.

PRACTICAL THEOLOGY: MISSIONS

C. Peter Wagner, area editor

MISSIONS

C. PETER WAGNER
McGavran Professor of Church Growth
Fuller Seminary School of World Mission

Introduction

Lausanne II International Congress on World Evangelization was the most highly visible missiological event of 1989. The congress was held in Manila, Philippines, on July 11–20. Over 4,000 participants, observers, speakers, and staff members were carefully selected from the top evangelical Christian leadership of some 190 nations and assembled for an intensive period of reflection, personal interaction, prayer, and strategy planning, centered on the evangelization of the world. Through plenary sessions, 450 workshops divided into forty-eight "tracks," national meetings, and ad hoc gatherings. The congress suggested the possibility of completing the Great Commission of our Lord Jesus Christ by the year A.D. 2000.

The congress slogan was "The Whole Church Taking the Whole Gospel to the Whole World." Fifteen years previously in Lausanne I (convened in 1974 in Lausanne, Switzerland), the major outcome related to the "whole world," stressing the priority of cross-cultural evangelism and the so-called "people approach to world evangelization." A lesser but also highly significant issue emerging from Lausanne I was clarifying the relationship between evangelism and Christian social responsibility within the total mission of the church. This issue was further developed in a Lausanne-sponsored consultation held in Grand Rapids, Michigan, in 1982.

Many have felt that the most significant contribution of Lausanne II may turn on the "whole church" part of the slogan. For the first time in the history of the Lausanne movement Pentecostal and charismatic leaders were made to feel involved in the inner workings of the event and assigned key places of input on the program. Another highly visible emphasis that emerged from Manila was the reaffirmation of the critical needs of the poor and oppressed, who are concentrated mostly in the urban areas of the world.

The theological focus of Lausanne II was on the "whole gospel." Able speakers from many parts of the world expounded on subjects such as guilt, grace, sin, lostness, the end times, and salvation. Two theological issues maintained a high profile during the congress: the uniqueness of Jesus Christ and conversion. I have selected these two topics for the current volume. In making the following choices, I received valuable assistance from my advisory board comprising some of America's most prominent missiologists: Norman E. Allison of Toccoa Falls College; J. Ronald Blue of Dallas Theological Seminary; Harvie M. Conn of Westminster Theological Seminary; Ralph R. Covell of Denver Theological Seminary; David J. Hesselgrave of Trinity Evangelical Divinity School; Donald Hohensee of Western Evangelical Seminary; L. Grant McClung, Jr., of the Church of God School of Theology; Marvin K. Mayers of Biola University; Kenneth B. Mulholland of Columbia Biblical Seminary and Graduate School of Missions; and Warren Webster of the Conservative Baptist Foreign Mission Society.

Lesslie Newbigin looks back on a long career as a missionary to India and as bishop of the Church of South India. He further distinguished himself as a professor at Selly Oak Colleges in Birmingham, England, and as director of the Commission on World Mission and Evangelism of the World Council of Churches. The rising approval of religious pluralism in many parts of the world concerns Bishop Newbigin deeply, and he expounds this concern in "Religious Pluralism and the Uniqueness of Jesus Christ."[1] The central issue for many, he asserts, is the abandonment of the belief that it is possible to know the truth. Facing squarely many of our contemporary authors and arguments, Newbigin, with finesse, concludes that there is objective truth and that the truth was embodied in Jesus Christ, who suffered under Pontius Pilate.

Arthur Glasser, Dean Emeritus of the Fuller Theological Seminary School of World Mission, deals with a related issue in "Conversion and the Kingdom."[2] He says that cultural pluralism and religious relativism have brought into question whether Jesus Christ is truly the starting point for the subject of conversion. After dealing with this question, he stresses the radical nature of true conversion and entrance into the kingdom of God. Drawing from reports from Africa, Glasser points out the dangers of superficial conversions to Western culture rather than genuine kingdom conversions.

Honorable Mention

I join with members of my editorial board in lamenting that *The Best in Theology* is not *The Best in Missions,* for many of the following articles could well have qualified as selections for reprinting. Fine, scholarly material on missions continues to appear in the standard missiological journals and other publications as well.

Editorial board members frequently mentioned three articles as exhibiting particular merit. Pamela S. Mann took a substantial risk when she wrote "Toward a Biblical Understanding of Polygamy."[3] Drawing on her experience in Cameroon, she offers such statements: "As an American woman who cannot imagine her husband with another woman, I was surprised to discover African women preferring polygamy." Mann contends that "It is in Jesus, not monogamy, that women will know the fullness of life."

Two other outstanding articles relate to the matter of the poor, which was a strong emphasis in Lausanne II in Manila. David Stravers looks at some benefits of Christian conversion in "Poverty, Conversion and Worldview in the Philippines."[4] In the article he examines some of the subtle cultural ripple effects of social ministries and says that "It is important that such ministries be designed to change *people* rather than merely their measurable income."

In "Serving Christ in the Slums,"[5] Owen Salter interviews Michael Duncan of Servants to Asia's Urban Poor, who also ministers in the Philippines. Duncan has joined those who have taken the radical step of moving in with their family among the slum dwellers and thereby identifying with them even on an economic level. Among other duties, Duncan feels that high-level spiritual warfare against territorial spirits is a part of their missionary responsibility. He and his colleagues believe that they have identified at least two of these spirits over Manila.

Additional important missions articles from the past year can be listed in ten categories:

1. *Current Trends in Missions.* As the end of the millennium approaches, a number of scholars are taking an assessment of where we have been in missiology and where we might be going in the future. Donald W. Dayton writes on pneumatology in "The Holy Spirit and Christian Expansion in the Twentieth Century,"[6] while Michael Pocock sees eschatology (particularly premillennialism) as a prominent theme in "The Destiny of the World and the Work of Mission."[7] Leighton Ford in "Confronting Changes in Today's World"[8] identifies and analyzes current trends. Howard A. Snyder likewise examines current trends in "Ten Major Trends Facing the World Church."[9] Arthur F. Glasser, author of one of our featured articles, looks down the road in "Mission in the 1990s,"[10] as does David B. Barrett in "Living in the World of A.D. 2000."[11] Finally, Sharon E. Mumper highlights a painful new issue in "AIDS Is Newest Chapter in the Missions Handbook."[12]

2. *Theology.* Year after year the topic of contextualization remains in the forefront of missiological theory and practice. Harold Netland in "Toward Contextualized Apologetics"[13] and Paul G. Hiebert in "Christianity in a World of Religious Turmoil"[14] provide important new contributions.

3. *Urbanology.* The fine journal *Urban Mission* affords a regular networking vehicle for the increasing number of urban missiologists. Two of its outstanding offerings during the past year were Craig Ellison's "Growing Urban Churches Biblically"[15] and Viv Grigg's "Squatters: The Most Responsive Unreached Block."[16]

4. *Evangelism and Outreach.* At the age of 92 the venerable Donald A. McGavran strongly appeals for increasing the evangelistic component of seminary curricula in "Beyond the Maintenance Mentality."[17] One of McGavran's disciples, Allen J. Swanson, contributes "Decisions or Disciples? A

Study of Evangelism Effectiveness in Taiwan."[18]

5. *Women in Mission*. Thomas Russell writes "Can the Story Be Told Without Them? The Role of Women in the Student Volunteer Movement."[19]

6. *Missions in the Past*. Two excellent analyses of people and events in missions history merit special mention: "American Protestants in Pursuit of Mission: 1886–1986" by Gerald H. Anderson[20] and "The Legacy of Roland Allen" by Charles Henry Long and Anne Rowthorn.[21]

7. *Leadership*. Kenneth O. Gangel puts his finger squarely on some of the most vital issues for world evangelization in "Developing New Leaders for the Global Task."[22]

8. *Pentecostals*. Writing as an insider, Russell P. Spittler identifies "Implicit Values in Pentecostal Missions."[23]

9. *Islam*. Two excellent contributions address the world's largest block of unreached peoples: "The Challenge of the Muslim World" by Robert C. Douglas[24] and "Christian-Muslim Dialogue" by George N. Malek.[25]

10. *Regional*. Three significant regional studies conclude our listing: "The Roots of African Theology" by Kwame Bediako,[26] "Distinctives of African Urban Ministry" by John J. Shane,[27] and "Christianity and Ancestor Practices in Hong Kong" by Henry N. Smith.[28]

Notes

[1] Lesslie Newbigin, "Religious Pluralism and the Uniqueness of Jesus Christ," *International Bulletin of Missionary Research*, Vol. 13, No. 2, April 1989, pp. 50–54.

[2] Arthur F. Glasser, "Conversion and the Kingdom," *World Evangelization*, Vol. 15, No. 53, July-August 1988, pp. 14–17.

[3] Pamela S. Mann, "Toward a Biblical Understanding of Polygamy," *Missiology: An International Review*, Vol. XVII, No. 1, January 1989, pp. 11–26.

[4] David Stravers, "Poverty, Conversion and Worldview in the Philippines," *Missiology: An International Review*, Vol. XVI, No. 3, July 1988, pp. 331–48.

[5] Owen Salter, "Serving Christ in the Slums," *Evangelical Missions Quarterly*, Vol. 25, No. 1, January 1989, pp. 6–15.

[6] Donald W. Dayton, "The Holy Spirit and Christian Expansion in the Twentieth Century," *Missiology: An International Review*, Vol. XVI, No. 4, October 1988, pp. 397–407.

[7] Michael Pocock, "The Destiny of the World and the Work of Missions," *Bibliotheca Sacra*, Vol. 145, No. 580, October–December 1988, pp. 436–51.

[8] Leighton Ford, "Confronting Changes in Today's World," *World Evangelization*, Vol. 16, No. 59, May–June 1989, pp. 8–10.

[9] Howard A. Snyder, "Ten Major Trends Facing the World Church," *World Evangelization*, Vol. 15, No. 52, May–June 1988, pp. 5–11.

[10] Arthur F. Glasser, "Mission in the 1990s," *International Bulletin of Missionary Research*, Vol. 13, No. 1, January 1989, pp. 2–8.

[11] David B. Barrett, "Living in the World of A.D. 2000," *World Evangelization*, Vol. 15, No. 55, November–December 1988, pp. 11–14.

[12] Sharon E. Mumper, "AIDS Is Newest Chapter in the Mission Handbook," *Evangelical Missions Quarterly*, Vol. 25, No. 2, April 1989, pp. 146–52.

[13] Harold Netland, "Toward Contextualized Apologetics," *Missiology: An International Review*, Vol. XVI, No. 3, July 1988, pp. 289–303.

[14] Paul G. Hiebert, "Christianity in a World of Religious Turmoil," *World Evangelization*, Vol. 16, No. 59, May–June 1989, pp. 17–19.

[15] Craig Ellison, "Growing Urban Churches Biblically," *Urban Mission*, Vol. 6, No. 2, November 1988, pp. 7–18.

[16] Viv Grigg, "Squatters: The Most Responsive Unreached Block," *Urban Mission*, Vol. 6, No. 5, May 1989, pp. 41–50.

[17] Donald A. McGavran, "Beyond the Maintenance Mentality," *Christianity Today*, Vol. 33, No. 2, Feb. 3, 1989, pp. 28–29.

[18] Allen J. Swanson, "Decisions or Disciples? A Study of Evangelism Effectiveness in Taiwan," *Missiology: An International Review*, Vol. XVII, No. 1, January 1989, pp. 53–68.

[19] Thomas Russell, "Can the Story Be Told Without Them? The Role of Women in the Student Volunteer Movement," *Missiology: An International Review*, Vol. XVII, No. 2, April 1989, pp. 159–75.

[20] Gerald H. Anderson, "American Protestants in Pursuit of Mission: 1886–1986," *International Bulletin of Missionary Research*, Vol. 12, No. 3, July 1988, pp. 98–118.

[21] Charles Henry Long and Anne Rowthorn, "The Legacy of Roland Allen," *International Bulletin of Missionary Research*, Vol. 13, No. 2, April 1989, pp. 65–70.

[22] Kenneth O. Gangel, "Developing New Leaders for the Global Task," *Evangelical Missions Quarterly*, Vol. 25, No. 2, April 1989, pp. 166–71.

[23] Russell P. Spittler, "Implicit Values in Pentecostal Missions," *Missiology: An International Review*, Vol. XVI, No. 4, October 1988, pp. 409–24.

[24] Robert C. Douglas, "The Challenge of the Muslim World," *World Evangelization*, Vol. 15, No. 55, November–December 1988, pp. 15–17.

[25] George N. Malek, "Christian–Muslim Dialogue," *Missiology: An International Review*, Vol. XVI, No. 3, July 1988, pp. 279–86.

[26] Kwame Bediako, "The Roots of African Theology," *International Bulletin of Missionary Research*, Vol. 13, No. 2, April 1989, pp. 58–65.

[27] John J. Shane, "Distinctives of African Urban Ministry," *Urban Mission*, Vol. 6, No. 5, May 1989, pp. 31–40.

[28] Henry N. Smith, "Christianity and Ancestor Practices in Hong Kong," *Missiology: An International Review*, Vol. XVII, No. 1, January 1989, pp. 27–38.

About the Area Editor

C. Peter Wagner (M.Div., Fuller Theological Seminary; Th.M., Princeton Theological Seminary; M.A., [Missiology] Fuller School of World Mission; Ph.D., [Social Ethics] University of Southern California) is the Donald A. McGavran Professor of Church Growth at the Fuller Theological Seminary School of World Mission. Previous to joining that faculty in 1971, he served as a missionary to Bolivia for sixteen years. He served as a charter member of the Lausanne Committee for World Evangelization 1974–1989. Wagner teaches an adult Sunday school class at Lake Avenue Congregational Church in Pasadena, California. He is the author of over thirty books on missions and church growth. Among the more recent are *Strategies for Church Growth* (Regal, 1987), *The Third Wave of the Holy Spirit* (Servant, 1988), and *How to Have a Healing Ministry* (Regal, 1988).

RELIGIOUS PLURALISM AND THE
UNIQUENESS OF JESUS CHRIST

LESSLIE NEWBIGIN
Retired Missionary and Bishop of
Church of South India in Madras

Article from *International Bulletin of Missionary Research*

In his 1987 Lambeth Lecture on "Religious Pluralism and Its Challenge to Christian Theology," the director of the World Council of Churches unit on interfaith dialogue, Wesley Ariarajah, speaks of "a current . . . about to become a flood," exercising an overwhelming pressure on people of all religions to "become aware of and to cope with a religiously plural world."[1] That pressure has already led a group of well-known Christians to announce—under the title *The Myth of Christian Uniqueness*—their conclusion that the claim for uniqueness must be abandoned.[2] The July 1988 issue of the *International Review of Mission (IRM)*, containing addresses and discussions centering on the celebration of the jubilee of the 1938 Tambaram Conference, gives further evidence of the power of this current.[3] It is fed, of course, not only by arguments that are, properly speaking, theological and philosophical, but also by the pervading feeling of guilt in the world of Western Christendom, and by the overwhelming sense of need to find a basis for human unity in an age of nuclear weapons. As always, there is a strong temptation to go with the current, but even a small acquaintance with history is enough to remind us that what seem to be overwhelmingly powerful movements of thoughts can lead to disaster. Critical reflection is in order.

No persons in their senses deny the need for human unity. Our world is in fact torn apart by rival programs for human unity. Washington and Moscow are both convinced that we need one world. Many years ago André Dumas drew attention to the obvious fact that any proposal for human unity that does not specify the center around which unity is to be constructed has as its hidden center the interests of the proposer. *The Myth of Christian Uniqueness* provides rich illustration of this. Gordon Kaufman in his essay starts from the need for human unity and takes it for granted, without argument, that the Christian gospel cannot provide the center. He goes on to say that "modern historical consciousness" requires us to abandon the claim to Christ's uniqueness and to recognize that the biblical view of things, like all other views, is the product of a particular culture (pp. 5–6). It is of course true that the biblical view of things is culturally conditioned: that does not require us to say that it is not true. "Modern historical consciousness" is also a culturally conditioned phenomenon and does not provide us with a standpoint from which we can dispose of the truth-claims of the Bible. Recognition of the culturally conditioned character of all truth-claims could lead to the abandonment of all belief in the possibility of knowing the truth; that is what is happening in contemporary Western culture. But this recognition provides no grounds upon which it is possible to deny that God might have acted decisively to reveal and effect the divine purpose for human history; and such a revelation would, of course, have to be culturally conditioned, since otherwise it would not be part of human history and could have no impact on human history. There are certainly no grounds whatever for supposing that "modern historical consciousness" provides us with an epistemological privilege denied to other culturally conditioned ways of seeing.

As Alasdair MacIntyre so brilliantly documents in his book *Whose Justice, What Rationality?*[4] the idea that there can be a kind of reason that is supracultural and that would enable us to view all the culturally conditioned traditions of rationality from a standpoint above them all is one of the illusions of our contemporary culture. All rationality is socially embodied, developed in human tradition and using some human language. The fact that biblical thought shares this with all other forms of human thought in no way disqualifies it from providing the needed center.

The authors of *The Myth* would go some way to accept this. For Paul Knitter, "Pluralism seems to be of the very stuff of reality, the way things are, the way they function. . . . There can never be just one of anything."[5] So there are no absolute values given to us; we must create them, but this must be a collective enterprise in which we all share. In similar vein Stanley Samartha calls upon Christians to contribute "to the pool of human values such as justice and compassion, truth and righteousness in the quest of different people for spiritual and moral values . . . to hold together different religions, cultures, languages and ethnic groups" (*IRM*, p. 323) and that "to claim that one religious tradition has the *only* answer to such a global problem [as the nuclear threat] sounds preposterous" (*IRM*, p. 315).

These and similar statements bring us, I think, to the heart of our matter, revealing as they do that loss of faith in the possibility of knowing objective truth, which is at the heart of the sickness of our culture. In the first place it is, of course, not true that the modern worldview of physics removes all absolutes. There are such absolutes as the speed of light and the value of Planck's constant. One might well say that it seems preposterous that these figures should be just so, no more and no less; but it is so. These are what we call in our culture "facts," about which we are not pluralists. It is in the realm of "values" that we are pluralists. Values are matters of personal choice; they are what people *want*. And human wants conflict. The idea of contributing to a shared pool of "values" conveys no coherent meaning. The question that has always to be addressed, surely, is the question about the facts, the question "What is the case?"—and on that question some answers will be true and others false. Rational people will see to it that their "values" are based upon what is the case, upon reality. "Values" that are not so based are merely personal wishes, and human wishes collide. It is precisely for "justice" that nations go to war.

The course of the present debate has illustrated the retreat from objectivity into subjectivity of which I speak. In his well-known use of the Copernican paradigm, John Hick advised us that we should learn to see God as the center of all reality, and abandon our culture-bound vision of Jesus as the center. Paul Knitter and others now suggest a further move, beyond a Christocentric and even a theocentric view to one that might be called soteriocentric—for why indeed should belief in God be the clue to reality? Thus Christopher Duraisingh writes: "It is not through our *a priori* doctrinal formulations on God or Christ, but rather through our collective human search for meaning and sacredness that the 'universe of faiths' could be adequately understood," and he goes on therefore to say, in agreement with Paul Knitter, that our approach to other faiths must be neither theocentric nor Christocentric, but must start from soteriology (*IRM*, p. 399). In Paul Knitter's words, interfaith dialogue "should not revolve around 'Christ' (or Buddha or Krishna), or around 'God' (or Brahman or Nirvana) but around 'salvation'— that is, a shared concern about and effort to remove the sufferings that rack the human family today" (*IRM*, p. 399).

The movement that Knitter and Duraisingh propose is indeed a natural extension of the movement initiated by Hick. He asked us to move from Jesus—the name of a man about whom there are historical records that can be read and probed and analyzed—to God, a name that has almost as many meanings as there are human beings. "God" as the center means not God as revealed in Jesus or in the Qur'an or in any other specific religious tradition but "God" as I understand God. It is a move from the objective to the subjective. The further move is natural—the move to my own search for wholeness, a search that is surely in some sense different for every human being. Hick in several places speaks of true religion as being turned from self-centeredness to reality-centeredness; but this is a move in the opposite direction, from objective reality to the self and its needs.

One might bring out the point by placing Copernicus in his historical context. Ptolemy's way of understanding the solar system had endured for 1,500 years. During that period it enabled astronomers to predict eclipses, cartographers to make accurate maps, and explorers to sail to far destinations. It satisfied human need for a very long time. When Copernicus proposed his alternative view, there was a debate (not then called "dialogue"), which lasted for many decades. It was not, of course, a debate between "science" and "religion"—an absurdly anachronistic portrayal of the matter. It was a debate within a society that had not yet relegated "facts" to a domain outside theology. It was a hotly argued discussion. In the end it was decided: Copernicus was right; Ptolemy—useful as he had been for so many centuries—was wrong. The suggestion that the argument might be ended by agreeing that there is a common search for truth or that the different views should be "pooled" would not have been accepted. And rightly so, because there was a concern for truth and a belief that it could be known.

I make this point (which I owe to Harold Turner) to illuminate what seems to me to be the central issue in this whole debate; it is the abandonment of the belief that it is possible to know the truth. There is indeed an ancient and venerable tradition that tells us that ultimate reality is unknowable. It is true that the human mind cannot comprehend God. But this true statement can be used, and is used, to disqualify any firm affirmation of truth. The true statement that we cannot know everything can be used to disqualify a valid claim to know something. The human mind cannot comprehend God, but we have no grounds for denying the possibility that God might make the divine known to human beings and that they might legitimately bear witness to what has been revealed to them.

And, of course, the writers whom I am criticizing would reply: "Yes indeed, but God has revealed God's self in many ways. Therefore, there are many gospels and many missions." I do indeed believe and am firmly convinced that there is no human being in whose mind and conscience there is not some whisper of God's word, and I have known many non-Christians who have a deep and often radiant sense of the presence of God. But I also know that many evil and horrible things are done in the name of religion and in the name of God. Does a claim to have a mission from God exempt the one who makes it critical questioning? And if there are to be questions, where do we find the criteria? Diana Eck, moderator of the WCC's Dialogue Unit, is severely critical of Hendrik Kraemer because he presumed to discuss the question of whether and how God reveals the divine to a Muslim; for the answer to that question, she says, we must go to the Muslim (*IRM*, p. 382). But does that apply to all those who claim to have a mission from God? Hitler, for one, was certain that he had a mission from God; do we take his word for it? If not, on what grounds do we deny his testimony? When Christians do evil things in the name of God, as they do, we can confront them with the figure of Christ in the Gospels and require them to measure their actions and motives against that given reality. But if it is denied that there is any such divinely given standard available to us as a part of our human history, what grounds are there for passing a judgment that is more than *ad hominem?*

This is not a merely rhetorical question. In *The Myth of Christian Uniqueness* one writer faces up to it. Langdon Gilkey asks the question: How, in a pluralist world, do we respond to a phenomenon like Hitler? His answer is interesting. He says that for such situations we need an absolute; only something like the Barmen Declaration is an adequate response. But the necessity for this absolute is a relative one. Gilkey's key sentence is: "paradoxically, plurality, precisely by its own ambiguity, implies both relativity and absoluteness, a juxtaposition or synthesis of the relative and the absolute that is frustrating intellectually and yet necessary practically" (pp. 45–46). Gilkey endeavors to cope with the intellectual "frustration" by appealing to "the venerable, practical American tradition" of pragmatism, and I confess I am simply unable to follow him. He is, of course, profoundly right in drawing attention to what he calls the demonic possibilities of pluralism. But I remain totally unconvinced by the idea of an absolute that is available on call when it is relatively necessary.

The point is that we do not need to go back to Hitler to find evidence for the demonic possibilities of pluralism. We surely know that our contemporary Western culture is in the power of false gods, of idols; that people are seeking salvation through the invocation of all the old gods of power and sex and money—"star wars," the "nuclear shield," the free market, the consumer society. There will come a point, perhaps not far in the future, when Christians will realize that something like the Barmen Declaration is needed. What deeply troubles me about the contemporary output of the "interfaith industry" is that it is destroying the only basis on which such a declaration could be made. There is certainly a common search for salvation; it is that search that tears the world to pieces when it is directed to that which is not God.

But Wilfred Cantwell Smith says that there is no such thing as idolatry. In *The Myth* volume he restates his familiar view that all the religions have as their common core some experience of the transcendent; that whether we speak of images made of wood or stone, or images in the human mind, or even of Jesus himself, all are the means used by the transcendent to make himself or herself or itself present to us humans. To claim uniqueness for one particular form or vehicle of this contact with the transcendent is preposterous and blasphemous. Much rather accept the truth so beautifully stated in the Bhagavadgita and in the theology of Ramanuja, that God is so gracious that he (or she or it) accepts all worship whatever be the form through which the worship is offered. Here clearly "the transcendent" is a purely formal category into which one can put any content that the mind can devise. Once again it is clear that we are in the world of pure subjectivity. There can be no such thing as false worship because no objective reality is involved. The question "True or false?" simply does not arise. We are witnessing the collapse of the whole glorious human enterprise of seeking to know the truth, to make contact with reality, to know God as God truly is. It is the mark of a culture that— in the words that Gilbert Murray used to describe the end of the glorious civilization of Greece—has lost its nerve. We are in the midst of a dying culture.

When the Greeks, worshiping "an unknown God," were confronted by a not very impressive man (see 2 Cor. 10:10) who told them, "What you worship as unknown, that I proclaim to you," they were naturally inclined to laugh. And of course God was not wholly unknown, otherwise there would have been no altar. And if God had been truly known, there would have been no need for many altars to many gods. God has indeed made the divine known in some way and in some measure to all human beings. Why, then, speak of one unique revelation? Eck tells us that her Hindu teacher was astonished to learn that Christians acknowledge only one *avatar*, and she goes on to say that while some Christians believe this, to many other Christians it is folly (*IRM*, p. 384). With Cantwell Smith, she deplores the idea that God's revelation is locked away in the past, and she quotes Smith as writing, "God is not revealed fully in Jesus Christ to me, nor indeed to anyone that I have met; or that my historical studies have uncovered" (ibid.). Now surely every Christian must confess that he or she has not fully grasped the length and breadth and height and depth of God's revelation in Jesus, and is seeking to comprehend more. Truly God makes the divine known in the soul and conscience and reason of the human person, but not in a purely inward spirituality, which is separate from the public history that we share. The Hindu can speak of many *avatars*, because none of them is part of public history; they are all ideas in the mind. There is no event in public history that can or could replace those events that we confess to have taken place under Pontius Pilatè. It is because of those events that we can recognize and rejoice in the intimations of God's presence in the experience of men and women of many religious traditions and (especially!) men and women who make no religious profession. What is here in question is not merely an inward experience of "the transcendent" but a series of events in public history by which the human situation is decisively changed. We enter into and grow into the inward experience of God's love and truth through participating in the rational discourse of the community that takes its rise from these events. This tradition of rational discourse enables us to find in these events not only the source of a growing inward experience of God, but also the clue by following which we are enabled to make sense of the world, to grasp its real nature with growing (though always very partial) sureness.

Of course, it is always possible to deny that these events have this significance. One might almost say that it is normal to deny it. There are no external proofs by which it could be shown to be indubitable. But every form of rationality or of spirituality is socially embodied in a particular tradition and language, and rests ultimately upon presuppositions that cannot be verified by reference to some reality external to it. The idea that the universe is so constructed that we can enjoy indubitable knowledge without the risks of personal commitment is an illusion, but this illusion is used to discredit the claims of a specific tradition of rationality such as is embodied in the Christian community. "True knowledge," says Paul Knitter (quoting Cantwell Smith), "is that knowledge that all intelligent men and women . . . can share, and can jointly verify, by observation and by participation" (*No Other Name?* p. 11). But truth is not the possession of majorities—even if the vote is unanimous. All knowing is reality, and supremely when the reality in question is God, is the work of people nurtured in a tradition of rational discourse.

The fact that the Christian affirmation is made from one such socially embodied tradition in no way discredits its claim to speak truth. To pretend to *possess* the truth in its fullness is arrogance. The claim to have been given the decisive clue for the human search after truth is not arrogant; it is the exercise of our responsibility as part of the human family.

There is, of course, one final objection. It was classically expressed in the saying attributed to Rousseau: "If God wanted to say something to Jean Jacques Rousseau, why did He have to go round by Moses to say it?" Why Moses and not Socrates or Confucius or Gautama? Why one people and not another? Should not "the transcendent" be equally and simultaneously available to every human being? Very clearly there lies behind the complaint that very ancient belief to which I have referred: the belief that in the last analysis I am a solitary soul with my own relationship with the Transcendent—whatever he, she, or it may be. And that belief is false. It rests upon an atomistic spirituality that contradicts what is most fundamental in human nature, namely, that our life is only fully human as we are bound up with one another in mutual caring and responsibility. When Stanley Samartha, in the Tambaram discussion, attacks the traditional work of missions because "conversion, instead of being a vertical movement towards God, a genuine renewal of life, has become a horizontal movement of groups of people from one community to another" (*IRM*, p. 321), he demonstrates his captivity to this illusion. We do not know God, in the sense of true personal knowledge, except as part of a community. The fact that the confession of Jesus as unique Lord and Savior is made by a particular human community among other communities provides no ground for denying its claim to speak truth. God's action for the salvation of the whole human family cannot be a series of private transactions within a multitude of individual souls; it is something wrought out in public history, and history is always concrete and specific. It is possible, as it has always been possible, to deny the truth of the Christian claim, as these writers do. But it is not possible to claim that the denial rests upon a kind of rationality superior to that which is embodied in the Christian tradition.

I think it is fair to say that the writers whom I am criticizing are not wholly to blame for this individualist perspective. I think that the whole debate about the uniqueness of Christ has for many decades been skewed by the notion that the only question at stake is the question of the fate of the individual soul in the next world. It is assumed that those who speak of the uniqueness of Jesus are saying that only Christians will be saved in the next world—which of course opens the way to destructive debates about who is a real Christian. It is enough to say that this way of thinking has lost contact with the Bible. This individualism, with its center in the selfish concern of the individual about personal salvation, is utterly remote from the biblical view, which has as its center God and divine rule. The central question is not "How shall I be saved?" but "How shall I glorify God by understanding, loving, and doing God's will—here and now in this earthly life?" To answer that question I must insistently ask: "How and where is God's purpose for the whole of creation and the human family made visible and credible?" That is the question about the truth—objective truth—which is true whether or not it coincides with my "values." And I know of no place in the public history of the world where the dark mystery of human life is illuminated, and the dark power of all that denies human well-being is met and measured and mastered, except in those events that have their focus in what happened "under Pontius Pilate."

There is indeed a powerful current in our time that would sweep away such a claim and insist that the story of those events is simply one among the vast variety of "religious experience" and that it can be safely incorporated into a syllabus for the comparative study of religions. The current is strong because it is part of the drift of contemporary Western culture (of what in every part of the world is called "modernity") away from belief in the possibility of knowing truth and toward subjectivity. The World Council of Churches has been asked, at two general assemblies, to accept statements that seemed to call in question the uniqueness, decisiveness, and centrality of Jesus Christ. It has resisted. If, in the pull of the strong current, it should agree to go with the present tide, it would become an irrelevance in the spiritual struggles that lie ahead of us. I pray and believe that it will not.

Notes

[1] S. Wesley Ariarajah, "Religious Plurality and Its Challenge to Christian Theology," *World Faiths Insight* (London), June 1988, pp. 2–3. Ariarajah is quoting from Wilfred Cantwell Smith.

[2] John Hick and Paul F. Knitter, eds., *The Myth of Christian Uniqueness: Toward a Pluralistic Theology of Religions* (Maryknoll, NY: Orbis Books, 1987).

[3] All quotations from the *International Review of Mission (IRM)* cited in the text of this article are from the July 1988 issue.

[4] Notre Dame, IN: University of Notre Dame Press, 1988.

[5] *No Other Name?* (Maryknoll, NY: Orbis Books, 1985), p. 6.

CONVERSION AND THE KINGDOM

ARTHUR GLASSER
Dean Emeritus
School of World Mission
Fuller Theological Seminary

Article from *World Evangelization*

The church has long understood her mission to involve working for the conversion of non-Christians. Disciples must be made of every people. Not a few biblical texts underscore this obligation. However, in our day influential voices have challenged this and argue that the conversion of non-Christians is neither necessary nor desirable. The reasons they advance are both many and formidable. First, nationalist movements in many countries regard the Christian movements in their midst as so identified with Western colonialism that to become a Christian is to identify oneself with something foreign and denationalizing. (Why should any citizen who loves his country and is concerned for her development seek identity with a religious system prominent among those who exploited her in the past?)

Second, increasing study of the non-Christian ethnic faiths has uncovered much of ethical and social value. Hence, the Christian missionary must look at them "with sincere respect [since they] often reflect a ray of that truth which enlightens all men."[1] This has caused some to speculate: If the Spirit of Truth has already been at work in these religions, the probability is that they more adequately meet the spiritual needs of their peoples. Christian missionaries should help them become more aware of the treasures they possess and more willing to utilize them for the humanization of their societies.

Third, disillusionment with the institutional church has become so widespread that the simplistic call has been widely heard and fervently accepted: "Forget the church! Join hands with those supporting the poor and the oppressed in their struggle for social justice and human values! That's where God is and that's where the action is!"

As a result of this ferment, the religious debate on conversion has shifted in many circles from individual conversion to Christ, followed by incorporation into the church, to speaking of "conversion" as involvement with a socially concerned community, whether or not its members profess any allegiance to the person of Jesus Christ. Cultural pluralism and religious relativism have diverted many from making Jesus Christ the starting point in their approach to the subject of conversion. Admittedly, there is a sense in which, as Stephen Neill has said: "Every person really needs three conversions—to Christ, to the Church, and to the world." By being converted to the world he means that the Christian needs to face outward and move "back to the world in witness and devoted service." He then adds:

> It is an observable fact that these conversions may come in any order. One man first finds himself challenged to surrender by the recognition of Christ as the supremely lovable and adorable Master. Another first finds the reality of Christian faith in the shared fellowship and mystery of the church. A third finds himself overwhelmed by the sorrows and sufferings of humanity and discovers in Jesus of Nazareth the pattern and the inspiration for a life of service.[2]

At this point we do well to turn to the Scriptures for their witness to the reality and essentiality of conversion. A key to its place in both testaments is found in the appearance of John the Baptist and his summons to radical repentance in view of the imminent approach of the Kingdom of God. This repentance was marked by submitting to baptism. Since John's preaching and baptism represented the continuation of the Old Testament prophetic call to return to the Lord—to turn back, to be converted—any biblical discussion of conversion should begin with a review of this tradition.

The prophets were essentially revivalists who sought to call the people of God to renew their covenant obligation to Yahweh. Although their call was to the people as a corporate unity, it resulted increasingly in the emergence of a remnant comprised of individuals who personally responded by "turning" (involving repentance) and recommitting themselves to the ordinances of worship and to the ethical standards of the Sinaitic covenant. The Israelites were originally converted to Yahweh when they accepted his purpose for them to turn from their slavery in Egypt and become his servants (Exod. 19:4–8). Generally speaking, specific expressions of obedience were involved in every reaffirmation of their relationship to Yahweh (e.g., their conversion as in Hezekiah's day—2 Chron. 29, 30). On occasion we come upon the record of a king (e.g., Manasseh in 2 Chron. 33:12, 13) going through a turning around (turning back) conversion experience. Since the prophets were invariably messengers of future hope, the thrust of the conversion experience was to focus attention on the ongoing movement of God's redemptive purpose toward its glorious consummation in the Day of Yahweh. It is this forward-looking stance that characterized John the Baptist with his proclamation that the Kingdom of God and the advent of the Messiah was "at hand."

Nothing is more important at this point than to take the full measure of the call to conversion uttered by Jesus following the imprisonment of John. He inaugurated the Kingdom as "already" though "not yet" with his proclamation that the time was fulfilled, that one and all should repent and believe the gospel. Lesslie Newbigin helpfully amplifies this proclamation in the following fashion: "Turn around! Look the other way! Believe, what I am telling you, namely that God's righteous reign is at the door."[3] Jesus' call to conversion involved turning around, accepting the reality of God's rule and then willingly becoming an expression and extension of that rule in fellowship with a local congregation of his people.

These three elements demand expansion: first, the spiritual reorientation of a person turning from all unworthy allegiances to Christ's lordship expressed by repentance and faith. One "turns to God from idols" (1 Thess. 1:9). Then, there is the behavioral transformation in which one consciously begins to participate in the activity of God, what Paul defined as "to serve a living and true God" (1 Thess. 1:9). Finally, there is the dimension of community. Solitary, individualistic Christianity has no place in the New Testament record. From this time onward—and underscored by the reference to baptism in the Great Commission—the call to conversion issued by the apostles involved radical repentance, submission to Jesus Christ, and baptism into a visible fellowship. The proclamation of the universality of Christ's lordship over all nations and over all creation, does not mean that it should be confined to his provision of the forgiveness of sins (Luke 24:47). Since the Great Commission primarily concerns "the Kingdom of God" (Acts 1:3), conversion to Christ does not mean that the nations should be left as they are. Individual Christians and corporate congregations are to be "signs of the Kingdom." And this can only mean being so responsive to the rule of Christ that they reflect in every way "his tomorrow" in the world of today.

Will the Kingdom in its final glorious manifestation reflect in fulness peace, justice, truth, and holiness? Assuredly! It follows then that his people today are to be peacemakers, concerned for reconciliation between all types of warring factions. They are to be involved in the struggle for social justice, deeply concerned to extend the knowledge of the truth of God (i.e., worldwide proclamation!) and themselves unmarred reflections of his holiness and his love. This is what conversion is all about! And it brings "great rejoicing" not only in the presence of God but among his people on earth (Luke 15:10; Acts 15:3, NEB).

Individual Conversions in Acts

So then, the biblical data is explicit. Conversion involves the decisive, Godward reorientation of a person's inner world that not only changes his/her basic relation with God but also enlists him in becoming a sign of the coming Kingdom.

Luke records in Acts the conversion experiences of five people of different background, nationality, temperament, prior religious experience, and sex: the Ethiopian eunuch (ch. 8), Saul the Pharisee (ch. 9), the Italian Cornelius (ch. 10), the merchant Lydia and the Roman jailer (ch. 16). Although their encounters with Christ are markedly different, we find striking similarities in the sequence of events that brought about their conversion. None were directly challenged to "convert to God," yet all were found by him in the context of the apostolic evangelistic witness—that God had reconciled the world to himself through Jesus Christ and was calling men and women to himself as an expression of his universal concern.[4]

First, all went through a period of preparation: the Ethiopian reading the Scriptures (8:28); Saul's knowledge of Judaism and the law (22:3; 26:5) and of the doctrine of those he was persecuting (7:2–53; 9:2; 22:4; 26:9–11); Cornelius was a God-fearer and a man of prayer (10:2); Lydia was a synagogue worshiper who had culivated the habit of prayer (16:13, 14); and the Roman jailer doubtless heard the witness of Paul and Silas during the considerable period ("some days") before they were imprisoned (16:12).

Second, all heard either preaching about Jesus or experienced his presence. Philip explained the good news of Jesus to the Ethiopian (8:35); Jesus himself formed the content of Saul's vision on the road to Damascus (9:5; 22:8; 26:15); Peter reviewed with Cornelius the highlights of Jesus' words and deeds (10:34–43; 11:14); Paul bore witness to Lydia (16:13) and Paul and Silas "spoke the word of the Lord" to the jailer and his household (16:32–34).

Third, all made some sort of response, generally an inquiry, in the process of their movement toward conversion. The Ethiopian questioned Philip about the passage he was reading (8:34); Saul sought the glorified Christ's identity (9:5; 22:8; 26:13) and, in one account, requested a commission from him (22:10); Cornelius asked the "angel" for an explanation of his vision (10:4) and the Roman jailer put the key question to Paul and Silas: "Men and brethren, what must I do to be saved?" (16:30).

Fourth, prominence is given to the activity of God. The Spirit is associated with the ministry of Philip and became the agent in the Ethiopian's conversion (8:29, 39); Saul encountered the glorified Christ directly (9:4–6) and at the hands of Ananias, also prompted by God (9:10–16), received the Spirit prior to his baptism (9:17, 18); Cornelius saw an angel of God in his vision (10:3, 30–32), and also received the Spirit before being baptized, evidenced by his speaking in tongues (10:44–48; 11:15; 15:8); the Lord "opened the heart" of Lydia (16:4) and everything about the unlikely conversion of the Roman jailer bears witness to God's intervention (16:25–34).

Fifth, the convert in each case received baptism (8:38; 9:18; 10:47, 48; 16:15, 33). This belonged inseparably to them all with its implicit confession of faith and its vivid representation of their having embarked on a "resurrection life" made possible through the risen Christ. It should be noted that none made explicit confession of faith apart from baptism. Scholars are largely agreed that Acts 8:37 is a late interpolation.

Finally, in each case one cannot but note the evident results of the conversion experience. The Ethiopian and the jailer rejoiced (8:39; 16:34); Saul proclaimed Jesus, saying, "He is the Son of God" (9:20, 22; 26:22, 23); Cornelius spoke with tongues, extolling God (10:46), and Lydia and the jailer displayed the Christian virtue of hospitality (16:15, 34; cf. 1 Pet. 4:9).

Despite the limitations of the biblical data, certain features are sufficiently common to these five accounts for us to make the following deductions. First, the spiritual experience in question is more than simply the work of a moment. Conversion is a process. Second, conversion is frequently occasioned by all that the New Testament includes under the rubric of "preaching." Third, some kind of intellectual activity, however elementary, takes place in the process. Fourth, Christian conversion involves the total personality, not merely intellectual apprehension. Fifth, the convert is normally brought into the total life of the church through baptism, and this is often directly related to the gift of the Holy Spirit. Finally, as fundamental to all that may be said about conversion in the New Testament, this work is from first to last a response to the *opus Dei* (work of God).[5]

Viewed externally, conversion involves "stopping, turning, attending, and pursuing a new course."[6] More is involved than mere repentance over the past and new resolutions touching the future. There is the deliberate disposition of heart and mind to surrender to the will and power of God through encounter with Jesus Christ, and then, under his direction, to turn from the things that are not of God. This reorientation of the whole life and personality is the *sine qua non* (essential condition) of entrance into the Kingdom of God (John 3:3). Paul struck a parallel with the death and resurrection of Christ: the convert has been "baptized into his death" and "raised to newness of life" in the Spirit (Rom. 6:2–4; Col. 2:12). And the conversion paradigm of repentance and faith, of death and life, becomes the subsequent pattern of the Christian life ("as you received Christ Jesus the Lord, so live in him"—Col. 2:6).

Another integrating concept is the centrality of baptism in the total conversion experience. Bishop Stephen Neill has pointed out the radical discontinuity involved in the conversion process by calling attention to the fact that admission to the churches of the apostolic age was "by faith *and baptism*" (his emphasis) and added: "The New Testament knows nothing of membership in the church by faith alone without this accompanying act of obedience and confession."[7] Luke's summary of Paul's ministry in Corinth was: "Many of the Corinthians hearing Paul, believed and were baptized" (Acts 18:8). His definition of a "Christian" would be: one who confesses Jesus Christ as Lord and Savior, abides in the teaching of the apostles through faithful study of the Scriptures and participates in the local *koinonia* of the people of God, sharing in their common life and service (2:42).

Furthermore, we must underscore the fact that at every level of the biblical evidence conversion demands commitment to conduct reflective of the coming Kingdom of God. This means the commitment to constructive action in history—the proclamation of the knowledge of God accompanied by those activities in society that adumbrate and forward God's purpose for his creation—the Kingdom in its full realization. Not mere membership in a saved community but participation as an agent of the work of God in history, which is not complete until all things have been summed up in Christ.[8]

Power Encounter

The central issue in God's confrontation of any person is his authority and Christ's lordship. This means that there is an inevitable "power encounter" between him and the reaction of the person being confronted and drawn by his love. Perhaps this is why Luke in his Gospel tells us that those whom God graciously overwhelms with his love and who enter his Kingdom do so "violently" (16:16). The thrust of the gospel is that Jesus Christ is not to be admired, but "received." This means a transfer of allegiance—a conscious submission to his rule—and it involves trauma, for one is thereby delivered from the Kingdom of darkness and transferred into God's Kingdom (Col. 1:13). The issue is one of power, as Alan Tippett has stated so well:

> Man is the victim. He is bound. He is under an enslaving authority, trapped and imprisoned. The situation is such that it is quite beyond human power for man to save himself or escape. In this desperate plight a Savior from outside must be introduced into the situation or man will perish. We are faced with the power (*dunamis*) of the enemy, we are entrapped in the works (*erga*) of the devil, we are victims of the craftiness or method (*methodeias*) of the devil, and we are under the authority (*exousia*) of Satan. Only through a greater power and authority can mankind hope for deliverance. . . . Hence Vicedom does not spare the pagan religions or advocate mere dialogue with them. "In the last analysis they are to be understood from the viewpoint of *the other Kingdom* set over against the mission of God. While they may contain much that is good, it is embedded in evil and covered over by evil.[9]

In the Gospels we have already found this dimension of power central to Jesus' proclamation of the gospel of the Kingdom. This has been challenged for there are those who have argued that he dealt with no two people in precisely the same way because of his respect for their differing temperaments and the different situations in which he found them. And yet, he was guided by certain universals and careful scrutiny of each separate interview will reveal that "He treated them all as being alike."[10] He never confined the good news of the Kingdom to mere talk: his Gospel always involved power, as Paul later affirmed (1 Cor. 4:20).

A few years ago Aylwaard Shorter warned missionaries serving in Africa of the dangers inherent in preaching a gospel that was devoid of power encounter. Ponder his portrayal of what might only be called "marginal conversion" in the African context. In his book, *African Theology: Adaptation or Incarnation*, he gives the following graphic description of marginal conversion in the African context.

During the past hundred years African traditional religion has been visibly sinking beneath the surface of modern social life in Africa, but what remains above the surface is, in fact, the tip of an iceberg. At baptism, the African Christian repudiates remarkably little of his former non-Christian outlook. He may be obliged to turn his back upon certain traditional practices which the church, rightly or wrongly, has condemned in his area, but he is not asked to recant a religious philosophy. The church, in any case, takes no cognizance of this philosophy. Consequently, he returns to the forbidden practices as occasion arises with remarkable ease. Conversion to Christianity is for him sheer gain, an "extra" for which he has opted. It is an overlay on his original religious culture. Apart from the superficial condemnations, Christianity has really had little to say about African traditional religion in the way of serious judgments of value. Consequently, the African Christian operates with two thought-systems at once, and both of them are closed to each other.[11]

The force of this was recently brought home to many missionaries serving in Africa upon learning that one of the African Church's most prominent pastors had virtually apostatized from the faith in his closing days. When told that he had terminal cancer and after being sent home from the church's Western hospital, he went to the village of a spiritist practitioner to live out the final few months of his life. After his death, a missionary who knew the circumstances well reminded us that Jacob Loewen spoke of this particular pastor in a plenary address at the International Congress on World Evangelization (Lausanne 1974). Loewen referred to a conference in Africa at which he had just finished discussing indigenous and foreign conversion models. Then this leading African pastor got up and said,

Sir, what you have said about conversion deeply moves me, because I must confess, I have not been converted that way. My deeper African values have not been changed. I have merely become an imitation European on the outside. I have not learned to listen to the Holy Spirit but, I have been trained to listen very carefully to what the missionary wants.[12]

We can only surmise the impact this man's reversion to the power of the spirits is currently having on the church in Central Africa.

Conclusion

No issue in mission theology or in mission methodology is so crucial as the issue of religion and conversion. We dare not be content merely to describe the gospel of the Kingdom. To preach it adequately is to issue the call to conversion. True, the gospel offers people hope: the new heavens and the new earth will certainly come and replace all that is old. But judgment precedes the glorious manifestation of the Kingdom. Hence, the importance of repentance and the conversion of the heart.

So then, we close this study with the reiteration of Jesus' words to Nicodemus on the essentiality of the conversion experience:

> Truly, truly, I say to you, unless one is born anew, he cannot see the Kingdom of God . . . unless one is born of water and the Spirit, he cannot enter the Kingdom of God (John 3:3, 5).

If Nicodemus, a well-trained Jewish rabbi, was given this stark and pointed statement of his spiritual need, who can say it is without universal application? Is it not also true that if a person is not born again, he may on the Day of Judgment wish that he had never been born at all?

Notes

[1] Abbott, Walter M., ed. *The Documents of Vatican II*, translated by Joseph Gallagher. New York: Geoffrey Chapman, 1966.

[2] Neill, Stephen. *The Unfinished Task*. London, Edinburgh House Press, 1957.

[3] Newbigin, Lesslie. "Conversion," pp. 30–43. *Religion and Society*, Vol. XIII, No. 4, December 1966.

[4] Kümmel, Werner George. *Man in the New Testament*, translated by John J. Vincent. London: Epworth Press, 1963.

[5] Smalley, Stephen. "Conversion in The New Testament," pp. 193–210. *The Churchman*, Vol. 78, No. 3, Summer 1964.

[6] Routley, Erik. *The Gift of Conversions*. London: Lutterworth Press, 1957.

[7] Smalley, "Conversion in The New Testament," pp. 193–210.

[8] Newbigin, Lesslie. *The Finality of Christ*. Richmond: John Knox Press, 1969.

[9] Tippett, Alan R. *Verdict Theology in Missionary Theory*. Lincoln, IL: Lincoln Christian College, 1969.

[10] Morgan, G. Campbell. *The Great Physician*. New York: Fleming H. Revell Company, 1937.

[11] Shorter, Aylwaard. *African Theology: Adaptation or Incarnation*. Maryknoll, NY: Orbis Books, 1977.

[12] Loewen, Jacob. "Response to Dr. Ralph D. Winter's Paper," pp. 246–52. *Let the Earth Hear His Voice*, J. D. Douglas, ed. Minneapolis: World Wide Publications, 1975.

PRACTICAL THEOLOGY: HOMILETICS

Haddon W. Robinson, area editor

HOMILETICS

HADDON W. ROBINSON
President, Denver Seminary

Introduction

According to the literature on homiletics, preaching is sick and everyone knows it. Preachers sense something has gone wrong, but they can't put their finger on it. They just don't feel that preaching is as healthy as it used to be. Preachers seemed stronger years ago, but now they look a bit pale and lack the energy they once possessed. While it's not polite to anticipate the death of the patient, some disease seems to be sapping its strength.

Friends who recognize the symptoms agree that something is wrong, but the diagnosis of the illness doesn't come easily. Writers on preaching don't agree on what must be done to bring the patient back to health.

Some authors believe that the audience may be part of the problem. In the first five issues of *Preaching*, Wayne Oates, Professor of Behavioral Psychology at the University of Louisville School of Medicine, invests some thought on the taut, nonverbal messages that go back and forth between the preacher and members of the congregation. According to Oates, a minister may unwittingly feed unhealthy and growth-damaging relationships. His articles deal with the dependent personality (January–February); the "packaged" personality (March–April); the scrupulous personality (May–June); authentic preaching versus clever manipulation (July–August); and authentic preaching versus homiletic narcissism (September–October). In an article in *Preaching* (March–April 1989), John Stott also talks about how modern audiences relate to biblical sermons.

Other articles insist that a major deficiency of modern preaching lies in its content or the way the sermon is put together. J. Grant Swank, a Nazarene pastor, discovered expository preaching twenty-five years into his ministry, and he writes about "Exciting Expository Preaching" in *Church Management* (August 1989). Other writers, however, are not convinced that an explained and applied biblical content are all that a preacher needs. For example, story sermons are in vogue now, while propositional preaching based on Greco-Roman rhetoric receives low marks. "Left-brain" ministers trained to handle texts in the traditional manner may not feel at home in a "right-brained" world. After expounding his philosophy of preaching in *Spirit, Wind and Story* (Word, 1989), Calvin Miller devotes about a quarter of his book helping his readers recast the old, old story. John R. McFarland, in *Christian Ministry*

(January–February 1988), decries abstractions in a sermon by insisting that "The Illustration Is the Point" and not merely an elaboration of the point. George G. Nichol discusses how exegesis and story serve each other in deriving and delivering the message from a scriptural text. He offers a helpful example of the process drawn from the conversation between Jesus and the woman healed by touching the fringe of Jesus' robe (*Expository Times*, July 1989). For those who stalk and store illustrations and want technology to help them, Clinton A. McCoy talks about "Computerizing Your Sermon Illustration File" in *Pulpit Digest* (May–June 1989).

While preaching on the Second Coming once drew crowds in evangelical churches, at present the emphasis on the end times has fallen on difficult times. David Grenshaw, in *The Journal for Preachers* (Easter 1989) insists that the most powerful preaching of the church is eschatological. There are no "good old days" for the Church. We live in hope, not nostalgia. Grenshaw struggles with the tricky question of how to preach the promises of God for the future without abandoning the present. For those who equate eschatology with detailed charts on the Tribulation, his article will have little appeal. Grenshaw, however, does offer some guidance on how to live in hope without falling into quietism.

Sometimes sermons fail either because they sprawl out like the Delta of the Mississippi instead of hitting like rifle shots, or because preachers don't actually expect their sermons to accomplish much in the lives of people who hear them. Bill Hybels helps focus the sermon in two articles that appeared in *Leadership* during 1989: "Well-Focused Preaching" (Spring 1989) and "Preaching for Total Commitment" (Summer 1989).

Surprisingly, very few writers this year felt that the demise of preaching should be traced to the character of the preacher. Those articles that touched on ethics, such as "Integrity of Preaching" by Nolan P. Howington in *Church Training* (July 1988), tend to offer keen insight into the obvious. Most of us believe we should be servants of the Word who faithfully deliver its truth with a life that reflects our message. Discussions on the integrity in the pulpit move little beyond that. Perhaps the reason is because we already know more than we practice.

S. M. Hutchens in *Touchstone* (Summer, Fall 1988) agrees that preaching among evangelicals seems more anemic now than in our recent past. In the first article that follows, he argues that evangelicals threw out the dog with the fleas when they abandoned fundamentalism. They need to be both narrower and broader, he says, to capture the glory of the pulpit again.

Some critics of preaching have felt that we place altogether too much emphasis on the person in the pulpit and not enough on the Holy Spirit. As Dietrich Bonhoeffer noted, "A concert audience doesn't come to watch the conductor but to hear the symphony; a congregation should not come to church to watch or listen to the preacher, but to hear the Word of God." Harry B. Adams, Chaplain of Yale University, delivered the first of the Leslie R.

Smith Lectureships in Preaching and Worship at Lexington Theological Seminary on the subject, "Creative Tensions in Preaching." They were reported in the *Lexington Theological Quarterly* (January, April 1989). His first lecture is on the tension between the work of the preacher and the working of the Spirit. It struggles with how God and the minister relate to one another in the preaching enterprise, and it is the second essay in this section.

About the Area Editor

Haddon W. Robinson (Th.M., Dallas Theological Seminary; M.A., Southern Methodist University; Ph.D., University of Illinois) has been president of Denver Seminary since 1979. He was ordained in 1955 by the Conservative Baptist Association. He was professor of homiletics at Dallas Theological Seminary from 1970–79. He is co-editor (with Duane Litfin) of *Recent Homiletical Thought* (1983); and author of *Biblical Preaching* (1980) and *Biblical Sermons* (1989).

THE CRISIS OF EVANGELICAL PREACHING

S. M. HUTCHENS
Episcopalian Layman
Sturtevant, Wisconsin

Article from *Touchstone*

In the Protestant world the vigor of the churches is to a large degree a function of the vitality of preaching. The Reformers' de-emphasis on the Mass as the principal means of grace in the divine service elevated the ministry of the Word in those churches which developed the most self-consciously Protestant frame of mind. When preaching languishes, the churches which are directly dependent upon it for their life and health will also decline. And indications that this is happening are legitimate cause for alarm.

There is little doubt that Fundamentalism and its Evangelical offspring are major repositories of the preaching tradition of Protestantism, not only because of the strongly Protestant character of these movements, but also because their roots are firmly fixed in a revivalist tradition to which the sacraments are essentially dispensable and the means of grace are to be found in the voice of the preacher rather than in the hands of the priest.

It had been my own impression for some time that rich and moving preaching among the Evangelicals was harder to find than it once was, but I tended to chalk that up to changes in myself rather than in the character and quality of the preaching. The question "Where have all our great preachers gone?" finally caught and held my attention when it was asked by a remarkable woman whose long career on the president's staff of a major Evangelical college had placed her at the center of its world and its preaching. She knew American Evangelicalism from the inside, and knew it very well. Behind her question I saw a uniquely informed perception which made the matter worthy of very serious consideration. Since she brought it to my attention I have heard a number of other Evangelicals complaining about the quality of preaching in their churches (see, for example, J. N. Akers' editorial "Bored to Fears" in *Christianity Today*, 22 April 1988). My friend's question pointed to a problem which I am coming to think may be epidemic and a very serious matter indeed among those churches formed and constituted by preaching.

I am old enough to remember her great preachers. I heard some of them speak when I was a boy and they were near the ends of their careers, for my family attended a large conservative Baptist church where I had the frequent opportunity to sit under them. I especially remember their power. I was a fairly attentive boy and heard them with the defenseless impressionability of early youth. They were memorable men. Theirs was the great preaching my friend remembered from the center of her life and I from my nonage. She was right—this sort of preaching seems to have all but disappeared from the Evangelical churches. We have heard well-crafted, uplifting, clever, and occasionally inspiring and edifying sermons—but the old power, without which no preaching can be called great, seems to be nearly exhausted.

Whence came the power? In one sense it was a holdover from the certitude and authority typical of the Evangelical preaching of the nineteenth century, which was itself inherited from revivals of earlier times. But what allowed it to survive in certain strains of conservative religion into this far more tentative age? For a large number of early and mid-twentieth-century preachers it was simply not optional. It was an essential part of the rhetorical panoply that a Fundamentalist needed to maintain his credibility and stand his ground during the controversies of the twenties, thirties and forties, to build great churches and other ministries out of the rubble of rejection and discredit. It was his sword and shield against the Menckens, Darrows, Fosdicks and Sinclair Lewis's of this world, the sound of well-cultivated conviction, confirming to the preachers and their congregations that they were right, not only about the gospel of Jesus Christ, but about the religious culture which they were creating around it—a culture in which only the gospel was deemed to move with freedom and power. These were strong men, and their sermons were strong, too. One came away from them tired, chastened, and yet strangely exultant, desiring to do better than one had been doing at the things that were important to us. (Yes, there was the guilt as well, but that must not be mentioned as if it were merely pathological, or the sum of it all.)

Where have these great ones gone? Why weren't the gaps which they left filled with vigorous young men made in their images? Why do so many Evangelical preachers now appear to rely primarily on the stimulative power of technique—which no longer really moves their people—rather than deep and infectious conviction? And why do so many of them, like the preacher to whom J. N. Akers referred, seem so dreadfully bored? Has the Spirit departed? My friend's question set me to thinking on all of this.

Those old warriors were Fundamentalists, ending their ministries in a day when a certain kind of conservative religion was in many quarters reassessing itself, and they were in a sense becoming vestigial parts of a new organism. In many places they were replaced by those who were not content to call themselves Fundamentalists. A new generation arose, the type of preachers that some of the older men were already becoming—that calmer, better educated, and far more accommodating breed: the Evangelical. My friend has moved principally in the Evangelical world since this changing of the guard, and what she has noticed is a difference in the tone of authority between Fundamentalist and Evangelical preaching. I think that if she were

returning to hear those who are still willing to call themselves Fundamentalists, she would find the same type of preaching that she remembered. Having
been for years an Evangelical, however, she would find it disappointing. For
the vigor she remembered would be there, to be sure—but I think she would
face reawakened memories of the narrowness, that is, of the theological
irresponsibility of Fundamentalist preaching which had originally propelled
her into the Evangelical camp. She desires the best of both worlds—the
better culture and more gracious manners of Evangelicalism and the power
and authority of Fundamentalism.

Why does Evangelical preaching appear to lack the virility and conviction and authority of Fundamentalism? It would seem that one of Fundamentalism's dire predictions concerning "neo-Evangelicalism's" descent down
"the perilous path of compromise and middle-of-the-roadism" has come
true—much of the power of conviction has dissipated. On the other hand, it
would seem that the Evangelicals were right in their criticism of the Fundamentalists—the power which they enjoy in their preaching, and from which
flows much of their self-confidence, is not all legitimately come by. It arises
not so much from the gospel itself as from the avidity of its style. It must be
granted that some of the strength of Fundamentalist preaching rests in the
power of the gospel, but there is also much by which the Evangelicals were
understandably repelled. This was part of the justification for the birth of
their own movement. This does not, however, excuse the weakness of the
Evangelical preaching.

At root, Evangelicalism has this dilemma: It does not wish to be confused
with Fundamentalism, but it lives in the theological shell of this movement of
which it is so embarrassed. Evangelicalism associates the power of Fundamentalism with its mistakes and refuses to be identified with it, but still finds
itself preaching a watered-down version of the Fundamentalist gospel.

For example, Evangelicalism is, like Fundamentalism, millenarian, but it
no longer displays much confidence in its inherited eschatology. (Dispensa-
tionalism was decidedly unpopular among students of the traditionally dis-
pensationalistic Evangelical seminaries that I attended.) It need hardly be
noted that the old system of traditional personal and social abstinences
(called "revised asceticism" by J. D. Hunter) is falling on hard times. Unwilling to adopt the authoritarian mannerisms and ascetic program from which
much of the distinctive character and power of Fundamentalism flows, Evangelicalism has failed to develop a similarly cohesive, integrated, and convincing shape of its own. Carl F. H. Henry, an Evangelical scholar of stature,
doubts whether adherence to the doctrine of biblical inerrancy, as important
as he considers this to be, should be regarded as the definitive mark of an
Evangelical, and thus places himself on the left side of a deepening rift in the
movement. Moreover, and perhaps most significantly, in light of its increasing recognition of the possibility of genuine and vital Christianity in the
liturgical, sacramentally oriented churches, it must even question the abso-

luteness of its revivalist soteriology. In the Evangelical world Fundamentalist theology is being modified, but it has not undergone the sort of transformation which would come with the development of a distinctive character of its own. Its preaching has suffered much from this irresolution, weakening in a day when strength is required, and in a world which needs—and has a right to expect—something far better from the Evangelicals.

What is to be done? Let me suggest first of all that Evangelicalism must gird up its loins and prepare itself to bear the burden of being mocked. This is a requirement of "mere Christianity" that Evangelicalism has been unwilling to bear for the fear of being denominated Fundamentalist by the liberal and secular world, the respect of which it has been desperately anxious to gain from the beginning of its existence. However dedicated it has been to ridding itself of the more obnoxious aspects of hyperconservatism, it should resign itself to accept the "Fundamentalist" stigma from its natural enemies with good grace. The Evangelical, although courageous enough in many things, is paralyzed by the fear of being mistaken for a Fundamentalist. But mistaken for a Fundamentalist he will be, no matter how sophisticated and free from the lingering echoes of Bible-thumping, proof-texting, and Fanny J. Crosby he considers himself. Part of the price he must pay for his orthodoxy is the acknowledgement of this lineage. He must accept the dreaded taunt and boldly make common cause with the Fundamentalist in areas where they can agree (as he is willing to do with others). If the Evangelical ever regains some of the courage to be ill-spoken of, he will recover the power to preach a message which the world by no means wants to hear.

But this alone would not solve the problem. I must return to say something about what I have called the theological irresponsibility of Fundamentalist preaching, an irresponsibility which Evangelicalism shares as long as it is marked by certain sectarian traits of its Fundamentalist heritage. Being more courageous is a good and necessary thing, but what, then, is to be preached? Evangelicalism has not really moved that far beyond Fundamentalism theologically. It picks and chooses what it can from the old Fundamentalist agenda. I am by no means suggesting that it sell its orthodox birthright for a mass of liberal pottage. I am suggesting that Evangelicalism needs to rediscover the Bible, and with this rediscovery find its place in the larger Church.

The tiresomeness of much Evangelical preaching belies the official conviction that the Bible is the Word of God, sharper than a two-edged sword and supremely powerful. In the Evangelical world the Bible has lost its power because it has been mastered—made too easy by Fundamentalism's interpretive shell, a shell which may be modified, questioned, or even replaced in private study, but must be adhered to in preaching. This "mastery" of the Bible has left the Evangelical academic and pastoral magisterium bored. This boredom is a root cause of the decline of the vitality of Evangelical preaching on one hand, and, on the other, the indulgence of many of its intellectuals (those who can afford to consider themselves liberated) in unconstructive Evangelical-bashing and conspicuous dalliance with causes and doctrines (like feminism) which offend the orthodox sensibilities of their fellows.

Is there a way out? Can Evangelicalism's strengths, preeminent among which may be its potential for preaching of the highest art, conviction, and authority, be saved before the movement falls into dogmatic slumber or heterodoxy, largely from the sheer weight of ennui? Perhaps—if Evangelicalism is willing to examine itself in light of the beliefs it shares with other Christians it considers essentially orthodox—if it would take some pains to rediscover the Bible in the light of a well-informed concept of the Church instead of merely assuming that its own movement is at the center of orthodox tradition. It appears to me that its errors lie at the very places where it is most distinctively *itself*, at the places where it prides itself on its differences with other groups whose doctrine it regards as essentially correct. (One might examine the final chapter of Thomas Howard's *Evangelical Is Not Enough* for some therapeutic suggestions along these lines.) It may well be that when Evangelicalism repents of closing out the rest of the confessing church (including the Fundamentalist) and purposes to join itself as much as possible, not just with other Evangelicals but with other *Christians*, a way might open for renewed doctrinal certitude. I am not speaking here of those of whom the Evangelical churches have traditionally entertained high suspicions. Indeed, Evangelicalism's tendency to seek the approval of the heterodox under the pretext of evangelizing them has been one of its greatest weaknesses from the very beginning—a sin against its own conscience, which the Fundamentalists have perceptively accused it of for many years. A more "catholic" Evangelicalism might find a theological confidence which is not so completely dependent on a particular theory of revelation as a binding force—and hence find a renewed power in its preaching.

I am calling here for a rebirth of the vision of the first generation of Fundamentalists which has been abandoned by Fundamentalist and Evangelical alike. For originally Fundamentalism (taken *in meliorem partem*, of course) was built upon an ecumenical ideal which sought to both purify and unite the church under the confessional head of a canon of *fundamental* doctrines to which all Christians should be able to subscribe. This could have been not only the proper response to modernism, but the beginning of a reexamination of the sectarian theologies of the original Fundamentalists. Unfortunately, it did not turn out that way. The Fundamentalists were willing to assert the existence of "fundamentals," but not at the cost of reconsidering their own private distinctives. They were willing to rid the house of liberals, but not to settle accounts with those others whom they recognized as orthodox. And they were willing to imagine, in order to build an effective anti-modernist coalition, that a solution for their own disunity could be put off indefinitely. In all of this, one of the most significant reasons for a purified *fundamental*-ism—the unified proclamation of a doctrinally unified church—was lost, and the essential question of what is really fundamental was given short shrift. This error needs to be corrected by the present generation of Evangelicals (with perhaps the exchange of some belated apologies with their Fundamentalist brethren.)

Of course, the prescription for Evangelicalism given here applies *mutatis mutandis* to every church that finds itself affirming the ancient faith against the spirit of the age and the religious modernism which serves it. They must all grant Evangelicalism its place in the sun and learn what it has to teach them. The point made here is that Evangelicalism has its own peculiar pilgrimage to make and that it had best get on with it. It is time for responsible Evangelical leadership (not just a few ornery voices in the wilderness) to reopen and pursue with full vigor the question about the essential nature of a truly biblical Christianity and thus to finish the job begun in the early part of this century. The decline in preaching—which is a symptom of a general malaise in Evangelicalism today—cannot be solved with anything less than critical self-examination along these lines. Nor can an increasingly moribund Evangelicalism be revived until a leadership emerges which is willing to challenge some of its characteristic pretensions in the name of "what has been believed everywhere, always, and by all."

CREATIVE TENSIONS IN PREACHING: PERSON AND SPIRIT

HARRY BAKER ADAMS
Chaplain of Yale University

Article from *Lexington Theological Quarterly*

Phillips Brooks delivered one of the most often quoted definitions of preaching when he wrote that "preaching is truth through personality." That is surely not a comprehensive definition of the craft, but then no adequate definition can be given in one brief sentence. It can be argued, moreover, that Brooks failed to focus on the central and crucial character of the preaching ministry. The statement obviously raises many issues. Is all communication which takes place through personality to be identified as preaching? Obviously not. Politicians, rock singers, door-to-door sales persons are not in the preaching business but they all seek to communicate by expressing themselves as persons. If persons standing in the pulpit succeed in communicating "truth" through the dynamic of their personality, does it necessarily follow that they have been faithful as Christian preachers? Not necessarily. For questions need to be raised about the kind of truth they have delivered. The definition certainly implies that the personality of the preacher is the key factor in authentic preaching. Is preaching best interpreted by that strong a focus on the person who stands in the pulpit? Does not the statement accentuate the risk that strong persons in the pulpit will nurture a personality cult to satisfy their own egos?

Such issues need to be raised in assessing the adequacy and emphasis of Brooks's definition of preaching. His statement does push forcefully the place of the person in the whole enterprise, but what is the proper role of the person in preaching? How much stress should be placed on this person who stands in the pulpit? To what extent should the preacher deliberately intrude his or her personality into the dynamic of a worship event? To those questions we turn our attention in this chapter as we reflect on the tension between the role of the person and the role of the Spirit in the preaching of the Christian community.

To Minimize the Role of the Person

Some interpretations of preaching seek to minimize the role of the person who actually delivers the sermon. There seems to be some unease that a person must be involved in the preaching enterprise, and every effort is made to reduce the opportunity for the uniqueness or distinctiveness or flair of the preacher to be expressed in the sermon. Both the congregation and the preacher want the human being to play as small a role as possible in the whole event.

Why would the role of the person in preaching be interpreted in this way? A number of arguments can be offered, from quite different perspectives. One kind of argument is that when the preacher as person is given too big a role, there is serious risk both that the pulpit will become focused on the person and that the sermon will become an ego trip for the preacher. There is no question that the risk is present. Pulpits have come to be known as Dr. X's pulpit or Dr. Y's pulpit. As the church seeks to reach out to people, the main attraction to be offered is the dynamic of the preacher. When the church advertises in the newspaper, the only feature highlighted is the preacher, complete with picture and flashy sermon title for this Sunday. The service itself clearly builds toward a climax which comes when the preacher mounts the stairs to the pulpit. After suitable dramatic delay, the lights dim, and what can only be called a performance begins. In large measure the congregation is held together and sustained only by their appreciation for and their loyalty to the one who preaches to them.

For the preacher, such a situation offers an almost irresistible opportunity for an ego trip. It is heady business indeed to have every eye focused on you. It is satisfying indeed to know that people come to church to hear you. It is rewarding indeed to carry the church by the power found in you. It is thrilling indeed to move people by the words which come from you. Few events are more exhilarating than capturing an audience by the power of the spoken word. There is always the temptation for the preacher to use the pulpit to satisfy personal needs for approval or acclaim.

Because the risks are so great both for the congregation and the preacher when the personality of the one in the pulpit is allowed free rein, the solution for some is to do everything possible to restrict the person. This must not become Dr. X's or Dr. Y's church, and to reduce that possibility there will be as little of Dr. X or Dr. Y as possible in the preaching. The sermon event must not become an ego trip for the preacher and so there will be as little of the preacher's ego as possible in the preaching.

Another kind of argument focuses on the issue of authority in preaching. The sermon does have authority in the Christian community, but the authority does not reside in the person of the preacher. The truth is not made true because the preacher declares it emphatically. The truth is not made true because the preacher believes it passionately. The truth is not made true because the preacher argues for it persuasively. When the sermon speaks with authority, it is because the sermon manifests some authority external to it and to the person who delivers the sermon.

In this view of the situation, people do not come to hear the preacher's ideas, but they come to hear witness to a reality which transcends anything the preacher as person could offer. And preachers do not seek to communicate anything of themselves, because the preacher's task is to serve as transmitter of truth, not as creator of truth. Preachers speak with authority only when they speak what is given to them to declare. Therefore the role of preacher as thinker, as committed believer, as passionate advocate is minimized. In fact, the ideas, commitments and passions of the preacher may serve only to obscure the genuine message which the sermon is intended to carry.

Yet another kind of argument roots in an understanding of the nature and meaning of preaching itself. In varied language an exalted view of preaching is articulated. Preaching is the very Word of God spoken to this people. Preaching is a sacrament by which God is present in the midst of this community. Preaching is an event in the ongoing relationship between God and persons. Preaching is God at work judging and redeeming not only the lives of persons but the whole creation. Preaching is an encounter between God and persons. To talk about preaching in such ways makes it immediately evident that preaching is beyond the capacity of any human being to achieve. No one can set out to create a sacrament by putting words together with brilliance and delivering them with passion. No one can orchestrate an encounter between God and persons by ringing rhetoric or dynamic delivery. So, if a sermon happens at all, it is not because of the person of the preacher.

Obviously then the person of the preacher is not important if one genuinely understands what a sermon is. At best, the person of the preacher may be an instrument used of God to accomplish what God intends. Instrument is a mechanical term, and if God needs a voice then the preacher's voice can be used, but God really does not need the passion, imagination, insight, ideas, convictions of the preacher, all those things which make the preacher a unique human being.

One final observation about the reluctance of many to stress the role of the preacher as person is not to note another argument but to note a feeling. If there are those who are prima donnas of the pulpit and supremely confident of their ability to pull it off, there are many who approach the pulpit with a great sense of their inadequacy for the task. Such people join a goodly company, of course. For when God called Moses to his mission to free the people of Israel from their bondage in Egypt, Moses protested vigorously and finally declared: "Oh, my Lord, I am not eloquent, either heretofore or since thou hast spoken to thy servant; but I am slow of speech and of tongue." When God called Jeremiah and told him that he had been appointed a prophet to the nations, Jeremiah demurred: "Ah, Lord God! Behold, I do not know how to speak, for I am only a youth." When God appeared to Isaiah to manifest an awesome holiness, Isaiah cried out: "Woe is me! For I am lost; for I am a man of unclean lips, and I dwell in the midst of a people of unclean lips; for my eyes have seen the King, the Lord of hosts!"

Those who come to the pulpit with great feelings of personal inadequacy will obviously be limited in their willingness and their ability to express themselves as persons. It takes a considerable level of confidence to offer one's unique gifts and insights in public. Without that confidence the person may seek some generally accepted way of doing things. Or the person may approach the pulpit with the kind of humility which leads one to believe that nothing he or she has to offer is really worthwhile.

For any number of reasons then, the view may be held that the person of the preacher should play a minimum role in the event of preaching, and that conviction gets expressed in different ways as preachers actually present themselves in the pulpit. Some people are hesitant to be themselves in the pulpit, for example. They adopt a style which is quite different from their ordinary speaking manner. They may be warm and exuberant in their relationships with others outside the pulpit, but somehow feel that they can't express that self in the pulpit and so become cool and reserved. Or they operate under an impression that there must be a "right" manner in the pulpit, a manner different from the way any ordinary human being would function in a nonchurchy setting. Or they pattern their style in the pulpit after some.person they happen to admire, and who seems to embody what a proper pulpit presence must be. Instead of being themselves they seek to emulate the way of another. The point simply is that much of what seems strained or mannered in the pulpit is the result of a conviction, perhaps unconscious, that people cannot be fully themselves in the act of preaching. Their normal humanity is somehow inappropriate or inadequate for the task, and they adopt styles which are quite different from those which they express in their ordinary, i.e., nonpulpit, relationships.

Or some people manifest their conviction about the need to minimize the place of the person in the pulpit by constant appeal to outside authority, both biblical and nonbiblical. The Bible plays a unique role in Christian preaching and does serve as an authorizing source for what is affirmed from the pulpit. But constant appeal to particular texts of Scripture to support every statement of the preacher surely reflects a conviction about the role of the person in preaching. The person who speaks has no right of insight or interpretation or application in the light of the contemporary situation; the person is to serve only as a transmitter of the authoritative word of the text of the Bible. Or in traditions which are less prone to root the whole sermon in biblical texts, preachers may seek support for what they say from the writings of theologians or philosophers or psychologists or newspaper columnists. Surely every preacher is dependent on the ideas and insights which come from reading. But there is a difference between the preachers who can incorporate the ideas and insights into a coherent and personal pattern of thought, and the preachers who must use the ideas and insights of others to authenticate what they are saying because they have no confidence that their personal convictions have a place in preaching.

The Place of the Person in Preaching

In spite of the reasons for minimizing the person in preaching, in spite of the risks of making a personality cult out of the church, Phillips Brooks was right. Brooks's definition of preaching as "truth through personality" is limited and partial, but his thrust is surely right that preaching involves a person who shares fully of himself or herself. The arguments in support of that statement can be made on several grounds. First, it can be made on theological grounds. A central theological conviction of the Christian faith centers on belief in the incarnation. God the Creator of the universe, God the awesome and holy One, God the mover and shaker of history, God the ultimate mystery of reality came into this world in the life of a person. The Gospel of John makes the declaration in this fashion: "In the beginning was the Word, and the Word was with God, and the Word was God . . . and the Word became flesh and dwelt among us, full of grace and truth; we have beheld his glory, glory as of the only Son from the Father. . . . And from his fulness have we all received, grace upon grace." The Apostle Paul makes the declaration in this fashion: "That is, God was in Christ reconciling the world to himself." The Letter to the Hebrews makes the declaration in this fashion: "In many and various ways God spoke of old to our forbears by the prophets; but in these last days God has spoken to us by a Son, whom God appointed the heir of all things, through whom also God created the world. He reflects the glory of God and bears the very stamp of his nature, upholding the universe by his word of power."

God came into the world in a person, the person of Jesus of Nazareth. Jesus shared fully in our human existence. He was a man in the midst of our history. Even as he manifested the love and power and character of God he participated completely in what it means to be a human being on this earth. The Word which was from the beginning became flesh. The God who reconciles persons did so in a man. The one who reflects the very glory of God and bears the very being of the nature of God lived as a person in the hills of Galilee. The astonishing claim of the Christian faith is that God came to us. To know God we don't have to enter some esoteric realm of pure spirit. To know God we look to the one in whom the divine is incarnate, even Jesus of Nazareth.

Preaching is the witness to that love and power and character of God made known in the man Jesus. If God chose to make the divine will and nature known in one man who lived in a particular place at a particular time, it is fitting that God chooses to continue to make the divine known through the medium of persons. It may be an offense that frail, fallible human beings can speak the Word of God, but it is the offense of the Gospel which declares that the love of God became fully manifest in a frail, suffering man who could be executed on a cross.

The person needs to be involved in preaching for it is through persons that God has chosen to make revelation of the divine nature, has chosen to set forth the divine will, has chosen to act on behalf of sinful humanity, has chosen to bring reconciliation with wayward children, has chosen to set persons free from the evil powers. To minimize the place of the person in preaching is to flee from the scandal of the God who became man. To affirm the place of the person in preaching is to take seriously the Christian claim of incarnation.

Second, argument in support of the statement that preaching involves the full personhood of the preacher can be made on the basis of the essential nature of the preaching enterprise. Preaching is a means of communication between God and persons. People have learned of God and God's ways through many evidences. The wonder of creation bears testimony to the power and glory of God. The freeing of the people of Israel from their bondage in Egypt bears testimony to the redeeming care of God. The witness of the prophets bears testimony to the claim and judgment of God. Above all, the person of Jesus Christ bears testimony to the character and love of God.

For the Christian community, preaching is a continuing witness to the good news made known in Jesus. God is not limited to persons in the manifestation of divine love and glory. The physical creation can be testimony to the Creator. But God does use persons, and preaching surely involves persons, and the interaction between persons. Preaching is not the delivery of stone tablets from heaven, but the word of a person to other persons. Preachers do not fulfill their call when they try to reduce their involvement as persons so that the "pure Word of the Lord" can be spoken. They misread their function if they seek to serve merely as a mechanical voice through which God can speak the Divine Word. By the very nature of the preaching enterprise, those who are called to it are to offer their whole person in this service—their ideas, their emotions, their insights, their learning, their passions, their gifts, their doubts, their sensitivities, their convictions.

Preaching in its essence is communication, but not just communication of ideas. To put on a screen in the front of the sanctuary the words of a great thinker might be a useful exercise and might provide helpful insights. But the words of even the most brilliant mind projected on a screen cannot be called preaching by any stretching of the definition of the enterprise. The communication of preaching involves dimensions which are possible only in the interaction of persons. The preacher as person speaks words which may be more or less helpful, but the preacher as person also communicates as genuine care is manifest for those who hear the words, as profound conviction is evidenced about the significance of what is going on as the people of God gather for worship. The preacher communicates as pain and sorrow are shared, as joy and achievement are celebrated. The preacher communicates as there is openness and vulnerability and not just cautious competence, as there is shared searching and not just absolute assurance. The more fully preachers dare to invest themselves in what happens in the preaching event, the more possibility they offer for the event to reach its full potential.

Then, because preaching is the word to be spoken to this congregation at this moment, the person of the preacher is crucial. Preaching is not the delivery of some timeless word which is eternally true and instantly meaningful. Preaching is the speaking of a word from the eternal truth of God into this unique situation. It can happen that sermons prepared for one place and one time can speak with authority and insight into another place and another time. By God's grace, all things are possible. But in general sermons do not travel very well, nor do most of them read very well. For the written words are merely instruments which might make possible the event when a sermon actually happens.

If words are to be formed which speak to this people at this time they must be crafted by a person who is open and sensitive to this people in their particular circumstance. Therefore preachers are called to use their imaginations, their insights, their sensitivities as they seek to find words which will speak the Word of God for this moment. Surely there is risk that preachers will be carried into odd flights of fancy by imagination; that they will misread the situation because their insights are inadequate; that they will blunder badly because their sensitivities are dull. But preaching is always risky business. The only sure way to fail is to refuse to use the capacities for imagination and insight and sensitivity in an effort to avoid the limitations inherent in the human situation. Only persons can preach. Only persons willing to risk their full personhood can speak the words which can become the Word of God for this people at this time.

Third, argument in support of the statement that preaching involves the full personhood of the preacher can be made on the basis of effectiveness. This argument is clearly subservient to the first two, for only if the place of the person in preaching has basis in theological understanding of God's work and in the interpretation of the meaning of preaching dare we make assessment according to what works. Powerful personalities have swayed multitudes by their speaking, but have not come anywhere close to the essential meaning of Christian preaching. Persons have used all their gifts to great effect in the pulpit, but they have done so for self-aggrandizement not for the glory of God. There is always the risk of using personal dynamics in order to manipulate others.

In spite of the corruption and the risks, however, the case for the full use of the person in preaching can be supported on the grounds that it is the effective way to proclaim the Gospel. When the words of preachers are invested with the sense that the truth offered has laid claim on those who speak it, there is a powerful reality present. When the words of preachers are delivered with the sense that they really care about the people who sit before them, there is a persuasive authenticity. When the words of the preachers are used not only to inform the mind but to grip the will of the hearer, there is a potential for transformation. Sermons delivered with dry detachment surely limit their impact. Only when the passion, the conviction, the compassion of the preacher as person come through does the sermon have a chance of reaching its potential for witness to the Gospel. The preacher as person needs to be in the sermon for that makes for effective preaching.

In marshalling the arguments for the significance of the person in preaching, there have been indications about how the preacher appropriately gets invested in the sermon, but we turn now to a more ordered statement about how that can happen, considering first the preparation of the sermon, and second the delivery of the sermon. What does it mean for the person to be involved in the preparation? To be personally invested in the preparation means that the ideas and insights of the preacher will be appropriately used in what is said. The preacher is not under obligation just to repeat the text, nor to seek the truth in what others have said. The preacher is not under mandate to preach the sermon which any other human being would deliver in the same circumstances. Preachers enter a dangerous domain when they begin to speculate on what a revered teacher or a renowned pulpiteer would say to their congregations this Sunday. We can learn from revered teachers and possibly even from renowned pulpiteers, but neither can tell the preacher what needs to be said to this congregation from this text on this Sunday. All of us are limited in our ideas and insights, and need to be constantly expanding them by sharing the wisdom of others. But finally it is not the wisdom of others which is to be shared in the sermon, but the ideas which have genuinely commended themselves to us or which we have arrived at by our own reflections. And deciding what needs to be said will be shaped by what the preacher knows of the situation of the congregation and the needs of the people. There is a place for the "visiting preacher" who travels around delivering sermons in special circumstances. But the sustained preaching for the community grows out of the shared life of minister and congregation. The preacher's individual insights and sensitivities about the issues with which people are struggling and the pains with which people are coping will inform the preparation of the sermon.

Then, to be personally invested in the preparation means that preachers must do their own reading of the text. Again we enter into a risky area, for people have made highly eccentric readings of biblical texts. People have forced texts to say what they wanted them to say, rather than letting the text speak for itself. Preachers are under mandate to be responsible in their reading of the Scripture. They must seek to grasp what the author is saying. They must try to understand what the text meant in the situation in which it was written. But they must also seek to hear what the word is saying to the people to whom they preach, and to do that they must let the words of the text speak to them. All of the tools of biblical criticism can be helpful in exploring the meaning of the word. Comments by others about what the text means can be helpful. But finally the preacher cannot depend upon anyone else to declare the meaning of the text for this congregation at this moment.

The text does not mean in this situation what the biblical scholar says that it means. The text does not mean what the creative commentator says that it means. The text must mean what the preacher hears from careful listening to the text itself as the word is sought which needs to be addressed to this particular people. This one person's assessment of the situation of the congregation and the meaning of the text is crucial if the preaching is to be done with point and with power.

To be personally invested in the preparation means also that preachers must be free and willing to find their own way of saying what they want to say. Preachers have different gifts in the use of language, and are under mandate to nurture the gifts which they do have rather than to imitate the gifts of another. Some preachers have poetic gifts, but not all. Some preachers can use language with exceptional grace, but not all. Some preachers can put words together so that they hit with enormous impact, but not all. Some preachers can articulate the most complex ideas with a crystalline simplicity, but not all. If the sermon is to express the person who is to deliver it, then it must be prepared by that person using all the resources that he or she has. But the preparation will be false if the preacher becomes enamored of the strengths of another person and seeks to prepare the sermon in a style fitting for the other. Most of us would like to write with poetic grace and power and simplicity. But we are called to develop the particular gifts which are ours, and to use them with as much skill and dedication as possible. We are not called to prepare the sermon as another would, nor to express ourselves in styles which are foreign to who we are and what we can do with integrity.

Finally, to be personally invested in the preparation means that we will find the process which enables us to produce as richly as possible, and not the process which others impose upon us because they find it useful for them. There are masters of the pulpit, and some not so masterful, who insist that their manner of sermon preparation is the ideal. They are quite prepared to mandate that topics for sermons should be worked out a year in advance, that background study will always involve translation of the text from the Greek or the Hebrew, that an outline must be prepared at least a week before the sermon is to be preached, that a full text must be written no later than Wednesday, that a revised manuscript will be prepared on Friday. People can offer helpful suggestions to others, and the ways in which "successful" preachers do their work may provide some useful ideas to be tried. But what works for one person will not necessarily work for another. Some preachers should spend their time every week translating the text from the original languages; others should not. Some preachers should write full manuscripts for their sermons; others should not. The point is that even in the process of preparing a sermon, the uniqueness of this preacher as person needs to be expressed, so that no "right pattern" can be mandated for every one.

Second, we turn to the question of the ways in which it is appropriate for the preacher to be personally involved in the delivery of the sermon. Metaphors which deny or minimize the role of the preacher as person fail to depict fairly the responsibility of one who preaches. To talk of the preacher as *instrument* of God's action, to talk of the preacher as *channel* of God's grace, to talk of the preacher as *transmitter* of God's Word is to use metaphors with primarily a mechanistic or nonpersonal orientation. The preacher can thus be conceived as merely a physical means by which the words get spoken, so that a computer programmed to speak the same words would do the job as well or better.

There are few who would seriously propose using a computer to speak the words, or even advocate installing a tape deck to play the words. But there are some who fear the role of the preacher as person in the pulpit. There is some reason for the fear, of course, for as has been mentioned earlier, the risk is real of the pulpit becoming a place where a personality cult is nurtured. Preachers can use the sermon to draw attention to themselves. They can seek to sway persons solely by the power of their personality. They can revel in the acclaim which is given to them when their "performance" in the pulpit is well received. They can subordinate the content of the sermon to the demand for a particular response.

But preachers as persons need to be involved in the event of a sermon. They need to be involved in the communication of the ideas. The ideas take on a seriousness when preachers speak with conviction because the ideas are important to them personally. Preaching is not about some vaguely interesting and mildly significant notions which people have developed. Preaching is the exploration of the insights and ideas which have shaped generations of persons, and which will have profound impact on those who take them seriously in this day. Preachers communicate as persons when it becomes clear that the ideas about which they speak have indeed had great impact on them personally.

Then preachers need to be involved in the communication of emotion and feeling. The sermon is not just an appeal to the intellect; it is a claim on the whole person. Persons are moved when they witness the emotional response of others to significant occasions. Preachers can enable the Gospel to lay powerful claim on persons when they find ways to share their own emotional investment in the revelation of God which has come to them through Jesus Christ. Emotion in preaching is not to be confused with emotionalism. Emotionalism is response to an event or a situation in which the feeling is disproportionate to the genuine meaning. Preachers who seek to invoke emotional involvement by sentimental stories have not realized the potential for genuine emotion, which can come as preachers are willing to risk their own feelings in the moment of preaching.

Perhaps most significant of all, preachers need to be involved as persons in genuine care for the people who sit before them. The potential of the sermon is gravely restricted when the congregation assesses that the preacher cares seriously neither for what he is saying nor for them as persons. Genuine care is communicated in real but subtle ways. If a preacher ever feels compelled to *say*, "now hear this because I really want you to hear it because I care about you," he or she needs to raise serious question about the relationship with the congregation in the preaching moment. The words should not need to be said, because in manner and personal involvement that care can be communicated at a level more compelling than words. How does the preacher communicate care? In many ways, but primarily by actually caring. A genuinely caring person comes across to others, and so when the preacher as a person really does care for those people who sit in the pew, that will somehow be manifest. And without the genuine caring relationship, all else will soon ring false.

The Spirit in Preaching

Nothing the preacher can do can guarantee that a sermon will happen. Nothing the preacher can do will insure that the Word of God will be proclaimed. Nothing the preacher can do can certify that God will be present in the midst of the worshipping congregation as the sermon is delivered. No matter what the person does in the sermon, the sermon is beyond all human creation. For a sermon is not one person sharing ideas with others. Nor is the sermon one person making affirmations about the meaning of the faith while others listen. There are people involved in the creation of a sermon, people who speak and people who listen. But finally the sermon is not within the capacity of a man or a woman to bring off.

In its essential meaning, the sermon is the creation of God. Only the Spirit of God can make a sermon. Only the Spirit can transform the words of a person into the Word of God. Only the Spirit can change the sermon from an encounter between the person of the preacher and the persons of the congregation into an encounter between the Holy One and all the people present. Only the Spirit can infuse the event of the sermon so that it becomes a sacrament, an occasion when the grace of God is ministered to the people. If God is present in the sermon, it is because God chooses to be present.

Every preacher has had the experience of knowing without any doubt that the sermon "worked." It worked not simply in the way that any public address might work. There are good speeches and poor speeches, speeches that reach the mind of the hearers and speeches that don't, speeches that excite people immensely and speeches that bore people excruciatingly. Preachers know about those good speeches and those lousy speeches too. But preachers also know about sermons that move beyond all human capacity until people encounter again the living God, and receive God's mercy and judgment, God's demand and promise. The evidence that sermons work is subtle and preachers don't always know when it happens. But there do come those marvelous occasions when the preacher becomes absolutely certain that God ministered to the people through the words spoken and the relationship established.

Preachers also know about sermons that don't work. The sermon may in fact be very good from every human standard—biblically sound, well structured, gracefully written, deftly illustrated, powerfully delivered. But the sermon didn't work and the preacher knows it. There was no sense of the power and presence of God in what happened on this occasion. Such occasions serve as stark reminder to preachers that the creation of the sermon in its most significant meaning is simply beyond the preachers' capacity. Finally, sermons either work or don't work because of what God does, not because of what persons do.

How does the Spirit work to create the sermon? If we thought we could answer that question, we would have missed one of the essential characteristics of the Spirit, namely, that the Spirit is not under our control. We cannot know exactly how the Spirit works to create the sermon. We cannot know what circumstances will make it possible for the Spirit to accomplish a sermon, and what circumstances will make it impossible for the Spirit to work. The story of Jesus' encounter with Nicodemus must be taken seriously by all who would grasp the way of the Spirit in the life of the Christian community, and specifically in the creation of a sermon. Jesus told Nicodemus that a person must be born anew in order to see the kingdom of God. Nicodemus wanted to know how this could be, and then Jesus said to him: "Truly, truly, I say to you, unless one is born of water and the Spirit, he cannot enter the kingdom of God. That which is born of the flesh is flesh, and that which is born of the Spirit is spirit . . . the wind blows where it wills, and you hear the sound of it, but you do not know whence it comes or whither it goes; so it is with every one who is born of the Spirit." The Spirit is not under the control of any person, and the preacher cannot mandate the presence of the Spirit by any action or word or preparation.

With a clear grasp that the Spirit works as God intends and not as we intend, we can then go ahead to make three comments about what can be discerned of the work of the Spirit in the creation of a sermon. First, the Spirit inspires the preacher in the preparation and delivery of the sermon. As the preacher works with the text and seeks insights and struggles for ideas, there needs to be the awareness that the Spirit can enable the preacher to move beyond human capacity to grasp the truth and reality of God. As the preacher speaks in the actual moment of delivery, there needs to be the awareness that the human words can be empowered by the Spirit to speak more than the preacher knew or intended. Part of the process of preparation then is openness to the movement of the Spirit, and a seeking of the presence of the Spirit. The sermon needs to be created with prayer, and with the willingness to wait for the Spirit of God to move within the mind and the spirit of the one who has been entrusted with the responsibility of speaking to the people of God.

Second, the Spirit moves within the life of the community as the words are spoken which might become a sermon. A sermon happens not only when words are spoken but also when words are heard, not only when the words of the preacher are transformed into the Word of God but also when the words are heard to be the Word of God. And so there needs to be openness in the people to the movement of the Spirit in their lives, and prayer that they may hear what God has to say to them in this moment of the preaching. The liturgy of the people of God at worship is not to be shaped exclusively as a build-up for the climax of the preaching. All that goes before the sermon in a service of worship is not just preparation for the main event of the sermon. Nonetheless, the whole liturgical movement of the worship can serve to prepare persons for the movement of the Spirit in the preached word. From a strictly human perspective, preaching which is not set within a liturgical context surely poses grave difficulties, for the people are simply not prepared to engage the words as are those who have prayed together and sung together and confessed together. Only when the Spirit moves within the minds and hearts of the people can the words spoken by the preacher be heard as the Word of God.

Third, the Spirit authenticates the whole event which is a sermon. When the Spirit is present a sermon happens. When the Spirit is present those who participate in the preaching and the hearing find themselves actually in the presence of God. Through the Spirit the words about forgiveness become the means by which persons experience the forgiveness of God. As the Spirit moves, assertions about the power of God get translated into the sustaining strength of God in the lives of persons. Words about the judgment of God become that judgment when the Spirit moves. Lives are so transformed that persons are made capable of "love, joy, peace, patience, kindness, goodness, faithfulness, gentleness, self-control" when the Spirit takes the vision offered by the preacher and enables persons to capture that vision for their own lives.

No human being can do for another what the Christian community has found the sermon capable of doing. Surely there are many sermons which fall short of the exalted potential being claimed here for preaching. There are dull sermons, and irrelevant sermons, and meaningless sermons. But in the ongoing life of the Church across the generations, the preached word has had enormous impact as it has brought people to the faith and sustained them in the faith. No human being can give the forgiveness and judgment and vision of God to another. Only the Spirit can bring the presence and power of God to a person.

Keeping the Tension of Person and Spirit

There is clearly a tension in the two major assertions which have been made in this chapter. On the one hand, the person of the preacher is crucially important in the enterprise of preaching. On the other hand, nothing the person does can create the sermon; only the Spirit of God can do that. Those two statements must be kept in some kind of creative tension if the preaching ministry is to realize its potential.

From one side the tension can be lost if the preacher believes that the creation of the sermon depends solely on human wit and wisdom. Preaching is surely a human enterprise, and some people do it better than others. The quality of the preaching does depend on the gifts of the preacher and the way in which the preacher uses those gifts. Sloppy preparation shows in a preaching ministry. Lazy study habits show in the kinds of sermons which come from the pulpit. Insensitivity to people and the world shows in what the preacher does. If the negative shows, so also do the positives. Good sermons reflect the careful preparation, the disciplined study, the sensitivity of the preacher.

Furthermore, the judgments about sermons are significant and meaningful judgments. Some sermons are in fact better than other sermons. There are good sermons and there are poor sermons. There are sermons which grab the attention of people at the beginning, which move with clarity, which relate the text to the people with creative insight, which state the ideas with power, which reach a moving climax at the end, and which are delivered with authority. And there are other sermons which seem to meander aimlessly and endlessly with little reference to either text or people. Some sermons are worthy of the comment made after a lecture by a theologian. One person asked another: "What was he talking about?" The other person responded: "He didn't say."

If some sermons indeed are better than other sermons, then the gifts and discipline of the preacher are clearly significant. The quality of the sermon depends on the person of the preacher, on the preacher's knowledge, wisdom, sensitivity and rhetorical skills. Therefore the success of a preaching ministry relates directly to the capacity of the person who does the preaching. Experience certainly demonstrates the truth of that statement, but when the ability of the preacher is made the only necessity for successful preaching, the creative tension between person and Spirit has indeed been lost.

From the other side, the tension is lost when the success of the sermon is attributed solely to the movement of the Spirit. A certain logic argues that if all depends on the work of the Spirit, then any human thought or effort becomes irrelevant. There have been preachers who have argued that they didn't want to prepare in advance because they wanted to leave room for the movement of the Spirit when the moment came to deliver the sermon. There have been preachers who have minimized their own efforts in preparation because they were sure that the Spirit could use whatever they offered from the pulpit. There have been preachers who are convinced that human judgments about good or bad sermons are meaningless because no person can determine what the Spirit can or cannot use. What is judged from a human point of view to be a poor sermon may in fact serve to lay God's claim on the lives of some people. What is judged to be a good sermon may be heard as witty, informed, insightful but may make no claim of God on the hearer.

How is the tension of person and Spirit to be kept creatively? Both things must be said: The person is crucially significant in preaching—everything depends on the work of the Spirit. The corollary of the assertion that everything depends on the work of the Spirit is not: therefore it makes no difference what the preacher does. The corollary of the assertion is: therefore the preacher must offer the best instrument possible. The preacher is under mandate to use the best gifts of mind and spirit to create the best possible sermon, all the while knowing that the best possible sermon will be no guarantee that the full meaning of what it means to preach will be realized. The tension of person and Spirit is kept only when the preacher is absolutely clear that the Spirit is never under the control of human effort. No clever insight, no fascinating structure, no moving illustration, no biblical quotation will mandate that the Spirit must use this vehicle.

The tension of person and Spirit is kept also only when the preacher is absolutely clear that God does use the instrument of preaching to nurture the life of the Christian community. In God's grace and mercy, the preached word does become the Word of the Lord to this people. In God's grace and mercy, the relationship between preacher and people gets transformed into a relationship between God and persons.

In the mysterious and wonderful way of preaching, all depends on the person of the preacher and all depends on the work of the Spirit.

PRACTICAL THEOLOGY: CHRISTIAN EDUCATION

Kenneth O. Gangel, area editor

CHRISTIAN EDUCATION

KENNETH O. GANGEL
Professor and Chairman of the Christian Education Department
Dallas Theological Seminary

Introduction

Twenty to ten to four—the excruciating annual process of selection for *The Best in Theology*—Christian Education. What changes will this fourth year yield? How has our discipline reordered its priorities as the last decade of the century trundles into view?

In actuality, not much. Battered some by financial exigencies in churches, colleges, and seminaries, the field of Christian education thrives at all levels. Old programs fade; new structures arise. Startling demographics call attention to growing and shrinking population groups as church leaders grapple with ministry revisions geared to meet the felt needs of a changing society.

But those educational trends mark the decade, not the year. Our scholarly concerns as reflected in "the literature" between mid-1988 and mid-1989 fall again into fairly standard, even predictable, categories. The best twenty titles represent the Christian educators' ongoing concerns with matters like teaching process, spiritual formation, adult ministries, leadership development, educational theology/philosophy, and special issues.

Congratulations to two journals. *Christian Education Journal* placed four candidates in the top twenty, and ETTA's new *Journal of Adult Training* offered two provocative articles in its first year while carefully avoiding treacly kitsch. I am amazed at the wide variety of theological journals that carry articles pertinent to this collection. Sixteen different sources provided the twenty pieces from which the final four were selected. Special thanks to professional colleagues who advised in the search—Drs. Robert J. Choun, Michael S. Lawson, Fred R. Wilson, and Professor David L. Edwards.

Church leadership still occupies a dominant concern among Christian educators. Perhaps the first-place item merely reflects curmudgeonly bias as well as the orientation of my own writings. *Mea culpa.* Nevertheless, I press on to name a *Pastoral Psychology* piece by Jack Balswick and Walter Wright: "A Complementary—Empowering Model of Ministerial Leadership." The authors view ministerial leadership as "the use of one's power to increase the maturity of another for Christian ministry," a view for which I admit a high degree of enthusiasm. They blend this premise nicely with self-denying discipleship to develop an attractive working model.

Rodney McKean serves as Associate Professor of Educational Ministries at Azusa Pacific University. His work reviews "Research on Teaching for Christian Education," and although the title seems a bit ambiguous, the article is not. McKean surveys assumptions, methodologies, and problems to conclude that "the only 'implications' for teaching that exist are implications that come from the study on teaching. . . . The task is ours to define and help provide the implications that will make us more effective in the central task of Christian education." Many journal articles are far too long; this one deserves additional space. Perhaps we can expect McKean II next year.

Less exciting than the first two but no less important is Zabilka's treatment of "Calvin's Contribution to Universal Education," appearing (most commendably) in *The Asbury Theological Journal* (44:1, Spring 1989). Zabilka writes like a historian (or perhaps like the registrar he was), chronicling the records of Calvin's educational system in a cool, dispassionate way that might surely please The Theologican himself. This work represents value not only for its historical insight, but more properly because Christians still struggle with schooling arguments and church/state issues to the present hour.

Linked closely thereto is the Michael Shepherd article "Home Schooling; Dimensions of Controversy, 1970–1984" (*Journal of Church and State*, 31:1, Winter 1989). Hardly a week goes by in which I don't receive some inquiry or question related to home schooling. Interestingly, Shepherd is public school trained and employed, an elementary teacher in the city of Dallas. His research is flawless, his objectivity without question, and his conclusions sound. Here are the final three sentences: "Whatever yardstick a state comes up with, it seems increasingly evident that more parents will experiment with home education in spite of official policy. The academic promise of home instruction as well as its protective aspects will persuade more parents to try it. With the advent of computers, the future of education as a whole may be a future of greater decentralization and allowance for individual diversity, not state imposed uniformity." To which many of us say, "Hear, hear!"

I find myself again in tune with the writer of Hebrews as he asks in seeming frustration, "What more shall I say? I do not have time to tell about Gideon, Barak, Samson. . . ." Many Gideons, Baraks, and Samsons might well have found their articles printed in these pages but for the limitations of space. This editor thanks all who have written during this past year to better inform our discipline and thereby advance the cause of Christian education in the Lord's church.

About the Area Editor

Kenneth O. Gangel (M.Div., Grace Theological Seminary; M.A., Fuller Theological Seminary; S.T.M., Concordia Theological Seminary; Ph.D., University of Missouri at Kansas City) is professor and chairman of the Department of Christian Education at Dallas Theological Seminary. He is an ordained minister in the Christian and Missionary Alliance. He edited *Toward a Harmony of Faith and Learning* (1983) and *The Christian Educator's Handbook on Teaching,* co-edited with Howard Hendricks (1988); and has written *Unwrap Your Spiritual Gifts* (1983), *Christian Education: Its History and Philosophy,* co-authored with Warren Benson (1982), and *Feeding and Leading* (1989).

A COMPLEMENTARY—EMPOWERING MODEL
OF MINISTERIAL LEADERSHIP

JACK BALSWICK
Professor of Sociology and Family Development
Fuller Theological Seminary
WALTER WRIGHT
President and Professor of Christian Leadership and Management
Regent College

Article from *Pastoral Psychology*

Although a key dimension of pastoral care is leadership, because of the complexity of congregational life and diversity of individual parishioner needs, effective ministry often demands a variety of leadership styles. This need for flexibility in leadership styles can tax the ability of ministers to have developed competency and comfort in a specific leadership style. We believe that the Bible is suggestive of what we might call a *complementary* model of leadership. A complementary model of leadership recognizes that although a variety of leadership styles or skills is needed within the same congregation, these need not necessarily reside in the same leader (1 Cor. 12:29–31). However, we further believe that from a biblical perspective all styles of leadership must be characterized by an attempt to *empower*, rather than to dominate and control. We believe that pastoral care will be most effective when the church is following a *complementary-empowering* model of leadership.

Before we give a full description of a complementary-empowering model of ministerial leadership we will first review a summary of the current social science wisdom on effective leadership styles. We believe that the accumulated social science research on leadership effectiveness comports well with a biblical view of leadership style.

Social Science Literature on Effective Leadership Styles

The attempt to systematically study leadership effectiveness began in the 1920s and continues to be a vital interest of social organization researchers and theorists today. Between 1920 and 1950 the emphasis was upon identifying the characteristics and traits of effective leaders. This classical view or "great man" approach to understanding leadership effectiveness began to give way to an emphasis on the importance of leadership *behavior* by the

1940s. Sashkin and Lassey (1983) identify the emergence of three different approaches to the study of effective leadership behavior.[1]

The *One-Dimensional* approach sought to place leadership behavior along a single continuum ranging from *people oriented* leadership at one extreme to *production oriented* leadership at the other, (see part 1 of figure 1). By the 1950s, the *Two-Dimensional* approach separated people oriented

Figure 1

One- and Two-Dimensional Approaches to Leadership

One-Dimensional Approach to Leadership

PEOPLE ——————————————————————— *PRODUCTION*
ORIENTED   *ORIENTED*
(Supportive, friendly,   (Directive, distant,
concern for   concern that work
subordinates' welfare)   be accomplished)

Two-Dimensional Approach to Leadership

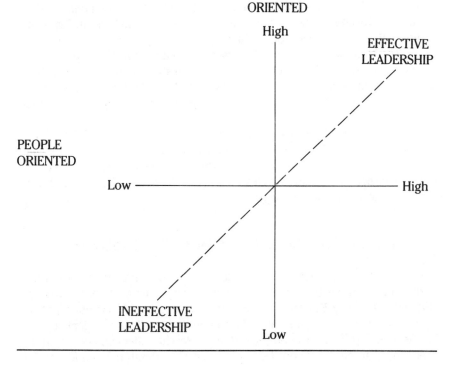

behavior and production oriented behavior into two separate dimensions which could be correlated with each other (see part 2 of figure 1).[2] Most of the research generated by the two-dimensional model demonstrated that effective leadership is characterized by a combination of high people and high production orientations, while ineffective leadership is characterized by low people and low production orientations. Although other attempts have been made to identify more specific types of leadership behavior, such as supportiveness, interaction facilitation, work facilitation, and goal emphasis,[3] these identified factors can still be assumed under the broad dimensions of people/relationship oriented behavior and production/task oriented behavior.

By the 1960s a variety of *systems* or *contingency theories* of leadership began to emerge. Contingency theories acknowledge that both relationship oriented and task directive activity are important in effective leadership, but in different proportions "contingent" on three situational conditions: (1) quality of leader-member relations; (2) amount of task structure; and (3) amount of the leader's legitimate authority.[4]

Situational Leadership Theory is similar to contingency theory except for the emphasis it places upon the importance of knowing the subordinate's level of "task maturity."[5] Task maturity is based on *job maturity*—the competence or ability to do a job, and *psychological maturity*—the confidence or willingness to do a job. The objective of leadership in this theory is the increase of the maturity of the members—their ability to operate independently with competence and confidence.

Each of these approaches is qualitatively similar to a general system theory understanding of organizational behavior, in which effective leadership is understood in terms of a complex interplay between leaders, members, and organizational structures. We must be content with this rather cursory review of the development of research on leadership theory, and move to a consideration of how leadership is portrayed in the Bible.

Empowering as a Biblical Model of Leadership Maturity

Although definitions of leadership differ, all definitions at their core include the concept of *power*, which is defined in the conventional social science literature as *the ability or potential to influence others.* Leadership behavior can be considered the actual exercise of that ability. We believe that *empowering* is the biblical model for the *use* of power. As Paul states in Ephesians 4:11–12, "And these were his gifts: some to be apostles, some prophets, some evangelists, some pastors and teachers, to equip God's people for work in his service, to the building up of the body of Christ." This is leadership as empowering—the use of one's power to increase the maturity of another for Christian ministry. It is the transfer of power—the delegation of authority—to the members that they might be able to lead out in ministry. This type of empowering leadership is contrary to the common use of power in many secular and Christian organizations. According to the research of Burke

> Empowering is not a simple process. Many, perhaps most, people believe that power is a zero-sum quantity; to share power, to empower others, is to lose a certain amount of it. This sharing of a precious commodity, especially for those who have a strong need for power, is a difficult act. Some would say that such an act takes courage.[6]

However, it is consistent with contemporary leadership theory. As Sashkin (1984) points out, it is an ethical imperative.[7] The use of one's power *for* others is not a natural human tendency, but it is a necessary corollary of membership in a community of persons who are bound together in covenantal relationships.

The biblical view is not that leadership resides in a person who stands off and away or over and above the body. On the contrary, the biblical leader is one who is part of the body of Christ and together with the other members form the *koinonia* of community. In Romans 12, the apostle Paul calls all Christians to a life of ministry and service, listing seven gifts that have been given to the body so that it may function as a healthy whole (Rom. 12:6–8). Leadership is listed, not as the first in order or the last but as one of the gifts, actually sandwiched between giving and helping! Paul clearly makes the point that leadership is only one of the gifts given to the church and persons with the gift of leadership like those with other gifts need to exercise it within the sober perspective of the community and not take themselves and their gift too seriously (Rom. 12:3). Persons who are gifted with leadership qualities are in relationship with the other believers in the community (Rom. 12:4–5). The Bible describes the nature of these relationships between believers in terms of covenant commitments. As Christ is unconditionally committed to the church as the body of Christ, so persons in leadership positions, as part of that body, are to be unconditionally committed to the other members of the body. All members of the body are to be committed in reciprocal (two-way) accountability relationships with each other (Rom. 12:9–16). Within these covenantal relationships, members of the body of Christ have the hope of living in an atmosphere of grace and forgiveness. Out of this atmosphere of grace, members of the body have the possibility of entering into mutually empowering relationship. Empowering is the fruit and not the basis of Christian commitment.

In living an empowering leadership model, Jesus provided a basis for all human relationships. In response to James's and John's request that they be permitted to sit on his right and left hand in glory, Jesus gave a radical reply, "Whoever wants to become great among you must be your servant, and whoever wants to be first must be slave of all. For the Son of Man did not come to be served, but to serve, and to give his life as a ransom for many" (Mark 10:43–45). Jesus redefined the understanding of leadership power by his teaching and by his action in relating to others as the servant. Jesus rejected the use of power to promote oneself over others. Instead he affirmed the use of power to serve others, to lift up the fallen, to forgive the guilty, to encourage responsibility and maturity in the weak, and to give power to the powerless. Robert Greenleaf develops this view of Christian leadership in his now classic book *Servant Leadership* (1977).[8]

Jesus' relationship to his disciples can only be understood in terms of his empowering of them. In preparing his disciples for his leaving, Jesus replies to their question, "Lord, are you at this time going to restore the Kingdom to Israel?" by saying, "You will receive power when the Holy Spirit comes on you" (Acts 1:8). As a result of the empowering which Jesus spoke of (Pentecost), it is worth noting the type of community his disciples developed in his absence. It is stated in Acts 2:44–45 that "all the believers were together and had everything in common. Selling their possessions and goods, they gave to anyone as he/she had need." The logical end result of taking Jesus seriously was to give up the very *resources* upon which conventional power is usually based, i.e., economic. Jesus defined power as strength for serving, rather than for controlling others.

The empowering leader will attempt to establish power in another person. Empowering leadership will not, however, merely yield to the wishes of another person, nor give up one's own power to someone else. Rather empowering leadership engages in an active, intentional process of enabling the acquisition of power in others. The person who is empowered has gained power—the ability or resources from which to lead—because of the empowering behavior of the leader, power which would not have been realized if it were not for the actions of empowering leadership.[9] Empowering leadership is the process of helping the other to recognize strengths and potential within, as well as encouraging and guiding the development of these qualities. It is assisting the other to develop the knowledge, skills, and competence with which to give leadership. Empowering leadership is the affirmation of another's ability to learn and to grow and become all that they are meant by God to be—mature in Christ.

A Complementary—Empowering Model
of Ministerial Leadership

By integrating contemporary social science theories of effective leadership and the biblical model of leadership as empowering, we are ready to examine what a complementary-empowering model of ministerial leadership would look like. Contained in figure 2 is a visual representation of this model. To begin with, it can be noted that the two separate dimensions of a minister's socio-emotional activity (represented as low at the bottom and high at the top of the chart) and a minister's directive task activity (represented as high at the left and low at the right) vary together to represent a minister's style of leadership. At the top of the chart, maturity of congregational members is represented as low at the extreme left, moderate in the middle, and high at the extreme right.

Empowering and Alternative Leadership Maturity Styles

The bell-shaped curve within the figure represents the *empowering curve*. At the extreme left end of the curve very little empowering is taking place among congregational members. This extreme can be considered congregational *dependence* upon leadership. At the extreme right end of the curve there is high *empowerment*, the opposite of dependence. From left to right, this empowering curve represents ministerial leadership maturity. Represented at different points on the empowering curve are four different ministerial leadership styles.

The leadership style at the extreme left is *preaching*, characterized by one-way communication in which the minister *tells* the congregational members what to do. This leadership style is needed for people whose Christian maturity is low. They are not sufficiently grounded in their faith to be able or willing to apply it to their lives or utilize their gifts in ministry. They need the clear directions and close supervision which a preaching style gives. In emphasizing high task/low relational activity, this style requires the minister to clearly define roles and to tell congregational members what, where, when, and how to perform tasks or live the Christian life. Socio-emotional activity is minimized, but present as a reward for compliance.

The *teaching* leadership style is for congregational members who are low to moderate in Christian maturity. These may be new Christians who are willing to take responsibility for specific tasks or function of ministry, but who do not know how. This ministerial style requires both moderately high directives and personal support and encouragement. Teaching differs from preaching in that communication can be two-way. Congregation members may ask questions, discuss, or even begin to give their own answers. However, most of the communication is done by the minister, who if skilled knows when to withdraw his/her own structuring behavior while giving high levels of caring supportive behavior.

In the *participating* leadership style the minister is like a "playing coach." Learning is still taking place, but proper behavior is *modeled* in addition to being taught. This leadership style is for congregational members who are moderate to highly mature in their Christian faith. Although members may have the ability to do certain tasks and carry out ministerial responsibilities, they may still lack the confidence and thus the motivation to

*Figure 2

A Complementary-Empowering Model of Ministerial Leadership

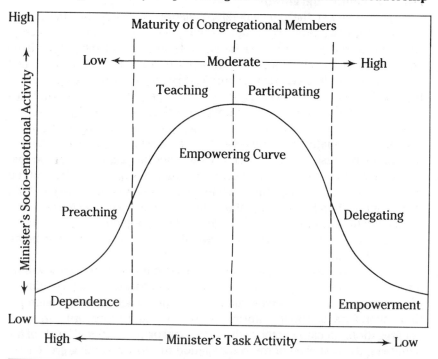

*This figure is a revision of the Situational Leadership Model presented in "The Impact of Situational Leadership in an Educational Setting," Paul Hersey, Arrigo Angelini, and Sofia Carakushansky, in *Leadership and Social Change*, 1983, edited by William Lassey and Marshall Sashkin.

do so. The participating minister encourages congregational members to begin doing things their own way and in the process further reduces the amount of directive task activity given in their behalf. Participating ministers encourage their congregational members to be their own persons, allowing them to learn, to make mistakes, while the minister walks alongside offering support when needed.

The *delegating* leadership style is for high maturity congregational members who are both able and willing to perform ministerial tasks as a natural expression of their Christian faith. In delegating responsibility and authority, leaders need not supply high levels of task or relational behavior. Continued high support could be taken as paternalism or a lack of confidence and thus hinder development. Ministers who are fortunate enough to be in delegating relationships with their congregational members are in a position where they in turn can be empowered. This is what James Macgregor Burns, in his Pulitzer Prize winning book, *Leadership*, calls transforming leadership—a relationship in which both the leader and follower are raised to new levels of maturity and growth.'[10]

Taken together, the four leadership styles of preaching, teaching, participating, and delegating constitute the complete continuum of leadership style. Ministerial leadership must incorporate all four leadership styles if the congregational members are to be brought to full Christian maturity and empowered for ministry. In some churches in which there is only a preaching leadership style, there will be a corresponding perpetuation of dependence of congregational members upon the preacher-leader. In congregations in which there is only preaching and teaching leadership, congregational members may never mature themselves to the point at which they too can share in the ministerial task of the church. On the other hand, a congregation that experiences only the delegating style of leadership may flounder without direction or mission, not being sufficiently grounded in the Christian faith and its application to life. It is in this collective sense, when *all four styles* of the leadership continuum are exercised in a congregation, that ministerial leadership is directly related to the potential development of Christian maturity in congregations.

We must realize, however, that ministers in different churches will be ministering to persons who possess different maturity levels. The readiness of a congregation for leadership maturity is dependent upon both congregational members' spiritual maturity and social cognitive maturity. In some congregations, because of the high educational or occupational levels of the members, the maturing of the congregation towards assuming greater responsibility for leadership tasks has great potential. In other congregations, the ministerial staff may need to go slowly in developing leadership among persons who have not had the benefit of being trained for personal responsibility, to say nothing of assuming the responsibility for someone else. In any growing congregation there will be a mixture of persons at different levels of Christian maturity. The discipling of Christians then must be geared to the potential of individual believers and not the organizational agenda of the leadership staff. At this point in our discussion, we need to look at the other dimension in our leadership model—complementarity.

Empowering and Leadership Complementarity

Leadership is a gift given to a particular minister for service in the body. Just as leadership research has demonstrated that no one leadership style can be thought of as the best or most effective style of leadership for every situation, any attempt to rank leadership gifts (or any other gifts within the church for that matter) must yield instead to the biblical model of complementarity

(1 Cor. 12:15–26). The body is made up of many parts, with not one being more important than the other. On the contrary, all four styles of leadership are important for the life of the congregation. Each style plays its critical role in the development of Christian maturity among congregational members and must be present for there to be complete and empowering leadership in the congregation. A church which is being led with only one style of leadership cannot increase the spiritual and leadership maturity of its members.

In a mass society such as exists today, Christian leaders who are especially gifted as good preachers can expect to successfully draw great crowds of people. If these ministers are equally gifted as teachers, modelers, and delegators, they can lead their congregational members into individual spiritual maturity, to the place where they themselves can empower others. Some good preachers may be equally gifted in each of these areas. However, the effort needed to move through all four stages with each member of a large congregation may require such ministers to spread themselves so thin that their total leadership effectiveness suffers or they wind up as candidates for "career burnout." On the other hand, some good preachers may not have these additional leadership gifts. If they seek to retain all of the leadership within their preaching style, they may successfully draw a large listening audience, but they may in actuality be retarding the spiritual development of individuals within their congregation. Due to their ability to attract great numbers of people, gifted preachers, more than any other leadership style, need to be sensitive to the complementary nature in which God intends for the church to function. In a society which takes great satisfaction from numbers, we need to keep in view the biblical model of leadership which measures the effectiveness of leadership by the maturity of the members. It is not the number of persons in the congregation that stands as the measure of effective ministerial leadership, but the number of persons who have been empowered for ministry and are now actively serving and leading themselves under a delegating style of leadership.

In order to make this happen it is necessary that the congregation include the full range of leadership maturity. If the preaching minister does not possess gifted abilities in teaching, modeling, and delegating, the congregation will need to identify persons in its midst who do have these skills. Complementarity requires that the congregation as a whole, not any single minister, have the complete continuum of leadership skills in order to empower its members. For most congregations this will involve a team of leaders rather than a single preaching minister. It is this team or community of leadership that provides the leadership needed to empower the members of the congregation and guarantees a continuity of leadership during staff transitions. In some churches the leadership team may be the ministerial staff. In other churches the team may be comprised of ministry staff and lay persons. In small churches where the preaching pastor does not possess gifts in all of the leadership styles it will be necessary for the lay members to provide the needed leadership for the congregation. Social science leadership theory helps us to understand the need to adapt our leadership style to the maturity of the members, but it is the biblical model of empowering leadership that raises up members gifted in each style of leadership to staff the complementary leadership team needed to empower members of the congregation for ministry.

Conclusion

In conclusion, we suggest that both contemporary leadership effectiveness theory and a biblical view of leadership empowering point to what we have called a complementary-empowering model of ministerial leadership. The varying levels of maturity to be found in any congregation require an adaptable leadership style that addresses each member of the congregation at his/her level of maturity and empowers that person for ministry and leadership in the church and community. The skills needed to lead persons at each of the maturity levels are not always given to every minister. Thus the complementarity of the body of Christ provides a variety of gifted leaders who together can empower believers for lives of service to the body of ministry in the community.

Notes

[1] M. Sashkin and W. Lassey. "Theories of Leadership: A Review of Useful Research," in *Leadership and Social Change*, edited by W. Lassey and M. Sashkin, 1983.

[2] R. Stogdill and A. Coons, eds. *Leader Behavior: Its Description and Measurement*, 1957. R. Blake and J. Mouton. *The Managerial Grid*, 1964.

[3] D. G. Bowers and S. D. Seashore. "Predicting Organizational Effectiveness with a Four-Factor Theory of Leadership," in *Administrative Science Quarterly*, 1966. 11:238–63.

[4] F. E. Fiedler. *A Theory of Effective Leadership*, 1967.

[5] P. Hersey and K. Blanchard. *Management of Organizational Behavior: Utilizing Human Resources*, 1982.

[6] W. Warner Burke. "Leadership as Empowering Others," in *Executive Power: How Executives Influence People and Organizations*, edited by S. Srivastva, 1986.

[7] M. Sashkin. "Participative Management Is an Ethical Imperative," in *Organizational Dynamics*, 1984, 12(4), 4–22.

[8] R. Greenleaf. *Servant Leadership*, 1977.

[9] P. Hersey. *The Situational Leader*, 1984. P. Block. *The Empowered Manager*, 1987.

[10] J. M. Burns. *Leadership*, 1978.

References

Blake, R., and Mouton, J. *The Managerial Grid*, 1964.

Block, P. *The Empowered Manager*, 1987.

Bowers, D. G., and Seashore, S. D. "Predicting Organizational Effectiveness with a Four-Factor

Theory of Leadership," in *Administrative Science Quarterly*, 1966. 11:238–63.

Burns, J. M. *Leadership*, 1978.

Burke, W. W. "Leadership as Empowering Others," in *Executive Power: How Executives Influence People and Organizations*, edited by S. Srivastva, 1986.

Fiedler, F. E. *A Theory of Effective Leadership*, 1967.

Greenleaf, R. *Servant Leadership*, 1977.

Hersey, P. *The Situational Leader*, 1984.

Hersey, P., and Blanchard, K. *Management of Organizational Behavior: Utilizing Human Resources*, 1982.

Sashkin, M. "Participative Management Is an Ethical Imperative," in *Organizational Dynamics*, 1984 12(4), 4–22.

Sashkin, M., and Lassey, W. "Theories of Leadership: A Review of Useful Research," in *Leadership and Social Change*, edited by W. Lassey and M. Sashkin, 1983.

Stogdill, R., and Coons, A., eds. *Leader Behavior: Its Description and Measurement*, 1957.

RESEARCH ON TEACHING FOR CHRISTIAN EDUCATION

RODNEY B. MCKEAN
Associate Professor of Educational Ministries
Azusa Pacific University

Article from *Christian Education Journal*

We all agree that teaching is an essential element for our task in Christian education. Recent books by Marlene LeFever and Howard Hendricks are further evidence of both our interest in teaching and our need to focus on it more carefully. Historically, teacher training and teacher preparation were the foundations of our Christian education endeavor. It used to be fashionable to study Jesus as the "Master Teacher."

But in the last couple of decades our field has been dominated more by an emphasis on "good curriculum" than on "good teaching." Why has this shift occurred? Why do we put more time and effort into looking for good curriculum materials (or complaining about the lack of them), than in concentrating on the quality of teaching that can overcome our dissatisfactions with the available curriculum materials? It may be that we have become lazy, and have allowed our ideas about teaching to be dominated by some accumulated assumptions about what is good teaching. What are some of these assumptions, and what are their origins?

Common Assumptions about Teaching

One common assumption about teaching is that teaching results from the acquisition of good content. This has been the common assumption of higher education for centuries. It is usually assumed that a person who has an advanced degree in chemistry is automatically the best person to teach chemistry. This assumption has also been borrowed in the ministry. It has been assumed that the person who knows biblical literature, biblical languages, and church history and doctrine will be the best person to pastor a church. In Christian education the assumption has been passed on that to be a good teacher a person needs to know about the Bible and Bible times—assuming that such knowledge will automatically make the person a better teacher.

Another assumption is that good curriculum materials will make a person a good teacher. In fact, when a person is recruited to be a teacher, one of the first questions that the person often asks is what curriculum materials are available. Or else the promise of material that makes teaching easy is usually part of the persuasion tactic in recruiting teachers. The companies that publish some curriculum material are often accused of trying to make their curriculum "teacher proof," meaning that they hope that good teaching will result merely from the effect of the curriculum materials themselves, regardless of who does the teaching.

Another assumption is that good teaching is the result of good character or a good personality. If a teacher is upright in character, it is sometimes assumed that he or she will be a good teacher. Or it is assumed that if a person has a bubbly personality, confidence, and get along well with kids, the person will make a good teacher. Even worse, we often recruit teachers who are merely "willing" to teach, out of a sense of duty or out of a love for kids. Related to this is another assumption that some people are just natural born teachers.

What are the origins of these assumptions? How reliable are these assumptions? How can we know if they are true or helpful? We can all come up with anecdotal stories in which we find examples and nonexamples of the truthfulness of these assumptions. We've each known some "natural born teachers," but can we rely on this to help us identify the best possible teachers? Stories and isolated past experiences aren't going to be the best source or the best justification for ideas about what constitutes good teaching. If we want to know what good teaching is, we are going to have to study teaching.

Research on Teaching

Theories about teaching that emerge from and are tested by research on teaching are likely to be the most reliable. One of the first major efforts to organize research on teaching was Gage's *Handbook of Research on Teaching* published in 1963. Since then research on teaching has become more diversified, more sophisticated, and more useful. Today, research on teaching is a major point of interest for many professionals, and for a large national organization like the Institute for Research on Teaching at Michigan State University.

It can be very helpful to those involved in Christian education to become familiar with some of the current areas of focus in research on teaching, some of the most consistent findings of research on teaching, the types of research methodologies that are being used, and the problems in research methodology. It will also be important for us to discover the implications of these research issues, findings, methods, and problems for our tasks as teachers of Christian education, and as teachers of teachers in the Christian education ministries of the church.

Research Topics and Findings

Though many different aspects of teaching have been or are being studied through research on teaching, the following three may have some of the most immediate connections to our tasks of Christian education: teacher effectiveness, teaching styles, and teacher decisions/planning.

Teacher effectiveness. Research on teacher effectiveness usually focuses on those things that teachers do to improve student learning. In the past fifteen years many studies have focused on different aspects of such research. In her review of research on teacher effectiveness, Amy Driscoll outlines the research topics as follows: academic learning time, classroom management, active teaching, praise, and questioning strategies.[1]

In Allan Ornstein's review of the research on teaching effectiveness, he summarizes the following elements of teaching as having a positive effect on student achievement: classroom management techniques, direct and structured learning strategies, academic focus and student opportunity to learn, flexibility in instructional planning and variability in media and methods, and democratic, "warm" behaviors, as well as teacher enthusiasm and teacher acceptance of students' ideas and feelings.[2]

Thomas Good summarized the findings of research on teacher effectiveness by offering the following conclusions:

(a) elementary school teachers do exert differential effects upon student achievement; (b) classroom management skills are exceedingly important; and (c) a pattern of teaching behavior called *direct instruction* seems to be a useful heuristic for describing effective elementary classroom teachers.[3]

David Berliner summarized the research by identifying such areas as the teacher's use of time, monitoring student work, structuring instructional activities, and use of questions.[4] Specific focus within teacher effectiveness has been given to such topics as time-on-task studies, cooperative learning, and intentional ways to structure teachers' instructional behavior such as the teaching plan often referred to as Hunter's Seven Steps.

Teaching styles. Research on cognitive styles has existed for over thirty years. Some of the earliest research on cognitive style suggested that a person's cognitive style influenced how that person learned. Now such research is also being used to study how people teach. Three different ways of looking at cognitive style and teaching style appear in the research.

Perhaps the best known and most influential research is that pioneered by H. A. Witkin and his associates. Their research indicates that there are patterns in the ways a person perceives information from his environment. These patterns are not related to a person's ability to learn, but to the way he learns and to the kinds of teaching to which he responds most effectively. Witkin and his associates have focused on field-dependent and field-independent cognitive learning styles. Witkin says that the evidence from educational research

> indicates, first of all that whereas relatively field-dependent teachers favor teaching situations that allow interaction with students, more field-independent teachers prefer teaching situations that are impersonal in nature and oriented toward the more cognitive aspects of teaching.[5]

Another way of understanding learning styles was developed by Kolb over a dozen years ago. Though his work has identified four different styles of learning, his emphasis was never on matching teaching styles with learning styles as much as making sure that teaching engaged learners in all four styles of learning.

More recently interest has focused on a personality typing scheme focusing on the Myers-Briggs Personality Type indicators. The personality type indicators are based upon some Jungian ideas about personality. The focus is upon four areas of personality described by a pair of opposite traits: extrovert—introvert; sensing—intuitive; thinking—feeling; and perceiving—judging. In reviewing and summarizing research about teaching styles and cognitive style, Kagan reports:

> Empirical research has, in fact, supported the theoretical connection between teacher behavior and cognitive style by revealing some consistent relationships between scores on the Myers-Briggs scales and a variety of teaching attitudes and behaviors. In general, results have indicated that higher scores on thinking or judging scales are associated with a tenuency to teach in structure, teacher-controlled formats, while higher scores on the intuition, feeling or perceiving scales are associated with more flexible and spontaneous teaching styles.

It should be noted that research on teaching styles is not very helpful for studying teacher effectiveness. This kind of research does not necessarily tell us what kind of teaching is better, or what kind of teaching a person should do. Rather, it helps to explain or predict why some teachers teach the way they do and why other teachers teach differently.

Teacher decisions. David Berliner indicates that much of what influences what a teacher does in the classroom are the decisions that the teacher makes before, during, and after times of instruction.[7] Driscoll reviewed the research by R. J. Shavelson and others on teacher decisions and teacher thinking and concluded that "teachers' beliefs about teaching affect their instructional decisions and that decision making may be the most basic teaching skill."[8] In arguing for a new approach to the methodology of research on teaching, A. S. Bolster refers to research findings which emphasize the importance of the teacher as a "situational decisionmaker."[9]

In their review of the research on teacher decisions and teacher thinking, Clark and Peterson organize the focus of the research into three areas:

(a) teacher planning; (b) teachers' thinking during the process of teaching—teachers' interactive decisions; and (c) teachers' theories and beliefs—including teachers' attributions for the causes of students' performance.[10] Some of their findings indicate that experienced teachers do very little planning on paper, and very little step-by-step planning. Rather, they are often guided in the actual instruction by a broad mental vision of what they think is important. In response to this finding they comment:

> The modest-to-significant roles of lesson planning reported by experienced teachers is interesting. Lesson planning is one type of planning that is addressed directly in all teacher preparation programs. Yet lesson planning is rarely claimed as an important part of the repertoire of experienced teachers.[11]

Research Methodologies and Problems

Much of the research on teacher effectiveness has used methodologies borrowed by the social sciences from the natural sciences. Some of them use control groups in their experimental design and statistical procedures such as t-tests or factorial designs. Many, however, use more simple correlational designs. In summarizing such research methods, Karen Zumwalt writes:

> Many researchers have focused on explaining the relationship between classroom processes (usually teacher behavior) and educational outcomes (usually measured by achievement tests). Dubbed "process-product" research, this research employing the scientific paradigm has generally, but not exclusively, relied on quantitative methods to yield correlational findings.[12]

Because of a desire for scientifically rigorous studies, often research on teacher effectiveness has limited its focus to an individual or a narrow set of teacher behaviors, and to summative student achievement measured by higher than expected group gains on standardized achievement tests. Because of the scientific research designs used in such research, the "treatments" that are administered are often done for only a short period of time ranging from a few class sessions to a few weeks. And then such treatments only account for a fraction of the teachers' behavior during the time period, and thus, a fraction of the learning experiences of the students. Another problem is that real-life teaching does not consist of discrete teaching behaviors, but of a mosaic of the teacher's personality, preparation, skills, and available resources. In some cases the treatments are administered and tested in laboratory or simulated settings, which are even less like real teaching.

Methods of quantitative data collection in addition to standardized achievement test scores include psychological (self-report) inventories, descriptive questionnaires, surveys and other schedules for quantifying observations, and Likert-type scales of attitudes, preferences, and beliefs.

Berliner raises concern over the helpfulness of this approach to research on teaching:

> A good deal of the research cited has been derived from correlational studies or studies of single variables as investigators searched for some effect on student attitude, behavior, or achievement. Teaching—real, live, honest-to-goodness teaching—is extremely complex and extremely dynamic. A very legitimate concern, then, is whether the factors mentioned are found to hold up *in situ.*[13]

Berliner goes on to identify some findings that do hold up in real teaching, and some that do not. But Bolster is not as optimistic as Berliner tries to be. He is afraid that much research can't have a positive effect on real teaching because

> researchers and school teachers adopt radically different sets of assumptions about how to conceptualize the teaching process. As a result, the conclusions of much formal research on teaching appear irrelevant to classroom teachers—not necessarily wrong, just not very sensible or useful.[14]

One response to the limited helpfulness of the scientific/quantitative approach to research on teaching has been to call for a more qualitative approach. Rogers calls for such qualitative and naturalistic approaches, and suggests how it can be done, and done rigorously.[15] Qualitative and naturalistic research is research that is done in real-life settings, observing real people doing real things, and trying to capture the full essence of what is going on—not merely those specific elements that can be parsed out and measured. Elliot Eisner expresses the need for such research by saying:

> If educational research is to inform educational practice, researchers will have to go back to the schools for a fresh look at what is going on there. We will have to develop a language that is relevant to educational practice, one that does justice to teaching and learning in educational settings, and we will need to develop methods of inquiry that do not squeeze the educational life out of what we study in such settings.[16]

One of the most helpful effects to come out of research on teaching, and especially a call for more qualitative and naturalistic approaches to research on teaching, is that it will help us focus more carefully on teaching itself. One of the most common practices in education, and maybe one of the most common weaknesses in education, is to assume that once we can define good learning, we automatically know what good teaching is. The field of education has been dominated in the past twenty-five years by educational psychology giving us theories of learning and human development. But these theories do not constitute theories of teaching, and cannot tell us what good teaching is. If we want to better understand teaching, then we have to study teaching itself. Qualitative and naturalistic approaches to studying teaching may come the closest to studying teaching as it actually exists.

Meaning for Christian Education

What does all of this mean for the task of Christian education? First of all it should be clear that teaching isn't just something that falls from the sky, or automatically emerges once we've signed up people and given them "the materials." Teaching is a complex enterprise that can be studied and can be done more effectively when adjustments are made in light of the findings of studying it. It is time for Christian education professionals to renew their interest in qualitative teaching and to respond to that renewed interest by some intentional research on teaching.

We can begin by asking what is effective teaching in Christian education. The answer will depend upon what important outcomes are identified, but the following could certainly be included: (a) biblical and doctrinal knowledge: (b) concept formation; (c) attitude change and development; (d) personal adjustment and interpersonal relationship skills; (e) ministry and service skills and abilities; and (f) character development. It is likely, based upon existing research, that different types of teaching will be effective for different types of desired outcomes. It no longer makes sense to believe that there is one best approach to teaching in Christian education, but only good research will tell us when to do what.

We can also begin studying what teachers in Christian education are actually doing. How do they spend their time? How do they organize their activities? How do they decide what to do, and what influences them to make those decisions—their personalities? Their learning styles? Or their beliefs about teaching, learning, or Christian living? Most of us are probably ignorant of how our current teachers prepare for teaching, use their time and resources during teaching, and evaluate the effectiveness or appropriateness of their planning and teaching. How can we help people do something better if we don't know what they are doing in the first place?

Another area of research on teaching for Christian education should focus on selecting, training, and supervising people who are teachers. How do teachers develop the skills and attitudes necessary for effective teaching? Are some kinds of people more likely than others to develop the necessary skills and attitudes? Are we getting the best possible people to be our teachers?

It is time for Christian education professionals to go beyond our debates about learning theories, cognitive, moral, and faith development, and psychological and sociological descriptions of spiritual maturity, to some intentional study of teaching. We have been long on prescriptions about teaching based upon our pet theories, or our pet curriculum designs, or our favorite organizational structure for educational ministry. We need more descriptions of what is really going on, what it yields, and how it can be improved. The only "implications" for teaching that exist are implications that come from the study of teaching. Suggestions that come from theology, psychology, sociology, or history provide only hypotheses for research on teaching. The task is ours to define and help provide the implications that will make us more effective in the central task of Christian education.

Notes

[1] Amy Driscoll, "The Influence of Research on Effective Instruction on Student Teachers' Thoughts and Behaviors," presented to the American Educational Research Association, San Francisco, 1986.

[2] Allan C. Ornstein, "Research on Teaching: Issues and Trends," *Journal of Teacher Education*, November–December 1985, p. 28.

[3] Thomas Good, "Teacher Effectiveness in the Elementary School," *Journal of Teacher Education* (vol. 30, 1979), p. 52.

[4] David C. Berliner, "The Half-Full Glass: A Review of Research on Teaching," *Using What We Know About Teaching* (Alexandria, VA: Association for Supervision and Curriculum Development, 1984), pp. 51–77.

[5] H. A. Witkin, et al., "Field-Dependent and Field-Independent Cognitive Styles and Their Educational Implications," *Review of Educational Research*, vol. 47 (Winter 1977), pp. 27–28.

[6] Dona M. Kagan, "Cognitive Styles and Instructional Preferences: Some Inferences," *The Educational Forum*, vol. 51 (Summer 1987), p. 395.

[7] Berliner, *op. cit.*

[8] Driscoll, *op. cit.*

[9] A. S. Bolster, "Toward a More Effective Model of Research on Teaching," *Harvard Educational Review*, vol. 53 (March 1983), p. 306.

[10] Christopher M. Clark and Penelope L. Peterson, "Teachers' Thought Processes," *Handbook of Research on Teaching* (American Educational Research Association, 1986).

[11] Ibid., p. 260.

[12] Karen K. Zumwalt, "Research on Teaching: Policy Implications for Teacher Education," *Policy Making in Education, NSSE Yearbook* (Chicago: The National Society for the Study of Education, 1982), p. 217.

[13] Berliner, *op. cit.*, p. 71.

[14] Bolster, *op. cit.*, p. 295.

[15] Vincent R. Rogers, "Qualitative Research—Another Way of Knowing," *Using What We Know About Teaching* (Alexandria, VA: Association for Supervision and Curriculum Development, 1984), pp. 85–106.

[16] Elliot W. Eisner, "Can Educational Research Inform Educational Practice?" *Phi Delta Kappan*, March 1984, p. 451.

CALVIN'S CONTRIBUTION TO
UNIVERSAL EDUCATION

IVAN L. ZABILKA
Educator
Lexington, Kentucky

Article from *The Asbury Theological Journal*

John Calvin's contribution to the development of common schools and universal education has been neglected by secular historians of education. He used religious motivations to bring about the civil promotion of education, yet scholars have been distracted from his significance. His theological system, his role in promoting French literary style, and his contribution to the relation of church and state have drawn attention away from his educational system. Another cause of neglect is that Luther was a more prolific writer upon educational topics, implying to some investigators a greater concern than Calvin's, but such is not the case. Luther was active in defending education against radical reformers who wanted to destroy all education to rid themselves of the supposed blight of Catholic education, while Calvin invested himself in developing a functioning educational system in Geneva. This concern was carried forward in the emerging education centers of the Reformed Church in Germany, particularly at Heidelberg and Herborn, where educational programs were fashioned with reference to the irenic, evangelical rubrics provided by the *Heidelberg Catechism* (1563).[1] Finally, the achievements in education of the French, Dutch, Scottish, and English reformers caused attention to be directed away from Calvin and the Genevan schools, even though the leaders of these movements were often trained in Geneva. Thus, at every point Calvin's contribution has been eclipsed.

Calvin's attitudes toward education are not presented in philosophical essays like those of Luther, but in working civil documents. I will survey these Genevan records, describe the schools founded under Calvin's guidance, and evaluate his influence upon education in other countries, especially during his own era.

Education for Leadership

Calvin's educational intentions are discerned in the first edition of the *Institutes of the Christian Religion*, the catechisms, the formal organization of schools, and were influenced by Johann Sturm and Calvin's own education.

The first edition of the *Institutes*, consisting of six brief chapters, appeared in 1536. Calvin's intent for the first edition was a simple introduction to the Christian faith that could serve to instruct anyone who wished to learn.[2] In subsequent editions the work gradually lost its teaching intent and became the comprehensive summary of his theology that resulted by 1560. The final form of the *Institutes* did contain his discussion of the teaching attitude of the minister.[3] Teachers, in Calvin's opinion, should exhibit kindness, prudence, and skill in giving advice. Advice-giving imparted information and supported the authority of church and state. He indicated that arrogance could not be a part of instruction, and harshness reduced its value.[4] Calvin emphasized that teachers must be honest, sincere, and an example to their students, both as scholar and spiritual leader. Wit and reason were presumed helpful. False teachers were a curse from God upon the authorities who failed to select well.[5] Even though these characteristics marked the minister as teacher, one may assume that such attitudes did apply to those who were directly involved in teaching activity. The emphasis upon kindness, while in contrast with Calvin's popular image, was consistently present in his attitudes toward children as learners.

While the *Institutes* provides some understanding of his view of teachers, the catechisms are more helpful with his methodology. The people of Geneva requested guidance in correct theology through the formation of a catechism, having seen the effectiveness of Luther's use of it. In February 1537, prior to his and Guillaume Farel's expulsion in April 1538 following their first efforts at reform, Calvin presented a long and tedious catechism to the city officials for use in the instruction of children and citizens. This initial effort serves primarily to illustrate Calvin's misapprehension of the amount that children or adults could master.[6] During his exile from Geneva, Calvin came under the influence of Johann Sturm in Strasbourg, who had begun the most effective gymnasium of the day. He invited Calvin to deliver theological lectures. While engaged, Calvin apparently learned from Sturm's example and from the limitations of his students. When he later presented a revised catechism in 1541, it was simplified and shortened. It still ran to more than fifty modern book-sized pages, but the questions and answers were short, and the student had fifty-five weeks in which to master it.[7] Clearly, the child or citizen had to be able to read the vernacular in order to master the expected theology, thus, elementary schools were necessary.

Calvin's progress in producing better catechisms points to the importance of brevity, clarity, and simplicity in educational methods, a perspective that appeared in his other writings as well. In a letter to Simon Grynacus he stated that the successful interpreter of the Scriptures, a major objective of education, must be clear and brief.[8] The interest in brevity and simplicity extended to any teaching tool, including writing, and consequently Calvin accused other commentators upon the Scriptures of being "much too clever."[9] Calvin's intent is refreshing, although his standard of brevity and simplicity is removed from that of the current century.

Several histories of education assume that Calvin was the originator of the Genevan schools, since he formed the "College" and the "Academy." The honor of founding the vernacular schools, however, must go to the reformers and city fathers responsible for leading Geneva from Catholicism prior to Calvin's arrival. The *Registres du Conseil* indicate that by unanimous action on May 21, 1536, provision was made for the education of all children, with the girls in separate schools, under the leadership of Antoine Saunier.[10] All parents were obligated to send their children, with instruction provided free to the poor. Calvin did not alter the plan of the vernacular schools and sought to aid in the selection of teachers. He was able late in life to aid in reorganizing them more efficiently, as will be seen.

An even more pressing concern to Calvin was the instruction of the people of Geneva in "correct" theology. The content of such "correct" theology was defined by Calvin in terms of a pious, reverential "knowledge of God and man," that had been disrupted by the fall into sin. Hence, the didactic character of theology was integral to all genuine Christian faith.[11] In Calvin's Geneva, education was subordinated to and motivated by this spiritual concern, a concern which appeared in the "Articles concerning the Organization of the Church and of Worship," presented on January 16, 1537.[12] In these Calvin claimed that preservation of pure doctrine necessitated that ". . . infants of tender age be so instructed that they be able to give reason for the faith. . . ." Such instruction was to be from "hand to hand" and "father to son," based upon a prepared catechism. At this time Calvin was emphasizing individual learning and the role of the family in instruction, but it was not working, for he also criticized parents who failed to do it, and recommended that a catechism be adopted and regular teaching instituted, events which transpired by 1541.

The *Ecclesiastical Ordinances* of September and October of 1541 provide direct evidence of Calvin's influence.[13] In the "four orders of office" for the government of the church, the second listed is "doctors" or teachers. The salary of these officials was to be provided by the state. Their role was clearly defined, so that they did not replace the teaching function of the "ministers" entirely, for the latter were responsible for the mid-Sunday instruction of young children in the catechism. Parents were required to bring their children to the classes.

The principal function of the teachers was the instruction of the faithful in true doctrine, not for citizenship or the Renaissance man. For this purpose lecturers in theology were appointed, one for each testament. Since profit from the lectures would result only from proper instruction in the languages and the humanities, a "college" for the preparation of ministers and civil officials was necessary. The form this took was a middle school, above the vernacular schools and eventually preparatory to the "academy" or University of Geneva. Calvin further recommended the payment of the vernacular school teachers from civil funds again, and the continued separation of girls from boys. The teachers were to be subject to the same discipline as the ministers.[14]

This brief presentation of the schools in 1541 does not give a full picture of their nature and development, but it does demonstrate that Calvin was active in promoting them at an early date. While all children attended the vernacular schools, it is apparent that a more select group was educated in the College for the ministry and leadership of state. There is no mention of girls, which is expected since they could not hold the positions for which the schools prepared. Even at this early date potential was developed for training more than just local leadership.

In 1547 Calvin returned to the problem of instruction in the catechism, when adjustments had to be made for the differing situation in the country churches around Geneva. The "Ordinances of the Supervision of Churches in the Country," which appeared on February 3, 1547, made provision for instruction in the catechism every other week in each church since the ministers had two churches.[15] Additionally, fathers were liable for their children's penalties for failure to appear at catechism.

As noted, the College was authorized in 1541, and opened shortly after. The next notice of activities related to the College appeared on the fifth of June, 1559, in the "Ordre du College de Geneva," a document which made formal the methods developed over the years. The final paragraphs discussed education beyond the seven levels of the college, and gave formal date to the founding of the University of Geneva. Combination of the schools in this document has caused some confusion of the two among educational historians.

A summary of the contents of this document does much to clarify the nature of Calvin's educational theory for the middle and upper levels. The basic classicism of the content of the instruction will be apparent.

The *Ordre* stipulated that the teachers would elect the rector who would then be approved by the ministers and the Council. (Geneva had three councils: The Little Council, The Sixty and The Two Hundred. Which was intended is not clear.) The teachers were also approved by the ministers and the Council. Students were to be present unless properly excused, circumspect in behavior, and diligent in the pursuit of learning. Rebelliousness and indifference led to punishment. Disputes were referred to the ministers and the Bible. In the treatment of students, teachers were expected to avoid crassness, rudeness, abruptness, and were alternatively to set a good example. They were to listen attentively to their students, and to remonstrate with their errors without losing control of the class.

Scholars were divided into four groups according to the section of the city in which they lived. They were also separated into seven graded levels. Lessons began at six in the morning in summer and seven in winter. Placements in the classes were determined by skill and not age. The hours for study, recitation, meals, and psalm singing were prescribed, including a 4:00 P.M. public session for the chastisement of those who failed assignments or broke rules. While the public reprimanding of disciplinary problems is poor from a modern perspective, the moderation of such methods from the usual corporal punishment of the day is apparent. Following this, the students recited the Lord's Prayer (in French), the Confession of Faith, and the Ten Commandments. On Wednesday they attended morning sermon and followed it with a question-and-answer session over the content. The Saturday schedule also varied with a special hour for student declamations, and a three-hour study of the catechism in the afternoon.

The curriculum was broadly defined for each year, with the seventh or lowest class expected to know the French and Latin alphabets and to be able to pronounce Latin and read French fluently. If the students were old enough at this level they also began to write.

The first half of the sixth class was spent on Latin declensions and conjugations. During the second half of the year they studied oratory and declamation, comparing French with Latin forms. Students were expected to begin speaking Latin among themselves.

The fifth class studied declamation and syntax using Virgil's *Bucolics*. Exercises in writing continued with simple original compositions expected by the end of the year.

The fourth class was expected to continue the study of syntax until it was mastered, using Cicero's *Letters* and various writings of Ovid. The study of Greek declensions and conjugations was begun.

On the third level emphasis was placed upon Greek grammar in a comparative approach to Latin, with attention to style. Materials used were Cicero's *Letters*, Virgil's *Aeneid*, Caesar's *Commentaries*, the *Parenthetic Orations* of Isocrates and other less-known works.

The second class studied history through the Latin works of Livy and the Greek works of Xenophon, Polybius, and Herodian. Propositional argumentation was studied through the *Paradoxes* and *Smaller Orations* of Cicero. The biblical book of Luke was read in the Greek.

The first class studied dialectics and rhetoric using Cicero's *Orations* and Demosthenes' *Olynthiacs* and *Philippics*. Special attention was paid to style and the Pauline Epistles were read in Greek. The objective of this curriculum was the thorough preparation of ministers to proclaim the "Word," in the best classical tradition.

The headmaster was responsible for maintaining the diligence of the faculty, and resolving minor quarrels. He was responsible for obedience to civil law, and the adherence to the articles of faith by the teachers. His term of office was for two years, and although not stated, it was renewable.

Further regulations governing students included an annual vacation of three weeks at the wine harvest, in addition to the first Friday of every month. The procedures for the promotion of students to the next level began three weeks before the first of May, when one of the academy professors proposed a theme in French for all students. The students had five hours to write upon the theme in Latin without the aid of books. The professors on the next level of the college evaluated the themes, and submitted them to the rector who made final judgments on the basis of the professor's recommendations. Prior to the first day of May, a conference was held with each student at which a vote was taken among the professors as to advancement. On May first, all the students and professors assembled at the Church of Saint Pierre, along with a councilman, the ministers and the regents of the school. The rector gave a lecture, after which the councilman congratulated those being advanced. The rector then offered words of encouragement to the students and they were dismissed for the day.

The next level upward was the "public lectures," which were the beginning of the academy. The ones giving these lectures were professors of Greek, Hebrew, and theology, whose obligations were discussed in the *Ordre*. They were expected to use Aristotle, Plato, Plutarch, and Christian philosophers. Students at this level were exposed to oratory, history, physics, and rhetoric. They had to register with the rector and confess their faith.[16]

From this summary, the importance of classical Greek and Latin authors is readily apparent. The role of declamation, debate, and rhetoric in the preparation of Calvin's ministers is also difficult to miss. The curriculum is similar to Sturm's at Strasbourg, for he also emphasized classical languages and literature, rhetoric, grammar, logic, and history. Sturm had less place for the sciences, and seems to have influenced Calvin, although Calvin did include the "physics of space."[17]

Calvin's own experience may have promoted the moderate discipline in the Genevan schools. He left his home in Noyon, France, in 1523 to enter the College de la Marche, at the age of fourteen. Classes began at five in the morning and continued with intermissions until eight in the evening. Calvin moderated these hours in Geneva. School started later and ended earlier with fewer intermissions. In addition to the more humane hours for young bodies, Calvin also worked in a more compact community where children lived with their parents, rather than in boarding schools, leaving the evening hours to the family. Albert Hyma indicated that "Corporal punishments were frequently inflicted [at the College de la Marche], even when the students were not guilty of serious offenses. . . ."[18] The exception to this pattern was Mathurin Cordier, or Corderius, who was a priest, humanist, and educator who taught Latin to the lowest level. He had originally taught at the upper levels, but he was so disappointed with the skills of those coming to him that he chose to inspire the beginners. He combined kindness with good teaching, avoiding corporal punishment. Cordier's educational principles involved grouping by age, gradual development, and emphasis upon the fundamentals.[19] All of these marked Cordier as a bit different from others, and although Calvin studied with him for perhaps no more than three months,[20] Cordier made such an impression that Calvin later secured him for Geneva, a further evidence of Calvin's satisfaction with moderation in the treatment of children. The only apparent difference is that Calvin grouped by skill where Cordier preferred age.

Following his brief time at the College de la Marche, Calvin moved on to the College de Montaigu, where he successfully studied the liberal arts and logic. He remained there approximately four years until 1527. He nominally studied for the priesthood by taking scholastic theology from Noel Beda. He also came under the influence of the reformers Nicholas Cop and Pierre Robert Olivetan, a distant relative.[21] Meanwhile, Calvin's father developed trouble with the Bishop of Noyon, to whom he was secretary. After completion of his initial studies his father told him to withdraw from Paris and study law, which Calvin obediently did. He moved to Orleans, where he studied law under Peter de l'Etoile, a successful case lawyer and logician, and under Melchoir Wolmar, another reformer. Upon completion of his studies, the university conferred upon him the doctor's degree. From Orleans, Calvin went to Bourges where he studied with Andrew Alciati, a well-known Milanese lawyer.[22] He returned then to Paris for further humanistic studies at the Royal College.[23] The humanism of his early and late education appeared in his love of the classics. The legal aspect of his education undoubtedly appeared in his love of order, in completeness of organization, and in the *Institutes* in many indirect ways that are beyond the scope of this study.

Throughout this discussion of Calvin's writings upon education, they have been presented as his alone. In actuality he always presented them to the city fathers as the work of the ministers, but Calvin was clearly the moving spirit. He may well have held first place in Geneva as far as influence goes, but he never sought public office, nor did he hold positions of superiority to the other ministers. Even in the schools, he placed others as rector and never held a position save as professor of theology. He may have been the leader in forming opinion, but he seldom left others completely behind. He emphasized the dangers of wealth and office, especially the generation of pride, which he associated with false teaching.[24]

This survey of Calvin's educational writing demonstrates that he wrote little upon the philosophy of education, save as it related to the formation of specific schools in Geneva. He was an organizer, with theory present only when the purpose of the schools was considered. He was primarily concerned with a method of organizing schools to accomplish the goal of training a Bible-reading laity and an effective clergy.

The Schools In Geneva

Having considered Calvin's perspective upon the education of children for leadership, it is appropriate to turn to the actual schools developed in Geneva and what they were able to accomplish. After a survey of the schools formed and the students who came to study, consideration will be given to the crucial issue for modern educators, that of ideological control. This issue will provide further insight concerning why Calvin has been neglected.

The development of the schools cannot be clearly understood without at least a preliminary glance at the relationship between the churches and the government in Geneva. Some difficulties in interpreting the significance of the schools are the result of a misunderstanding of the government of Geneva and Calvin's role in it. The ministers and a large segment of the population came to view Geneva as a theocracy where both the church and the state were responsible to God. Even though a majority view, the interpretation of the implications remained a chronic ground for differences of opinion that were often expressed actively and even violently. The ruling church body was the "Consistory," which included the company of the ministers and a dozen lay members selected from The Little Council or The Two Hundred.[25] The Consistory was the primary source of contact with the civil government, and there is no denying the influence that Calvin was able to wield in this body. However, political control always resided in the civil councils, that of The Little Council, The Sixty or Senate, and The Two Hundred, elected representatives of the people. The dominance of the ministers and Calvin among the members of these groups fluctuated with every election. Early efforts by the ministers met with stiff resistance, and Calvin was expelled for three years. After returning he was only once in that specific danger, but he did not always achieve his objectives. An example is the modification of who had final control over the selection of teachers. The Council of the Sixty changed the proposal of 1541 so that they had the final determination.[26] Other proposals were similarly revised and occasionally defeated. Calvin has been called the "undisputed" dictator of Geneva.[27] Any consideration of the activities of the Councils is sufficient to show that this is certainly an exaggeration, for Calvin was even reprimanded upon occasion. While he did seek to eliminate opposition, usually through persuasion, the effort was directed toward accomplishing what the most learned citizens of the city deemed best. While the number of citizens burned or expelled is appalling, it is necessary to keep in view that the civil authorities tried and executed such acts.

Similarly, Calvin did not exercise control over the schools, but responsibility was divided between church and state.[28] The state's responsibility was control and provision of support, while the education was definitely for the benefit of the church and only indirectly for the state.

As a result of this system of relations, the first schools established were the vernacular schools which were scattered about the city under the direction of Saunier, as previously noted. In these schools the children were taught to read and write French, and the rudiments of arithmetic necessary for daily transactions. After Calvin clearly understood that family teaching of the catechism was not effective, the schools also taught it.[29] The pastors recognized that success in developing a strong church was difficult with an uneducated laity.[30] This was the core of the contribution of Calvin and Geneva to education: the responsibility of the state to promote literacy by providing schools.

Calvin soon recognized the advantages of more advanced instruction for the pastors. He circulated a prospectus in 1537 for a higher school.[31] Following his expulsion and stay in Strasbourg, the proposal was revised in the light of his experiences with Sturm and presented in 1541, as previously noted. Under this regulation Sebastian Castellio revived the College de la Rive between 1542 and 1544.[32] The document of 1559 was a formalization or revision of the school system, including the reduction of the vernacular schools to four, and the founding of the Academy.

William Boyd indicated that the early progress of the College did not satisfy Calvin, so in 1556 he returned to Strasbourg to evaluate Sturm's school again with an eye to improving his own.[33] Calvin did not slavishly follow Sturm, for there were only seven classes instead of ten, and Calvin used the vernacular in the four lower classes, where Sturm had pressed for the exclusive use of Latin. The difference in number of classes may be explained by the fact that Sturm had no antecedent vernacular schools as Calvin did. While Cicero was still prominent at Geneva, Calvin placed less emphasis upon his works than did Sturm. During Sturm's lifetime his school overshadowed Calvin's efforts, but Calvin was able to achieve more lasting results.[34]

In 1558, the Council approved a plot of ground for a permanent location for the college and academy. Calvin solicited gifts and effectively encouraged the inclusion of the schools in wills. The partially completed building was dedicated and put into use under the forms of the 1559 *Ordre*, although it was not finished until 1563.[35] The academy was not divided into classes as the college was. There were no promotions and no degrees. Students were given attendance certificates and character references. Gifts and government funds allowed the instruction to be free. Arts and theology faculties existed in Calvin's day, and law and medicine were added after his death.[36] Before he died, Calvin was able to place the academy upon firm foundations.

The three levels of schools, the three separate founding dates, and different leaders such as Saunier, Castellio, and Theodore de Beza have caused confusion among educational historians. Other problems appear as well, for example, Frederick Mayer, in a standard history of education, listed the courses taught in the academy and included mathematics, although this was not mentioned in the *Ordre*, as was the rest of his list.[37] This may have resulted from Calvin's having a well-known mathematician on the faculty, even though he was teaching philosophy. Similarly, Calvin has often been gently chided for being deductive, even though Francis Bacon was four years old when Calvin died. Cordier has often been cited as rector of Geneva's schools, although there is no evidence that he ever had the position of leadership.[38] Discipline has been called severe in the schools, and it was, compared to the permissive classroom; but compared to the sixteenth century, it was mild.[39]

One of the most significant contributions that Calvin made to the schools was the recruiting of good teachers. Since the essential purpose of education in Geneva was the religious preparation of the people for service to the church and the city, the Ordinances of 1541 included the teachers under the same discipline as the ministers. They had not only to be adequate pedagogues, but theologically learned and orthodox as well. While this seems restrictive to the present age, it was not unusual then. In addition to Saunier and Cordier, another significant addition was Castellio, who served as headmaster of the college, but whose quarrelsomeness led to difficulties. He resigned because of an inadequate salary, and sought a pastorate. He was found to have a mildly heretical view of the Song of Solomon and the creed, and was denied the pastorate.[40] He developed a deep resentment toward Calvin, whom he felt was responsible for his problems, and in May 1544 he accused the ministers of being guzzlers and licentious, charges he could not prove. For this he was expelled from Geneva and his resentment turned to hate, leading to attacks from a distance over the following years.[41] Calvin exercised some moderation here, for the usual result of heresy was death. Fewer problems resulted from Calvin's efforts to staff the academy in the late 1550s. After failing to secure some outstanding French scholars he wished, growing problems at Lausanne led Beza to move to Geneva. A short time later Calvin gained several faculty from the academy at Lausanne who had resigned over Bern's assumption of secular authority over spiritual discipline.[42] These men were Calvinists and gave the academy an instant faculty of repute.

Opinion varies widely among historians regarding the number of students enrolled in the College and Academy in 1559. The uniform agreement upon the number from the rector's books is 162, but whether this is both schools or the academy alone is not clear. Four years later there were 300 enrolled in the academy and 1200 in the college. From these figures, some scholars have assumed extremely rapid growth. Alternatively, Paul T. Fuhrman claims that the 162 refers to the academy, and that there were approximately 800 enrolled in the combined schools.[43] William Monter supports this, indicating that there were 280 in the first class of the college, and Emanuel Stickelberger said there were 900 in the combined schools.[44] If these figures are correct, it would present a more realistic view of growth, doubling over a four-year period, and would also make provision for the fact that the college was functioning prior to 1559.

Prior to the reorganization, students were primarily from Geneva and France.[45] Following 1559, students began to come from all over Europe.

Many of them were excellent scholars who contributed to the intellectual ferment in Geneva, and then returned to influence their native lands. Among the most illustrious were John Knox, the reformer from Scotland; the tutor of King Henry IV of France; Thomas Bodley, later of Oxford University; Caspar Olivianus, co-author of the *Heidelberg Catechism* (with Zacharius Ursinus); and Marnix of Saint-Aldegonde, a leader of the Dutch revolt against Spain.[46] Indirect evidence of the penetration of Calvinistic thought through Geneva's schools appeared in a 1625 list of eminent men of Louvain, Belgium, one-fourth of whom studied in Geneva.[47]

The value of the schools has been variously assessed. J. G. Compayré has suggested that the College was little more than a school for the study of Latin.[48] Another has suggested that the primary function was to ". . . safe-guard and advance the interest of his particular church. . . ,"[50] raise the question of the significance of Calvin's progress toward free and useful education, and the issue of freedom of thought. John T. McNeill, one of the most prolific modern writers about Calvin, made a fine distinction, suggesting that while Calvin was not egalitarian he was not necessarily thereby anti-democratic. As a consequence, at the lower levels, the young had equal educational opportunity regardless of birth or wealth.[51] At the upper levels, since the education was for church and community leadership, women were not admitted, and the wealthy or distinguished had an advantage.

Another aspect of the freedom of thought is the assumed Protestant emphasis upon the right of the individual to interpret the Bible without the intermediation of the church. Such a manner of stating the problem is not quite accurate from Calvin's perspective. He emphasized the right of "under-standing" more than the right of "interpretation," and the necessity of cor-rect belief more than freedom of belief. Subordination did not disappear from Calvin's system; it was directed to correct belief and true spiritual teachers rather than to Rome. In the light of this, Calvin wrote little about education to "interpret the Bible," but he did emphasize the necessity of education so that the Bible could be studied and true interpretation recognized and under-stood.

The use of the catechism made clear that, for the majority of citizens, the learning of specific answers to specific questions was thought the most effective method of teaching the material needed for the defense of the faith. Luther had so ably demonstrated the effectiveness of the catechism, that both Calvinists and Catholics adopted the method with little comment.[52] The catechism, the *Institutes*, expulsions and persecution make clear that there were definite bounds to freedom of thought in Geneva.

Still another element in the limitation of freedom resulted from Calvin's view of man. From classical sources the Humanists had adopted the view that man could raise his estate through education. While Calvin had Human-ist influences in his own educational background, he apparently reacted against them in a considerable measure, moving beyond the Catholic view that man could be raised by grace administered through the Church, to a position where grace administered solely by the will of God was the only hope. For Calvin, education was not a panacea for solving the ills of the race, but it was still necessary to educate children concerning their evil state and their obligations to God. Since Calvin did not regard children as partakers of grace until they were able to comprehend it, they could be especially evil.

Because of Calvin's "failure" to understand education in a modern secular light, some have claimed that he did comparatively little to further education, and that he produced no "new education" independent of the clergy and its authority.[53] This supposedly resulted from a failure to fully grasp the meaning of private judgment, and thus Calvin failed to apply Protestant principles and was not fully Protestant.[54] This is one of the most glaringly antihistorical perspectives in modern educational writing, completely missing the theological consistency of Calvin, and implying that one is not Protestant if the concept of freedom does not coincide with that based upon four hundred years of additional thought about the problem.

Nicholas Hans made an apparent error on the opposite extreme; that is, too favorable to Calvin. He claimed that, while the Calvinist tradition was "essentially progressive," the appearance of rote use of catechisms in Scotland was evidence of degeneration ". . . into narrow and intolerant dogmatism."[55] This view ignored Calvin's and Luther's use and promotion of catechisms.

A final aspect of the issue of freedom of thought is the different interpretations of Calvin's willingness to allow the study of science. As previously noted, physics was present in the curriculum of the college, but science in the form of medicine did not enter the curriculum of the academy until after Calvin's death. Calvin opposed astrology and palmistry as inimical to seeking God's will by more orthodox means, but, while against some forms of superstition, he did not necessarily endorse science.[56] Some scholars have asserted that there was implicit in Calvinism an impulse toward free inquiry, not necessarily obvious in Calvin, but that found fruition in his followers, leading to the dominance of science by Calvinists as suggested by Robert K. Merton.[57] This is the natural result of the Calvinistic view of natural revelation combined with the right of the student to freely examine and prove all things, an idea that grew among Calvinists. Calvin did have the mathematician Tagaut as a faculty member shortly after the founding of the academy, although he taught philosophy. Copernicus was ignored, and John Holywood (Sacro Bosco) was the thirteenth-century astronomical authority at Geneva.[58] Calvin was more pre-Copernican than anti-Copernican in scientific matters. Science did not develop among the Calvinists until the sense of professionalism could be combined with the Calvinist sense of call in the following century.

The rejection of Calvin's views on method and freedom contributed to the neglect of his more important contribution to the practical provision of the means to enlist civil support for education.

A Spreading Influence

Whatever the limitations of Calvin and his thought, he firmly believed in spreading the gospel by educating learned and zealous pastors. This was the goal of Genevan education. The pastors were further taught, at least by example, that an educated laity was essential to the strong church. As the Calvinistic influence expanded, the growth of schools was not far behind. The Genevan pattern of educating citizens and ministers together predominated, until the university level became the normal pattern wherever Calvinistic thought permeated. While Calvinism is narrow by modern standards, it was based on the new learning of the time (save the sciences), and thus appeared dynamic and progressive.

France was the first objective of the Calvinists. Calvin never forgot his homeland, becoming a Genevan citizen only late in life. His first love outside Geneva was the French Reformed Church. The majority of early enrollees in Geneva's schools were French. These students returned to France to strengthen the growing Huguenot movement. Between 1555 and 1566 a minimum of 161 pastors returned to France from Geneva. The flood reached the point that Charles IX asked the magistrates to stop the supply, but his request was refused.[59] By 1559, when Calvin wrote the Gallic Confession for the use of the French Church, the French Protestants numbered over 400,000.[60] By 1561 there were 2,150 churches.[61] When Calvin died in 1564, a religious war was in progress and persecution growing. Huguenots were numerous, powerful, and in a position to dispute the kingdom with the Catholics. The Geneva-trained did not seem to advocate subversion, but persuasively argued the Reformed cause.

The high point of the penetration of Calvinism came with the Edict of Nantes of 1598. The Huguenots had religious freedom and control of some two hundred towns where they were able to develop the schools on the lowest levels.[62] Later they developed thirty-two colleges and eventually eight Huguenot universities, including the best known at Nimes, Montauba, and Saumur. The Geneva standards were observed: the poor and the laity were educated, synods made liberal appropriations for the universities, supervision of both faculty and students was present, and use was made of the Bible and the vernacular.[63] Following the revocation of the Edict of Nantes, the schools were suppressed and the Huguenots began to flee France. Education in France among the Protestants never became compulsory, as it had been in Geneva, on any basis other than a local one. Power was never concentrated enough for that. The impact upon France was great, but only temporary, and the longer lasting influences of Calvinistic education came from other countries.

Calvinism entered to a limited extent into Italy, Austria, Poland, Hungary, and Bohemia, but there is little available evidence that any lasting achievements were made in education. Slightly better results were obtained in the Palatinate, as has been noted, and some of the other German states. The Palatinate became significant primarily through the universities of Heidelberg and Marburg, the former the most significant Calvinist university other than Geneva. It excelled Geneva in law, medicine, and philosophy.[64] Frederick III, especially, promoted Calvinism at the university and was responsible for the authorizing of the *Heidelberg Catechism* in 1563,[65] as well as establishing the lower schools in each village. In some of the western German states, schools were established under the German Reformed Church, especially in such locations as Strasbourg, Nassau, Bremen, Hesse, Baden, and Anhalt.[66] These efforts were modest, and they were eventually absorbed into Lutheranism. An exception would be the academy at Herborn in Nassau, which attained the status of a university. Several precursors of modern "nonscholastic" educational theory taught there, including the Christian encyclopedist, Johann Alsted, and John Annos Comenius, the seventeenth-century intellectual leader of the Czech Brethren, who were the catalysts for igniting the national spirit of that land. Under the impact of Pietism, this school also became the center of the foreign missionary efforts of the German Reformed Church in the eighteenth century, especially through the ministry of Philip Wilhelm Otterbein.[67]

The major development of school systems came in Holland and Scotland, where compulsory education was adopted on a nationwide scale. In Holland, where some schools were in existence before the Calvinists came to power, the Dutch merely adapted these schools to their needs and expanded them to make them universal.[68] Freeman Butts, the educational historian, indicated:

> The Synod of the Hague in 1586 provided for the establishment of schools in the cities, and the Synod of Dort in 1618 provided for the establishment in all villages of schools under control of the civil magistrates, to give free instruction to the poor.[69]

The salaries of schoolmasters were paid with civil funds.

The middle class had assumed the leadership role in the struggle against Spain, and Calvinism was found to fit very well with their design on both political and religious freedom from Spain. As in Geneva, parents were called upon to read the Bible and teach the catechism to their children. The schools extended religious instruction as well as the more secular elements of education. Only Reformed Church members could instruct in the schools.[70] Pastors were made the superintendents of the schools and were required to inspect them regularly. Some of the provinces passed school taxes based on the number of eligible children, and not those actually attending. Eventually some pastors were designated as truant officers to make sure the children were in school.[71] Such were some of the familiar innovations that are now regarded as commonplace. They were developed in response to the needs of accomplishing the typical Calvinist objectives of educating the citizenry to carry out their task.

The Calvinist influence naturally reached the University, as Geneva became the example for the University of Leiden. Holland became the prime example of that wedding of Calvinism and middle-class mercantilism that reached fruition in New England. Comenius's views on raising sunken humanity through education found especially fertile soil in Holland as well.[72] Leiden was founded in 1575 and was quickly followed by Franeker, Groningen, Utrecht, and Harderwijk. All were Calvinistic centers and began to attract foreign students in the fashion of Geneva, especially as zeal declined in Geneva and the center of Calvinism shifted northward. Holland became the major center for the exporting of Calvinism.[73]

A national system of education also developed in Scotland. There the system was more under the influence of one man, John Knox, as had been the case in Geneva under Calvin. Consequently, education in Scotland seems more narrow then in Holland, and more subject to the limitations of Knox's influence. The Scottish schools were not unnoticed or failing in influence, but Scotland never became as great a center as Holland in propagating the faith. Part of this may also be that they were less a seafaring and trading people than the Dutch.

As in Holland, the Scottish schools did not have to be started. In the fifteenth century James I decreed the maintenance of public schools, but little had been accomplished. The catalyst for Scotland was the time John Knox spent with Calvin in Geneva around 1556.[74] Knox observed the relation between Church and State and the power of the school system capped by the academy. Such a system, he believed, would promote the reformation in his homeland as well. Knox advocated educating girls in the same schools, and the right of every child of talent to any level in the system.[75] In 1560 the General Assembly of the Presbyterian Church recommended to the Scottish Parliament that primary schools be established in connection with each church, and middle schools in every town of importance. Many years passed before this was realized, but in 1616, 1633, and 1646, laws were passed which provided for schools in each parish.[76] Knox had hoped to finance the schools from the old church and monastic foundations, but the nobles also had designs upon that income, and Knox was unsuccessful. Some schools were begun on the local level during his lifetime; he died in 1572, but the fruition came after his death. In 1567, Parliament caused the Presbyterian Church to appoint visitors or superintendents for the existing schools, and when the church was established in 1592, these visitors became responsible for licensing teachers.[77] Presbyteries received the right to tax for the schools in 1640, but exercised the right in only a limited fashion. In 1646 the erection of schools became mandatory, a law that was poorly observed.

The influence of Geneva was also apparent in the founding of the University of Edinburgh. Unlike the medieval autonomy of the faculty and nations of the medieval university, Edinburgh was placed under the civil administration and the ministers of the city. This meant much more control of the curriculum and faculty. The university was intended to serve the Church.[78] The success of the Scottish schools was much longer in coming than in Holland, and failed to have as much impact subsequently, but it is notable that the schools that were in existence were nearly as available to the poor as to the rich. There was an egalitarianism that is not quite so apparent in any other European country.

England was not without the Puritan influence stemming from the writings of Calvin. The academy was again the pattern for Emmanuel College at Cambridge. Calvinism made its initial inroads through the gradual adoption of Calvinistic ideas by Thomas Cranmer, and the subsequent influencing of the Church of England by Calvinism, culminating in the mild Calvinism of the Thirty-Nine Articles. The effects of Calvinism in England upon education of the very young were less spectacular than Holland and Scotland. England had much greater difficulty breaking away from the idea that education was for the wealthy. Religious strife also prevented the development of a comprehensive system at an early date.

While a survey of the influence of Calvinism upon American schools is clearly beyond the scope of this paper, it is necessary to note that the founding of schools in every parish in New England is a direct influence of the Calvinism of the early settlers, as were schools in the Carolinas where Huguenots were settling, and the schools of the Scotch Presbyterians in the central colonies. These early American colonists were influenced by what they had seen in Switzerland, Holland, and Scotland. The Dutch influenced the formation of the same kinds of schools in New Netherlands. The strongest schools, and those broadest based, tended to be in the colonies with the greatest Calvinist influence. The expansion of education clearly shows the remarkable influence of one man and the schools he promoted in Geneva.

Conclusion

Calvin was extremely influential in developing concepts of Church and State that provided the means of promoting universal elementary education. There is a correlation between the presence of Calvinism and the development of state-supported schools. Calvin wrote little on education, but provided an example of a working system that spread his theological ideas very effectively. His contribution appears to have been neglected or ignored because of the narrowness of his views and the unpopularity in more enlightened ages of the rigorous pursuit of theological and moral error in Geneva.

Notes

[1] J. S. O'Malley, *Pilgrimage of Faith: The Legacy of the Otterbeins*, ATLA Monograph Series, No. 3 (Metuchen, N.J.: Scarecrow Press, 1973) Part 1.

[2] J. K. S. Reid, "Introduction," *Calvin: Theological Treatises* (Philadelphia: Westminster Press, 1954), Volume 22 of the Library of Christian Classics, and Williston Walker, *John Calvin* (New York: Schocken Books, 1906, 1969), p. 137.

[3] John Calvin, *Institutes of the Christian Religion* in two volumes (Philadelphia: Presbyterian Board of Christian Education, 1936, 7th American ed.), trans. by John Allen.

[4] John Calvin, *Christian Theology: Selected and Systematically Arranged: With a Life of the Author by Samuel Dunn* (London: Tegg and Son, 1837), p. 332.

[5] Ibid., pp. 335, 342.

[6] Walker, *John Calvin*, pp. 192–94.

[7] Reid, *Calvin*, pp. 88–139.

[8] Simon Grynacus (1493–1541) was a Swabian scholar working in Heidelberg. Joseph Haroutunian and Louise Pettibone Smith, eds., *Calvin: Commentaries*, The Library of Christian Classics (Philadelphia: Westminster Press, 1958), 23:73.

[9] Ibid., p. 203. Commentary on 1 Thessalonians.

[10] Volume 29, Folder 112. Quoted in H. D. Foster, *Collected Papers* (Privately printed by the Scribner Press, 1929). See also John T. McNeill, *The History and Character of Calvinism* (London: Oxford University Press, 1954), p. 192, and Wilhelm Oachsli, *History of Switzerland 1499–1914* (Cambridge: The University Press, 1922), p. 152. Translated by Eden Paul and Cedar Paul.

[11] See John Calvin, *Institutes of the Christian Religion*, I, 1, I and III.

[12] John Dillenberger, *John Calvin: Selections from His Writings* (Garden City, N.Y.: Doubleday, 1971), pp. 48, 54.

[13] Ibid., pp. 233, 240.

[14] Ibid., p. 234.

[15] Ibid., pp. 77–78.

[16] John Calvin, *Calvini Opera*, vol. 10 (New York: Johnson Reprint Corporation, 1964), pp. 65–146.

[17] William K. Medlin, *The History of Educational Ideas of the West* (New York: Center for Applied Research in Education, 1964), p. 63.

[18] Albert Hyma, *The Life of John Calvin* (Philadelphia: J. P. Lippincott, 1944), pp. 20–21.

[19] Paul T. Fuhrman, *God-Centered Religion* (Grand Rapids: Zondervan Publishing, 1942), p. 26.

[20] Quirinus Breen, *John Calvin: A Study in French Humanism* (New York: Archon Books, 1968), p. 16.

[21] Franklin Charles Palm, *Calvinism and the Religious Wars Development of Calvinism* (Grand Rapids: Eerdmans Publishing, 1959), p. 10.

[22] Ibid., p. 11, and Dunn, *Christian Theology*, p. 12.

[23] A. Mervyn Davies, *Foundation of American Freedom* (New York: Abingdon Press, 1955), p. 27.

[24] Haroutunian and Smith, *Commentaries*, p. 381. Commentary on Micah.

[25] William Monter, *Calvin's Geneva* (New York: John Wiley, 1967), pp. 136–37.

[26] Hyma, *Calvin*, p. 68.

[27] Edward Hartman Reisner, *Historical Foundations of Modern Education* (New York: Macmillan, 1927), p. 435.

[28] James Hastings Nichols, *Democracy and the Churches* (Philadelphia: Presbyterian and Reformed Publishing, 1951), p. 237.

[29] R. Freeman Butts, *A Cultural History of Western Education* (New York: McGraw-Hill, 1955, 2d ed.), p. 213.

[30] Davies, *Foundation*, p. 25. The Catholic scholar Gerald L. Gutek expressed the objectives in the following fashion: "Calvinism also required a literate and educated laity. Since laymen were empowered as trustees of their churches, they were responsible for the collective consciences of their congregations" (*A History of Western Educational Experience* [New York: Random House, 1972], p. 127).

[31] Christopher J. Lucas used this document to indicate the "dual function" of schools as follows: "Although we accord the first place to the Word of God, we do not reject good training. The Word of God is indeed the foundation of all learning, but the liberal arts are aids to the full knowledge of the Word and not to be despised." Further, education is indispensable to guarantee "public administration, to sustain the Church unharmed, and to maintain humanity among men" (*Our Western Educational Heritage* [New York: Macmillan, 1972], p. 254).

[32] McNeill, *Calvinism*, p. 192.

[33] William Boyd, *The History of Western Education* (London: A. & C. Black, 1950, 5th ed.), pp. 199–200.

[34] Frederick Eby, *The Development of Modern Education* (New York: Prentice-Hall, 1934, 1952, 2d ed.), pp. 92–93.

[35] Henry R. Van Til, *The Calvinistic Concept of Culture* (Grand Rapids: Baker Book House, 1959), pp. 114–15.

[36] Hyma, *Calvin*, pp. 103–04.

[37] Frederick Mayer, *A History of Educational Thought* (Columbus, Ohio: Merrill Books, 1960), p. 191.

[38] Robert Whitfield Miles, *That Frenchman, John Calvin* (New York: Revell, 1939), p. 147. See also Breen, *Calvin*, pp. 156–57, and Frank Pierpont Graves, *A Student's History of Education* (New York: Macmillan, 1922), p. 131.

[39] Mayer, *Educational Thought*, p. 191.

[40] Dillenberger, *Calvin*, pp. 6–7.

[41] Roland H. Bainton, "New Documents on Early Protestant Rationalism," *Church History* 7 (1938): 180–83. See also Emanuel Stickelberger, *Calvin: A Life* (Richmond, Va.: John Knox Press, 1954), p. 101. Trans. by David George Geizer.

[42] Van Til, *Culture*, pp. 114–15.

[43] Fuhrman, *Religion*, p. 63.

[44] Monter, *Geneva*, p. 112, and Stickelberger, *Calvin*, p. 134.

[45] Van Til, *Culture*, pp. 115–16.

[46] Hyma, *Calvin*, p. 104.

[47] Ellwood P. Cubberly, *The History of Education* (Boston: Houghton-Mifflin, 1920), p. 331, n.

[48] Jules Gabriel Compayré, *The History of Pedagogy* (Boston: D. C. Heath, 1890), pp. 113, 528.

[49] Isaac Doughton, *Modern Public Education* (New York: Appleton-Century, 1935), p. 52.

[50] Arthur Dakin, *Calvinism* (Philadelphia: Westminster Press, 1946), p. 129.

[51] John T. McNeill, "The Democratic Element in Calvin's Thought," *Church History* 18 (1949): 167.

[52] John S. Brubacher, *A History of the Problems of Education* (New York: McGraw-Hill, 1947), p. 326.

[53] Edward J. Power, *Main Currents in the History of Education* (New York: McGraw-Hill, 1962), p. 316.

[54] Thomas Davidson, *A History of Education* (New York: Charles Scribner's Sons, 1900), pp. 182–83.

[55] Nicholas Hans, *New Trends in Education in the Eighteenth Century* (London: Routledge and Kegan Paul, 1951), p. 55.

[56] Robert Holmes Beck, *A Social History of Education* (Englewood Cliffs, N.J.: Prentice-Hall, 1965), p. 69.

[57] Robert K. Merton, *Science, Technology and Society in Seventeenth-Century England* (New

York: Harper & Row, 1938, 1970).

[58] Breen, *Calvin*, pp. 155–56.

[59] A. M. Fairbairn, *The Cambridge Modern History*, vol. 2 (New York: MacMillan, 1918), A. W. Ward, et al. eds., p. 373.

[60] C. Gregg Singer, *John Calvin* (Philadelphia: Presbyterian and Reformed Publishing, 1975), p. 21.

[61] Cubberly, *History*, p. 332.

[62] Reisner, *Foundations,* p. 438.

[63] Hans, *New Trends*, p. 154, and Cubberly, *History*, p. 333.

[64] Claus-Peter Clasen, *The Palatinate in European History 1559–1660* (Oxford: Basil Blackwell, 1963), p. 39.

[65] Dakin, *Calvinism*, p. 137.

[66] Butts, *History*, p. 208.

[67] O'Malley, *Pilgrimage of Faith.*

[68] Butts, *History*, p. 208.

[69] Ibid.

[70] Reisner, *Foundations*, pp. 440–41.

[71] Cubberly, *History*, p. 334.

[72] Eby, *Development*, pp. 267–68.

[73] Dakin, *Calvinism*, pp. 38–39.

[74] Stickelberger, *Calvin*, p. 142.

[75] Bratt, *Rise and Development of Calvinism* (Grand Rapids, Mich.: William B. Eerdmans, 1959), p. 202.

[76] Butts, *History*, p. 256.

[77] Reisner, *Foundations*, pp. 442–43.

[78] Ibid., p. 444.

HOME SCHOOLING: DIMENSIONS OF
CONTROVERSY, 1970–1984

MICHAEL S. SHEPHERD
Educator
Dallas Independent School District

Article from *Journal of Church and State*

Criticism of the public schools and alienation of parents from the public schools are among the most fundamental reasons why home schooling has gained growing public support since the late seventies. Gallup polls generally show a steady decline in public confidence in the public schools from 1969 to 1978. Declining discipline, busing for purposes of racial integration, and declining test scores have been cited by George Gallup as important alienating factors.[1] The United States Supreme Court, in *Pierce v. Society of Sisters* (1925), upheld the rights of parents to use private schools to educate their children.[2] However, many parents who were alienated from the public schools during the seventies and eighties could not afford to pay for a traditional private school while paying taxes to support the public school. As attorney Gerrit H. Wourmhoudt observed, "The *Pierce* decision was handed down . . . at a time when a great many Americans could afford to pay the price of both public and private education for their children . . . today relatively few parents can afford to shoulder the costs."[3]

The impressions of home-education advocate John Holt as well as the survey results of doctoral research by Gunnar Gustavsen of Andrews University of Michigan and Norma Jean Freeman Linden of East Texas State University all indicate that very few home-schooling families are affluent.[4] Thus, today's home-schooling movement may be partially explained as an attempt by families of modest means to provide the kind of education they feel their children need, which they are convinced the public schools not only deny but in significant ways openly subvert.

Home-tutoring advocates consistently argue that the academic quality of home instruction is superior to that of traditional classroom instruction. Standardized test results are frequently cited in court cases[5] and in comparative studies[6] as evidence of academic quality. The fact that students perform well on tests after home instruction while public school students often do poorly on the same standardized tests has been used to discredit arguments that there is a need for state control of home schools.[7] Also frequently cited are the personal success records of individual home-tutored students who have been admitted to such institutions as the University of California at

Berkeley[8] and Harvard University.[9] In some home-schooling court cases, however, prosecutors have argued that the very process of home education fails to allow adequate access to certified teachers, proper materials, or acceptable curriculum and thus fails to meet state requirements. In these cases prosecutors are often unable to argue successfully that the educational results are inadequate. Advocates of home schooling counter this by insisting that states put their own academic house in order in the public schools before trying to exercise control over private education.[10]

Partisans of home teaching list famous people in America who were taught wholly or for the largest share of the time at home. Presidents Woodrow Wilson, Franklin Roosevelt, and George Washington studied at home. Andrew and Jamie Wyeth did not attend school outside their artistic home; John Quincy Adams went directly from home to Harvard; and Frank Vandiver, a distinguished Civil War historian and until recently president of Texas A&M University, studied at home.[11]

Attorneys John Whitehead and Wendell Bird assert that "an important part of the educational effectiveness of home instruction is the proved tutorial method that it embodies."[12] The tutorial method, argues developmental psychologist and home-school promoter Raymond Moore, is superior to group instruction because a child has greater opportunity to get answers to his questions.[13] The classroom teacher, no matter how good he may be, simply does not have the time for individual concern and attention that a parent has.[14] Moore further holds that tutoring makes much more efficient use of time; indeed he insists that a child can learn more in two hours or less by being tutored than in a whole day of classroom group instruction.[15] A former school teacher who began home teaching her children stated that the "hurry up or busy work" atmosphere of group instruction is eliminated by home tutoring.[16]

Advocates hold that home schooling provides the child with time to explore and discover things on his own, something that may be lacking in a structured classroom curriculum. Holt argues that children are naturally curious learners but that formal schooling tends to stifle this natural learning instead of promoting it.[17] Creative, aggressive learners like junior playwright Ishmael Wallace of Ithaca, New York, appear to thrive in more relaxed, informal home settings with limited structure and plenty of time to read freely.[18] Alternative-school promoter Hal Bennet contends that individualized learning is more meaningful for the child.[19] Holt reiterates that the only true education is that in which an individual is motivated to learn for himself and the only true teachers are those who encourage the individual to pursue his interests.[20] Many educators concur that free exploration can benefit the child. Without the all-day regimentation of the classroom the child can become more of a free explorer and thinker than a restricted regurgitator of books, which to him are often more barriers than facilitators of learning. In an article in *Teachers College Record*, Moore summarizes the academic benefits of home instruction:

1. Home schools are characterized by parents who have enough concern for their children to take on the task of systematically teaching them.

2. Parents provide the partiality that young children need, but schools cannot allow.

3. Children thrive on routines that involve a few children who share the same family values.

4. A child in the home school daily experiences from ten to a hundred times as many personal adult-to-child responses as he would in a formal school; such responses—along with adult example—mean educational power far more than do books.[21]

It must be pointed out that some administrators and judges criticize the academic quality of home instruction, and the issue of teacher certification is a key element in this criticism. If a parent is not certified by the state, the argument goes, then the instruction offered is not sound.[22] Six states have passed laws requiring that a home tutor be certified to make a home school legally acceptable; other states simply require that instruction be given by a "qualified" person.[23] After observing a number of home schools, Brigham Young University researchers David Williams, Larry Arnoldsen, and Peter Reynolds concluded that parents often have doubts about their competency to teach. They may ask: "Do I know enough to teach my children?" or "Can I answer all of my children's questions?"[24] School district authorities or the state may answer "no" to these questions. Certified teachers are viewed as essential to the process of instruction by the National Association of School Boards.[25] Indeed, lack of certification has been cited as grounds for rejecting home schools in both Florida and Iowa.[26]

Court cases, of course, have established that noncertified teachers (parents) have often been successful in teaching their children at home using correspondence materials. In one case, the state attempted to prove that a correspondence school education was an "inferior education." The parents, a mother with a high school education and a father with a tenth-grade education, used a curriculum purchased from the Calvert School of Baltimore, which had begun its correspondence school in the early 1900s and was accredited by the state of Maryland. The state could not prove that the home-schooled children were receiving an inferior education. In fact, according to a newspaper report, "Lee Joyce Richmond, Associate Professor of Education at Johns Hopkins University, who tested the children, said Terry, Jr., a fifth-grader, was reading at a tenth-grade level and his sister, a second-grader, was reading at a fifth-grade level."[27] It was the judgment of the court that the

Calvert correspondence course was justified by its academic results and that the parents (uncertified teachers) were, indeed, competent.[28]

Some school administrators in the private "Christian school movement" also deny the quality of home tutoring. When Marge Schaeffer, for example, tried to take her third-grader out of church school, the principal was completely unsympathetic. In Schaeffer's words, "He said we were foolish, we were fanatical. He said we couldn't possibly offer our children the resources that the school had. If everybody did what we were doing, there'd be a bunch of fruits running around."[29]

Another housewife who followed Raymond Moore's advice and kept her son at home until age eight encountered opposition from a church school teacher.[30] The problems continued when the child entered the church school at age eight and was placed in first grade. The child, fortunately, was able to prove his ability to the teacher, who then allowed him to move quickly to more advanced materials.[31]

Arguments against home schooling may be inferred from court decisions against parents who simply failed to provide an acceptable curriculum. A number of courts have upheld state authority in setting minimal curricular standards. "Parents may not replace state educational requirements with their own idiosyncratic views of what knowledge a child needs,"[32] a federal court ruled in the case of *Scoma* v. *Chicago Board of Education* in 1974. In another case, children whose parents refused to send them to school because the school did not teach Indian heritage or culture but who provided no appropriate alternative to public schooling were declared "neglected children."[33] Another parent's complaint that the public-school curriculum ignored and belittled a student's Indian heritage was deemed an insufficient defense for an attendance law violation.[34] Not only did the home-school curriculum have to be "equivalent" but also approved by the superintendent of schools, according to a ruling in the case of *City of Akron* v. *Lane* in 1979.[35] On the other hand, a New York court deemed home instruction to be equivalent for a first-grade child but held that it might not suffice for children in "more advanced grades."[36] Thus, even while some home learning arrangements were approved, many judges gave the state, not the parents, the final word on what must be taught. Whether it is the parents or the states that actually set genuine academic standards is an open question.

Some contend that the home, not the conventional school, may promote the child's physical health just as it promotes his academic advancement. Moore has argued that starting school before eight to ten can damage a child's health. It can especially damage the eyes, explains Moore, because developmentally the child is not ready for "close work."[37] Some parents feel that discipline in school is not conducive to a child's good health, and one court allowed the children of one mother to be excused from truancy when she insisted that she did not want her children "beaten up" in school.[38]

Emotional health has sometimes been a factor in the removal of a child from the public school, and parents have recorded the improvement of their children's dispositions when they have been taken out of the classroom.[39] Holt has received letters from parents who have removed their children from the public school for health reasons. Excerpts from such letters follow:

> One day I decided to take L out of school (after weeks of one or two days per week attendance due to various "complaints"—headache, bellyache, sore throat).

> The changes that have occurred in Ishmael since we took him out of school have been unbelievable. Gone are the fits of temper that erupted every day around 4:00 p.m., gone are the headaches, the lines of tension around his mouth, and gone is his depression.

> Let me tell you what happened to our son after we removed him from a local public school's first grade last November. He stopped wetting his bed, he stopped suffering from daily stomach upsets and headaches, and he has not had a cold for six months, although he averaged one cold a month while attending school.[40]

Some home schools, to be sure, have been found inadequate in safeguarding the child's health. *West Virginia* v. *Riddle*, 1982, is a case in point. Here a West Virginia court failed to approve a home school in part because of the failure of the parents to provide proof of medical screening (vaccinations, for example). It was argued that the state's interest in the child's health was not being met.[41]

In addition to the debate about academic quality and the health of children, the social environment of the school as a place to learn has been both praised and maligned. Socialization, defined as contact with other children, is a major issue in the debate over the legitimacy of home schooling. It is argued that children taken out of school miss the opportunity to enjoy vital contacts with their peers: "Beginning home-schooling parents find that their children often miss their friends. The most important dimensions of school to some of these children were their peer relationships. Now that they are in home school, they feel lonely and sometimes have difficulty making friends with their own family members."[42]

There may well be serious damage to psychological or emotional growth, the argument continues; for example, the child may come to consider himself either inferior or superior if kept out of school. Indeed, schoolmen and psychologists argue the need for social contact with peers as a compelling reason for school attendance.[43] Schoolmen often state that children need to be out in the "real world" as represented by the school. One disillusioned veteran of overprotective parental concern, who was taught at home up through the eighth grade during the forties, agrees: "Sooner or later kids have to mix it up in society. I wouldn't say I regret being taught at home but Christianity has to be lived in the real world. You can't avoid the four-letter words forever."[44]

Home schoolers of the seventies and eighties reject the socialization argument. Moore distinguishes between positive socialization, based on a stable family life, and negative socialization, a me-first attitude, peer dependency and the rejection of family values. Schools tend to provide too much negative socialization, says Moore; and with preschooling unhealthy forms of peer dependency come at even earlier ages.[45] A survey of home-schooling parents reveals general agreement with Moore's view of socialization:

> This [socialization] is one of the major reasons that many home schoolers want to take their children out of the school. As one home-schooling mother said, "We want our children to be peer-independent." These parents want their children to be family-socialized and have their family be the center of the children's social world, at least until they are old enough to be on their own socially. This attitude does not preclude children from associating with other children; most parents do encourage social encounters, either with other home-schooling families or with neighborhood children . . . most home-school parents see home school as a means of protecting their young from the rivalry, ridicule, competition and conflicting moral values they believe are associated with much of the socialization that takes place in schools.[46]

Holt suggests that peer groups in school have a negative effect on children—that children learn from peers that it is "smart" to smoke cigarettes, drink alcohol, and even turn to drugs. These children also face other tensions in school social life.

> When I point out to people that the social life of most schools and classrooms is mean-spirited, status-oriented, competitive, and snobbish, I am always astonished by their response. Not one person of the hundreds with whom I've discussed this has yet said to me that the social life at school is kindly, generous, supporting, democratic, friendly, loving, or good for children. No without exception, when I condemn the social life of school, people say, "But that's what the children are going to meet in real life."[47]

Some courts have been reluctant to accept socialization as a justification for compelling students to attend school; in fact, this very argument was ruled out as a legitimate consideration in the *Perchemlides* v. *Frizzle* (1978) case in Amherst, Massachusetts.[48] Emphasis is now being placed on academic success, not on social equivalency.[49]

The socialization issue is directly related to the issue of family life. Joel Spring, assistant professor of education at Case Western Reserve University in Cleveland, Ohio, argues that compulsory attendance, even as it took over much of the educational role from the parents and gave it to the schools, actually strengthened family life. This was done, he says, by prolonging the required number of years of schooling and thus making the children economically dependent on parents for a longer period of time.[50] Attorney

Brendon Stocklin-Enright argues to the contrary. He points out that home schooling, not compulsory attendance, strengthens the bonds of family life by requiring parents to devote more time and energy to their children.[51] Holt accuses the schools of simply getting children out of the way of adults.[52] Of course, the mother who does not want her children "out of the way" may have difficulty adjusting her schedule to teach them at home and may encounter the criticism of unsympathetic neighbors, as evangelical journalist Dean Merrill points out:

> Home schooling, in the end, amounts to a tradeoff of sorts: family closeness is gained at the expense of the varied experiences of school. Controlling the input means the mother (or some one) must streamline her schedule and say no to competing activities. The flexible scheduling is a bonus, but neighbors and friends are likely to misunderstand.[53]

A number of energetic parents are not deterred by the challenge. Some, Williams, Arnoldsen, and Reynolds point out, enjoy being parents watching their children learn, and even learning with them. Further, "they believe they are not stunting their children's growth by keeping them at home. . . ."[54]

A variety of activities takes place in home schools. Moore contends that "true homework is work at home—chores and industries done with parents." He lists more than two hundred cottage industries that home-schooling families conduct—from agriculture to bicycle repair. "Such manual labor," Moore explains to parents, "provides your child with badly needed balance for a tired young brain; and," he continues, "there should be as much of this work as study."[55] Peter Yarema, a public-school teacher, describes the activities of his own children as they are being taught at home:

> The education here is broader than they could ever get in the classroom. Molly, who's eight, sews on all the buttons in this family. Kathy's made an apron. If Char [Mrs. Yarema] asks her to make muffins for lunch, she can do it. All three kids use ledger sheets with their allowances so they know exactly where their money is going. You'd have a much harder time getting around to these things if your kids are gone two-thirds of the day.[56]

Families often work together in learning, using diverse media. One parent explains:

> We have our religion class, sometimes a lesson, sometimes a cassette tape. Then Mom reads from the American Classic Series: Thomas Jefferson, after which each of the kids has a turn reading aloud from their respective *McGuffey's Reader* while the others are doing independent study. . . . On Thursdays and Fridays Dad does PE times with the kids—running, basketball, jumping rope, rope climbing, etc. Independent study consists of reading, writing, math, algebra, shorthand, typing, sewing, crocheting, cooking, and using the Sinclair computer. Also science, gardening, music, and merit badges. Mom also checks the educational TV programming guide and assigns appropriate programs for viewing during the week.[57]

It should be noted that home schoolers face difficulties in realizing their goals of cooperative family life. Parents fluctuate between exhaustion and total dedication. "They often admit," says Williams, Arnoldsen, and Reynolds, "that being both a parent and a teacher to their children, especially when there are more than one or two children, can be an extremely demanding role."[58] Finding ways to separate home from school can, indeed, be a problem. Williams, Arnoldsen, and Reynolds explain as follows:

> When a parent is playing both a parent role and a teacher role and the children are playing both the child and student roles in the same setting, potential problems arise. Relationships may become complicated, especially when the parents feel anxious about how well the children are learning and realize that they are taking the responsibility to make sure that those children learn certain things. Some parents are not able to stand back and give the children the support that they expect themselves to be giving as parents because they are at the same time demanding certain things as teachers.[59]

Other problems may also arise in home-schooling families. For example, parents sometimes have difficulty in striking a balance between Holt's concept of spontaneity and their own felt need for scheduling and structure.[60] In addition, parents may feel unsure about their children's progress; sometimes one parent may have difficulty with a spouse who does not support the home school. Choosing or obtaining teaching materials pose problems for others. Moreover, some children have been discipline problems, "fighting, complaining, or wasting a lot of time." Parents desire to "teach their kids to think on their own and be independent and self-disciplined"[61] but some express doubts about knowing how to accomplish this.

Home schooling is a religious enterprise for many families throughout the United States. Some parents are less interested in creating the ideal family life here on earth than they are in making sure their children get to heaven. Many cite the biblical call to Abraham as reason for their action: "For I have chosen him, so that he will direct his children and his household after him to keep the way of the Lord by doing what is right and just. . . ."[62] The command to the Israelites to pass the law of Moses on to their children is also cited: "Only be careful, watch yourselves closely so that you do not forget the things your eyes have seen or let them slip from their heart as long as you live. Teach them to your children and to their children after them."[63]

Home schooling is a logical activity for parents who do not want to compromise their religious beliefs. Looking at the Bible as a direct source of guidance in education, Blair Adams and Joel Stein have authored a series of books entitled *Education as Religious War* in which they criticize state control of education and justify private nonaccredited schools and home schools.[64] Many of the curricula being sold to home schoolers are overtly "Christian," sometimes with a rigid sectarian or denominational orientation. Moore, author of several books on home instruction, is a Seventh Day Adventist. Merrill, in the evangelical journal *Christianity Today*, emphasizes the advantage of home schooling for religious parents: "Parents," he says, "get to instill their values and spiritual commitments directly, without countermanding."[65]

Parents not only argue that religious teaching is a parental responsibility, but that home schooling is a constitutional right. Since the First Amendment to the U.S. Constitution guarantees "the free exercise" of religion, devout Amish Americans have been successful in claiming that the free exercise of religion includes their exemption from compulsory high school.[66] A Michigan family successfully argued their First Amendment right to teach younger children at home. The judge in the case ruled as follows:

> Freedom of religion is, of course, a fundamental constitutional right which occupies a "preferred position" in our constitutional framework (*Murdock* v. *Pennsylvania*, 391 U.S. 105, 115, 1943). The government can only punish acts taken pursuant to sincerely held religious beliefs in extraordinary circumstances. Criminal or civil sanction of religion-based action must be based on a compelling State interest. Furthermore, there must be no "less restrictive means" available to achieve the legitimate State interest while maintaining the integrity of the citizens' religious beliefs.[67]

The court added that the state's teacher certification requirement for home tutoring did not pass the "less restrictive means" test.[68]

Religious convictions, it must be noted, have not always been held to supersede state law. Religious parents who have not requested and received permission from school authorities to teach their children at home have sometimes been judged guilty of attendance violation.[69] In a case in Wisconsin the religious appeal was unsuccessful for other reasons. Home schooling, in this instance, it was held, did not merit First Amendment protection, since the parents in the case were motivated merely by an ideological, philosophical belief.[70] In *Hanson* v. *Cushman*, a Michigan court denied the need to show a "compelling interest" for enforcing the attendance law. It held that the teacher certification law merely needed to be reasonable. Home study, the court ruled, was not a constitutional right.[71] Acting on that assumption, Texas school officials have repeatedly prosecuted religious parents in spite of their religious claims.[72] The results are mixed, some judges ruling with the parents, others with the school authorities.

Viewed as a religious or secular activity, the controversy over home schooling is a classic case of individual rights pitted against the modern regulatory state. Parents seem willing to try anything they think may help their children; state officials, on the other hand, claim to be acting solely in the interest of these same children. If it is assumed that the state does have a legitimate interest in the education of its citizens, then perhaps that interest could best be served by allowing parents the freedom to teach their children at home, employing different teaching methods. Not all Americans agree, of course, on the role the state should play in regulating private education; and it may be that a logical, case-by-case approach will be the best way to judge the quality of education provided by parents. Certainly broad policies, such as certification and accreditation requirements, in no sense automatically guarantee educational quality.

Since academic and social success for students is more important than the means of education, it might be wise as well as less expensive for states to allow parents whose children are progressing well at home to pursue this private alternative of home schooling. A child's progress could be measured through testing, observation or other procedures. Whatever yardstick a state comes up with, it seems increasingly evident that more parents will experiment with home education in spite of official policy. The academic promise of home instruction as well as its protective aspects will persuade more parents to try it. With the advent of computers, the future of education as a whole may be a future of greater decentralization and allowance for individual diversity, not state-imposed uniformity.

Notes

[1] Stanley M. Elam, ed., *A Decade of Gallup Polls of Attitudes Toward Education, 1969–1978* (Bloomington, Ind.: Phi Delta Kappa, 1978), 1.

[2] *Pierce* v. *Society of Sisters*, 268 U.S. 510 (1925).

[3] Gerrit H. Wourmhoudt, "Supreme Court Decisions," *The Twelve Year Sentence*, William F. Rickenbacker, ed. (La Salle, Ill.: Open Court Publishing Co., 1974), 65.

[4] John Holt, *Teach Your Own* (New York: Delacorte Press, 1981), 15; cf. Gunnar Gustavsen, *Selected Characteristics of Home Schools and the Parents Who Operate Them* (Ann Arbor: University Microfilms, 1981) and Norma Jean Freeman Linden, *An Investigation of Alternative Education: Home Schooling* (Commerce, Tex.: East Texas State University, 1983).

[5] Patricia Lines, "Private Education Alternatives and State Regulation," *Journal of Law and Education* (April 1983), 189–234.

[6] Raymond Moore, "Home Schooling: An Idea Whose Time Has Returned," *Human Events* (15 September 1984), 12–13.

[7] Blair Adams and Joel Stein, *Who Owns the Children?* (Grand Junction, Colo.: Truth Forum, 1983), Chapter 1.

[8] Wendy Priesnitz, "Schooling at Home," *Orbit* 11 (June 1980), 3–5.

[9] "Harvard Freshman," *Houston Post* (29 August 1983), B1.

[10] Moore, "Home Schooling," 12–15.

[11] Raymond and Dorothy Moore, *Home Style Teaching* (Waco, Tex.: Word Books, 1984), Appendix. Kirk McCord, Speech at Home School Book Fair, Richardson, Texas, 27 April 1985.

[12] John Whitehead and Wendell Bird, *Home Education and Constitutional Liberties* (Westchester, Ill.: Crossway Books, 1984), 98.

[13] Moore, "Home Schooling," 12–13.

[14] Dean Merrill, "Schooling at Mother's Knee: Can It Compete?" *Christianity Today* (2 September 1983), 19.

[15] Moore, "Home Schooling," 12–13.

[16] Merrill, 19.

[17] John Holt, *Teach Your Own* (New York: Delacorte Press, 1981), Chapter 1.

[18] Nancy Wallace, *Better Than School: One Family's Declaration of Independence* (New York: Lawson Publishing Co., 1983).

[19] Hal Bennet, *No More Public School* (New York: Random House, 1972), Chapter 1.

[20] John Holt, *Instead of Education: Ways To Help People Do Things Better* (New York: E. P. Dutton, 1976), Chapter 1.

[21] Raymond Moore, "Research and Common Sense: Therapies for Homes and Schools," *Teachers College Record* 84 (Winter 1982), 372.

[22] J. J. Harris and R. E. Fields, "Outlaw Generation: A Legal Analysis of the Home Schooling Movement," *Education Horizons* 61 (Fall 1982), 26–31.

[23] Whitehead and Bird, *Home Education and Constitutional Liberties*, 68.

[24] David Williams, Larry Arnoldsen, and Peter Reynolds, *Understanding Home Education: Case Studies in Home Schools*, Conference Paper (New Orleans, La.: American Educational Research Association, April 1984), 22.

[25] Ed Nagel and Tom Shannon, "Should Parents Be Allowed to Educate Their Kids at Home?" *Instructor* 89 (October 1979), 30.

[26] *F. and F.* v. *Duval City*, 273 So.2d 15 Fla. Dist. Ct. (1973); *State* v. *Morehead*, 308 N.W. 2d 60 Iowa (1981).

[27] Marianne Kryzanowicz, "Home Teachers Acquitted" (Annapolis, Md.: *Evening Capital*, located in NewsBank [Microform], Education, 1984, 43:G8, Fiche).

[28] Ibid., G8.

[29] Raymond and Dorothy Moore, *Home Spun Schools* (Waco, Tex.: Word Books, 1982), 25.

[30] Ibid., 83.

[31] Moore and Moore, *Home Spun Schools*, 85.

[32] *Scoma* v. *Chicago Bd. of Education*, 391 F. Supp. 452 N.D. 111 (1974), 454.

[33] *In re McMillan*, 226 S.E. 2d 693 N.C. Ct. App. (1976).

[34] *In re Baum*, 401 N.Y.S. 2d 514 N.Y. App. Div. (1978).

[35] *City of Akron* v. *Lane*, 416 N.E. 2nd 642 Ohio Ct. App. (1979).

[36] *In re Falk*, 441 N.Y.S. 2d 785 Fam. Ct. (1981), 789.

[37] Raymond Moore, "Another Bulletin from Hewitt Research . . . A Synopsis" (Washougal, Wash.: Hewitt Research Foundation, 1984), 1.

[38] *In re Foster*, 330 N.Y.S. 2d 8 N.Y. Fam. Ct. (1972).

[39] Ibid.

[40] Holt, *Teach Your Own*, 30–31.

[41] *West Virginia* v. *Riddle*, 50 U.S.L.W. 2397 U.S. (1982).

[42] Williams, Arnoldsen, and Reynolds, *Understanding Home Education: Class Studied in Home Schools*, 26.

[43] Harris and Fields, *Education Horizons* 61.

[44] Merrill, *Christianity Today* (2 September 1983), 19.

[45] Moore, "Another Bulletin," 2.

[46] Williams, Arnoldsen, and Reynolds, *Understanding Home Education: Case Studies in Home Schools*, 5.

[47] Holt, *Teach Your Own*, 49–50.

[48] *Perchemlides* v. *Frizzle*, No. 16641, Mass. Super. Ct. (1978). Transcript of decision in letter to author from Rockland Independent School District.

[49] James W. Tobak and Perry A. Zirkel, "Home Instruction: An Analysis of Statutes and Case Law," *University of Dayton Law Review* 8 (Fall 1982), 1–60.

[50] Joel Spring, "Sociological and Political Ruminations," *The Twelve Year Sentence*, William F. Rickenbacker, ed. (La Salle, Ill.: Open Court Publishing Co., 1974).

[51] Brendon Stocklin-Enright, "The Constitutionality of Home Education: The Role of the Parent, the State and the Child," *Willamette Law Review* 18 (1982), 563.

[52] Holt, *Instead of Education*, Chapter 1.

[53] Merrill, *Christianity Today* (2 September 1983), 21.

[54] Williams, Arnoldsen, and Reynolds, *Understanding Home Education: Class Studies in Schools*, 7.

[55] Moore and Moore, *Home Style Teaching*, 122.

[56] Merrill, *Christianity Today* (2 September 1983), 20–21.

[57] Williams, Arnoldsen, and Reynolds, *Understanding Home Education: Class Studies in Schools*, 8.

[58] Ibid., 23.

[59] Ibid., 24.

[60] Ibid.

[61] Ibid., 25–26.

[62] Genesis 18:18–19, NIV.

[63] Deuteronomy 4:8–9, NIV.

[64] Blair Adams and Joel Stein, *Who Owns the Children?* (Grand Junction, Colo.: Truth Forum, 1983).

[65] Merrill, *Christianity Today* (2 September 1983), 19.

[66] *Wisconsin* v. *Yoder*, 406 U.S. 205 (1972).

[67] *Michigan* v. *Nobel*, 57th Dist. Ct., Allegan Cty., Michigan. In *Teach Your Own* by John Holt (New York: Delacorte Press, 1981), 293.

[68] Holt, *Teach Your Own*, 294.

[69] *West Virginia* v. *Riddle*, 50 U.S.L.W. 2397 U.S. (1982).

[70] *State* v. *Kasubaski*, 275 N.W. 2d 101 Wis. Ct. App. (1978).

[71] *Hanson* v. *Cushman*, 490 F. Supp. 109 W. Dist. Mich. (1980).

[72] "Parents Keep Students Home," *Dallas Morning News* (15 November 1984), A43.

ABOUT THE AUTHORS

HARRY BAKER ADAMS (B.A., Yale College; B.D., Yale Divinity School) is Yale University Chaplain and Master of Trumbull College. He has written curriculum materials for the American Baptist Church, Presbyterian Church, and United Methodist Church. He is affiliated with the Christian Church (Disciples of Christ).

JACK BALSWICK (B.A., Chico State College; M.A., Ph.D., University of Iowa) is professor of sociology and family development and director of research for Marriage and Family Therapy at Fuller Theological Seminary. His publications include *Why I Can't Say I Love You* (Word, 1978) and *Life in a Glass House: The Minister's Family in Its Unique Social Setting* (Zondervan, 1989). He also co-authored a book with his wife Judy entitled *The Family: A Christian View of the Home* (Baker Books, 1989).

BRUCE A. DEMAREST (B.S., Wheaton College; M.S., Adelphi University; M.A., Trinity Evangelical Divinity School; Ph.D., University of Manchester [England]) is professor of systematic theology at Denver Seminary. He ministered in fifty countries as theological secretary for the International Fellowship of Evangelical Students. He is co-author of *Challenges to Inerrancy: A Theological Response* (Moody, 1984) and *Integrative Theology*, volumes I and II (Zondervan, 1987, 1989; volume III is forthcoming).

JAMES B. DE YOUNG (B.A., East Texas Baptist College; B.D., Th.M., Talbot Theological Seminary; Th.D., Dallas Theological Seminary) is professor of New Testament language and literature at Western Conservative Baptist Seminary. He is co-chairman of The SaltShakers and has been a visiting professor at Tyndale Theological Seminary in Badhoevedorp, The Netherlands.

TAMARA C. ESKENAZI (B.A., M.A., University of Denver; Ph.D., Iliff School of Theology/University of Denver) is assistant professor and director of the Institute for Interfaith Studies, Center for Judaic Studies, University of Denver. She has written *In An Age of Prose: A Literary Approach to Ezra-Nehemiah* (Scholars Press, 1988).

ARTHUR F. GLASSER (C.E., Cornell University; B.D., Faith Theological Seminary; S.T.M., Union Theological Seminary) is dean emeritus and senior professor of theology, mission, and East Asian studies, Fuller Theological Seminary, School of World Mission. He is an ordained minister in the Presbyterian Church in America, and has authored (with D. A. McGavran) *Contemporary Theologies of Mission* (Baker, 1983).

369

MONIKA K. HELLWIG (LL.B., C.S.Sc., Liverpool University; M.A., Ph.D., Catholic University of America) is professor of theology at Georgetown University. She is associate editor of the *Journal of Ecumenical Studies*, and has written numerous books and articles including *Sign of Reconciliation and Conversion* (Michael Glazier, Inc., 1982) and *Christian Women in a Troubled World* (Paulist Press, 1985).

DANIEL A. HELMINIAK (B.A., St. Vincent College; S.T.B., S.T.L., Gregorian University [Rome]; M.A., Boston University; Ph.D., Boston College and Andover Newton Theological School) is director for spiritual growth and pastoral counselor at the Omega Point Counseling Center in Austin, Texas. He is affiliated with the Roman Catholic Church and is currently pursuing studies toward his second doctorate, specializing in human development and personality. He has written *The Same Jesus: A Contemporary Christology* (1986) and *Spiritual Development: An Interdisciplinary Study* (1987), both published by Loyola University Press.

S. M. HUTCHENS (B.A., Oakland University; M.Div., Th.M., Trinity Evangelical Divinity School; Th.M., The Lutheran School of Theology at Chicago; Th.D., Lutheran School of Theology) has recenty completed his doctorate. He was ordained in the National Association of Congregational Christian Churches in April, 1984. He is affiliated with the Episcopal Church.

CHRISTOPHER LASCH (B.A., Harvard; M.A., Ph.D., Columbia) is the chairman of the department of history at the University of Rochester. He is the author of *The Culture of Narcissism* (Norton, 1979) and *The Minimal Self: Psychic Survival in Troubled Times* (Norton, 1984).

RODNEY B. MCKEAN (B.A., Simpson College; M.A.R., Asbury Theological Seminary; M.A., Ph.D., Michigan State University) is professor of educational ministries at Azusa Pacific University. He is affiliated with the Evangelical Covenant Church. He has written several journal articles in the area of Christian education and youth ministries.

HENRY F. MAY (A.B., University of California; M.A., Ph.D., Harvard) is the Margaret Byrne professor emeritus of history at the University of California, Berkeley. He has authored *The Enlightenment in America* (Oxford University Press, 1976) and *Coming to Terms: A Study of Memory and History* (University of California Press, 1987).

D. LOUISE MEBANE (B.A., California State University at Northridge; M.A., Ph.D., Fuller Theological Seminary) is a psychology intern at Children's Hospital in Boston. She is also a fellow in clinical psychology at Harvard

Medical School. She has co-authored numerous journal articles and has been an interpreter for deaf and blind adults.

LESSLIE NEWBIGIN is a retired bishop in the Church of South India. He recently served as minister in the United Reformed Church in the UK. His books include *Foolishness to the Greeks* (Eerdmans, 1986) and *The Gospel in a Pluralistic Society* (Eerdmans, forthcoming).

MARK A. NOLL (B.A., Wheaton College; M.A., University of Iowa; M.A., Trinity Evangelical Divinity School; M.A., Ph.D., Vanderbilt University) is professor of history and theological studies at Wheaton College. He has written journal articles and books, and is author of *Between Faith and Criticism: Evangelicals, Scholarship, and the Bible in America* (Harper & Row, 1986) and *One Nation Under God? Christian Faith and Political Action in America* (Harper & Row, 1988).

ALBERT C. OUTLER (A.B., Wofford College; B.D., Emory College; Ph.D., Yale University), recently deceased, was a college professor. He taught theology successively at Duke, Yale, and Southern Methodist University. He was affiliated with the United Methodist Church and editor of *The Works of John Wesley*, Volumes I-IV, *The Sermons* (Abingdon, 1984–87). The late Dr. Outler died September 1, 1989.

CLARK H. PINNOCK (B.A., University of Toronto; Ph.D., University of Manchester) is professor of systematic theology at McMaster Divinity College. He has written numerous books including *The Scripture Principle* (Harper & Row, 1985), *Three Keys to Spiritual Renewal* (Bethany House, 1986), and *A Case for Faith* (Bethany House, 1987).

VERN SHERIDAN POYTHRESS (B.S., California Institute of Technology; M.Div., Th.M., Westminster Theological Seminary; M.Litt., University of Cambridge; Ph.D., Harvard; Th.D., University of Stellenbosch, South Africa) is professor of New Testament interpretation at Westminster Theological Seminary. He is affiliated with the Presbyterian Church in America and is associate editor of *Westminster Theological Journal.* His publications include *Symphonic Theology: The Validity of Multiple Perspectives in Understanding Dispensationalists* (Zondervan, 1987) and *Science and Hermeneutics* (Zondervan, 1988).

CHARLES W. RAUP (B.S., Pennsylvania State University; Th.M., Dallas Theological Seminary; M.A., Psy.D., Rosemead Graduate School of Professional Psychology) is assistant professor of counseling at Denver Seminary. He has worked with programs designed to rehabilitate drug abusers, and serves as psychotherapist at the Vernon Grounds Counseling Center in Denver.

HOWARD L. RICE (B.A., Carroll College; M.Div., McCormick Theological Seminary) is professor of ministry and chaplain at San Francisco Theological Seminary. He was ordained by the Presbyterian Church U.S.A. in 1956.

CHARLES R. RIDLEY (B.A., Taylor University; M.A., Ball State University; Ph.D., University of Minnesota) is associate professor at Fuller Theological Seminary. He is a licensed psychologist and has taught at Indiana University and the University of Maryland. He has written *How To Select Church Planters* (Charles E. Fuller Institute, 1988).

MICHAEL S. SHEPHERD (B.A., University of Texas; M.A., Ed.D., East Texas State University) is a teacher in the Dallas Independent School District. He has worked with Wycliffe Bible Translators in Bolivia, and now provides information to parents and school districts regarding home schooling.

GARY S. SHOGREN (B.S., Philadelphia College of Bible; M.A., M.Div., Biblical Theological Seminary; Ph.D., Aberdeen University) is pastor at Penacook Bible Church, Penacook, New Hampshire, and teaches New Testament and hermeneutics at Conservative Baptist Seminary of the East.

DANIEL B. WALLACE (B.A., Biola University; Th.M., Dallas Theological Seminary) is assistant professor of New Testament studies at Dallas Theological Seminary. He is a Southern Baptist minister and a Th.D. candidate at Dallas.

GORDON J. WENHAM (B.A., M.A., Cambridge University; Ph.D., London University) is senior lecturer at The College of St. Paul and St. Mary in Cheltenham, England. He is affiliated with the Church of England. He has authored *Numbers: Introduction & Commentary* (InterVarsity Press, 1981) and *Genesis 1–15 (Word Biblical Commentary*; Word, 1987).

WALTER WRIGHT (B.A., Simpson College; M.Div., Ph.D., Fuller Theological Seminary) is president and professor of Christian Leadership and Management at Regent College in Vancouver, B.C. He is an ordained minister with the Evangelical Covenant Church and is a member of the adjunct faculty at Fuller Theological Seminary and North Park Theological Seminary.

IVAN L. ZABILKA (A.B., Asbury College; M.Div., Th.M., Asbury Theological Seminary; M.A., Ph.D., University of Kentucky) is a seventh-grade math teacher in Lexington, Kentucky. He was ordained by the Evangelical Methodist Church and has taught at Asbury College and the University of Kentucky. He has written *A History of the Creation/Evolution Controversy* (Bristol Books, 1990).

DON H. ZINGER (B.A., Augustana College; M.Div., S.T.M., Chicago Lutheran Seminary) is professor of religion and philosophy at Grand View College in Des Moines. He is an ordained minister in the Evangelical Lutheran Church in America.

ACKNOWLEDGMENTS

Harry Baker Adams. "Creative Tensions in Preaching: Person and Spirit." *Lexington Theological Quarterly* 24/1 (1989): 1–16. Used by permission.

Jack Balswick and Walter Wright. "A Complementary-Empowering Model of Ministerial Leadership." *Pastoral Psychology* (Fall 1988): 3–14. Reprinted by permission of the publisher, Human Sciences Press.

Bruce Demarest and Charles Raup. "Recovering the Heart of Christian Spirituality." Reprinted from the *Criswell Theological Review* 3/2 (1989): 321–26. Used by permission.

James B. DeYoung. "The Meaning of 'Nature' in Romans 1 and Its Implications for Biblical Proscriptions of Homosexual Behavior." *Journal of the Evangelical Theological Society* 31/4 (December 1988): 429–41. Reprinted by permission.

Tamara C. Eskenazi. "The Structure of Ezra-Nehemiah and the Integrity of the Book." *Journal of Biblical Literature* 107/4 (1988): 641–56. Reprinted by permission of the Society of Biblical Literature.

Arthur Glasser. "Conversion and the Kingdom." Reprinted with permission from the July-August 1988 issue of *World Evangelization*, published by the Lausanne Committee for World Evangelization.

Monika K. Hellwig. "In Spirit and In Truth: A Catholic Perspective on the Holy Spirit." *Quarterly Review: A Journal of Scholarly Reflection for Ministry* 8/2 (Summer 1988): 36–48. *Quarterly Review* is a publication of the United Methodist Board of Higher Education and Ministry and the United Methodist Publishing House. Reprinted by permission of the publisher.

Daniel A. Helminiak. "Spiritual Concerns in Erich Fromm." *Journal of Psychology and Theology* 16/3 (1988): 222–32. Copyright 1988 by Rosemead School of Psychology, Biola University. Used by permission.

S. M. Hutchens. "The Crisis of Evangelical Preaching." *Touchstone* (Summer/Fall 1988): 28–31. Reprinted with permission from *Touchstone, A Journal of Ecumenical Orthodoxy*, 4637 N. Manor Ave., Chicago, IL 60625. Copyright, 1988, B'rith Christian Union.

Christopher Lasch. "The Obsolescence of Left & Right." *New Oxford Review* (April 1989): 6–15. Reprinted by permission.

Rodney B. McKean. "Research on Teaching for Christian Education." *Christian Education Journal* 9/2 (Winter 1989): 11–19. Copyright 1989, Scripture Press Ministries. All rights reserved. Used by permission.

Henry F. May. "Jonathan Edwards and America." From *Jonathan Edwards and the American Experience*, edited by Nathan O. Hatch and Harry S. Stout. Copyright © 1988 by Oxford University Press, Inc. Reprinted by permission.

D. Louise Mebane and Charles R. Ridley. "The Role-Sending of Perfectionism: Overcoming Counterfeit Spirituality." *Journal of Psychology and Theology* 16/4 (1988): 332–39. Copyright 1988 by Rosemead School of Psychology, Biola University. Used by permission.

Lesslie Newbigin. "Religious Pluralism and the Uniqueness of Jesus Christ." *International Bulletin of Missionary Research* (April 1989): 50–54. Copyright 1989 by International Bulletin of Missionary Research. Reprinted by permission.

Mark A. Noll. "Jonathan Edwards and Nineteenth-Century Theology." From *Jonathan Edwards and the American Experience*, edited by Nathan O. Hatch and Harry S. Stout. Copyright © 1988 by Oxford University Press, Inc. Reprinted by permission.

Albert C. Outler. "A Focus on the Holy Spirit: Spirit and Spirituality in John Wesley." *Quarterly Review: A Journal of Scholarly Reflection for Ministry* 8/2 (Summer 1988): 3–18, a publication of the United Methodist Board of Higher Education and Ministry and the United Methodist Publishing House. Reprinted by permission of the publisher.

Clark H. Pinnock. "Climbing Out of a Swamp: The Evangelical Struggle to Understand the Creation Texts." *Interpretation* 43 (April 1989): 143–55. Used by permission.

Vern Sheridan Poythress. "Christ the Only Savior of Interpretation." *Westminster Theological Journal* 50/2 (1988): 305–21. Reprinted by permission.

Howard L. Rice. "Feasting and Fasting in the Reformed Tradition." *Pacific Theological Review* 22:1 (Fall 1988): 6–16. Printed with permission of *Pacific Theological Review*, a publication of San Francisco Theological Seminary.

Michael S. Shepherd. "Home Schooling: Dimensions of Controversy, 1970–1984." Reprinted from *Journal of Church and State* 31 (Winter 1989): 101–14.

Gary S. Shogren. "Will God Heal Us—A Re-Examination of James 5:14–16a." *The Evangelical Quarterly* 61/2 (April 1989): 99–108. Published by The Paternoster Press, Exeter, England. Reprinted by permission.

Daniel B. Wallace. "'Ὀργίζεσθε in Ephesians 4:26: Command or Condition?" Reprinted from the *Criswell Theological Review* 3/2 (1989): 353–72.

Gordon J. Wenham. "The Place of Biblical Criticism in Theological Study." Reprinted with permission from *Themelios* 14/3 (April 1989): 84–89. *Themelios* is an international journal for theological students produced by the Religious and Theological Studies Fellowship and the International Fellowship of Evangelical Students.

Ivan L. Zabilka. "Calvin's Contribution to Universal Education." *The Asbury Theological Journal* 44/1 (1989): 12–13. Reprinted by permission of *The Asbury Theological Journal*, Asbury Theological Seminary, Wilmore, KY 40390.

Don H. Zinger. "Are Grace and Virtue Compatible?" *Lutheran Forum* 23/1 (1989): 12–13. Reprinted from the Lent, 1989 edition of *Lutheran Forum*, the largest independent Lutheran journal of opinion in North America today.

RECOVERING THE HEART OF
CHRISTIAN SPIRITUALITY

BRUCE A. DEMAREST
Professor of Systematic Theology
Denver Seminary
CHARLES W. RAUP
Assistant Professor of Counseling
Denver Seminary

Article from *Criswell Theological Review*

In the Christian scheme of things the study of Scripture or theology and the pursuit of piety should constitute a single, seamless garment. A casual reading of St. Paul, Augustine or Calvin reveals that leading saints of old related to God with both their minds and their hearts. Historically, orthodox Christians seldom reflected on Christian truths independently of knowing God in a vital, experiential relation. For many Christian giants of the past the disciplines of the mind and the heart were inseparable.

I. The Heart of the Problem

As time went on, however, Western Christianity tended to conceptualize the faith and divorce theology from the lived experience of God. Late medieval Christianity forfeited the earlier integration of head and heart by separating dogmatic theology from mystical theology. Descartes in the 17th century fostered intellectualism in Europe by identifying truth as clear and distinct ideas. Post-Reformation Lutheran and Calvinist authorities in the 17th and 18th centuries ("scholastic Protestantism") adapted to the rationalistic mindset by constructing rigorous systems of theology that seemed to have little relevance to the believer's experience of God. In our century influential European theologians promote "scientific theology" (*wissentschaftliche Theologie*), which is chiefly an intellectual and academic discipline with no evident experiential component. Add to the above an overreaction to the emotional and ethical excesses of some Pentecostals (cf. contemporary electronic evangelists), and we understand why contemporary evangelicalism primarily stresses the intellectual and moral dimensions of the faith to the neglect of the mystical or experiential.

Protestantism suffers from the scourge of *intellectualism* when it believes that deepest human needs can be satisfied by right thinking about God.

Some evangelicals identify Christianity with a formally correct theology or a coherent world view. A few even define the person, as image of God, exclusively as the power of a rational mind![1] Christendom furthermore suffers the scourge of *moralism* when it believes that ethical achievements, apart from a vital relation to God, constitute the heart of the Christian life. Not uncommon in conservative circles is the belief that a Christian attains mature spirituality by legalistically adhering to a set of rules or a code of conduct. M. Kelsey sums up the present state of affairs with the following astute observation: "In Protestantism, God became a theological idea known by inference rather than a reality known by experience."[2]

II. The Problem of an Undernourished Heart

Surely the Christian faith requires sturdy intellectual foundations. Who God is and what He has done for humankind in Christ constitute the non-negotiable foundation of true spirituality. Similarly the Christian faith embraces right moral action. Good works, as the letter of James emphasizes, represent the inevitable fruit of a heart that is properly related to God. However, conceptual knowledge of God and good works must be joined with an experiential knowledge of God nurtured in an atmosphere of faith and commitment. C. Jung, who was not an evangelical Christian, observed that the religion of many professing Christians was largely intellectual, lacking in vital experience of God. Jung concluded that as a result of this imbalance many Christians were spiritually and emotionally ill. Persons created in the image of God are not adequately nourished by a faith that is primarily intellectual or moralistic. For example, the mere thought of food will not satisfy a hungry person. Nothing short of actual partaking of food will suffice. So it is that Christians hunger and thirst for a participation in God that strikes a chord of reality in their total, lived experience. Believers need personally to discover and relate to the God who not only engages their minds, but who also lovingly reveals himself to their hearts.

The contemporary rush of Christians to psychotherapists suggests that many believers, some of whom have been saved for decades, have deep-seated needs that are not being met. The Christian therapist assists the broken and hurting individual to come into a healing relationship with God, with himself and with others. Significant numbers of Christians in our day need to bring their head knowledge of God into the heart in the form of a total experience that fulfills them as renewed image-bearers of God. Human spiritual hunger must be satisfied. People who do not engage the true and living God in a fulfilling, lived experience are vulnerable to transcendent experiences offered by Eastern religions, the New Age Movement, Satanism, or hallucinogenic drugs. Thus, some fault for the contemporary drift to the East and to the cults may lie at the doorstep of the church with its intellectual and legalistic approach to the Gospel. Evangelicalism in its predominately rationalistic and moralistic modes is a church still in bondage in Egypt.

III. Heart Intimacy with God

During the last two decades many Roman Catholics and a variety of Protestants outside the Pentecostal tradition have eagerly embraced "charismatic" renewal movements. This phenomenon cannot be dismissed as an interest in the exotic or offbeat. Nor can it be viewed as an attempt to substitute mindless experience for theology. Rather the contemporary interest in "charismatic" renewal movements testifies to a significant void in contemporary Christendom. Neither the intellectualism and moralism of Protestantism nor the ritualism of Catholicism satisfies the hunger for an experiential relationship with Christ. Christians of all stripes hunger for the best God offers—and that is a living, experiential intimacy with himself.

Consider a few biblical examples. The first human couple personally communed with God in Eden (Gen. 3:8). The patriarch Abraham had numerous personal encounters with the Lord (Gen. 12:3; 13:4; 15:5). Jacob wrestled with God in human form at Peniel (Gen. 32:30). Moses encountered God personally when called to lead Israel out of Egypt (Exod. 3:6). In the Gospels many persons had life-transforming encounters with Christ. Acts records numerous incidents of intimate experiential contact with God through the Holy Spirit (Acts 2:4; 4:31; 6:10). In the epistles Paul expresses his deep heart yearning for experiential intimacy with Christ. Noteworthy is Philippians 3:10: "I want to know Christ and the power of his resurrection and the fellowship of sharing in his sufferings, becoming like him in his death." Paul's yearning for an intimate experience with Christ is not unlike that of many contemporary Christians. But we note a significant difference. Paul desired that his intimate relationship with Christ would be increased; today the cry is to discover an experiential intimacy that has been lost.

How can we recover the lost heart of Christian spirituality? The tradition of "devotions" is a natural place for evangelical Protestants to begin. But the customary "devotions" should give pride of place to the cultivation of *heart-intimacy* with God. In general, a person achieves intimacy by listening intently and by being completely open and available to another. By listening to the voice of God and by opening the heart to him, the Christian can maximize experiential intimacy with Christ. The desired intimacy with Christ can be enhanced by employing helpful spiritual disciplines that foster listening, openness and availability to God.

First, Christians can heighten their ability to listen intently through the discipline of reverent quiet. God in wisdom has chosen to speak to his children by quiet promptings and whispers (1 Kings 19:11–12). Thus, stillness of heart is necessary to detect the voice of God (Hab. 2:20). The Lord's command to all who would know him experientially is, "Be still, and know that I am God" (Ps. 46:10). Waiting silently and expectantly before the Lord, we should pray for a calm spirit and an uncluttered mind (Ps. 131:2). To facilitate listening to God the old Christian "prayer of quiet," or what John of the Cross called the "prayer of loving attention," often proves helpful. For a few moments the seeker silences all distractions and focuses his heart and mind entirely on the Lord himself.[3] Augustine referred to this discipline as "a loving gaze of the spirit directed toward God." Historically the preceding is called "centering prayer," which many older Christians have found to be a valuable doorway to God. In his book on the discipline, M. B. Pennington describes "centering prayer" as follows: "Centering Prayer is an opening, a response, a putting aside of all the debris that stands in the way of our being totally present to the present Lord, so that he can be present to us. It is a laying aside of thoughts, so that the heart can attend immediately to him."[4] We agree wholeheartedly with D. Bloesch who writes that, unlike Eastern religions, silence or the prayer of quiet "is to be used not to get beyond the Word but to prepare ourselves to hear the Word."[5] The Lord Jesus stands at the door of the believer's heart waiting to be admitted (Rev. 3:10). To fellowship with the risen Christ the believer needs only to prepare his heart in the proper way.

Second, Christians can increase openness and availability to the Lord by appropriate forms of prayer. This aspect of intimacy might begin with the "Jesus Prayer," widely practiced in the early church. Here the believer communicates his *desire* to fellowship with Christ by uttering from the heart the simple prayer, "Lord Jesus Christ, come to me," or "Lord Jesus Christ, have mercy on me" (cf. Mark 10:47). Or one may choose another prayer that genuinely expresses total heart desire for him. Believers ought not be deterred by a prayer of this nature, for Jesus denounced only the repetition of meaningless or "vain" words (Matt. 6:7, AV). A feature of pious Judaism was the prayerful repetition of the *Shema* (Deut. 6:4) in the daily liturgy.[6] Moreover, David employed the reverent repetition of spiritually meaningful words in his worship of God: e.g., "His love endures forever," which occurs 26 times in Psalm 136. Following this kind of preliminary prayer of desire one should meditate prayerfully on the person, the perfections, and the promises of God revealed in the Scriptures. It will be especially helpful to focus on God's unreserved acceptance, unlimited forgiveness, and unfailing love and concern for us. Availability to God can be further enhanced by praying for awareness of secret sins that grieve his Spirit, or for understanding of those fears that limit our unreserved openness to him. Lastly, we can reaffirm our availability by totally committing ourselves to the One upon whom we are entirely dependent—our Creator, Sustainer, and Redeemer God. Many devout believers of old have found that true prayer begins with a relationship with God. Before uttering words of petition for oneself or words of intercession for others, the earnest Christian quietly cultivates a heart-to-heart